THE FEMALE KING OF COLONIAL NIGERIA

THE FEMALE KING
OF COLONIAL NIGERIA

AHEBI UGBABE

NWANDO ACHEBE

Indiana University Press
Bloomington and Indianapolis

This book is a publication of

Indiana University Press
601 North Morton Street
Bloomington, Indiana 47404-3797 USA

www.iupress.indiana.edu

Telephone orders	800-842-6796
Fax orders	812-855-7931
Orders by e-mail	iuporder@indiana.edu

⊛ The paper used in this publication meets the minimum requirements of the American National Standard for Information Sciences—Permanence of Paper for Printed Library Materials, ANSI Z39.48-1992.

Manufactured in the United States of America

Library of Congress Cataloging-in-Publication Data

Achebe, Nwando, [date]–
    The female king of colonial Nigeria : Ahebi Ugbabe / Nwando Achebe.
        p.   cm.
    Includes bibliographical references and index.
    ISBN 978-0-253-35538-6 (cloth : alk. paper) — ISBN 978-0-253-22248-0 (pbk. : alk. paper) 1. Ugbabe, Ahebi. 2. Women, Igbo—Biography. 3. Sex role—Nigeria. 4. Igbo (African people)—Kings and rulers—Biography. 5. Nigeria—Kings and rulers—Biography. 6. Nigeria—History—1851–1899. 7. Nigeria—History—1900–1960. I. Title.
    DT515.77.U43A65   2010
    966.9'403092—dc22
    [B]

                                                        2010022842

1 2 3 4 5   16 15 14 13 12 11

In memory of Professor A. E. Afigbo
and for
My friend and guide, Mr. Erobike Eze

The tortoise on setting out for a long journey said to his people: if usual things happen, do not send for me; if the unheard of happens, call me.

—*Igbo proverb*

CONTENTS

The Igbo have a saying that coming and going keeps the road from getting cold. Like that insightful proverb, my journey into researching and writing King Ahebi's world has required several comings and goings to navigate and complete. I owe a debt of gratitude to my family, friends, and colleagues who have all in one way or the other supported and nurtured my journey. I am particularly grateful to the late Professor Boniface Obichere, under whose guidance I first discovered Ahebi. I have also benefited from the unflagging encouragement and unwavering support of the late Professor A. E. Afigbo, to whose Nigerian residence I first pilgrimaged in the summer of 1995 and subsequently every summer starting in 2006—all in an attempt to learn from a true master and live up to that perceptive Igbo adage that proclaims that a child who stays near an adult does not chew pepper but rather chews kola nut. Professor Afigbo, thank you so very much for your intellectual support of me. I will forever treasure our conversations and your kind words and e-mail communications.[1] This book is dedicated to you. This book is as much for my friend and guide, Mr. Erobike Eze, who twice dropped everything to accompany me into the research field, and without whose assistance and support this study could never have been completed. Mr. Eze, words are not enough to thank you for your commitment to this project. This book is also dedicated to you.

Funding for my research came from several sources and funding agencies. I thrice received the Sesquicentennial Research Fund for Historical Research and Publication of the history department at Michigan State University (MSU). Collection of source materials was further facilitated by MSU's Special Foreign Travel Fund and the Summer Research Fellowship of MSU's International Studies and Programs. I also received MSU's Intramural Research Grant Program award, which bought me a semester with no teaching, and the Wenner-Gren Postgraduate Fellowship, which allowed me to dedicate an entire academic year to writing. Without this support, I would never have been able to put Ahebi's story into writing. Likewise, this study could not have been completed without the support of Mark Kornbluh, the former chair of the history department, who approved the financial support from my department and accommodated my request for time away from teaching when I received external awards. Special mention must also go to my present acting chair, Keely Stauter-Halsted, who has seen to the continued support of my project by providing funds for an indexer.

Heartfelt appreciation goes to all my collaborators in Enugu-Ezike (especially Umuida), Unadu, Ofante, and Idah, who, over the fifteen years that I have been working on this project, have shared their experiences and memories of King Ahebi. I would be remiss, however, if I did not single out several collaborators for special mention. Mr. Samuel Ezeja, a teacher from Enugu-Ezike, first accompanied me to the Ahebi Primary School in 1996; thank you so very much for your time. That same year, the now-deceased Wilfred Ogara very graciously welcomed me into his home in Umuida, spending more time than I could ever have hoped explaining Ahebi's world to me. Alice Akogu (formerly Ahebi) also welcomed me on several occasions, cooking for me and sharing remembrances of her deceased "mother-in-law" Ahebi. I am particularly indebted to Nwoyeja Obeta (Felicia Ugwu Agbedo), now deceased, who first introduced me to the inner life of King Ahebi's palace. She too spent several hours with me, cooking, singing, and dancing King Ahebi's world. I will never forget how comfortable she made me feel. A world of thanks goes to Abodo Nwa Idoko of Ikpamodo, Enugu-Ezike, who on September 29, 1998, let me in on the "community secret" and by so doing gave me the space to critically reconstruct the life of the remarkable woman Ahebi. Honorable Fabian Azegba is warmly acknowledged for his dedication and support and for receiving me on numerous occasions. He also introduced me to his "big brother," retired army sergeant Samuel Apeh, who in turn shared memories of the day-to-day world of the Ahebi Palace School—which he attended as a youngster—recalling the songs they were taught so many years ago. Speaking of songs, I am most indebted to the now-deceased Oshageri, professional musician extraordinaire, who in 1998 twice entertained me with food and song. He composed and performed a special song in my honor, then performed King Ahebi's court music for us to enjoy. In the same year, I received every cooperation from Ahebi's great-great-grandson, Bernard Ameh, who generously loaned photographs of Ahebi's descendants to me. I would later meet with Ahebi's great-grandson, Bedford Okpe, who in July 2007 graciously came to my residence in Lagos so that I could interview him.

In Igala country, I benefited from the kindness and hospitality of several people. Usman Mangwu served as my interpreter in the field, and Musa Ejeh translated and transcribed my Igala interviews for me word for word on my return to Nsukka. Prince Nwatuluocha provided the car and driving services that enabled me jostle from Nsukka to Enugu-Ezike, Unadu, Ofante, and several towns in Igalaland. In Idah, Mr. F. C. and Mrs. Eucharia Omeje, Mr. Erobike Eze's friends, provided a place to sleep during our stay in the Kogi State capital. I was also well received by P. E. Okwoli, who loaned me copies of his published works; HRH Dr. A. P. Opaluwa (JP), the Eje Ofu, Onu Ugwolawo, and chairman of Ofu Local Government Traditional Council, Ugwolawo, Kogi State; as well as HRH Igwe F. U. Chukwuemeka, the Igbo community leader of Ankpa, Kogi State.

During each research trip to Nigeria, my cousins Professor Nnaemeka (Nwachinemelu) and Nkechi Ikpeze hosted me. Their home at the University of Nigeria, Nsukka, became my home away from home. I could always count on being able to stay in "my room" on the second floor. Thanks so very much for your kindness and hospitality. My profound thanks also go to my aunt and godmother, Mrs. Elizabeth Onuorah, who also provided a home for me while I was in Enugu and whose caring support I will cherish always. I owe a world of thanks to Dr. Chris U. Agbedo of the Department of Linguistics, University of Nigeria, Nsukka, who painstakingly translated the intricate words of King Ahebi's court music for me. Mrs. Justina Ekere helped secure a driver for me as well as made arrangements for a student artist to accompany me into the research field in Enugu-Ezike and Igala. I owe many thanks to the artist Chinedu Chukwurah for sitting with members of the Umuida community and reconstructing and then sketching images of Ahebi, her palace, and her palace grounds with their help.

My research was facilitated by several archivists and librarians around the world. I am particularly indebted to my friend and colleague Peter Limb, one of two Africana bibliographers at Michigan State University, who helped me locate hard-to-find primary sources and maps. In Nigeria, I benefited from being granted access to various libraries at the University of Nigeria, Nsukka. Particular thanks goes to Dr. Uchenna Anyanwu, head of the history department, for granting me access to the history department library, where I consulted numerous B.A. and M.A. theses as well as some Ph.D. dissertations. Uchenna also introduced me to capable undergraduate research assistants who helped gather secondary sources for me while I was in the Igala field. Many thanks also go to Professor Chinedu Nebo, the former vice-chancellor of the University of Nigeria, Nsukka, for allowing me access to the university's main Nnamdi Azikiwe Library.

In view of the limited time I had at the National Archives of Nigeria, Enugu, I am particularly grateful to the late Mr. Christian Uzor and Mr. Innocent Ede for their assistance. Although he was one of the most senior officers at the archives, Mr. Christian Uzor took over the job of bringing me documents so that I could complete my search in a timely manner. Many thanks also go to Maria Chinyere, Chinyere, and all of the staff at the National Archives of Nigeria, Enugu for their support of my work since my 1995 student days. Thanks also to Chief E. I. Nsoro, the zonal director of the National Archives of Nigeria, Enugu, for accommodating my many requests.

Other people made completion of this biography possible. Sarah J. AcMoody, cartographer extraordinaire of MSU's Remote Sensing & GIS Research and Outreach Services, deserves special mention. She went far beyond the call of duty, checking and rechecking plotted maps to ascertain that my narrative of Ahebi's journeys in fact matched up with the period-specific road maps. She also calculated all the distances that Ahebi traveled. Scott Pennington, the head of digitization and African projects at MSU's MATRIX, helped restore old photographs. Many friends, colleagues, and doctoral students provided encouragement and responded generously to my requests for advice, information, and assistance. Many thanks to Claire Robertson, David Estrin, my two "blind" reviewers, and my students, Joe Davey, and Harry Odamtten, who read various drafts of this biography and provided feedback. Claire Robertson deserves special mention for providing detailed comments. Joe Davey meticulously notated all the King Ahebi court music used in this biography, and Harry Odamtten worked tirelessly at the very last moment to create the charts that I initially submitted to the publisher. Thank you both for your time and dedication. I am most appreciative. I am also indebted to Ndubueze Mbah and Winifred Nwaefido, who served as my research assistants, both in the Nigerian field and at MSU. They both conducted interviews on my behalf and transcribed numerous interview tapes. Menna Baumann and Richard Yorku also served as my research assistants, scanning and digitizing numerous photographs as well as typing up the oftentimes-illegible Nsukka Division court proceedings and notes. I would be remiss if I did not mention the assistance of my colleague Gordon Stewart, who helped me attempt to identify the origins of Ahebi's helmet/crown. He sent my request to Michael Unsworth, history librarian at MSU, who in turn got in touch with Peter Harrington, the curator of the Anne S. K. Brown Military Collection at Brown's John Hay Library, who ran it by renowned uniformologist Alfred Umhey. Together these scholars were able to offer insight into the origin of Ahebi's helmet.

Very special thanks go to my childhood friend, Jane Nwakoby, for capturing the likeness and essence of King Ahebi in painting; and to

Darcy Greene for photographing it. The cover illustration is an expression of Jane's talents. To my friends Bridget Teboh, Bronwen Watts and Andrew Burge, DeBrenna Agbenyiga, Paula Somohano and Carl Boehlert, Pero Dagbovie, Daina Ramey Berry, Geneva Smitherman (a.k.a. Dr. G), Gloria Smith, Darlene Daniel, Dalia Golchan, Clare Membiela, and Father Paulinus Odozor I say a big thank you for your support and friendship.

In the task of analyzing and interpreting the Igbo world, I derived stimulus and insights from discussions with my father, Chinua Achebe, and my mother, Christie Chinwe Achebe, who were but a phone call away. Mommy and Daddy, words are not enough to say thank you. *Dalu nu* to the world's greatest mom and dad. I hope that you both enjoy this one. To my siblings, Chinelo Achebe Ejeuyitchie, Ik and Chidi Achebe, many thanks for your moral support. This book could not have been completed without the cooperation, support, and love of my husband and best friend, Folu Ogundimu, who took on far more than his fair share while I was researching and writing Ahebi's worlds. Thank you so very much for being my rock. At age 12, my daughter Chino is as sweet and loving as she was the day she was born, and to this day, she tells me just how much she loves me and endows me with more hugs and kisses than I can count. Thank you, sweetie; mommy loves you more than words can say.

Many thanks also to Dan Connolly for creating my index, and to Peter Froehlich, the assistant sponsoring editor at Indiana University Press, who made himself available to ensure that my manuscript was ready for copyediting. Brian Herrmann, also of Indiana University Press, saw my book through the production process to publication. Thank you for being such a great project editor. Last, but not least, I am deeply indebted to Dee Mortensen, Senior Sponsoring Editor at Indiana University Press, whose support and enthusiasm was matched only by her consummate professionalism. Thank you so very much for believing in this project from the very beginning. I could not have been blessed with a better editor.

THE FEMALE KING OF COLONIAL NIGERIA

❧ *Nkwado* / THE PREPARATION

All Trees Grow in the Forest, but the Ora Singled Itself Out

The Discovery . . .

"No one will grant you a Ph.D. for writing another history of the women's war." With this stern chastisement and a dry chuckle, my mentor and advisor, the late Professor Boniface Obichere, plunged me into a state of nervous trepidation. It was a sunny afternoon, that day in March 1995, and the "women's war" my mentor so ungraciously denounced, was of course, the Igbo women's war of 1929, that systematically organized rebellion that the women themselves called *ogu umunwanyi* (war of the women) but the colonial government disparagingly dismissed as a women's riot. It was the war that was in fact responsible for the vast number of colonial reports on Igboland and culture, a war that fueled an overwhelming preoccupation among British colonialists with trying to determine for themselves what it was about Igboland and its culture that would encourage Igbo women to behave in so uncouth a manner. But I digress.

Why the curt reprimand from my advisor? Well, I had just confided that I really hadn't the foggiest idea of what it was I wanted to write my doctoral dissertation on. Actually, that is not all together true, because I did know that I wanted to write a history of Igbo women, but which Igbo women and what history? I had no intelligent answer for myself or my tough thesis advisor. It would take me another few months to be able to give voice to my own rhetorical question about which women and what Igbo history, and answer it I would, with much confidence.

My newfound self-assurance stemmed from uncovering, albeit after a painstaking process of wading through hundreds, no make that thousands of pages on Igbo anthropology and ethnography, a female voice. This process of exploration that my mentor had sent me on was a nerve-wracking three-month ordeal—a process during which I would silently (and sometimes audibly) curse him every few hundred pages or so of not finding any tangible information on Igbo women. "Pray tell me," I would question myself in sheer exasperation, "why is Professor Obichere insisting that I plow through these oppressive pages? After all, he and I know that these British colonial anthropologists and ethnographers had not the slightest interest in Igbo women! What a fruitless activity!"

But then, there it was, tucked away in the first paragraph of the 158th page of C. K. Meek's *Law and Authority in a Nigerian Tribe*. Eleven words that introduced me, and, of course, the rest of Meek's readers, to a nameless king of female persuasion. It read: "The village-group of Ogurte is distinguished by having a female Eze."[1] It was this remarkable woman who had transformed herself into a man who would, from that point on, consume many of my waking thoughts. It is this *eze* on whom my critical biography is based.

The Female King of Colonial Nigeria focuses on the life and times of Ahebi Ugbabe, the only female warrant chief and king in colonial Nigeria (and arguably in British Africa).[2] It fills a considerable gap in African and gender studies scholarship by introducing readers to critical perspectives on women, gender, sex, and sexuality, and the colonial encounter. More innovatively, this biography seeks to encourage new ways of seeing, reading, and interpreting African worlds beyond received categories of analysis. In important ways, it complicates, problematizes, and challenges presumptions of homogeneity within the categories of "woman," "prostitute," and "slave." It does this by offering new theories that recognize a multiplicity of African female masculinities—female headman, female warrant chief, female king, and female husband— while delineating the limitations of such gendered transformations.

The term female masculinity was first used by Judith Halberstam in her 1998 book of the same name.[3] In simple terms, Halberstam defines female masculinity as "women who feel themselves to be more masculine than feminine."[4] She positions herself as one such (wo)man, while scrutinizing the politics of butch lesbians, "dykes on bikes," transgendered dykes, and drag kings—"counterproductions" that she argues serve as cultural affirmations of masculinity in women. She tells us what masculinity is not—the social, cultural, and political expression of maleness— and argues instead for a conceptualization and reimagining of masculinity "without men."[5] Like Halberstam, I adopt the concept of female masculinity to address notions and intersections of gendered power, legitimacy, and privilege within society—in this case, a distinctly African community. My conceptualization, however, departs from Halberstam's study in the sense that it does not espouse an uncomfortable relationship with men. It rather flourishes in heterosexual culture, finding expression therein.[6]

Likewise, I adapt the notion of gender as performance, a concept originated by philosopher Judith Butler[7] and then tailored for African

Studies by Paulla A. Ebron,[8] in my analysis of the performance of gendered transformations in precolonial and colonial Nigeria, specifically in Igboland. The idea of performing gender, far from being alien, permeates Igbo consciousness. It is first evoked at the beginning of life to usher newborns into the land of the living. It is also evoked to dramatize social distinctions and roles, as realized in the making, evolving, and/or transformation of girls into women and boys into men[9] and into full men, evolutions that are formally performed through age grades (*ogbo*) and initiation (*ikpo ifu mma*). Similarly, the construction of social, economic, and political status or class can also be viewed as a performance. Social, economic, and political status is realized in the performance of marriage rites when a female husband marries a wife. Social and political status or class was also dramatized in the performance of praise-songs, the blowing of praise flutes, and the beating of *okanga* praise drums by court musicians in honor of their female Igbo king.[10] Yet it is the performance of gender, communicated in the performance of female masculinities —female headmen, female warrant chiefs, female kings, female husbands, and female fathers—that this study is most concerned.[11]

The Female King of Colonial Nigeria also introduces the concept of "wife of deity" and extends the analytical category of "autonomous sex worker" as models through which to engage with continuities and changes in conceptions of female enslavement and independence as well as competing and overlapping definitions of prostitution in an African context. Taken together, these theories contribute greatly to advancing the study of masculinities in Africa as well as African gender systems and the flexibility thereof. There is no comparable biography on an African woman. Evaluating this study therefore against, or in dialogue with existing African women's (auto)biography and African gender history completes the story.

Women in the First Person: African (Auto)biography and Personal Narrative

Ever since M. F. Smith documented the life of a Muslim Hausa woman in her 1954 book *Baba of Karo: A Woman of the Muslim Hausa*,[12] the bibliography on African women's (auto)biography and personal narrative has grown incrementally. The earliest examples of women's (auto) biographical scholarship centered on making them visible. These texts, however, tended to represent women in the ethnographic present, zeroing in on them as both productive and reproductive subjects and as victims of male manipulation.[13] More recent scholarship has focused on asking more profound questions. These researchers have not only sought to capture the voices and life stories of "real" women, they have also sought to make these voices relevant and central to the reconstruction of African history as a whole. The outcome of this scholarly odyssey has been the production of texts as rich as they are varied.

The pioneering work of Margaret Strobel[14] fits this mold. Using a mix of oral and archival evidence, Strobel was able to show in the first of two important studies on women in Mombasa that poor women participated considerably in Kenya's economy and were not restricted by the values of Islam. Ten years later, in 1989, she collaborated with Sarah Mirza to document the life stories of three Swahili women, Bi Kaje, Ma Mishi, and Mwana Kutani, each of whom represented a different reality in society. They were African, Arab, freeborn, and enslaved. Each presented a "narrative of rebellion,"[15] offering Strobel's readers a more comprehensive understanding of the cultural, social, and religious norms of the community she had presented in her earlier work. In the same year, Jean Davison published *Voices of Mutira: Lives of Rural Gikuyu Women*.[16] A collaborative effort between the researcher and the researched, Davison's book presented the lives of seven Kikuyu women who were active participants in the making of their own histories, showing how the choices they made affected their gender roles, ethnic identity, family planning, and education. Apart from the introduction and conclusion, however, the book consists almost entirely of the translated words of the Kikuyu women and provides little or no interpretive vision. As a result, it produced more questions than answers.

Southern African women have also found voice in this body of literature. Marjorie Shostak's *Nisa: The Life and Words of a !Kung Woman* (1981)[17]—a pioneering model of anthropological research "for and by women"—is one such monograph. In it a 50-year-old !Kung woman, Nisa, recalls events of her daily life. Consumers of Nisa's story are also introduced to the vagaries of ethnographical fieldwork in which the anthropologist researcher battles tiredness, homesickness, frustration, and impatience and at times allows her judgmental attitude to get in the way of scholarship. Another monograph, *Women of Phokeng: Consciousness, Life Strategy, and Migrancy in South Africa, 1900–1983*,[18] published ten years later, focuses on a single cohort of Tswana women from relatively prosperous Christian peasant families. Penned by Belinda Bozzoli, individual narratives are choreographed to tell how these women perceived their times, especially their experience of change in South Africa's political economy. While the book is centered on the theoretical framework of "consciousness," it does not necessarily confront divergences between women's memory and historical fact.

Recent (auto)biographical inquires, in the best tradition of scholarship, have dovetailed with previous studies, adopting the good and advancing the field significantly. These studies have ranged from full-length monographs of individual women to engagements with women's personal narratives as backdrops of specialized studies. Claire Robertson's critically acclaimed study on Ga female traders, *Sharing the Same Bowl: A Socioeconomic History of Women and Class in Accra, Ghana* (1990),[19] is an example of this latter endeavor. While situating itself within the economic reality of the Ghanaian marketplace, Robertson's book masterfully interweaves women's personal testimonies throughout the histories presented. *Strategies of Slaves and Women: Life-Stories from East/Central Africa* (1990)[20] is another such study. In it, Marcia Wright elevates her scholarly narrative by engaging a treasure trove of seldom-before-consulted court and mission records to reconstruct women's experiences of enslavement and freedom in the temporal and geographical border regions between lakes Nyasa, Tanganyika, and Mweru. She complicates the truisms of slavery, showing how the survival strategies enslaved women and men evolved to fight the uncertainty of their condition were also at times adapted by the free. Patricia Romero's *Profiles in Diversity: Women in the New South* Africa (1998)[21] shares the stories of twenty-six South African women of varying age, class, and racial backgrounds. From Johannesburg to Pretoria, Kwa-Zulu Natal to Vryburg, the life histories encompass the diverse experiences of women in the new South Africa. What is missing, however, is an in-depth engagement with, or analysis and contextualization of the narratives presented.

Lack of analysis and contextualization has not necessarily been the bane of African women's (auto)biography. In fact, several (auto)biographical texts have proved the contrary. Two recent studies document the life and times of Sara Baartman, the Hottentot Venus.[22] In the more scholarly of the studies, Clifton Crais and Pamela Scully chase down obscure archival and genealogical references and unearth Baartman's life as a person, moving beyond locating her as a victim of scientific, racial, and sexual politics. Other (auto)biographical studies have also moved the genre forward. Of these texts, Wambui Otieno's *Mau Mau's Daughter: A Life History* (1998),[23] Mamphela Ramphele's *Across Boundaries: The Journey of a South African Woman Leader* (1999),[24] Cheryl Johnson-Odim and Nina Mba's *For Women and the Nation: Funmilayo Ransome-Kuti of Nigeria* (1997),[25] and Susan Geiger's *TANU Women: Gender and Culture in the Making of Tanganyikan Nationalism, 1955–1965* (1997)[26] immediately come to mind. Taken collectively, these studies represent vibrant investigations into the lived experiences of a diverse group of African women.

Two texts, *Mau Mau's Daughter* and *Across Boundaries,* stand out as reflective odysseys into being in which each author plays an important role in setting her personal agenda about what to include and what to exclude, reminding us that biography can be as much subjective as objective. In *Mau Mau's Daughter,* Wambui Otieno positions herself as one of the few female operatives working during Kenya's liberation movement, intimately describing women's roles as couriers, spies, and sexual agents. Otieno clearly has an agenda in telling her story, and it is to set the record straight—first about her great-grandfather, Waiyaki wa Hinja, who had been described in literature as a colonial collaborator, and second, about being legally silenced and vilified during the burial saga of her late husband, S. M. Otieno. In the final analysis, the success of the book is also its failure; a measure of self-serving in the accounting. In a South Africa of great poverty, racial oppression, and cultural destruction, Mamphela Ramphele documents her struggle to resist the apartheid state. In more ways than one Ramphele's agenda is similar to Otieno's. She elevates the centrality of her role in the Black Consciousness movement while also advancing the "legitimacy" of her adulterous relationship with Steven Biko. Making and creating agendas is the prerogative of individuals who write about themselves. Unfortunately, the unbiased critical voice is often missing from these constructions.

Clearly articulated personal agendas aside, Susan Geiger's *TANU Women* and Cheryl Johnson-Odim and Nina Mba's *For Women and the Nation* further advance our knowledge about African women's involvement in the nationalist struggles of their countries. Embracing the mantra of "the personal is political," Geiger documents the roles of women in Tanganyikan nationalism. She argues that women were up front and center in the struggle, registering voters and campaigning for equal rights. She also introduces her readers to the performative nature of nationalism in her assessment of the various ways TANU women confronted the colonial state by performing songs, selling TANU membership cards, and campaigning at rallies. The statement that the personal is political can also be used to describe the biography of Funmilayo Ransome-Kuti, who is best known for her leadership in the anti-tax campaigns of Nigerian market women. Mba and Johnson-Odim introduce us to the life and times of Funmilayo, a remarkable organizer and campaigner for Nigerian women's rights. Funmilayo Ransome-Kuti also fights tirelessly for voting rights for women and founds some of the first regional and national Nigerian women's organizations.

Of the (auto)biographical studies on African women in print, a number —including studies on Funmilayo Ransome-Kuti, Mamphela Ramphele, Wambui Otieno, Adelaide Smith Casely Hayford,[27] Winnie Mandela,[28] and, most recently, Wangari Maathai[29]—have focused on elite women. An underlying theme that connects the histories of these elite women is their belief in education as an answer to societal ills. They have each—to varying degrees—used the education of women as a platform through which to address competing women's concerns. Adelaide Smith Casely Hayford, a Sierra Leonean of mixed African and European ancestry who became the second wife of renowned Gold Coast lawyer and nationalist J. E. Casely Hayford, is one such woman. Like Funmilayo Ransome-Kuti of Nigeria, she struggled to build a vocational school for girls in Sierra Leone. However, unlike Funmilayo, who derived her sense of nationalism from her Yorubaness—as evidenced through her name, her choice to communicate in her mother tongue, and her clothing— Adelaide prides herself on being more European than African; she does not have an African name, speak an African language, or wear African clothes. Hayford's life presents biographer Adelaide Cromwell with the unique opportunity to explore contradictions intrinsic within settler populations in Africa. Sadly, however, this study, like several before it, tells us little about creole society and even less about the indigenous peoples on whose land the creoles settled.

While there is no doubt that the existing literature on women's (auto) biography and personal narrative has substantially enriched African and gender studies scholarship, significant gaps remain within the field. *The Female King of Colonial Nigeria* advances that narrative by centering the performance of orality in several of its manifestations—origin traditions; migration and settlement; traditions of kingship; the performance of naming (*igu afa*); geo-mapping; proverbs; the performance of songs; material culture; life stories; and, of course, topical interviews—while championing an interdisciplinary approach to the study of biography. It moves the field forward, expanding the theoretical debates on sex, sexuality, gender and enslavement; (auto)biographical practice; oral history; and the narrative conventions that come to bear on critical constructions of self.

To be sure, Ahebi's story complements the existing literature on the lives of elite African women in the sense that she was accomplished, motivated, and confident. However, beyond these descriptions, Ahebi's life seems to serve up a very different narrative. She was not educated (even though she clearly valued education), and her politics were quite different from the political agendas of the female leaders the studies discussed above focus on. Furthermore, Ahebi cannot be described as a nationalist. She is, in a sense, a deviant, perhaps even a collaborator. She recognized in the British new and enhanced opportunities for political power and might in the form of the offices of headman and warrant chief, and she claimed them with a singleness of purpose, performing in the process transformations into two distinct female masculinities. Moreover, she reaped these benefits at a time when African women rarely negotiated with the invading European colonial authorities. In a different vein, Ahebi's life could be said to straddle the world of the haves and the have-nots. She was in this sense an everywoman. She lived through subjugation, sexual exploitation, humiliation, and exile—many of the predicaments that we see everyday African women confront in existing studies. It is these experiences that helped shape the (wo)man that she became.

As previously discussed, what tends to be missing from autobiographical texts is the critical voice. Ahebi Ugbabe did not have the luxury of a formal education nor did she have the luxury of constructing her own life story to suit her purpose.[30] Consequently, this biography tries to avoid many of the unarticulated agendas that typically appear in (auto) biographies. Instead, it marries the best that autobiography and personal narrative offer, revealing a text that does not have an obvious personal agenda. It offers a narrative constructed through the prism of performance, of constant movement and negotiation between the researcher, the researched, and the audience, reminding us that a spectator in a masquerade dance—in this case, the researcher and the "spectator" audience —cannot appreciate the performance of the dance by standing in one position.

I owe a great deal to Susan Geiger. It was her pioneering work on Tanganyikan nationalism that first gave me permission to tell Igbo women's stories, and tell them I have for the past fifteen years. My methodological approach also evolved from her work. In the best tradition of scholarship, *The Female King of Colonial Nigeria* has been painstakingly pieced together out of myriad sources—some familiar and others quite new—and then contextualized and situated within broader historical events.

Becoming *Nwada*/Daughter [of the Lineage]: The Journey, The Process . . .

How does one piece together and construct a life out of scattered vignettes? How does one construct one (wo)man's world out of scanty documented evidence that is no more than a sentence or so in an old ethnographical study? This journey, this process of piecing together—building—what appears to be a seamless life narrative out of multiple, seemingly unrelated anecdotes is the exercise that I embarked upon as an oral historian, an Igbo historian, and a would-be daughter (of Enugu-Ezike).

In 1996, I was granted a Ford Foundation pre-dissertation grant to go to Nigeria to conduct research for three months. My first stop was the National Archives of Nigeria at Enugu. Much like the journey of "discovery" that my mentor started me on, I was again in search of a female voice—any information that I could locate about women in old Nsukka Division. The dissertation that I had conceived would explore the politics of gender and the evolution of women's power over the first six decades of the twentieth century.[31] However, I soon came to the realization that I needed to "tweak" my topic. I decided, for instance, that it made the most sense to focus on female power—something that I called the "female principle"—instead of on women.[32] This expansion of my research topic enabled me consider all expressions—human and spiritual—of female manifestations in Nsukka Division. Even so, after a month and a half at the archives, I had not uncovered anything substantial about Nsukka women, or about the "female principle," for that matter. Moreover, the only mention of the female king Ahebi Ugbabe that I could find at the time was a relatively short section in V. K. Johnson's "Intelligence Report on the Peoples of Enugu-Ezike."[33] This particular document, although thin on evidence about Ahebi, confirmed two important facts I had already garnered from A. E. Afigbo's short treatment of the female king;[34] namely, that Ahebi had been made warrant chief by the British and the year when that happened. Giddy with excitement at being able to corroborate Afigbo's assertions with primary evidence, I decided that it was time to make my way into Ahebi's community of Enugu-Ezike. I spent the next two and a half months going from research site to research site, interviewing as many oral history collaborators[35] as I could identify. It was during this time that I was able to piece together a skeletal outline of the life story of the female king I was interested in.

However, something had gotten in the way of my information gathering. It seemed as though the community either would not, or could not, tell me all that I needed to know. They seemed to have constructed a barrier that try as I might I could not penetrate. The community had a secret that they were not about to let me in on, at least not during this particular research trip. They would make me wait two more years, as though insisting that I earn the right to know.

In 1998 I was back in Enugu-Ezike. The Fulbright-Hays dissertation fellowship I had secured allowed me a year to attempt to gain the trust and confidence of individual collaborators. I hoped that somewhere along the way I would be able to make a breakthrough. And break through I did on September 26, 1998—the day I became *nwada* (daughter [of the lineage]).

My conversation that day with Abodo Nwa Idoko started like any other interview. There I was sitting across from one of the most powerful *dibias* (medicine men) in the community. Something about his persona, the way he carried himself, made me pose yet again the question that the people of Ahebi's town had been having difficulty answering:

> *Nna anyi* [Our father].[36] . . . Since 1996, I have been going around this village, talking to people who knew Ahebi. They have told me many things about Ahebi. They have told me that when she was young she got lost. And when I have asked how a young girl gets lost, they have shrugged their shoulders in uncertainty. And if pushed harder, they have said that she became a prostitute *after* she ran away. Thus still not answering my "how did she get lost?" question. Because of this, I have become frustrated. Do *you* happen to know how Ahebi got lost?[37]

Abodo Nwa Idoko looked me straight in the eye, cleared his throat loudly, and chuckled. It was a dry chuckle. When he spoke, he said this to me: "I see that our people have been giving you the runaround. Did you say you were here in 1996?" I nodded. "Wonderful! You've tried oh!"[38] [Pause.] "Well, they have done so because they are afraid to tell you the truth." He reached into the pocket of his shirt and brought out a small round tin container of *utaba* (snuff), which he opened with much drama. He lifted a fingerful of the brown, almost black, ground substance into his left nostril. He then closed the container, tapped on it with his index and middle fingers, reopened it, and lifted another fingerful into his right nostril. "*Ehh . . . ehh . . . ehh . . .*" he cleared his throat and let out a sneeze. Then, with as much drama as before, he pulled out a handkerchief and noisily blew his nose. He continued: "I am not afraid. No one and nothing can harm me. I am a powerful medicine man." He then paused for dramatic effect. "Ahebi *did not* get lost. Do you hear what I am saying to you? If anyone asks you, tell them that I, Abodo Nwa Idoko, said it. She *did not* get lost." [Pause.] "She ran away." Idoko then told me in no uncertain terms why Ahebi had run away (*o gbapu*)—a detail I discuss at length in chapter 1.[39]

I felt as though a boulder had fallen on me. I did not, could not, speak for some time. It all made sense now. But why had the people of

Enugu-Ezike hidden this fact from me or at least remained silent about it? Why had it taken the better part of two years for someone to reveal this pertinent detail to me? What did the silence around Ahebi's flight (*mgbapu Ahebi*)[40] say about community memory and the reconstruction of that memory?[41]

Perhaps not everyone knew, I reasoned, trying to explain away the community silence. After all, what happened to Ahebi was not a community event but a private one, and as such neither she nor her family was under any obligation to discuss it. Nonetheless there must have been other people who, like Abodo Nwa Idoko, knew.[42]

It was only after I had reentered the community, Abodo Nwa Idoko's revelation in hand, that the community's reception of me changed. In my post-"reveal" interview with one of Enugu-Ezike's most educated sons, Boniface Abugu, he was only too happy to corroborate Abodo's assertion. His confirmation came in the form of a riddle: "All I know," he began, "is that Baba killed Giwa, but if you insist on adding -*ngida* to Baba, then who am I to disagree with you?"[43] Abugu was of course alluding to Nigeria's corrupt and underhanded head of state, Ibrahim Babangida, who it was widely believed had, in October 1986, killed *Newswatch* editor-in-chief Dele Giwa with a letter bomb bearing the Nigerian government's official insignia. In evoking this riddle, Boniface Abugu confirmed, first, the factor that led up to Ahebi taking flight (*mgbapu Ahebi*), and, second, the reason most of my oral history collaborators had previously not admitted to having any knowledge of this fact: fear. Boniface Abugu admitted in the same conversation that he was not immune to the community fear himself but felt strongly that because he was simply confirming evidence I had already gathered no harm would come to him.

In the final analysis, it had taken a fearless individual, a powerful *dibia* (medicine man) and herbalist, to reveal society's secret. From that point on, collaborator after collaborator wasted no time in not only corroborating his assertion but also confiding other "unsavory" facts—oftentimes in whispered tones—about the female king that I was researching.

My relationship with the community had indeed changed. I was no longer a stranger, visitor, or guest (*onye obia*); I had become *nwada*—a daughter (of Enugu-Ezike) who could be trusted with all information.[44] It was as a result of this earned change in my positionality that I was granted the wherewithal to piece together—through community memory —the life story of this remarkable woman, Ahebi Ugbabe. And I am most appreciative to the Enugu-Ezike community for this opportunity.

Becoming *Onye Obia*/Visitor, or an Igala-Sanctioned Guest

In July 2007, when my research guide, Erobike Eze, my Igala interpreter, Mangwu Usman,[45] and I arrived in Igalaland, I was on a quest
to corroborate evidence already collected about Ahebi Ugbabe from
Igbo country. Igalaland featured prominently in Ahebi's story, as she
had spent the better part of twenty years there, growing into maturity.
Thus, there was no way that I could fail to visit Igalaland to witness
for myself, to feel, to sense the landscape that would have affected the
female king I was researching. Our first stop was the *attah*-Igala's (Igala
king's) palace in Idah. We went there to request permission from him to
conduct research in his kingdom.

When we arrived the palace, we had to stop at its front office first.
There we met Friday Ocheni, the Attah-Igala's administrative officer,
who received us well. After I had informed him of my mission, he asked
that I write an official letter to the Attah-Igala, Aliyu Obaje, requesting
permission to conduct research in his kingdom. I was of course happy
to oblige. I sat in the small office ruled paper in hand, and penned the
letter below:

[no date]
His Royal Majesty
Alhaji (Dr.) Aliyu Obaje (CON, CBE, FIAMT, CFR)
Attah-Igala

~~Dear Sir:~~ *Gabaidu,*[46]
Permission to Conduct Oral Research in Igala Kingdom
My name is Nwando Achebe and I am an Associate Professor
of African History at Michigan State University, USA. My area of
expertise is Women's History. I am in the process of writing my
second book on King Ahebi Ugbabe of Enugu-Ezike, the only
female warrant chief in all of colonial Nigeria, and arguably British
Africa.

King Ahebi not only lived in Igalaland from approximately
1894–1915, but she was crowned king by the *Attah-Igala* in the
1920s. I am interested in documenting her sojourn in Igalaland—
for instance, the name of the *Attah* who made her king, and the
reasons that he did.

I would be most grateful for any assistance you can provide
me.

Respectfully,
Nwando Achebe, Ph.D.[47]

I handed the letter to Mr. Ocheni, who instructed us to come back the following morning, at which time he was certain the *attah* would have an answer for me.

We returned bright and early the next morning and were informed that the *attah* had granted me permission to conduct research in his kingdom. He also confirmed, through his spokesperson, that his own father, Attah-Obaje (senior), had crowned Ahebi king.[48] The *attah* offered the services of his aged aunt, Ago Obaje, a beaded chief, who would be able to tell me more about the coronation her brother Attah-Obaje had performed.

After my conversation with Attah-Obaje's sister, the *attah*'s palace provided me with names of additional people to interview. In a foreign land, this direction and the permission to proceed with my inquiries was essential, because I could now say to individual collaborators that I had visited their king and that he had given me permission to conduct research in his kingdom. King Obaje's permission was a badge of approval, a declaration to all that I was indeed an *onye obia,* a guest.

At the end of my sojourn in Igala, I had interviewed a cross-section of individuals, some of whom were connected to the *attah* but just as many who had no connection to the royal house. My sojourn as an *onye obia* sanctioned by the Igala royal crown was indeed fruitful.

Nkolika—Recalling Is Supreme

In her recent book, Stephanie Newell has strongly rebuked me for what she deemed my conscious lack of engagement with issues of same-sex desire as well as with theoretical perspectives in my writing. Here in part are her words: "As a result of Achebe's refusal to engage with sexual desire, sexual coercion, and African 'cultures of discretion' is that her vivid story of the female king Ahebi Ugbabe, who transformed herself into a 'man' in the early twentieth century, remains highly narrativized and situated outside theorization or analysis."[49] Newell's charge that I have somehow deliberately skewed evidence against a supposed lesbian sexual preference on Ahebi's part in order to present an Africa devoid of homosexuality is not only false but is rooted in a Eurocentric (mis)understanding of African social institutions. Let me first state that I in no way ascribe to the fiction of a purely heterosexual Africa. Homosexuality exists in all societies.[50] However, woman-to-woman marriage in Africa has *absolutely nothing* to do with homosexuality. It instead speaks to the performance of social and economic status and class as well as to the performance of a female masculinity—a (wo)man's prerogative to assume the gendered position of husband—within a culturally sanctioned relationship. My discussion of the Igbo institution in chapters 1 and 4 place it firmly within its cultural, social, and economic cosmos and, by so doing, counters Newell's misinterpretation.

What I would like to address, however, is the author's reprimand that I, an African historian, an Igbo historian, somehow do not have the right to simply tell the Igbo story without the imposition of faulty, misinformed, interpretive models that originated in Western consciousness. Drawing inspiration from Filomina Chioma Steady's recent chapter on gender research on Africa in which she chastises Western scholars for placing "high value on theory and theory-building at the expense of pragmatism and relevance,"[51] my response to Newell is that there are some stories that simply need to be told. And as a people's historian, I have positioned myself to tell these stories in a way that the people who shared them with me will understand and appreciate.[52] To this end, my theorizing, when I have found it necessary to engage with theory, has originated from a deep-seated awareness and understanding of African culture and institutions and has thus come from within.[53]

People who have been lucky enough not to have had their stories told by others without respect might not fully understand nor appreciate the gift of being able to tell one's story on one's own terms. I come from a world where our story has been told almost exclusively by others. Therefore, in my own writing, I have worked to privilege the indigenous point of view so that in the final analysis, the people who entrusted me with their histories and lives can see themselves emerge within the text. *The Female King of Colonial Nigeria* contributes to this effort.

Don't Ask of Oral History That Which Oral History Cannot Answer

I have already spoken of one of the challenges of using oral history, that of community silence. Other issues—including how and why things are remembered the way they are, why some things are remembered and others forgotten—also beg attention. It seems to me that the fact that certain events are remembered by the community tells us something about indigenous reconstructions of history—namely, that the community deems those events important and therefore remembers them. Silence, as witnessed above, can be interpreted as society's way of protecting itself from acknowledging (or identifying with) unpalatable events or people and in so doing distancing itself from catastrophes that it would much rather forget. In both circumstances, the community functions as what Christie Chinwe Achebe has termed "custodians of memory,"[54] remembering and reliving (and, in some cases, choosing to forget) individual and group memories, anecdotes, vignettes, and histories that, when transmitted to an oral historian such as myself, metamorphose into an ordered indigenous metanarrative. However, A. E. Afigbo has cautioned us in an important article not to ask of oral history that which oral history cannot answer.[55] My own research among the men and women of Nsukka Division is rife with examples of the folly of falling into this pit; when this occurred, the individuals I interviewed were quick to call my attention to the absurdity of my line of questioning. Case in point: one collaborator, Oliefi Ugwu-Ogili, pointed out to me that when Ahebi was alive, she attended two courts, one to which "she was carried on men's heads to" (i.e. the colonial courts) and the other in which "she judged cases in her palace." When I asked a follow-up question about whether there was a difference in the types of cases that were judged in the courts "where King Ahebi was carried on men's heads to" and the cases "she judged in her palace," Ugwu-Ogili responded rather dismissingly, "Did I follow her to those courts to know the types of cases?"[56] Another collaborator, when asked whether he knew who had fathered Ahebi's descendant, Arikpu (whom he had previously discussed), had this to say: "I do not know. I shall not say what I do not know."[57] Even the boastful medicine man Utubi[58] recoiled when asked a question about the girl Ahebi: "Can I say anything about my mother[59] when she was young or small? This person [pointing to Alhaji Sarikin Akpanya] narrated the story his father told him [about her]. Neither of us can tell you how Ahebi was or what she was when she was young."[60]

However, when members of these same communities had something to contribute, these indigenous transmitters of history were not shy about sharing what it was that they knew. And when I was fortunate enough to corroborate indigenous knowledge with written primary evidence, my excitement was palpable because a conventional source had helped validate an avant-garde oral one. A somewhat confusing and rambling conversation in 1998 in which Alice Akogu (formerly Ahebi) recalled the *attah*-Igalas (kings of Igalaland) who visited Ahebi provides an example of this. The information that she provided corresponded with written sources on these kings, and the written sources validated the recollections of this custodian of memory. She not only informed me that two *attah*-Igalas visited Ahebi Ugbabe when she was warrant chief and king, she provided their names and physical characteristics. The one she described as Attah-Ameh Oboni was light in complexion and tall (in fact, she called him "huge"). She indicated that this particular *attah* visited Ahebi after "the first one . . . the dark and [equally] huge *attah*," who she identified as Attah-Obaje. It was this *attah* who, according to her, made Ahebi king. Hear her words:

> I know two *attahs* who came to Ahebi's palace: the first one and the other who succeeded him after his death. One was fair in complexion, tall and huge. The first one was dark in complexion and huge. Ameh Oboni was one; and Obaje Ocheje[61] was the other *attah*. Ahebi was installed king by the dark Attah-Obaje Ocheje. Ameh killed himself. After each *attah*'s visit, Ahebi gave him gifts at the time of his depar-ture. She gave goats to the *attah*'s entourage. After all, she had very many cows; and as many as seven died a week without Ahebi notic-ing. She offered kola nuts and a cow to the *attah*, and goats to his attendants. . . . To each of the two *attahs* who came to her palace she gave a cow. Ameh Oboni was the fair-complexioned one. The one who came first was dark. He made her king. The other one [Attah-Ameh] was fair and handsome.[62]

Documented evidence tells us that Attah-Obaje reigned from 1926 to 1945.[63] With the aid of oral and written evidence provided by the current *attah*-Igala, I was able to confirm that Attah-Obaje was indeed the *attah* who made Ahebi king.[64] Evidence also indicated that Attah-Ameh, who reigned from 1945 to 1956, would have been the second *attah* to visit Ahebi, just before her death in 1948.[65] He also would have been the *attah* who attended her funeral around 1946—a detail that Alice Akogu also mentioned during my long interview with her. Akogu's last point that I could substantiate is the fact that Attah-Ameh committed suicide[66]—the circumstance of which I discuss briefly in chapter 2.[67]

When oral evidence checks out, the experience is magnificent. However, oral historians more likely than not will be faced with the community's uncertainty and lack of clarity at one point or the other. It was during these times that I found that marrying oral knowledge collected from the custodians of memory with available written sources completed the story. This is the strategy I adopted in researching and writing Ahebi's world. For example, during my fieldwork, custodians of indigenous memory were able to tell me about Ahebi's responsibilities as court president in general terms but for the most part were unable to provide intricate details about particular cases or exact judgments. It became clear to me that I would have to marry the oral sources with archival ones to reconstruct a balanced and complete account. Thus, I embarked on yet another trip to the National Archives of Nigeria in

Enugu. My task was specific: I was looking to corroborate the indigenous memory of a particular case in which Ahebi took her community to court that most likely occurred in the early to mid-1940s. This was my sixth trip to the National Archives of Nigeria since 1996, and I was now on a first-name basis with many of the staff. I had one month available to me to look through all the judgment books—criminal and civil—that I could lay my hands on for Nsukka Division covering the period that Ahebi sat on the court as warrant chief. I also consulted all the Native Court Cause Books[68] and Native Court General Note Books[69] that covered the period when Ahebi was warrant chief.[70] I was able to accomplish this huge undertaking with the help of two archivists, Mr. Christian Uzor (now deceased) and Mr. Innocent Edeh, who kept replenishing my stack of Native Court books as quickly as I could go through them. In all, I consulted one out of a total of five civil and criminal judgment books (covering Nsukka Division's five area courts,[71] each one containing at least 300 individual cases), seventy-two out of a total of eighty-eight criminal judgment books (covering the same court areas and containing the same number of cases as the civil and criminal judgment book) and twenty-seven out of a total of thirty-one civil judgment books (also covering the same court areas and containing the same number of cases as the judgment books above).[72] Of the criminal judgment books, 14/1/67, 14/1/68, 14/1/77, 14/1/79, 14/1/80, 14/1/81, 14/1/87, and 14/1/88 were missing.[73] Two of the civil judgment books covering the time period I was investigating were missing: 16/1/24 and 16/1/28.[74] Of the missing criminal judgment books, two case books covered the periods 1937–1943 and 1943–1954—time periods that coincided with the possible date of the particular case that I was seeking. In the end, even though I was unable to find the specific case that I sought, my search revealed numerous cases in which Warrant Chief Ahebi presided either as president or member of the Native Court. As a result, my analysis of Ahebi's work as warrant chief in chapter 3 of this study is greatly enriched.

All in all, I can say without hesitation that my *nkwado,* the preparation that I embraced in order to successfully complete this biography—a preparation that challenged me to listen, hear, and process variant voices, both oral and written, through time and space—was worth the effort. It was a painstaking process that lasted over fifteen years, a true blending of interdisciplinary approaches. I hope that the end product like the (wo)man on whom the study is based, will stand the test of time. I now invite you to sit back and enjoy King Ahebi's story.

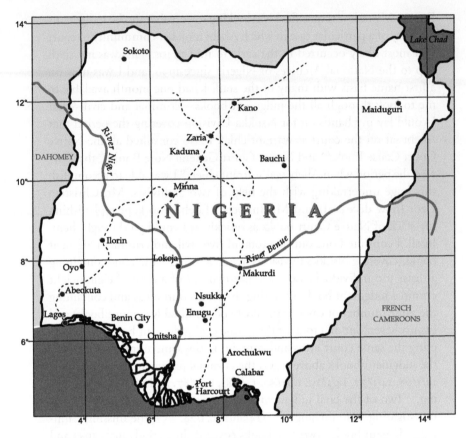

MAP INTRO. 1. Nigeria in the Early Twentieth Century. *Remote Sensing & Geographic Information Science, Michigan State University.*

Nkowa / THE INTRODUCTION

Unspoken, Blame the Mouth; Unheard, Blame the Ear

The remembered history of the people of Nsukka Division from the earliest times can be sorted into a series of memorable events, definite landmarks or, put differently, "public disasters of the greatest magnitude"[1] that have been passed down orally from one generation to the next. In some cases these events were recorded by the first British administrative agents to have converged on to the area. In 1934, one such officer, J. Barmby, charted these remembered epochs in an intelligence report on the peoples of the Igbodo group of Nsukka Division in the following manner:

(1) The founding of the village by a traditional ancestor

(2) Petty raids by surrounding towns *of which there are no details* (emphasis added)

(3) The coming of the Government in the person of a white man nick-named Otikpo, the destroyer

(4) The influenza (1919)

(5) The Ochima Patrol (1924)

(6) Taxation 1928[2]

Barmby's documented delineations most certainly provide the historian of Nsukka Division, Igboland, and arguably colonial Nigeria, a rare opportunity to gain insight into historical reconstructions from an indigenous point of view. Nevertheless, I would argue that in the case of Enugu-Ezike, it does not tell the entire story. In important ways, it unintentionally skews the measured perspective of the indigenous knowledge being expressed. Thus, a modification of his reading in particular locations to account for this oversight is necessary. Barmby's first identified cataloging of how indigenous memory constructed and privileged the founding of a village by a traditional ancestor is not only sound but firmly centered on Enugu-Ezike consciousness. The people of Enugu-Ezike recall in various tellings the founding of their town by an ancestor known as Ezike, a point that I will expound upon shortly. I would

MAP INTRO. 2. Nsukka Division and Surrounding Regions. *Remote Sensing & Geographic Information Science, Michigan State University.*

propose an addition here, though, that would allow for the centering of the "naissance of the [extended] family"[3] as an addendum to that of the village, thus giving prominence to the collective histories of the individuals who make up the village group. I am convinced that such an elucidation is necessary because in these Igbo parts, the conventional wisdom is that the foundation of the village or village group extends from the family—a unit through which the social, political, and reli-

MAP INTRO. 3. Nsukka Division. *Remote Sensing & Michigan State University.*

gious organization of Igbo communities can be traced.[4] C. K. Meek, another European documenter of Barmby's time, supports this point of view when he argues in his 1930 report that "the basic social unit" in all Igbo communities "is the group of patrilineal relatives who live together in close association and constitute what is known as *umunna* i.e. the children of a common forefather."[5] The term *umunne* (children of one mother) is also used to delineate one or more distinct but related extended family—families that make up what anthropologists have called a kindred. It is this kindred or, more precisely put, several kindreds living in close proximity, according to Meek, that occupy an area that can be described as a village. Furthermore, the unity of the village group is "based on a sense of common ancestry [i.e., the extended family], the possession of a common territory, and home, [as well as] common customs."[6] It is from this reading that my case for this initial modification of Barmby's conceptualization is extended.

   In response to Barmby's assessment of the importance of "petty raids . . . *of which there are no details*" to Nsukka's indigenous reconstruction of history, I take exception to his reduction of the interwar period[7] to a phase of "petty raids," as well as the second half of his statement, by arguing that in the case of Enugu-Ezike, as was true of most Igbo towns of the period, the minutiae of these so-called "petty raids," in actuality, inter-village slave-raiding, kidnapping, and warring, were not only remembered, but have, in fascinating ways, complicated the way in which each community's collective history materialized. The outcome of this pillaging of human beings, was the adoption of survival mechanisms that were constructed by each community to help "fight the slave trade"—mechanisms that Sylviane A. Diouf has in an important study characterized as defensive, protective, and offensive strategies.[8] I would in fact take Diouf's analysis a step further and contend that in the wake of these wars, these now weakened, fragile, and depopulated Nsukka Division communities (e.g., Enugu-Ezike, Idoha, Alor-Uno, and Obukpa) sought protection from their raiding enemies—as well as recompense from these same tormentors—by creating supernatural protector spirits that would simultaneously protect society and repopulate it by marrying human beings in a process known as *igo mma ogo* (becoming the in-law of a deity).[9] The introduction of these new deity-to-human marriages encouraged the creation of what amounted to new "slave"[10] systems, a reality that directly affected the life of the young Ahebi and one that I will develop more fully in chapter 1.

Barmby's next case for indigenous periodization centers on "the coming of the Government in the person of a white man nick-named Otikpo, the destroyer." The essential idea conveyed by this argument was realized in Enugu-Ezike as well as in Ahebi's life. For it was Ahebi Ugbabe who brought Otikpo, the destroyer, into her community, and it was with Ahebi's help that this socially constructed "he" was able to claim Enugu-Ezike as a colonial territory. Moreover, it was this coming of "government" that enabled Ahebi Ugbabe to perform her first gendered modification into female headman and would consequently pave the way for her second and more powerful modification into female warrant chief. Ahebi Ugbabe's life indeed tells us much about the shifting bases of gendered power under the British, as well as the important ways African women and men helped shape and remap the colonial terrain. An examination of colonialism as a gendered and gendering process will be developed and extended in chapters 2 and 3.[11]

Barmby's fourth, fifth, and sixth identified periods of Nsukka historical classification—namely, the Great Influenza, the 1924 Ochima Patrol, and the 1928 institution of direct taxation—I would argue, although important and certainly remembered in Enugu-Ezike, were not as significant as these same episodes would have been elsewhere in Nsukka Division. The reason can be traced back to the subject of this critical biography Ahebi Ugbabe. It is my contention that because there was an Ahebi Ugbabe in Enugu Ezike during these time periods—a woman who would assume elevated and mythical proportions—the construction of history in this part of Nsukka Division was shaped and overtaken by the memory of some of Ahebi's more outrageous and contentious actions. It is from this understanding that I offer yet another modification of Barmby's historical cataloging in which I substitute the Great Influenza of 1918–1919 with the coronation of Ahebi Ugbabe as warrant chief. The performance of this female masculinity, which also took place in 1918, moderated the overwhelming magnitude of the disaster of the influenza—one of the otherwise most important determinants of dating in Igboland—in the collective memory of Enugu-Ezike indigenes, creating in its stead the recollection of another *ife di egwu* (thing of great incredulity) in which Ahebi Ugbabe materialized as the only female warrant chief in all of colonial Nigeria. For Ahebi's coronation as warrant chief to have modified the sway of Igbo dating around the influenza, it seems possible that in the processing of indigenous knowledge over the years, Enugu-Ezike people privileged individual feat over the recollection of a disaster that affected so many—thus, perhaps, rendering them nameless. Consequently, this very Ahebi Ugbabe performance, realization, and reclassification of the office of warrant chief—an institution that not only had exclusively been constructed as male, but had effectively changed the focus of indigenous recalling—will be probed, scrutinized, and investigated in chapter 3.

The Ochima Patrol of 1924, a patrol which saw to the burning of an entire community of people to the ground[12]—a community far removed from Enugu-Ezike, and as a consequence, the corollary of which was not readily recollected by the Enugu-Ezike populace—will be excluded entirely from this historical reconstruction. In its stead, I will examine Ahebi Ugbabe's coronation as *eze* (female king), the third in her series of gendered performances, which was premised on the reality that in precolonial Igboland gender and sex did not coincide. Instead, gender was flexible and fluid, allowing women to become men and men to become women. This created unique Igbo female masculinities such as female husbands[13] and female sons and male femininities such as male priestesses.[14] To be sure, Ahebi's transformation into a female king was unprecedented, an *ife di egwu* (thing of great incredulity) that perhaps surpassed

her coronation as warrant chief or at the very least lent increased legitimacy and support to her colonial transformation. But what was even
more incredible was the fact that Ahebi was able to achieve this feat in a
society in which kings had no place; the institution was viewed almost as
an affront to the Igbo belief in egalitarianism in which the community
led itself. This Igbo perspective about kings had not emerged from a
vacuum. The Igbo knew about kings—after all, they were surrounded by
societies that had kings.[15] Perhaps it was their witness of kings in action
that supported their philosophy, which was clothed in sayings that were
meant to warn about the excesses of such an autocratic enterprise. One
such saying warned, "If you want to be a king, you can be a king in your
own father's backyard." In other words, "do not think that you can lord
your governing over others. Igbo society has no place for that." The Igbo
maintained very clearly that *Igbo enwe eze* (the Igbo have no kings).[16]

Finally, I will touch upon the 1928 taxation levied on Igbo men in
colonial Nigeria. As warrant chief, Ahebi supervised this new tax. The
new policy set into motion responses that led to the dismantling of
the institution of warrant chief in British Africa and the concomitant
reduction in Ahebi's political clout. However, this 1928 tax was not the
incident that stood out most for the Enugu-Ezike people. What the
community remembered most vividly during this period was the role
that Ahebi played three years later, during the 1931 "palm kernel census."
The community also recalled Ahebi's ingenuity and foresight in reimagining the use of the many buildings constructed for the census workers
as future educational structures for Umuida children as they came of
age.[17] In fact, Ahebi established the first school of learning in her palace,
as most warrant chiefs of her time were known to have done.

The next epoch of history Enugu-Ezike people recalled was characterized by Ahebi's virtuoso performance in regrouping and repackaging
herself as female king extraordinaire and, a few years later, as though
capitalizing upon that transformation, the launch of her most ambitious gendered performance yet, this time into a full man.[18] It was this
particular gendered performance, occasioned by her "bringing out" and
introducing to her community a masked spirit called Ekpe Ahebi, that
had the most immediately devastating and lasting effect on gendered
relationships in Enugu-Ezike, and would be evoked to the devaluation
of the 1928 taxation that affected all of Nigeria. The importance of the
masquerade cult in Igboland (as well as elsewhere in Africa) provides the
answer to the question: "why such a devaluation?" As A. O. Onyeneke
has argued, the masquerade cult was an institution that worked to dif-

ferentiate men from women.[19] More important, I contend that it differentiated regular men from full men. In fact, the social definition of full man in most West African communities has been constructed as the ability to control a masked spirit.[20] The focus of chapters 3, 4, and 5 will be centered on the ways that King Ahebi was able to maneuver and manipulate these gendered processes.

This book will follow in a methodical manner Enugu-Ezike people's conceptualization of their history, a process informed by a systematic colonial charting in 1934 of the historical progression of events in an Nsukka Division locality from an indigenous point of view. It is this delineation, this mapping, of what the people themselves held as important that I will privilege in my own construction and retelling of King Ahebi's story. Put differently, the memorable events, definite landmarks, and "public disasters of the greatest magnitude" that Enugu-Ezike people constructed as important *oge Ahebi* (during the time of Ahebi)[21] will form the milieu of this critical biography. Thus, I will first present and analyze the creation traditions that were handed down in Ahebi Ugbabe's town of Enugu-Ezike *oge gbo gbo* (a long, long time ago);[22] then I will chart the naissance of the Ugbabe extended family. The incessant warfare, raiding, and kidnapping that occurred during Ahebi's childhood years in Enugu-Ezike and that consequently led to the development of "slave" systems previously unknown to the area will be set as a backdrop to my analysis of the institution of *igo mma ogo* (becoming the in-law of a deity), an institution that had a decisive effect on Ahebi's life choices. I will use the creation and consolidation of the colonial government (*oge otikpo*)[23] as a lens through which I will unpack the thinking that must have gone into Ahebi's decision-making process vis-à-vis her relationship with the British. The rest of the biography will be devoted to fleshing out Ahebi's various gendered performances of the female masculinities of female headman, female warrant chief, female king, and, finally, full or "complete" man, all of which occurred *oge Ahebi*. These themes and more will be navigated throughout the text as I conceptualize and reconstruct the life of this extraordinary woman called Ahebi.

Situating Enugu-Ezike

Enugu-Ezike, which is situated at the northernmost tip of present-day Enugu State, Nigeria, made up a significant part of the geographical expanse called Nsukka Division during the period under investigation, ca. 1880–1948. According to the Nigerian census of 1911,[24] the town of Enugu-Ezike had approximately 11,460 inhabitants.[25] By 1931,

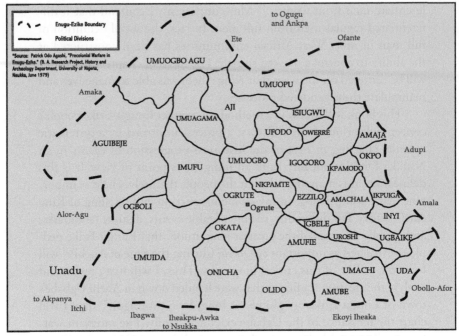

MAP INTRO. 4. Political Divisions of Enugu-Ezike. *Remote Sensing & Michigan State University.*

Enugu-Ezike had spread over an area of ninety-five square miles and had a total population of 27,919. The population density was approximately 294 people per square mile as compared to the 217 people per square mile for all of Nsukka Division or the 91 people per square mile in the Southern Provinces.[26] The people of Enugu-Ezike collectively remember this 1931 census count, when King Ahebi asked all the adults to take one palm kernel to the administration for each individual in a household. Michael Idoko, the headmaster of Ahebi Primary School in the mid-1990s, describes what transpired: "During the census of 1931, everyone was instructed to bring one kernel and through that exercise, people were counted. In a family of seven, each person was to bring one kernel each, [for a total of] seven kernels. In fact, nobody knew that what was being done was a census count. [It was arranged like this because] at that time, there was not enough labor to do the counting."[27]

This particular census, locally recalled as "the palm kernel census,"[28] informed how Enugu-Ezike people remembered and constructed their history *oge Ahebi*. The census figures stayed much the same in 1934, the year that Enugu-Ezike was described as "one of the most promising groups in the [Nsukka] Division" in an annual report on the Onitsha Province.[29] By 1937, the population had risen slightly to 28,423.[30] Twenty six years later, Enugu-Ezike's population had risen to 82,213 and it was one of the largest rural towns in colonial Nigeria.[31] Its land mass had also grown, extending approximately 260 kilometers; and the population density was about 625 persons per square mile.[32]

Oge Ahebi, the town itself was made up of four large village groups of thirty-three villages, including the Ezeodo group made up of Uda and Uroshi villages; the Umuitodo[33] group made up of Amufie, Amachalla, Igbele, Ikpuiga, Imufu, and Olido; and the Essodo group made up of Aji, Umuagama, Umu-Ogbo-Uno, Umu-Ogbo-Agu, Umu-Ogbu-Ekposhi, and Ufodo. The fourth and largest village group, Umuozzi, was the area where King Ahebi's power and clout was felt most directly. It included Amaja, Abuibeje, Amube, Ezzilo, Igogoro, Ikpamodo, Inyi, Isiugwu, Nkpamte, Ogrute, Ogboli, Ogbodu, Okata, Onicha, Okpo, Owerre Eze, Umachi, Umuida, and Umuopu.[34] In fact, Ahebi's village of birth, Umuida, was the largest of all the villages of Enugu-Ezike.[35]

The town of Ahebi's birth, Enugu-Ezike, shares common boundaries with the Akpoto-speaking Ete,[36] an ethnic group of Igala extraction, and with Ofante and Ankpa on its northern Igala side and the following towns on its Igbo side: to its south, Ekoyi, Iheaka, Iheakpu, and Ibagwa; to its east, Obollo; and to its west, Unadu, Itchi, and Alor-Uno.[37] Its inhabitants, though Igbo, speak a dialect of the language that reveals strong Igala and Akpoto influences—an influence that, according to V. K. Johnson, is "apparent in their manners and many of their customs."[38] A relatively small "stranger" population of Hausa, Nupe, and Yoruba had settled in the village of Amufie for trading purposes.[39]

The Enugu-Ezike of Ahebi's time was mostly undulating country, rising, according to V. K. Johnson's intelligence report, "from 900 feet above sea level in the west to 1500 feet in the east."[40] Its topography, as its name suggested (*enugu* means "on top of a hill" or "hill top") was hilly, like much of Nsukka Division. The Ugwueka hill (at Amube) and the Elele hill (at Olido) were concentrated in the southern part of Enugu-Ezike, whereas the Alumu and Ekposhi hills were located at the center of the town. The Amona Eje and Egija hills were located at Agbibeje and Amara villages, respectively.[41] The reward engendered by this hilly topography featured prominently in the creation traditions of the people of Enugu-Ezike that had been handed down from *oge gbo gbo,* a point that I will return to shortly.

Oge Ahebi, the source of livelihood for Enugu-Ezike people was farming and trading. Palm wine tapping was the main occupation of men; it was the vocation of Ahebi's father. Enugu-Ezike people used all parts of the palm tree and palm produce, trading locally as well as with "middlemen traders of foreign extraction," who then sold the pro-duce to European firms at Ogurugu, about fifty miles away.[42] Palm oil, palm kernels, and palm wine were popular both locally and far away, bestowing upon the people of Enugu-Ezike the title of the palm-tappers extraordinaire of Nsukka Division—an assessment that seems to have lasted the test of time; even today Enugu-Ezike is the place to go to buy good palm wine. Women were active in the local cloth-making indus-tries, specializing especially in spinning and weaving. Farming, on the other hand, tended to be practiced on the subsistence level; indigenes produced cassava, yams, and tobacco from Enugu-Ezike's poor, sandy soil for their daily consumption. These crops were typically not valuable commercially.[43]

The Founding of the Village by a Traditional Ancestor: Traditions of Origin, Migration, and Settlement in Enugu-Ezike

Two principal traditions of origin, migration, and settlement have survived in Enugu-Ezike and have been handed down from one gen-eration to the next. One tradition traces Enugu-Ezike's first ancestor to the Kingdom of Benin and the other to the capital city of the Igala kingdom at Idah. In the first tradition, the progenitor of Enugu-Ezike was a man from the Benin royal family known as Enugu-Ezike Oba Atta Igara bi Igbo N'ime, or Ezike Oba[44] for short. When one attempts to deconstruct this name, a number of variables emerge. The first is its literal translation, which would be: "Enugu-Ezike, son of Oba [of Benin], the king of Igala lives [or simply is] inside Igbo." This transla-tion means little without unpacking the sensibilities of the people who did the naming. The Igbo expression *ibi n'ime* (to live inside)—as in Atta Igara bi Igbo N'ime—is most profound and is layered in its mean-ings. The Igbo tongue twister *Mpili kata mpi. Mpi di mpi n'ime. Mpi mkpi pulu* (Horn greater than horn. *Horn inside horn.* Horn grown by he-goat), for instance, highlights this idea of "something being inside something else." Another expression, *Igbo di Igbo n'ime* (Igbo that is inside Igbo), perhaps more clearly than any other, speaks to this idea of layered meanings. It conveys most directly and efficiently the notion of "something being inside something [else]," which is a way that the Igbo talk about the "realness of a thing." The expression is used to indicate a purity, a genuineness that contrasts sharply with something that is fake. Therefore, *Igbo di Igbo n'ime* would be an allusion to "the real Igbo." The name Atta Igara bi Igbo N'ime (the king of Igala who is inside Igbo) would thus be suggestive of a very close and "real" link between the Igbo and Igala.[45]

According to the tradition, Ezike Oba was a hunter who was believed to have migrated from Benin to Onitsha through Asaba and then settled for some time at Enugwu Ukwu. Ezike Oba crossed the Anambra River to Igabada and continued his journey to Idah, both of which are in Igala country. He settled in Igalaland for some time, honing his hunting skills by joining the seasonal hunting expeditions of Igala menfolk. One day, Ezike Oba shot a huge elephant and followed the track of the wounded animal from Odaru and Agbokete in Idah all the way to Ibagwa Ani-Ekoyi grove in Igbo country and then up the Ugwueka hill at Amube, where the animal fell dead.[46] The priest of Ugwueka, Attama[47] Ugwueka, found him there and gave Ezike Oba a piece of land on the hill where his game died. He settled there. For this reason, the village of Amube occupies a position of seniority in relation to all the other Enugu-Ezike villages and Amube elders have the honored place of "most senior" during all Enugu-Ezike gatherings.[48]

Attama Ugwueka introduced Ezike Oba to a woman named Nogbo Omogbo,[49] a daughter of Ekoyi Ikojo of Iheaka, whom Ezike Oba eventually married. They had four sons: Ezeodo, Itodo, Eseodo, and Ozzi. In time these sons married and had children of their own, eventually creating an extended family of thirty-three. These thirty-three descendants of Ezike Oba and Nogbo Omogbo eventually made up the thirty-three villages of Enugu-Ezike.[50]

One of the reasons hunter Ezike Oba chose to settle at the Ugwueka hill, the tradition reveals, was because he could easily spot game from the top of the hill. Soon he earned the name Elugwu (meaning "on top of the hill" or "hill top") and his descendants thus became known as Elugwu Ezike Oba. In time, the Oba portion of the name fell into disuse and his descendants became known as simply Enugu-Ezike.[51] (The letters "l" and "n" are often interchangeable in Nsukka Igbo.)

A slight variation to the tradition suggests that Ezike Oba gave part of his kill to Attama Ugwueka for allowing him to settle in the area. The *attama* then reciprocated by sending Ezike Oba gifts. However, as this telling reveals, Attama Ugwueka did not know Ezike Oba's name, so he told his servants to deliver the gifts to Onye Elugwu (the hill dweller).

As a result, the descendants of the man Ezike Oba became known as Enugu-Ezike; that is, "[the people of] Ezike's hill"[52]—a name that has survived to the present.

The second tradition of origin differs slightly from the first, naming the progenitor of Enugu-Ezike as a man from Idah, Igalaland, called simply Ezike. The man Ezike, like his counterpart in the Benin version, was said to have traveled to Enugu-Ezike on a hunting expedition. In this version, however, he commenced his journey at Idah. He also killed an elephant at the Ugwueka hill, meeting the Attama of Ugwueka in the process, who allowed him to settle there. Ezike, as in the first tradition, eventually married and had four sons: Ezeodo, Itodo, Esodo and Ozzi, the fathers of Ezike's thirty-three descendants. In this telling, Ezike, the man from Idah, is the original father or ancestor of Enugu-Ezike.

Both traditions allude to the fact that after Ezike was married his in-laws gave him a strip of land called Ufu. He later descended from the hill and settled there with his wife and children. Ufu is still revered by the descendants of the father of Enugu-Ezike, so much so that when an *onyishi*[53] was appointed, he was expected to offer sacrifices at Ufu to the ancestors of the Enugu-Ezike people.[54]

So how does one read these traditions of origin? Should they be understood simply as intricate truths, or perhaps, as folktales spun for entertainment? Do the people of Enugu-Ezike, for instance, actually believe that there was in fact an Ezike, or an Ezike Oba, who killed an elephant, settled in Amube Enugu-Ezike, and fathered the original ancestors of Enugu-Ezike? I would argue, most probably not—not about this tradition or any traditions of origin, for that matter. However, it would be a mistake to categorize these traditions as folktales or myths, which in their constructions are fictive inventions of creative minds. Rather, like Stephen Belcher, I would argue that traditions of origin although not the same as the history of the past, are shared perceptions of the past that articulate the content and meaning of that earlier period[55] (*oge gbo gbo*) and "how [these contents and meanings] connect to the present world."[56]

These traditions, Belcher further articulates, are distinguished by "their cultural importance."[57] Elders preserve them to educate their young about who they are, enhance the prestige of a community, or untangle questions about property rights or community prohibitions.[58] Traditions may also be evoked to fill the need, as A. E. Afigbo has suggested, for small-scale societies (such as Enugu-Ezike) to create perceptions of alliances with more powerful kingdoms (e.g., the Igala kingdom) as a means of boosting their own status or image[59] or perhaps, in my own estimation, to anticipate protection from these kingdoms, especially during periods of great uncertainty, such as the interwar period, when individuals could be enslaved at the drop of a hat. Similarly, the Benin "connection" could be read as an attempt by Enugu-Ezike people to unite themselves with the famous and powerful Kingdom of Benin by inventing fanciful stories that would support an ancient blood tie with Benin. These explanations fall in line with Belcher's argument that traditions of creation tend to be "reconfigured with every new generation that learns it"[60] and to change "in the face of new cultural needs and new information."[61]

But there might be some historical memory built into these traditions as well. History tells us that at the end of the seventeenth and the beginning of the eighteenth centuries, the Igala controlled the adjacent part of Igboland south of Igala country and that the *attah*'s (king's) power and influence extended south into Nsukka.[62] During this period politically autonomous Igbo groups used the *attah*'s prestige to get their own local title-holders confirmed by his office.[63] However, there seems to be very little in Enugu-Ezike that connects the town with the Kingdom of Benin, except for the appendage of the name Oba to the Enugu-Ezike ancestor Ezike, which in itself does not accord any authenticity to the claim that Enugu-Ezike was connected to the kingdom.

A. E. Afigbo, writing on the place and importance of the traditions of origin of so-called segmentary communities, has argued that these traditions do not actually speak to the origin of the first individual nor do they necessarily speak to actual migrations to particular regions. Instead, he suggests, they are constructed by communities to explain the "constellation of culture traits"—language, political organization, family systems, inheritance, birth and burial rites, and methods of socializing children—"that distinguish the Igbo from their immediate neighbors."[64] To be sure, they are there to explain the cultural borrowings or contacts of varying intensities; what Afigbo calls "the amalgam of culture traits"—be they religious, political, or social—between the Igbo heartland and their non-Igbo neighbors *oge gbo gbo*. These borrowings are especially pronounced, Afigbo says, in borderland towns such as Enugu-Ezike.[65] His argument makes sense; neither of these traditions make any claims that their so-called ancestor was actually the first person to have inhabited their region. Instead, both traditions claim that Ezike (or Ezike Oba) met Attama Ugwueka at Ugwueka hill and that it was this priest who gave him land and introduced him to his future wife.

In their recollection, the people of Enugu-Ezike make no reference to vacant or barren land, nor do they suggest that the land was sparsely inhabited. In fact, the traditions are silent about what the population density of the area might have been at the time.

What these remembered narratives therefore convey (particularly the Igala connection), in my view, is a mixing or blending of bloodlines and cultures—a reality that was realized and has been historically corroborated in the borderland community of Enugu-Ezike, which has a fusion of Igbo, Igala, and Akpoto customs. Some of the borrowings and adaptations that have been embraced by both the Igala and the Igbo include farming techniques, especially shifting cultivation; fishing and hunting techniques, particularly the use of bows, arrows, and traps; pottery techniques and decoration; weaving techniques, including the use of horizontal and vertical broadlooms; iron-smelting techniques; and religious artifacts, such as gongs and Ikenga figures.[66]

There are also numerous marked similarities between the Igbo and Igala languages. This is evident in everyday expressions, such as the term for goat, *ewo* in Igala and *ewu* in Igbo. The words for the days of the week are similar in Igbo and Igala. Both languages use the word Eke; in Igbo it is the first day and in Igala it is the fourth day. Afo is the third day of the week in both Igbo and Igala. And Nkwo is the fourth day of the week in Igbo, which is very similar to Ukwo, the first day of the week in Igala.[67] Borrowings are also evident in many of the Igala-derived names that Enugu-Ezike people bear—a point that I will discuss in greater detail in chapter 1. These political, social, cultural, and religious borrowings are suggestive of a relationship between Igbo and Igala that may date from the very early period (*oge gbo gbo*) but are also indicative of more recent contacts, according to archaeologists Philip Adigwe Oguagha and Alex Ikechukwu Okpoko.[68]

The story of the elephant dying in Amube and Ezike Oba being offered land may well have been constructed to explain the coming together of two distinct peoples by negotiation (or even by force) and may allude to a contest between the indigenous and the settler community. The privileging of the kill—as in the killing of the greatest of all animals, the elephant—might also be metaphorical, constructed to privilege achievement or victory in a great event. It is possible that the people of Enugu-Ezike constructed Amube as a site of negotiation after a great war where blood was shed.[69] Thus, when one attempts to make sense of the sum of these variables, one can conclude that the actual origin of the first Enugu-Ezike ancestor, be he Bini or Igala, is not as important as what the traditions were constructed to evoke, the blending or negotiation of two or more distinct cultures.

J. S. Boston offers another interesting angle of interpretation in his discussion of the place of the hunter in Igala legends of creation—an analysis that might help contextualize the centrality of the hunter in Enugu-Ezike constructions of their own traditions of origin. He writes that hunting in Igalaland was an activity that had a pronounced influence on several Igala villages, which took their names from the kind of game that were plentiful in their areas. Hunting was also represented in the ritual cycle of the Igala year—the Igala were known to inaugurate the new year by burning grass outside their land shrine, which they would use for hunting.[70] Moreover, hunters in Igalaland were believed to possess outstanding ritual power and technical expertise. A great hunter was therefore a ritual specialist who was able to combine technical and ritual skill—for instance, in the preparation of arrow poison (*olo*), a process that involved using different ingredients and observing particular prohibitions. The hunter was also expected to invoke the poison at various stages during its preparation to activate it and to prevent it from obeying any other system of spiritual commands. Thus, according to Boston, the hunter in these traditions developed as a symbolic figure who was significant in the context of political[71] (and, in the case of Enugu-Ezike, religious) organization, evolving into an idiom that found expression and achieved fruition through Igala-derived Enugu-Ezike institutions such as the *asadu*[72] (political) and the *attama* (religious). In fact, *oge Ahebi*, any Enugu-Ezike person who wished to take an important title—or, as in the case of Ahebi, become a king—had to go to Idah for the conferment.[73] Therefore, these traditions of origin should be read, analyzed, and understood as lenses through which the Enugu-Ezike conceptualized their religious, cultural, and social makeup.

Igu-Afa: The Performance of Naming

The Igbo give their newborns the names Amaechina (may my path not be closed) and Obiechina (may my [male] house not be closed)[74] to acknowledge and celebrate the cherished space that children occupy in Igbo homes.[75] They are progenitors, the continuers of bloodlines, and as such they are constructed as extraordinarily special. This encourages would-be parents to look to spiritual powers to actualize the realization of this gift of children.[76] During the time period covered in this book, the Igbo performance of naming (*igu afa*) usually followed the birth of the child and was an important ritual that the entire community celebrated.

The privilege of naming a child was typically performed by the head of the extended family[77] in a ceremony that was scheduled at various times after the delivery of the child.[78] G. T. Basden, Amaury Talbot, C. K. Meek, Daryll Forde, and G. I. Jones[79]—anthropologists writing in the early twentieth century—provide evidence about naming practices that occurred in many different areas of Igbo country *oge Ahebi*. For instance, the southern Ngwa named a child on the day that she or he was born, whereas a child born of parents from Obollo Division was named after the day her or his mother came out of seclusion.[80] In Oru, Owerri Division, a child was named when she or he was able to sit up.[81] In some parts of Okigwe Division, naming did not occur until the teeth began to appear.[82] In Ahebi's birthplace of Nsukka Division, the naming of a child generally occurred on the twenty-fourth day after delivery.

Before a newborn was initiated into a kindred *oge Ahebi* the kola nut ritual was performed to beckon the ancestors and other deities to take their proper place in the celebration. The presence of the ancestors was important to ensure their protection and blessing on the family.[83] C. K. Meek reports that the new mother's relatives would be expected to congregate on the twenty-fourth day for the naming ceremony, bringing calabashes of palm wine and a supply of yams—items that they would offer for sale, at a considerable price, to the new father. A feast would usually follow, and the new mother's relatives would be given gifts. Once they had been adequately fed, all relatives would congregate outside, at which time the head of the extended family, who was believed to be closest to the ancestors and therefore privileged to perform the ritual, would take the newborn in his arms.

We can look to other scholars of the Igbo world to provide supporting and corroborating evidence as well as the nuanced meanings behind some of these practices. George Oranekwu, an Igbo scholar of divinity, explains the significance of kola nut and libation in the naming ceremony of a newborn. He reports that after prayers are offered by the eldest man in the kindred, that man breaks the kola. He throws some pieces to the ancestors, and the rest of the kola is shared between the witnesses gathered. A palm-wine libation is also poured to the gods as a token of hospitality, fellowship, and respect and as a symbol of family continuity.[84] The infant is then turned skyward and instructed, *"Nne gi gwa gi okwu, nulu ife! Nna gi gwa gi okwu, nulu ife! Were efife mulu anya!*

Ma gi were anyasi laru ula" (When your mother speaks to you, listen to her! When your father speaks to you, listen to him! Open your eyes in the day! And sleep at night!) The reason the child is turned skyward during this performance is so the sky and earth deities (*igwe na ani*), can bear witness to the fact that the child is well received and welcomed into the family. It is after this moral instruction, according to Oranekwu, that the child is named.[85] In C. K. Meek's 1937 telling, the oldest relative takes the newborn outside and lifts him or her in the air four times while saying "My [child], grow up strong and ever give ear to the behests of your father and mother." At this point, the elder asks the new father by what name the child is to be known. The father then picks a name.

For the purposes of this illustration, let us say that the name the father picked was Udoka. Meek informs us that the head of the family would peer at the newborn and say "[Udoka.] That is the name by which you shall answer our call. May long life be yours."[86] It is worth exploring the factors that might lead up to the choice of a name such as Udoka by a family. Udoka (which means peace is greater than all things) might be selected if the family had been embroiled in a long and protracted quarrel with another family that had totally tired them out. The wisdom that the family would be evoking in the performance of this naming would be a loud and clear statement: "Enough is enough. Let bygones be bygones. Peace is greater than all things." With the naming of the child, the newborn was initiated into the corporate community. According to Oranekwu, the performance of naming was "the seal of the child's separation from the spirits and the living-dead, and its integration into the community of human beings."[87]

In Igbo country *oge Ahebi* both boy and girl babies were given two or more names during a performance that was observed with feasting and rejoicing.[88] A number of factors influenced the choice of name given to a child. Parents did not pick out fanciful, cute, or nice-sounding names for their child before birth; instead, the conditions of birth often influenced the choice of appropriate name. Some names were determined by the day of a child's birth; the circumstances, events, or prevailing conditions at the time of a child's birth, as in the case of the choice of the name Udoka; the experiences of people who were intimately connected with the parents; the child's resemblance to a deceased relative; or the birth order of the child. All of these factors could direct the names that parents bestowed on their children.[89]

The first name of an Igbo child *oge Ahebi* was typically a combination of the word *nwa* (child) with the name of the day on which the child was born. The male names Nwafo (a child born on Afo day), Nwankwo (a child born on Nkwo day), Nwoye (a child born on Oye day), and Nweke (a child born on Eke day) all exemplify this wisdom. Other names were variants of this rule. The name Okoroafo, for instance, was also given to a boy born on Afo market day. The female equivalent was Mgbafo. Likewise, Okonkwo or Okoronkwo were names given to male children born on Nkwo day. Mgboye (female) and Okoye (male) were alternatives to the Nwoye name and were given to children born on Oye day, just as the name Okereke was given to a boy child born on Eke day.

A mother who had a particularly difficult pregnancy or birth *oge Ahebi* might name her child Chukwuemeka (God has been wonderful) as a thanksgiving to the Creator for Her/His mercies.[90] Parents who had waited a long time to be blessed with a child would often name that child Ifeyinwa (there is nothing like a child). The names Ozoemena (let [death] not happen again) and Onwubiko (let death forgive or, more directly, death, please!) were given to a child born after the death of previous children. The wisdom that each name evoked called on all that was good to intercede on life's part. The name Unoalo (the house has settled) was given to the youngest female child—a child who symbolically completed the family. The sentiment in the naming was that of well-balanced soup, of a well-balanced family that had been blessed with both male and female children.

Thus, the performance of naming—which bestowed a life force upon a newborn—separated the infant from the world of the spirits and living-dead. It introduced and initiated the child into the world of humans—the corporate community—as a functioning and contributing member of society. Furthermore, the names selected bore witness to encoded meanings about that child that would be released into the world to guide and direct the newborn throughout life.

In the next chapter I will piece together Ahebi's family history with the help of oral evidence. I will analyze and search for hidden meanings embedded in the names borne by Ahebi's ancestors. However, exploring hidden meaning will not be the sole purpose of Chapter 1; I will also reconstruct Ahebi Ugbabe's early childhood years in her mother's village, Unadu, focusing on the few years she spent in her birth town of Umuida, Enugu-Ezike, before she went into exile to Igalaland at the tender age of about 14 or 15.

❧ ONE

Oge Nwatakili:
The Time of Childhood, ca. 1880–1895

Umunne na Umunna:
Genealogy and Naming in the Ohom Eguru Elechi Clan

What has survived of Ahebi Ugbabe's family genealogy is at best imprecise and at worst sketchy. However, much like the Igbo philosophy of naming, *igu afa,* the Ugbabe family observed a similar ethos in their selection of names for their descendants. The family's choice of names tell us something about the circumstances of birth, as well as the prevailing events or conditions occurring at the time of a child's birth, thus serving to inform and document in its own way, something of the history of this particular family. Ahebi's oldest remembered ancestor was Ohom Eguru Elechi. I have been unable to fully deconstruct the meanings behind this name. However, we know that Eguru means "blacksmith" and that it was a name often given as a praise-name,[1] while Elechi asks the question, "Where is tomorrow?" or "Where is my *chi?*" Ohom Eguru Elechi was a man steeped in the mysteries of the occult. For it was said that whoever knew him would dare not cross or walk behind him because of his involvement with the supernatural.[2] It is to this great ancestor that Ahebi's commitment to the occult can be traced and attributed. It is not clear, however, nor can it be ascertained with any kind of exactness, when Ohom Eguru Elechi lived, a gap that does not unduly bother the owners of the history, who remember him as having lived *oge gbo*—"during the early days" or at least "a long time ago."

Ahebi's paternal grandmother, Ayibi Nwa Owo of Ohom Eguru Elechi, is easier to place in historical time, because she is but two generations removed from Ahebi Ugbabe (whom I estimate was born during the latter part of the nineteenth century).[3] Therefore, it is with approximate precision that one is able to place the birth of Ayibi Nwa Owo (who was said to have come from the town of Unadu at the outskirts of Umuida[4]) in the mid-nineteenth century. Furthermore, the town where Ahebi's paternal grandmother and mother were born (*be ikwu nne Ahebi*), as we will see below, played a crucial role in the upbringing and framing of the child Ahebi.

The process and performance of naming among the Igbo allows us another glimpse into Ahebi's ancestry, for the word *nwa* in Igbo means "child." Ahebi's paternal grandmother, Ayibi Nwa Owo, was therefore, as her name revealed, Ayibi, "child of" Owo, sex unknown. It was this Owo, Ahebi's great-grandparent, who most likely lived in the early nineteenth century and was most directly related to the spiritually powerful Ohom Eguru Elechi.[5] The name Ayibi Nwa Owo has roots in both the Igbo and Igala languages. Therefore, it would be impossible for us to pinpoint the linguistic origin of Ahebi's great-grandparent with absolute certainty. We are, however, certain of some facts: First, that the town of Owo's birth was situated on the outskirts of the old Nsukka Division, sharing common boundaries with Igala country, a detail that further blurs the exact origin of this ancestor. Second, that Ahebi's known lineage is littered with Igala ancestry, a point I will discuss more fully in the next few paragraphs. In my search for meaning, I consulted with both Igbo and Igala linguists. Igala historian and author P. E. Okwoli was of the view that "Ayibi" and perhaps "Ahebi" could have been derived from the Hausa/Arabic names for "Saturday"—Dan Asabe (male) or Assibi, Asabe (female).[6] In this positioning, "Ayibi" or "Ahebi" would mean "a child born on Saturday." In its Igala derivation, the name "Owo"—which also has both Igbo and Igala roots, as far as I can discern—refers either to the word for "hand"[7] or to the ceremony of Idel Fitri and Idel Kabir and is most probably given to a child born during these ceremonies.[8] Therefore, when we consider the Igala-derived variables, "Ayibi Nwa Owo" could mean "a child born on Saturday who is the daughter of a child born during the Idel Fitri or Idel Kabir ceremony."

Ahebi Ugbabe was born to Ugbabe Ayibi, a farmer and palm-wine tapper from Umuida, Enugu-Ezike, and Anekwu Ameh, a farmer and trader from Unadu, located on the outskirts of Enugu-Ezike. Ahebi's family name, Ugbabe, is found in both Igala and Igbo languages and means "a giant vulture."[9] In a 2007 interview, Igala historian P. E. Okwoli elaborated on the meaning of the Ugbabe family name:

> I know of Ugbabe. Giant vulture, that is what it means in Igala. It attacks carcasses. When an animal falls dead, it is Ugbabe that will go there first before other vultures. The regular vultures are afraid because they do not know whether the animal is living or dead, but after Ugbabe surveys the carcass, it strikes with its long beak, indicat-

ing to the other vultures gathered that it is safe to eat. If Ugbabe does not descend on it, then the other vultures will be afraid to go. But you know Igalas have strong names like the Igbos, names that exhibit power.[10]

The Enugu-Ezike Igbo express the same sentiment in the adage *ugbabe tubalu udene, udene elibe*—the giant vulture descends first on the carcass and opens it up for the rest of the vultures to follow suit and eat.[11] Without trying to read too much into naming and its implications here, it might be worth noting that the prominence of Igala names in Enugu-Ezike speaks cogently to the linguistic borrowings associated with borderland societies, as I discussed in the *Nkowa* chapter.

Ahebi had two brothers, Obeta Nwa Ugbabe and Onoja Nwa Ugbabe, and no sisters. The meaning of the name Obeta was described to me in two ways. One was that it was a shortened form of an Enugu-Ezike expression, *o be taa na o chie* (if things begin to get better today [i.e., immediately] or if identified problems are solved today, that would be sufficient).[12] Ahebi's nephew, Barnabas Obeta, suggested that his given name was the "way children were called as families grew."[13] Interestingly, both interpretations—one academic and the other familial—speak to the calming of the waters, which would allow children to survive and families to grow. Ahebi's second brother, Onoja, was given an Igala name—a name that could be deconstructed as *onu* (chief) and *oja* (public or the masses).[14] Thus, the wisdom behind Onoja Nwa Ugbabe's naming would have been Ahebi's parents' wish to announce to the world that a special person, a "chief of the people," had been born to the Ugbabe family.

When her siblings came of age, Ahebi married wives for them. For Onoja, she married Nwoye Ugwanyi; for Obeta, she married Omada Nwa Areji.[15] The precedent that allowed Ahebi to marry for her brothers could be found in the fact that in Igboland *oge Ahebi* exceptional and menopausal women were often constructed as male (gender, not sex) and in that capacity could marry wives for themselves, for their husbands (if they were already married), for their sons, and/or for their siblings. Marrying for another person in this society elevated a person's status. It meant that the woman doing the "marrying" would have to pay the bride-price, *ego nwanyi*—a performance better understood as child-price—in place of the actual future male spouse. I will use the term child-price, first coined by Ifi Amadiume,[16] in this biography to describe the transfer of money from husband to wife and from female husband to wife. Like Ifi Amadiume, I argue that child-price is a more appropriate description for the practice, since the transfer of money has nothing to do with the wife. Instead, as in the case of Ahebi's brothers, the negotiation and subsequent transfer of the child-price from the woman husband surrogate (that is, Ahebi) to the father of the bride officially sealed the marriage contract and transferred all rights over the children yet to be born to Ahebi's brothers.

Ahebi's brother Obeta had at least one child, a daughter, Nwojeja Obeta, who in her married years became known as Felicia Ugwu Agbedo. Ahebi's brother Onoja Nwa Ugbabe had at least three children, including Oyima Obeta Nwa Ugbabe, Barnabas Obeta Nwa Ugbabe, and Uroko Obeta Nwa Ugbabe.[17]

"Oyima" is an Enugu-Ezike name given to a woman who was a "friend"[18] of the Omabe masquerade or, as in the case of Ahebi's niece, a child born *oge oso Omabe* (during the run of the Omabe masquerade), which occurred once every two years and symbolized the return of the dead to life. The Omabe masquerade was the most powerful masked spirit in Enugu-Ezike. Functioning in the arena of political leadership and organization, it served as part of the executive-legislative process and was actively utilized as an agent of social control.[19] In its former usage, "Oyima" was used to distinguish a woman of high repute and bravado. Oyima Obeta, the child born during the run of Omabe, is the only surviving daughter of Onoja Nwa Ugbabe and is said to be the "spitting image" of her Aunt Ahebi, whom Oyima Obeta affectionately called *nnenne*. Although *nnenne* literally means "my mother's mother," the term is not often used in reference to that relationship. Instead, it is evoked as a pet name, a name that a mother often bestowed on a favorite daughter, or in this case, a niece on an aunt. Ahebi's other niece, Nwoyeja Obeta, also called Ahebi *nnenne*, as did Barnabas Obeta, Ahebi's nephew.

Oyima's younger brother Uroko was named after the tall and mighty iroko tree; in Enugu-Ezike, *uroko* is the word for iroko. The name connotes strength, courage, and power. The tree also had some religious relevance, as individuals were known to worship and leave sacrifices at the foot of the *uroko* for the unseen spirits to "eat."[20] Moreover, medicine men in Enugu-Ezike were known to name their most powerful medicines *uroko*.[21]

Ahebi had one biological daughter by the name of Oriefi Eze. Oriefi, literally "the eater of a cow," is a titular name that refers to somebody who has killed a cow in honor of another person or event. The name could also be given to a child born on the day such a cow was killed.[22] Perhaps Ahebi's daughter Oriefi was born on the day that Ahebi or someone close to Ahebi "killed a cow"—a killing that would indicate the performance of social and political class.

Oriefi's father was Eze Nwa Ezema. When one attempts to deconstruct this name a number of variables emerge. As previously discussed, *eze* is the Igbo word for "king"; *ma* means "spirit," "deity," or "masquerade." Therefore, "Ezema" means "the king of the masquerades" (praise-name) or "chief priest of a deity" (position).[23] Depending on the source, Eze Nwa Ezema was either a husband whom Ahebi divorced and then "unceremoniously abandoned" or he was simply Oriefi Eze's father. According to Ahebi's great-grandson, Bedford Okpe:

> Ahebi had a husband Eze Nwa Ezema. He was Oriefi Eze's father. However, when Ahebi became so powerful that she could not stay under somebody, she divorced Eze Nwa Ezema. She was living with Eze Nwa Ezema in Umugwaba in Enugu-Ezike. When she decided that she no longer wished to live with him, she went back to her own Umuome.[24]

Ahebi's niece, Nwoyeja Obeta, who was known by her marital name Felicia Ugwu Agbedo in 1998, was less precise. She knew that Ahebi had a daughter but was not certain whether or not Ahebi was married to her daughter's father: "Ahebi was pregnant sometime in her life. She had a daughter called Oriefi Eze Nwa Ezema. I do not know whether she was formally married to Eze Nwa Ezema or not. Eze Nwa Ezema was a native of Umuome."[25]

There was also a disturbing suggestion that Oriefi might have been conceived out of a rape:

> Eze Nwa Ezema was able to trick [Ahebi] to Enugu-Ezike to the Ojobo meeting and made her pregnant. Yes, Eze Nwa Ezema went to Unadu to meet Ahebi's mother. There he requested that she allow Ahebi to accompany him on a trip—that is, to carry his bag and accompany him to Ojobo—the meeting of his age grade. When it was night, Eze Nwa Ezema overpowered Ahebi and she conceived Oliefi Eze because she had been defiled by Eze Nwa Ezema. Ahebi did not marry Eze Nwa Ezema.[26]

No other collaborators made mention of a rape, and I was unable to corroborate this allegation, which was relayed to me by the wife of Ahebi's "slave son" Stephen, Alice Ahebi (now Akogu), who claimed that Ahebi

Ugbabe related the above events to her. I put the term "slave son" in quotes because although Stephen Ahebi was Ahebi Ugbabe's "slave" for all intents and purposes, she took him as the son that she never had and never treated him as a slave. Moreover, the institution of indigenous slavery in northern Igboland was much more benign than any New World counterpart. In fact, in some systems of slavery—for example, *igo mma ogo* (becoming the in-law of a deity)—the "slave's" power was enhanced as a result of his or her association with the spiritual world. In any event, it is possible that Oriefi was conceived in this way. Moreover, I do not believe that Alice Akogu, who was close to Ahebi, would make up such a story. Thus, I report this and other "truths" for the reader to consider in their evaluation of the overall narrative of Ahebi's life.

There was also the suggestion that Eze Nwa Ezema did not actually father Oriefi and that no one really knew who Oriefi's father was because Ahebi conceived her while working as a prostitute in Igalaland.[27] This telling goes on to report that because Ahebi was married to Eze Nwa Ezema, he became Oriefi's "legal" father. It is my opinion that this last claim, like the one before it, might have some legitimacy to it, partly because the information came from Ahebi Ugbabe's great-great-grand-child (who ought to have been eager to keep such "damaging" informa-tion from the public) but mainly because all the evidence points to the fact that Ahebi indeed became a prostitute[28] in Igalaland. Furthermore, support for this allegation can also be found in Igbo cultural norms that maintain that whoever pays child-price has the "legal right" to all children born during the marriage, regardless of whether the child/chil-dren was/were biologically his or hers. The tenets that encouraged this practice found expression in the reality that in this culture, biologi-cal parentage was often subordinated to "social" parentage. It was this law (*omenani*) that allowed Ahebi to perform the female masculinity of becoming female "father" to the numerous children who would bear her name. In this positioning, therefore, the exact identity of Oriefi Eze's biological father becomes almost irrelevant and indeed subordinated to the more significant fact that Ahebi Ugbabe—either through a sexual or "marriage" association with Eze Nwa Ezema (or with an unknown lover, for that matter)—gave birth to her only biological child, Oriefi Nwa Ezema.

After she came of age, Oriefi Eze bore two daughters and a son. These children had different fathers and did not bear their fathers' names. Instead, they bore the first name of their maternal grandmother (Ahebi) or, in the case of Ogara, his mother's name, Oriefi. These names confirm, first, the almost inconsequential character of biological father-hood and, second, the implicit expressions of female power in the Igbo practice of identifying children through the maternal side. Oriefi's great-grandson, Bernard Ameh, provided additional background on some of the circumstances that might have informed Oriefi's choices during her childbearing years:

> Oriefi gave birth to three children when she was moving around because she did not live or stay long with a man at any particular time. After each delivery, Oriefi complained that her mate did not treat her well, so her mother Ahebi removed her from the situation. Ahebi could do this because she was wealthy. She had a lot of money. That was why Oriefi gave birth to children with three different fathers. Yes, two daughters and one son, with a father for each—no two of them had one man as their father.[29]

Oriefi's children were Arikpu Ahebi, Oyibo Ahebi, and Ogara Nwa Oriefi. The names "Arikpu" and "Oyibo" Ahebi suggest that they were born in a foreign place: Arikpu and Oyibo were indeed born to Igala men in Igalaland. The name "Oyibo" literally means "a fair or white person" or, as articulated above, "a foreign place." The name could be given to a child born as a result of a contact with a white man or at the dawn of colonialism. It could also be given to a child born in a foreign land, as was the case with Oriefi's daughter. Arikpu's father was Inegedu, an Akpoto from Ankpa Aariga;[30] the names of the fathers of Oyibo and Ogara are lost to history.

Arikpu in turn gave birth to five children, two daughters and three sons. Her first two children—a daughter, Aminetu Nwa Arikpu, and a son, Atabo—were born in Igalaland to an Igala man by the name of Achimugu Agwuije.[31] Atabo, Igala for "a diviner or chief priest in charge of an oracle,"[32] was a military man who fought in World War II as well as for Biafra during the Nigerian/Biafran Civil War of 1967–1970 (during which he provided protection for his great-aunt Nwoyeja Obeta, who was then known as Felicia Ugwu Agbedo).[33] The first name of Atabo's sister, Aminetu Nwa Arikpu, was a Muslim-derived Igala name that means "honest, faithful, truthful, and trustworthy."[34] She gave birth to Bernard Ameh, whose father was Ameja Eze, also from Unadu.

Arikpu's last three children—two boys and one girl—were born after she had returned to Unadu and remarried, this time to an Igbo man named Igiga Okpe, with whom she had Okpanachi Nwa Okpe, Bedford Okpe, and Abu Nwa Okpe. It appears that Arikpu and Igiga paid tribute

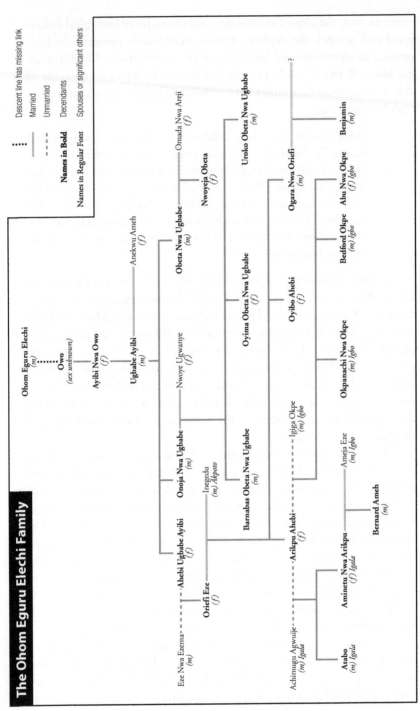

FIGURE 1.1. The Ohom Eguru Elechi family. *Prepared by author.*

FIGURE 1.2. Oriefi Eze Nwa Ezema (Ahebi's daughter), no date. *Photograph courtesy of Bernard Ameh, Unadu.*

FIGURE 1.3. Oyibo Ahebi (Ahebi's granddaughter), no date. *Photograph courtesy of Bernard Ameh, Unadu.*

FIGURE 1.4. Atabo Ahebi (Ahebi's great-grandson), ca. 1967–1970. *Photograph courtesy of Bernard Ameh, Unadu.*

FIGURE 1.5. Bedford Okpe (Ahebi's great-grandson), Lagos, Nigeria. *Photograph by Nwando Achebe, July 2007.*

to Arikpu's Igala roots by naming their first son Okpanachi, which is Igala for "during the reign of" or "in the era of." Okpanachi was a name that was often bestowed on a child born during the time of a great ruler or event.[35] Of these children, only Bedford Okpe, *igwe*-elect[36] of Unadu, still lives.[37]

Early Sojourns in Unadu and Return to Umuida

When Ahebi was a young girl, she lived in Unadu, *be ikwu nne ya* (her mother's town), for a brief period. Few details of Ahebi's sojourn or series of sojourns in Unadu were recorded in any of the numerous and enormously rich accounts of local knowledge about Ahebi. It was only when I systematically reviewed the collected oral data that usable vignettes of the times Ahebi spent in her mother's town began to reveal themselves.

Here is what we know: The years that Ahebi spent in her mother's town seemed to be happy ones. Moreover, all evidence points to the fact that she visited with her mother's people more than once during her childhood years. Alice Akogu revealed that when Ahebi was a child living in Unadu she considered herself a lucky person who was destined

FIGURE 1.6.
Bernard Ameh
(Ahebi's great-
great-grandson),
Unadu.
*Photograph by
Nwando Achebe,
September 1998.*

to become great one day. In a 1998 interview, Alice reminisced about an incident in the life of Ahebi that captured this predisposition:

> Ahebi Ugbabe was created great by God from her early childhood. She told me that she collected *udala* [star apple] when she was young. She was so small that she could not outrun her playmates to pick the *udala* as they fell down. But she was a lucky person and each of her playmates would give her a share of their *udala* fruits. This was the kind of good luck that Ahebi had, and she knew then that she was destined for great things.[38]

FIGURE 1.7. Barnabas Obeta Nwa Ugbabe (Ahebi's nephew), holding King Ahebi's helmet/crown, Umuida, Enugu-Ezike. *Photograph by Nwando Achebe, November 1996.*

Igbo consciousness had its own explanation for this assumed destiny, which is revealed in the performance of naming (*igu afa*). For instance, one of the names the Igbo bestow on their daughters is Ifesinachi (things that happen to a person are determined beforehand by the disposition of that person's *chi*). This celebration of *chi* in Igbo perception is revealed in another name given to girl children, Chioma or "good *chi*." *Chi* in

FIGURE 1.8. Oyima Obeta
Nwa Ugbabe (Ahebi's niece),
Umuida, Enugu-Ezike.
*Photograph by Nwando
Achebe, November 1996.*

Igbo cosmology refers to a person's personal spirit that protects and guides the person throughout life. The Igbo believed that *onye kwe chi ya ekwe* (if an individual said "yes" to his/her *chi*), their *chi* would say "yes" too).[39] Therefore, to the Igbo mind, Ahebi's good luck with the *udala* fruits as well as the humanity of the friends who eagerly shared what they had with the tiny and disadvantaged girl, would seem to point to Ahebi's innate predisposition for great things, an affirmation of the Igbo belief in *chidera,* the belief that once one's *chi* has inscribed or destined something, it can never be denied. Ahebi Ugbabe not only had a good *chi,* she had also said a resounding "yes" to it.

Ahebi Ugbabe's girlhood friends in Unadu included Okpe Nneze. According to Onyishi Augustine Abutu, the oldest man in Unadu, "when [Ahebi] came here [to Unadu], she picked friends as young boys and girls did, playing together with Okpe Nneze and others. . . . Okpe Nneze was of the family of Ijiga Nwa Oko here at Unadu. Ahebi was friendly with them then."[40]

From all indications, a good number of suitors came to ask the young Ahebi for her hand in marriage when she lived in Unadu. This information helps determine what might have been Ahebi's chronological age when she lived there. During the time under investigation, it would have been common for young men to ask for a girl's hand in marriage when that girl was between 13 and 14 years old. As was stipulated by custom, such a marriage would not be consummated until the said bride had "seen her menses."

During this time, Ahebi Ugbabe rejected suitors who had asked for her hand until Eze Nwa Ezema came to her mother and requested that Ahebi be allowed to accompany him to a meeting some distance away. According to Alice Akogu, it was during this ill-fated journey that Eze Nwa Ezema raped the young Ahebi.[41]

The theory that a rape occurred at this time that then led to the birth of Ahebi's child creates a timetable for Oriefi's birth that, I must admit, does not fit as neatly as I would like into the trajectory of this part of Ahebi's life. Therefore, I feel justified in allowing myself room for further speculation. Indigenous knowledge corroborates that Ahebi visited her mother's town several times when she was young.[42] It is thus my belief that the coming of suitors as well as the rape of Ahebi most likely occurred during one of her subsequent visits to Unadu. This is an important consideration because there is no evidence to suggest that the Ahebi who returned to her father's town soon after her initial stay in Unadu was pregnant, nor is there evidence to suggest that she had a child during the short time that she lived in Enugu-Ezike after her return. In fact, all evidence points to the fact that she was *not* pregnant at that time.

In any case, Ahebi Ugbabe soon returned to the town of her birth, Umuida. But within the space of a few years, she had escaped to Igalaland.[43] There are divergent views as to how and why Ahebi absconded to Igalaland. Indigenous knowledge bearers, however, agree on one thing: Ahebi Ugbabe *fulu efu*—she got lost. When asked about Ahebi's childhood years in Umuida, collaborators would often use the language "she got lost" to account for the fact that Ahebi Ugbabe had left home at a young age. This statement, however, creates a dilemma about clarity for the researcher. The words "she got lost" are vague and do not say much about the root cause of why Ahebi Ugbabe was away from home. In other words, how did Ahebi Ugbabe get lost? I am convinced that the phrase was constructed and then passed down and recollected as a palatable explanation to give voice to a family or perhaps even to conceal a village silence/secret about what really happened to the young Ahebi Ugbabe—a silence that might have been nurtured by the consolidation of British colonial rule and the introduction of new laws that made certain indigenous modes of being and punishment unacceptable. I will consider this point more fully shortly.

In response to my question "How did Ahebi Ugbabe get lost?" some collaborators contended that the young Ahebi was sold into slavery into Igalaland.[44] The most prominent of these voices was A. E. Afigbo.[45] In fact, Afigbo's view informed my initial reconstruction of Ahebi's life story—and in consequence, my line of questioning—when I was a graduate student researcher in 1996. It was frustrating, however, that Afigbo had failed to document who his oral source(s) were—he merely footnoted them as "oral tradition collected from Enugu-Ezike."[46] The vagueness of Afigbo's citation made it difficult to investigate the authenticity of his claims. After weighing the evidence I had collected, it was my informed opinion that Afigbo's argument, although reasonable, was flawed. Ahebi Ugbabe was *never* a slave—a fact that many of my collaborators corroborated.[47] Unearthing this information, however, was not enough for me. My determination to dot all my *i*'s and cross all my *t*'s led me to visit with Professor Afigbo in Owerri, Imo State, on the unseasonably cold morning of October 3, 1996. I needed to make sense of the contradictions manifest in the oral information the two of us had collected. Professor Afigbo received me eagerly and well, and after we had talked and I had shared my preliminary evidence on Ahebi's early life with him, the professor indicated that the evidence that I had unearthed indeed seemed sound.[48]

Other collaborators maintained that Ahebi Ugbabe *walu anya* (was a wayward girl who was skilled in the art of seduction) and that it was prostitution that led her to Igalaland.[49] This assertion is not without merit. However, it is important to differentiate one of the outcomes of Ahebi's exile from her *reason* for running away from home. All the collaborators I interviewed confirmed the fact that Ahebi was never a prostitute in Enugu-Ezike before she left for Igalaland, and that she had not shown any signs of having an inclination toward prostitution during that time. Therefore, I maintain that prostitution could not have been the reason why she absconded to Igalaland. We do know, however, that Ahebi Ugbabe became a prostitute/"free woman" after she reached

Igalaland. I contend that Ahebi Ugbabe was forced to become a sex worker in order to survive in a foreign and perhaps unfriendly land.

When Deities Marry

It was only after I had spent several months asking questions and gaining the trust and confidence of individual collaborators that I began to get a sense of what really happened to Ahebi. Apparently, when Ahebi Ugbabe was young—probably about 13 or 14 years old[50]—her family was experiencing a lot of misfortune. Their farms were yielding little, their trading did not flourish, and illness plagued various members of their household. In describing the chaos that enveloped Ahebi's family during this time, famed Enugu-Ezike medicine man and healer Chief Abodo Nwa Idoko put it like this: "There is a way that our people say it—that her lineage was becoming extinct."[51]

In an attempt to trace the origin of these ill fortunes, Ahebi's father sought the expertise of a diviner (*oje gba afa*). This was a common practice at that time. Diviners (*ogba afas* or *ndi ogba afa*) were believed to be endowed with the skill to unearth secrets, perceive the unknown (both present and future), and discern the will of the gods. *Igba afa* meant that a person or persons sought out the diviner, whose specialty it was to divine the root cause of their problems. In some cases, they would find out who a newborn baby really was and whether she or he was someone returned from the dead. If the *ogba afa* determined that the baby had in fact reincarnated, the parents would likely give the child the name of the ancestor who had been reborn in the child. *Igba afa* was an accepted way for individuals to find out why certain misfortunes (or, in some instances, good fortunes) surrounded them and if these could be attributed to invisible powers.[52]

The *ogba afa* was considered to be the master of all esoteric knowledge and wisdom. The words *ogba afa* mean "the maker of *afa*" or "the interpreter of *afa*." *Igba*, in this context, means "the investigation," "the performance," or "the procedure" of finding out the unknown. The Igbo language is littered with phrases that express this sensibility of performative discovery, including *igba ama* (to reveal someone else's secret), *igba egwu* (to perform a dance), *igba mgba* (to [perform the] wrestle), and *igba uta* (to shoot from a bow).[53] Because the Nsukka Igbo (indeed, all Igbos) see the spiritual world and its forces as supremely important, divination is a crucial practice within their culture.

The Igbo basically recognize two worlds—the spiritual unseen world (*ani mmo*) and the human visible world (*uwa*). The unseen world is supreme, and the Igbo ascribe most serious occurrences in the visible world to the unseen beings that inhabit the spiritual world. In an attempt to understand this unseen spiritual world, individuals seek out the services of a diviner, who reads signs by casting or throwing divination seeds or cowries and then interpreting the codes that these objects reveal. The following is an assessment of the true meaning of *afa* to the Nsukka Igbo, constructed out of indigenous memory that Austin Shelton collected in 1965:

> The *afa*-caster is important in every place, not because he is rich or powerful like an *eze* [king] or like an *onyisi* [*sic*] or like an *attama* . . . but because all people who are sick must go to him first to discover what spirit made them sick and what they must do to end the sickness. If somebody is bothered by witches who are trying to hurt him, he must go to the *afa*-caster, even if the person troubled is [the] *onyisi* [*sic*] or some other big man. If an *attama* dies, or before he dies, the people must take the sticks of the lineage men and boys to the *afa*-caster who will find out from the *afa* which stick belongs to the next *attama*. For all the unknown things, the people must go to the *afa* to learn the meaning, and it is only the *afa*-caster who can read the *afa* and tell them the truth. If he does not tell them the truth, the *afa* will kill him.[54]

Ani oma ogba afa, bu ani ojoo mmadu: A good time for the diviner is a bad time for the individual. After consulting his beads, the diviner delivered the revelation. Ahebi's father had committed a grave crime against a kinsman, and consequently the goddess Ohe, whom he had offended, was exacting a punishment on his entire family. Ohe was the goddess of creation, fertility, and protection. She was known to punish individuals for inappropriate and offensive behavior such as murder, thievery, and adultery.

Ohe's *attama* (chief priest) acted on her behalf by collecting the debts owed her, placing taboos on disagreeable behavior, and carrying out her oaths. Pius Idoko, the fifth *attama* of Ohe, explains her function in society:

> Nnenne [Mother] Ohe is a goddess who protects the world. She is worshipped by all [in Enugu-Ezike]. . . . Ohe does not encourage injustice nor prevent justice. She protects her children and gives them long life. Ohe's worshippers believe that both Ezechitoke [God] and Ohe guide and protect them. Ohe works for Ezechitoke. A barren woman who consults Ohe will start bearing children. If a person commits a crime and Ohe is consulted, that person will be killed by the power of Ohe. If a person poisons another or forcefully takes their

FIGURE 1.9. Entrance to Ohe's shrine, Imufu Enugu-Ezike. *Photograph by Nwando Achebe, September 1998.*

FIGURE 1.10. Pius Idoko, the fifth *attama* of Ohe, Imufu, Enugu-Ezike. *Photograph by Nwando Achebe, September 1998.*

land and Ohe is consulted, Ohe will kill that person. If a person com-
mits a crime and wants to be pardoned, they can either slaughter a
cow, sheep, dog, cock, or goat to pacify the great goddess. Even a priest
who does not perform his or her rituals will be killed. Thus, I am not
exempt. I know this much.[55]

Ohe also played a central role during war. She was said to protect her
people, the Imufu, from their enemies. However, her likeness was never
carried onto the battlefield; she acted from a distance. Ohe is married to
another deity called Idenyi Ohe, a less powerful god in the Enugu-Ezike
religious pantheon. In physical representations of Idenyi Ohe, he typically carried a knife, with which he was expected to look after and protect
Ohe's shrine.[56]

Ohe was worshipped on Oye and Afo market days. On those days,
her parishioners would keep vigil before her and present her with sacrifices. They also gathered to eat, drink, and sing songs in her honor. In
addition, Ohe served as a vehicular deity that could be moved from her
shrine to wherever her service was needed. The act of moving and thus
transferring Ohe's power was called *ikpo* Ohe. *Ikpo* in the Igbo language
either means "to call" somebody or something or "to peg" something
to the ground. Attama Ohe contextualized this vehicular function in a
1996 interview:

> Ohe is taken everywhere she is needed. She has been carried to far off
> places like Onitsha and Benin, and many other places, when crimes
> have been committed there. It is my family that carries her. Those
> worshippers who take part in her vigils can also carry her as well. We
> carry Ohe on our heads if we do not need to take her far.[57]

One way that people could compensate for their crimes was to present a freeborn human being in "marriage" to the goddess. Attama Pius
Idoko rejected the notion that his goddess demanded that human beings
be offered as living sacrifices to her; he insisted that offenders, often out
of their own volition, offered their daughters to Ohe in recompense for
their transgressions.[58] Other observers contended that diviners, acting
upon their visions, instructed offenders to offer their daughters to Ohe
in marriage so that the parent could *igo mma ogo* (become the in-law of
a deity). Whichever was the case, these demands were adhered to scru-
pulously. Nsukka society rationalized its concessions to these demands
by evoking the boundaries imposed by society on individuals to atone
for their sins. The Igbo insisted that the enormity of a ritual sacrifice was

in direct proportion to an offender's atonement. Francis A. Arinze put it best:

> If [a diviner or deity] says that a sheep is to be offered, then a sheep is to be offered. If the client tries to change the prescriptions unnecessarily, the [diviner] will tell him: *Mmuo na-eli asaa, enye ya asato o ju!* [The spirit that eats seven refuses when he is given eight!] If the person is poor, his relations sometimes help to procure the necessary victim, especially in an expiatory sacrifice to remove abomination, for in this case they are convinced that they also are implicated in the impending chastisement and that *ofu mkpulu aka luta mmanu ozue nine* [when one finger gets mixed up in oil, the oil reaches the others too].
>
> The worshipper does not pit himself against the [diviner] or the spirits to bargain for a smaller and smaller victim, for the Ibos believe that the larger the victim and the more cheerfully one gives it the more happy and pleased will the spirits and ancestors be.[59]

Ohe accumulated several "wives" or dedicatees in this manner. These dedicatees were known as *igberema* and were mostly beautiful young women.[60]

The historical precedent that encouraged deities to marry human beings in Nsukka Division had its roots in the period following the beginning of the abolition of the international slave trade in 1805. The communities of the Biafran hinterland had previously served the slave market well by acquiring human beings for the market on the West African coast. This procurement of human beings for the Atlantic slave trade led to chaos, an unimaginable insecurity for settlements in the Igbo heartland. Entire communities were devastated by this pillaging of souls. In the town of Alor-Uno, Nsukka Division, for instance, this looting of human beings led to a migration of people to Alor-Agu, "the Alor in the hills," a mass movement that in essence was the group's way of fighting the slave trade. For in moving to these hard-to-find hills, the people of Alor-Uno became inaccessible to the Aro and Nike slave raiders, some of the most vicious headhunters of the time. As a consequence Alor-Uno as well as other communities in Nsukka Division, including Obukpa, Idoha, and Enugu-Ezike, adopted (or constructed) new deities and new spiritual forces to help them fight the slave trade and defend the people who were left behind. These deities were primarily female and worked to protect and repopulate the societies that owned them, thus filling the female-gendered roles of "mother" and "protector." However, these deities could not repopulate society on their own. They needed human beings, women who could physically bear children. Hence, the Igbo hinterland communities were quick to adopt another distinctly Igbo institution, the performance of woman-to-woman marriage, which allowed exceptional women the space to "marry" other women and perform the gendered role of female husbands and fathers. It is important to note that these relationships were not lesbian in nature but based on the verity that in precolonial Igboland, sex, and gender did not coincide, and therefore biological women could be categorized as social males.

The philosophical basis of woman-to-woman marriage is located in the Igbo philosophies of *amaechina* (may my path not be closed) and *obiechina* (may my [male] house not be closed),[61] which spoke forcefully to the Igbo individual's unqualified desire for children. Children were the reason why child-price was paid in Igboland; moreover, they were essentially the reason for a man and a woman to get married. A union that was not blessed with children was considered unfortunate, quintessentially cursed. This was why if the barren spouse was the woman, she compensated to right things by either marrying for herself or marrying for her husband. If the husband was the affected spouse, his wife would often discreetly find an "outside" lover who would act as a sperm donor in her husband's place and thus allow the couple to be blessed with children "of their own." In a situation such as this, even if the wife's lover were to be revealed, he would have no rights over the child/children because he had not paid her child-price. It was this culture of privileging the payer of child-price that encouraged some collaborators to suggest that even if Oriefi Eze had been conceived when Ahebi worked as a prostitute, Eze Nwa Ezema, who had paid Ahebi's child-price, would always be regarded as Oriefi's father.

The tenets of this elevated woman-to-woman marriage were modified to allow female deities the prerogative to also marry women in a process known as *igo mma ogo* in order to repopulate society. In this way, the female deity performed the social function of female husband to the women that she married and female father to the children that would be born. Children born of deities often bore their deity "parent's" name, as was the case with the children of the goddess Efuru of Idoha, Nsukka Division, who bore the name Nwiyi, meaning "child of *iyi* [Efuru]," or "Efuru's stream." The women married to the deities were essentially enslaved to them, because as wives of spirits they were beholden to their deity "husbands" and were not allowed under any circumstance to marry freeborn men. They could, however, have sexual relationships with freeborn men; indeed, they were encouraged to do so, for their female deity husbands needed the assistance of human male sperm donors to realize their desire to become female fathers. This was the institution that became prominent in Imufu, Enugu-Ezike, and evolved around the goddess Ohe.

Ohe typically demanded human beings in retribution for a number of crimes, including murder, manslaughter and thievery. When a thief stole or took possession of another's land, the wronged person could curse the thief in the name of Ohe, in essence appealing to Ohe to take from the thief all that was dear to him/her, including his/her possessions and especially that which was most dear, the thief's daughter.

It is not clear what Ahebi's father's crime was. Abodo Nwa Idoko, however, claimed that "it was discovered that her family was under a curse."[62] Boniface Abugu added his thoughts:

> I cannot tell you exactly what happened, but perhaps her father took possession of another man's land by force and he was cursed in the name of Ohe. Ohe would then demand the man's daughter for this reason—normally when you pronounce a curse, you tell Ohe that the culprit shall take to her all things dear to you.[63]

A great injustice was unleashed when the seer revealed the mysteries of his divination: In order for things to get better, Ahebi would have to be offered as a living sacrifice to appease Ohe.[64] Boniface Abugu noted: "Ahebi was dedicated [to Ohe] because of something her father did,"[65] and Abodo Nwa Idoko contributed, "They dedicated her to the goddess [Ohe]. . . . Ahebi had developed breasts when the dedication happened. Yes, she had developed breasts when her lineage was becoming extinct and hence they decided to hand her over to the priest of Ohe to appease his goddess."[66]

The historical record remains clouded on what Ahebi's father's reaction to this news was. What we do know, however, is that when Ahebi was informed of the impending dedication, her reaction was anything but predicable. Ahebi Ugbabe—*nwatakili walu anya* (the difficult and conceited girl who did not listen to reason)—did something extraordinary. She *refused* to be dedicated. Her actions were an expression of overt resistance. Her defiance was twofold—first, she was revolting against the institution of domestic "slavery" and all its oppressions and subjugations; and second, she was rejecting the patriarchal authority and tenets of her culture that allowed guiltless individuals to be victimized by such dedications. In refusing to be dedicated, Ahebi Ugbabe was in essence rejecting the restrictions that society imposed on individuals, especially young girls and women. Her actions pitted her against her society, and as a result, she was forced to bear the consequences of her decision—she could no longer live in Enugu-Ezike. By rejecting the norms for group living her society imposed, Ahebi Ugbabe had committed a cardinal sin. Her only alternative was to remove herself from that community. Ahebi escaped to Igalaland; she took flight (*o gbapu*).[67]

In the next chapter, I will attempt to paint a portrait of what Ahebi's exile in Igalaland might have been like. Along the way, I will present vignettes from the lives and times of three extraordinary Igala women, women who most likely would have influenced the choices that Ahebi would make in her own life. She would become a prostitute, a trader extraordinaire, and, at some point in time, would have dealings with the Attah-Igala as well as the British colonial officers, who were attempting to advance into northern Igboland in their quest to consolidate their colonial occupation. Ahebi's sojourn in Igalaland would have profoundly influenced the impressionable 14- or 15-year-old teenager who then spent the next twenty to twenty-one years of her life—the period when she advanced from her formative adolescent years to adulthood—there. These narratives and more will form the crux of "*Mgbapu Ahebi:* Exile in Igalaland."

TWO

Mgbapu Ahebi: Exile in Igalaland, ca. 1895–1916

The Igala monarchy, one of the oldest and most formidable king-doms in central Nigeria, is centered on the office of the *attah*-Igala, who was regarded as the "father" of all Igala people.[1] However, one of the earliest *attah*-Igalas (kings of Igalaland) in living memory was a woman named Ebulejonu, meaning "woman" (Ebule) "that became chief or king" (Jonu).[2] Called Ebule for short, she was the only female king who was said to have reigned in the sixteenth century.[3]

Attah-Ebulejonu was the daughter of Attah-Abutu Eje, who, accord-ing to the Wukari tradition[4] of Igala kingship, was half-human and half-leopard. As the tradition goes, the king of the Jukun Kwararafa kingdom of Wukari had a daughter who collected firewood from the forest every day. One day, she was confronted by a leopard, which terrified her and transfixed her to the spot. While she stood frozen, the leopard was said to have metamorphosed into a handsome young man. The princess was immediately smitten and mesmerized by this young man's splendor and visited with him many times. Soon the two decided to get married. Once the princess's parents learned about their daughter's love interest, they wanted to meet him. A few days later, the princess took them into the woods, where her handsome suitor once again appeared as a leopard, ter-rifying the king and queen into flight. However, the love-struck princess was undeterred. She continued to visit her "prince" and soon their love blossomed, was consummated. Many moons later, the princess gave birth to a baby boy whom they named Abutu Eje ("leopard" in Igala).

Abutu Eje was said to have grown up in Wukari to become a man of great courage and charm. His insecure father-in-law king, however, eventually drove him away for fear that he might usurp his throne. Abutu Eje, according to one telling, wandered away to Idah, where he established a royal throne. His power impressed the Igala people around him, who addressed him as Attah (Father).[5] Another telling of this tra-dition states that Abutu Eje did not make it to Igalaland but died en route, thus paving the way for his only child and daughter Ebule to rule as female king.

I share this tradition here not because of its claims regarding dynastic origin but because it introduces an element of spiritualism and the supernatural by suggesting that Abutu Eje's father was half-human and half-leopard. Leopard symbolism has survived to the present day in Igala political life in the form of a leopard emblem and represents the oldest demonstration of authority in the Igala kingdom. It is also featured prominently during the burial ceremonies of the *attah* and individuals related to the king.[6] This symbolism and the construction of Ebulejonu's grandfather as part animal was translated four centuries later by Ahebi Ugbabe in her performance of colonial court justice and performance of praise-names—Agamega (female leopard)[7]—a title by which she was said to celebrate her political, economic and social status.

The Attah-Igala had a counterpart, a prime minister of sorts, called the *achadu,* who was the leader of the *Igala mela* (the nine traditional groups that were said to have first settled in Idah). According to tradition, the *achadu* was an outsider, an Igbo hunter[8] of "slave" origin called Acho Omeppa who was captured and brought before the female king Ebulejonu. King Ebule, entranced by Acho, decided to spare his life and to the horror of her subjects, befriend this man of lowly status. They thus branded him with the name "Achadu" (Acho the slave). Nevertheless, King Ebulejonu remained steadfast in her love for the Igbo "slave," Acho Omeppa, whom she later married. The tradition informs us, however, that because Omeppa was a keen hunter, he would not live with Ebulejonu. He built a compound for her at Ajuwo Atogu while he resumed his hunting activities in Akpanya, Unadu (Ahebi's mother's town), and Okpuje.

When Attah-Ebulejonu died, her brother, Agenapoje, asked Achadu Omeppa to transfer his sister's title to him because Ebule had not given birth to any children of her own. Omeppa agreed, but with one stipulation: that Agenapoje perforate his ears like a woman.[9] The act of perforating one's ears could be read as a gendering performance—a modification from an overt masculinity (king) to a tempered female masculinity (king with female traits)—in which the male king was expected to adopt the quintessence of Omeppa's female king wife, Ebulejonu, and by so doing, embody the true essence of womanhood. This tradition of ear perforation has carried on to the present day; the very validity of the office of *attah* rests firmly upon the performance of this ancient ritual.[10]

Attah-Ebulejonu, like Hatshepsut of Egypt before her, ruled as (and was remembered as) a king, not queen, perhaps setting the precedent for the coronation of another female king, Ahebi Ugbabe, about four centuries later. It is important to note that this female Attah-Ebulejonu's power was tempered by the influence of her husband, the male Achadu, whose permission was required for the transfer of the kingly powers upon his wife's death from sister to brother. Ahebi's coronation would be different. This time, the female king would not rule in the Igala kingdom nor would she be of Igala origin. Instead, the king would be an Igbo woman who had lived in Igalaland for many years, who had come of age and matured there and in the process had imbibed the cultural values and mores of the people with whom she had lived in exile. She would then force the office of individualized male autocratic authority on a people who had no kings—a people whose leadership ideal was a gerontocracy in which power was shared between male and female elders in a complementary fashion.

The Ahebi who escaped into Igalaland was a mere girl, a teenager of no more than 14 or 15 who could not possibly have had any support networks in her town of exile. She most likely knew no one. She had to find a way to navigate what must have been a foreboding place for a girl of her age.

This chapter seeks to unpack and then piece together what Ahebi's journey into Igalaland might have been like, reconstructing the choices she made that kept her alive. From what we know, this voyage began in Umuida, Enugu-Ezike, from whence she moved around a lot, ending at some point in time at Idah, the capital city of the Igala kingdom. I have also been able to determine by painstakingly piecing together oral evidence that Ahebi spent a considerable period of her life—between twenty and twenty-one years—in exile, making her about 36 years old when she returned to Nsukka Division. The circumstances that might have propelled her to the places that she visited; her vocation as sex worker, petty trader, and then trader extraordinaire; and the circumstances that encouraged her to interact with the Attah-Igala and the British colonial officers working in the area will be considered and analyzed in this chapter.

First, a little about the geographical expanse called Igalaland. It is situated on the east side of the confluence of the Niger and Benue rivers. The Igala speak a language of the same name that belongs to the Kwa group of the Niger Congo languages. They are members of a monarchy that dated back to the eighth or ninth century CE and was led by a paramount king, the Attah-Igala, who resided in Idah and was regarded as the father of all Igala people. At its apogee in the sixteenth century, the Igala kingdom included northern Igboland (the Nsukka area) in the

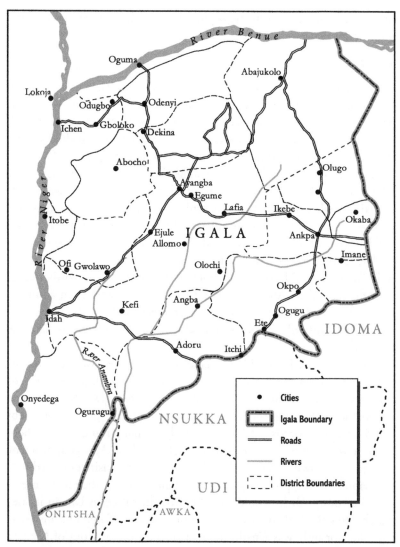

MAP 2.1. Igala Division. *Remote Sensing & Geographic Information Science, Michigan State University.*

south; Koton-Karfe (including areas north of Lokoja) in the north; parts of western Idomaland in the east; and parts of Etsakor in the west.[11] The Igala people were fierce warriors who fought many wars and obtained tributes from any kingdom they defeated. It is because of this warring nature that the history of Igalaland is forever entwined in the histories of two important Igala martyr princesses. In the final section of this chapter I will discuss the lessons that Ahebi most likely learned from their lives. But let us start from the beginning, and chart *ije Ahebi*—Ahebi's journeys in Igalaland.

Ije Ahebi

Charting the exact routes Ahebi took on her journey into Igalaland is a difficult task for a historian working over a century after the fact, partly because much remains unknown and therefore must be assumed. One reason for these historical gaps can be traced back to the fact that the Ahebi who escaped into Igalaland was a mere teenager, a few years removed from childhood. Is it any wonder that the people of Igalaland—I refer in particular to the individuals inhabiting the known towns Ahebi visited—Angba, Ankpa, Ayangba, Ejule, Idah, and Lokoja[12]—could not remember her? How many people would remember a child, a foreign child at that, who lived in their midst for unspecified periods starting in the late 1890s? To expect oral history to remember these events, we are, as A. E. Afigbo has said, asking too much of the source.[13] It is worth noting, though, that when Ahebi journeyed back to Igalaland as an adult—a woman who had challenged the norms of society and country by becoming the first and only female warrant chief in colonial Nigeria—she was remembered.

Nevertheless, I was able to make significant headway into reconstructing Ahebi's history in exile by using some unlikely sources of evidence. A detailed map of the Igala area *oge mgbapu Ahebi*[14] proved invaluable in charting Ahebi's possible routes and the places that Ahebi could have lived or visited. There are only so many routes[15] that Ahebi could have taken to end up at Idah, Angba, Ankpa, Ayangba, Ejule, or Lokoja—the towns where oral evidence tells us she visited or lived.

Moreover, it is possible—and, I contend, it makes the most sense—that the young Ahebi would have first sought solace in Unadu immediately after she had run away from Enugu-Ezike. Why? The answer is twofold: not only was Unadu the first stop on the way out of Nsukka Division and Igboland when traveling to Igalaland but the town also was a known quantity to Ahebi in an otherwise unknown and almost certainly overwhelming world. It was *be ikwu nne* (a mother's town of birth) for Ahebi, and in Igboland, a mother's hometown was always a place of salvation. A conversation between Uchendu and Okonkwo in Chinua Achebe's classic *Things Fall Apart* captures the essence of *be ikwu nne* in Igbo consciousness.

Uchendu, Okonkwo's maternal uncle, unhappy that his nephew has been full of self-pity, listlessly moping around, calls a family meeting to address Okonkwo's presence in his homestead. He poses the following question to Okonkwo and the members of his extended family:

> Why is Okonkwo with us today? This is not his clan. We are only his mother's kinsmen. He does not belong here. He is an exile, condemned for seven years to live in a strange land. And so he is bowed with grief. But there is just one question I would like to ask him. Can you tell me, Okonkwo, why it is that one of the commonest names we give our children is Nneka or "Mother is Supreme?" We all know that a man is the head of the family and his wives do his bidding. A child belongs to its father and his family and not to its mother and her family. A man belongs to his fatherland and not to his motherland. And yet we say Nneka—"Mother is Supreme." Why is that?[16]

A puzzled Okonkwo is unable to answer the question; neither is he able to answer a follow-up question about why it is that when a "woman dies she is taken to her home to be buried with her own kinsmen." Uchendu uses the opportunity as a teaching moment and provides the following rationale:

> It's true that a child belongs to its father. But when a father beats his child, it seeks sympathy in its mother's hut. A man belongs to his fatherland when things are good and life is sweet. But when there is sorrow and bitterness he finds refuge in his motherland. Your mother is there to protect you. . . . And that is why we say that mother is supreme.[17]

The Igbo name Nneka (mother is supreme) has no father equivalent. The name captures the culture's expectation about the position of mothers as well as a child's relationship with his or her mother, which is strict. In *Things Fall Apart*, human salvation, especially male salvation, is presented as matrifocal. It is through Okonkwo's mother's lineage that honor and dignity are restored to the exiled warrior. It is for this same reason that the first stop of the young and most likely petrified Ahebi in exile would most probably have been her mother's natal town, Unadu.

Let us now—with the aid of a period-appropriate colonial geographical and road map[18]—attempt to chart what must have been Ahebi Ugbabe's route into Igalaland. In precolonial Nigeria, communities were connected by complex networks of roads that were constructed by hunters, farmers, and traders for various reasons. Hunters built them to create tracts for game; farmers, to create footpaths to their farmlands; and traders, to create footpaths so that they could sell their goods in faraway places. Toyin Falola and G. O. Ogunremi suggest that long-distance trade encouraged communities to build more roads.[19] During a time when wheeled traffic was nonexistent, individuals made their way on foot and on animals.[20]

Oge mgbapu Ahebi, roads consisted primarily of leveled gravel or earth footpaths that were constructed out of existing precolonial trade routes by widening them.[21] With the advent of motorized transportation in the early twentieth century, the colonial government, under the supervision of its district officers, used forced Nigerian labor to reconstruct networks of gravel or earth roads, feeder roads, and tarred roads from the existing precolonial trade routes. They also constructed a small number of Class III roads. Class III roads were roads for which the government assumed responsibility through its Department of Public Works. Consequently, their construction, according to Gilbert James Walker, "conform[ed] generally with the minimum standard laid down in the Official Manual of Road Construction and Maintenance."[22] The Class III road, however, like most roads constructed *oge mgbapu Ahebi,* followed the line of the old footpaths and village labor was used to maintain it. Eastern Nigeria, which was densely populated and had a sizeable labor force, had more than its share of Class III roads connecting villages to towns.

In Nigeria, the first road for motorcars was built in 1906; it connected Ibadan to Oyo. By 1914, 3,200 kilometers of roads for motor vehicles had been constructed.[23] *Oge mgbapu Ahebi,* no tarred roads existed along the Enugu-Ezike-Igala axis. The roads in these parts, like the roads in much of Nigeria, were untarred and most people traveled by foot or horseback. By the second decade of the twentieth century, however, motorized transportation on lorries and motorcars had become a viable mode of navigation.[24]

Ahebi would have set out from her birth town of Umuida and would have trekked west on a leveled road—in all likelihood, a footpath—approximately 6.7 kilometers[25] to Unadu, her mother's natal village.

An astute observer might wonder why Ahebi did not spend all her years in exile in her mother's village. After all, she could have expected (and would have most likely received) the support and assistance of her extended family in coping with the curse that the goddess Ohe would have put on her for running away from the decreed marriage between deity and human. History informs us, though, Ahebi did not spend all of her years in Unadu. Instead, she escaped farther north to Igalaland.

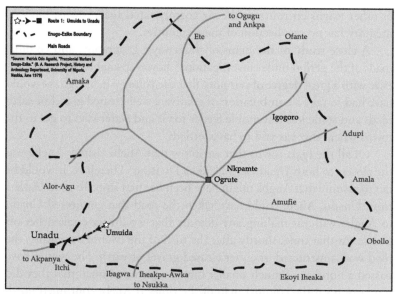

MAP 2.2. Ahebi Route 1: Umuida (Enugu-Ezike) to Unadu. *Remote Sensing & Geographic Information Science, Michigan State University.*

Although the historical record does not tell us why Ahebi chose to do this, there is room for speculation. My first guess would be that if Ahebi was indeed raped, she might have felt uncomfortable about continuing to live in a town that brought back painful memories of the incident that resulted in the birth of her only child and, in some tellings, marriage to the rapist. Thus, she most likely wanted a change of scenery. A second hypothesis would be that although the town of her mother's birth may have offered the solace that this teenager desired, it might not have been far enough removed from Enugu-Ezike for Ahebi to have felt safe from the vengeance of the powerful goddess Ohe. Regardless of her motivations, we know that Ahebi left Unadu for Igalaland in short order.

The possible routes that she might have taken from Unadu when she left Nsukka Division and traveled to Igalaland are more difficult to chart than is her route from Umuida to Unadu. Oral memory from Ahebi's Igbo relatives and friends in Enugu-Ezike and Unadu and from the Igala family of her "slave son" Stephen identify six Igala towns Ahebi lived in or visited during her exile: Angba, Ankpa, Ayangba, Ejule, Lokoja, and Idah (the town where Ahebi was coronated as king several years later). It is not only possible but likely that Ahebi visited and perhaps settled in other towns en route to the six corroborated Igala towns, but oral memory has no recollection of these vicinities.

A close study of the maps of waterways, geography, and colonial roads of the period under investigation,[26] however, enables us to hypothesize with a great degree of certainty that the young Ahebi Ugbabe would have had to take a combination of relatively well-cleared gravel or earth roads and some less traversable feeder roads and waterways to get to the towns where she was said to have settled.[27]

Of all the Igala towns that we know that Ahebi visited, Angba was the closest to both Unadu and Nsukka Division. Therefore, it would be fair to assume that Angba might have been her first stop. To get to Angba from Unadu, Ahebi could have taken the road that connected Unadu to Angba without making any detours that would have taken her off course. At that time, shortly after the turn of the twentieth century, the road was constructed of either cleared gravel or earth. She would have passed a number of much smaller towns—towns so small that they did not appear on the colonial map of the time. If Ahebi continued north on the earth road from Angba for a distance of about 36 kilometers, she would have eventually ended up in Ejule, after having passed through the town of Allomo.

Two options would have been available to the teenager when she traveled from Angba to Ankpa.[28] The first, which would have been the more arduous, would have involved sailing up the Anambra River by canoe from Angba north to Olochi and then continuing north on the Anambra all the way to Imane. She would have then had to proceed to Ankpa on a land route from Imane. This would have been a journey of 74.2 kilometers. If she chose not to do this, she would have had to journey south by road and return to Unadu. She would then have been able to travel by a north leveled gravel or earth road from Unadu to Ete, then from Ete to Ogugu, from Ogugu to Okpo, from Okpo to Imane, and then finally from Imane to Ankpa; this route would have been a total of 102.3 kilometers.

The journey to the capital of the Igala kingdom, Idah, from Ankpa or Angba would have been much longer; it could have taken days to complete. Angba was much closer to Idah and was perhaps an easier journey than the trip from Ankpa to Idah. Four options would have been available to Ahebi. The first would have taken her about halfway by waterway and the remainder by land. If she chose this option, she would have set out on the Anambra River from Angba, first canoeing south and then continuing west until she arrived at an unnamed[29] locale between Adoru

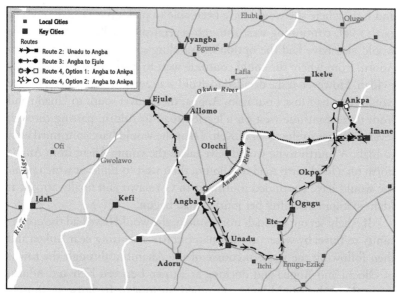

MAP 2.3. Ahebi's Routes 2, 3, and 4: Unadu to Angba, Angba to Ejule, and Angba to Ankpa. *Remote Sensing & Geographic Information Science, Michigan State University.*

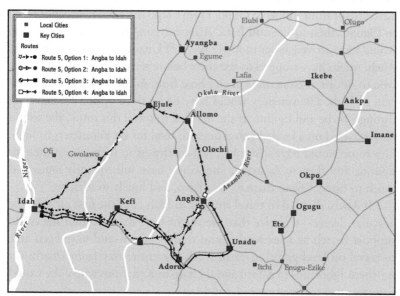

MAP 2.4. Ahebi's Route 5: Angba to Idah. *Remote Sensing & Geographic Information Science, Michigan State University.*

and Kefi, where she would have been able to pick up a cleared gravel or earth road, continuing west through several small villages to Idah. She would also have had the option of traveling south on a feeder road to Adoru, from where she could continue west to Kefi and then eventually to Idah. However, if she decided to avoid waterways and feeder roads, she would have had to set out from Angba, then travel south to Unadu and from there continue west on a leveled road to Adoru, passing through several villages to the town of Kefi. Then she would have continued west to Idah. A fourth route would have taken the young Ahebi from Angba north on a level earth road to Allomo, then west to Ejule, at which point she would have continued southwest to Gwolawo and finally arrived at Idah 79 kilometers after her journey had begun.

If Ahebi set out for Idah from Ankpa, she would have had the opportunity to travel by water on the Anambra River, starting near Ankpa and then following the western course of the Anambra through the towns of Olochi and Angba and docking at a town between Kefi and Adoru. From there she would have continued on foot or by horse or motorized transportation toward Idah. Alternately, if Ahebi wanted to avoid the waterways almost entirely, she would have had to brace herself for a 131-kilometer journey. She would have first traveled south on gravel or paved roads from Ankpa to Okpo. From Okpo she would have journeyed to Ogugu, then to Ete and Itchi. After traveling several kilometers, she would have arrived at her mother's town of Unadu. It is conceivable that Ahebi might have stopped to rest there before setting out again, this time west to Adoru, then setting sail on a boat from Adoru to her final destination of Idah. The runaway would have had a third option for traveling through Ikebe and Egume. If she decided to travel this route, she would have traveled on a leveled gravel or earth road for 121 kilometers to Idah. Her route would have first taken her northwest to Ikebe, from there to Egume, and then to Ayangba. She would have subsequently journeyed south to Ejule,[30] from there to Gwolawo, and finally to Idah.

If Ahebi decided to travel straight to Idah after she first escaped the oracular decree—a choice that she might have made so that she could support herself as a sex worker and trader—she would have been able to travel on level gravel or earth roads the entire way from Unadu (in northern Igboland) to Adoru and then up to Kefi, from where she would have traveled many more miles to Idah.

Oral evidence informs us that Ahebi traveled to Lokoja.[31] To get to this town, Ahebi would have had to travel through the all-important city of Ayangba. A question that arises is whether the exile would have

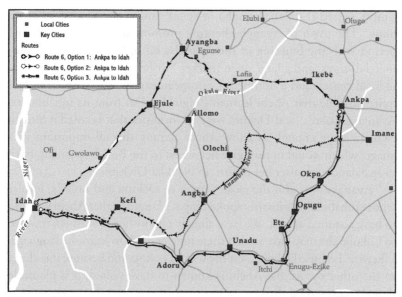

Map 2.5. Ahebi's Route 6: Ankpa to Idah. *Remote Sensing & Geographic Information Science, Michigan State University.*

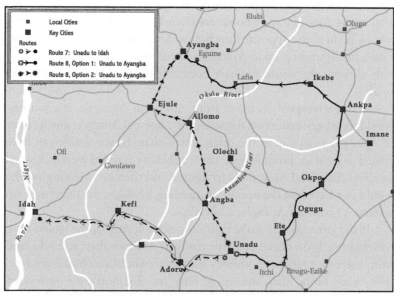

Map 2.6. Ahebi's Routes 7 and 8: Unadu to Idah and Unadu to Ayangba. *Remote Sensing & Geographic Information Science, Michigan State University.*

simply passed through Ayangba or spent time there. Here is what we know. The town of Ayangba became prominent during the colonial period with the building of the Ayangba oil mill, a number of commercial stores, and a large open market.[32] It became a flourishing commercial center, and a number of European expatriates lived there. It is quite possible that Ahebi learned Pidgin English from its inhabitants. Ayangba, Lokoja, and Dekina were all localities that boasted a foreign element large enough to allow Ahebi acquire this all-important language, which would in turn give her access to the British colonials, both in Igalaland and, after her return, in Nsukka Division.

Ayangba was also the closest town to Dekina and Lokoja, locales whose inhabitants primarily spoke Nupe, a language that Ahebi was said to have acquired as well. We have already established that Ahebi traveled to Lokoja; she may have settled there long enough to learn the language. Likewise, because Dekina is on the way to Lokoja and because it is closer to the other towns that Ahebi is known to have visited, it is plausible that she also settled there.

What might have been her route to Ayangba, Dekina, and Lokoja? Let us start with Ayangba. From Unadu, Ahebi would have had to travel north on gravel or earth roads to Ete and Ogugu, from where she would have had to travel to Okpo, then to Ankpa, Ikebe, and Egume, finally arriving at Ayangba 124 kilometers later. She could also have traveled from Unadu in the opposite direction to Angba and then to Allomo and Ejule, finally ending up in Ayangba. These routes would have been her only choices; she would not have been able to travel by water or feeder roads.

If she attempted to travel from Ankpa to Ayangba, the journey would have been easier to navigate, for the town of Ankpa is much closer to Ayangba than any of the other towns that she was known to have visited or lived in. From Ankpa, she would have traveled west on leveled roads to Ikebe and from there to Egume and then on to Ayangba. She would not have had the option of traveling by water, for there were no waterways between Ayangba and Ankpa.

If she attempted to make this journey from Angba, she would have traveled north on gravel or earth roads to Allomo, then to Ejule, and from there to Ayangba. A journey from Idah would also have been relatively easy. From Idah, she would have traveled northeast on leveled roads to Gwolawo, from Gwolawo to Ejule, and then to Ayangba.

What might Ahebi's journey from Ayangba to Dekina or Lokoja have looked like? From Ayangba, Ahebi would have been able to travel

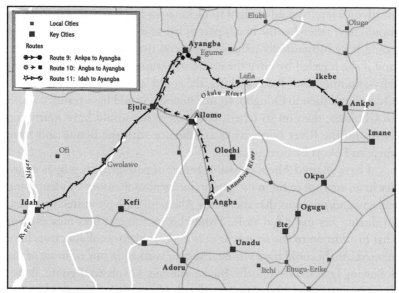

MAP 2.7. Ahebi's Routes 9, 10, and 11: Ankpa to Ayangba, Angba to Ayangba, and Idah to Ayangba. *Remote Sensing & Geographic Information Science, Michigan State University.*

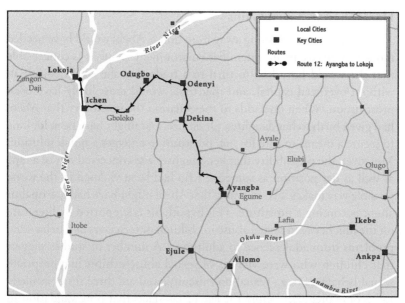

MAP 2.8. Ahebi Route 12: Ayangba to Lokoja. *Remote Sensing & Geographic Information Science, Michigan State University.*

north on a leveled road straight to Dekina—a 26-kilometer journey that would have taken her the better part of five and a half hours on foot. She could have substantially reduced her travel time by traveling on horse, and if she traveled by lorry the entire trip would have taken only about fifty-two minutes.[33] From Dekina, she could have continued on west to Odenyi and then to Odugbo, from where she would have traveled south to Gboloko, then on to Ichen. From there she would have journeyed north up the River Niger to its confluence with the Benue and from there to Lokoja by boat or canoe.

I have charted Ahebi's possible routes of passage within Igala country in an attempt to fill in the gaps in indigenous memory by identifying villages and/or towns that the young Ahebi might have visited or settled in during her extended exile. From this exercise, it becomes evident that in addition to the six towns that my oral history collaborators have named, Ahebi could have visited, lived, or worked in one or more of the following Igala towns: Olochi, Imane, Allomo, Gwolawo, Egume, Ikebe, Ete, Ogugu, Okpo, Kefi, Adoru and perhaps, Dekina, Odenyi, Odugbo, Gboloko, and Ichen. Therefore, we must consider all of the towns Ahebi passed through as places where she might have traded goods—and her body—for money.

Hard Choices, Great Gains

As a young girl running away from home, Ahebi would have needed money to survive in an unfamiliar environment. Thus, it is conceivable that she would have had to turn to a trade that she could engage in without overhead capital, and that trade would most likely have been prostitution. When one adds to the equation the possibility that Ahebi had given birth to her daughter, Oriefi Eze, and might have been looking to secure a means to care for her, prostitution emerges a quick solution. Moreover, the probability that her daughter was conceived out of a rape as well as her position as someone who had been violated in the worst possible way makes it conceivable that Ahebi might have had few qualms about becoming a prostitute. This hypothesis is supported by literature on the link between sexual abuse in children or teenagers and behavioral problems from adolescence to adulthood. A number of studies suggest that children who were victims of sexual abuse exhibit inappropriate sexual behaviors (e.g., sexual promiscuity) and are three times as likely to become pregnant before the age of 18—facts that bore validation in Ahebi's own life. What is particularly relevant to Ahebi's story is that several studies suggest that more than three-quarters of sexually abused teenagers go on to become prostitutes.[34]

The task of reconstructing Ahebi's years in exile is difficult partly because of the dearth of oral evidence about these years of her life. Although I was able to plot and travel the routes of Ahebi's possible Igala journeys in 2007, I had little success with unearthing information on the Igala side about her whereabouts or what types of activities she had engaged in. The only concrete information that I was able to secure came from Idah, where the Attah-Igala[35] and his royal retinue remembered her well; they recounted her coronation as king in detail. Their account gave me the opportunity to compare and contrast information on the same event from two distinct geographical areas (Igbo and Igala). But I have gotten ahead of myself, because this coronation happened many years after Ahebi's exile to Igalaland.

We know from oral evidence that Ahebi visited *be ikwu nne ya* (her mother's village) in Unadu more than once. In chapter 1, I shared remembrances from Ahebi's childhood years (*oge nwatakili*) in Unadu, sketching out recollections of the play dates that Ahebi had with her childhood friends as well as her ill-fated trip to Ojobo. I also suggested that if Ahebi was indeed raped by Eze Nwa Ezema, it seemed plausible that the rape occurred during a later trip to Unadu, a trip that would have taken place after Ahebi went into exile. This premise fits more neatly into my reconstruction of this part of Ahebi's life, for there is no evidence to suggest that Ahebi Ugbabe gave birth to a child before the oracular decree that attempted to give her in marriage (*igo mma ogo*) to Ohe.

We are however certain about one piece of the Igala puzzle: how Ahebi accumulated her initial wealth in Igalaland. There is ample evidence on both the Igbo and Igala sides to suggest that Ahebi was involved in prostitution.[36] One does not have to search far to understand why this would have been so. To a young, destitute, unskilled, and uneducated girl, prostitution was a means of survival, a means to an end. Sex work allowed her access to the financial capital she would need to set herself up in trade and to important and influential people, the most significant of whom was the reigning Attah-Igala and (by the end of her sojourn in Igalaland) perhaps some European colonists.[37]

Understanding Prostitution in Nsukka and Igalaland

Luise White, who writes about prostitution in colonial Nairobi, Kenya, argues that sex work as a full-time form of labor was invented during the colonial period.[38] She contends that in colonial Nairobi, it was a form of self-employment that was much more profitable than the wage labor available to women. Nairobi prostitutes essentially leased their domestic labor and services. They engaged in conversation with clients;

provided clients with a place to sleep, food to eat, and bath water; and sold sexual favors.[39] White's description is fundamental to understanding the nature of prostitution among the Nsukka Igbo and Igala.

In the Nigerian context, though, prostitution was not merely an invention of the colonial era; it existed in a distinctive form during the precolonial epoch. Before colonialism, prostitution in Nigeria was most often rural in orientation, and one of its distinguishing features was the fact that the sex worker was confined to a private space—she worked out of her natal home. The sex worker in the precolonial context was also constructed[40] as single,[41] and society had taboos (nso) in place that guarded against men engaging in sex with married women.[42] However, as was true of the Nairobi women in Luise White's study, Igbo and Igala prostitutes responded to reduced work opportunities during the colonial period by transforming their sexual labors into an organized and lucrative occupation that surpassed any economic opportunity available to them in rural areas. In fact, a colonial British official described prostitution in Nigerian cities as "extremely profitable" and characterized the Nigerian women who worked as prostitutes as "itinerant gold mines."[43] Colonialism thus offered rural prostitutes increased opportunities to separate themselves physically and emotionally from their otherwise infertile rural economies. Some women took advantage of this real or imagined potential of the colonial city by relocating to urban prostitution zones such as motels and brothels. Others stayed put, though, continuing to perform sexual services for money from their rural bases. The conditions under which these stay-at-home prostitutes functioned tended to mimic patterns of precolonial autonomous sex work. The urban colonial sex worker, however, perhaps as a result of her dislocation from home and community, was forced to rely heavily on the services of a madam, who essentially played the role of a pimp.[44] But I have gotten ahead of myself.

In order not to be held captive by inappropriate translations, it is necessary to put an Nsukka Igbo and Igala face on the institution as it was constructed oge mgbapu Ahebi. First, consider the words the Nsukka Igbo used to designate the concept "prostitute." These were varied and seem to have changed over time. Whether or not these names evolved successively or were used interchangeably or concurrently will require further investigation. Here is what we know. One of the words used was mgboto (person who goes naked). Oge mgbapu Ahebi and before, Igbo women were said to manifest "very little interest in personal apparel."[45] G. T. Basden, a missionary working to save Igbo souls in the first quarter of the twentieth century, observed that during this time "there was little inducement for [Igbo women] to [wear personal apparel because] there was no such thing as a manufactured garment in the country-side . . . Strips of home-woven cotton were all that were available and, in some parts, these were scarce."[46] The females that Basden observed were actually girls and adolescents. The term *mgboto* (person who goes naked) was used *oge mgbapu Ahebi* to separate such girls from women.[47] It appears that Nsukka people adopted the term *mgboto* for prostitutes because of the ease with which prostitutes were believed to disrobe. These *mgbotos* operated from "the comforts of home"[48] *oge mgbapu Ahebi* but seem to have evolved during the colonial period into the more elaborately ordered *adana*. The term *mgbotos* seems to have fallen into disuse after the precolonial period.

The *adana*, who also operated *oge mgbapu Ahebi*, did not get married. Like the *mgboto*, she entertained her patrons from "the comforts of home." The *adana* had few clients, but the clients were regulars and the women often treated them to palm wine, *kai kai* (undistilled alcohol), cigarettes,[49] and a wide variety of provisions. The *adana* normally set up shop in front of her home, which helped attract prospective clients. Some *adanas* maintained palm-wine parlors, and others ran full-fledged eateries, called *mama puts*.[50] It is important to emphasize, however, that not all *mama puts* were run by *adanas*. *Adanas* were known to cultivate long-term relationships with their clients, and many had children from these unions. They collected payment for their services in money or in kind. Some clients would cultivate their *adana's* farm, buy foodstuffs for their "lovers," or contribute to the building or maintenance of the homes of their "mistresses."[51]

The colonial period seems to have ushered in a shift in the nature and perhaps the practice of prostitution in Nsukka Division as well. Prostitutes, who no longer seemed to be concerned by their community's constructions of and constraints on public displays of sexual aggressiveness, boldly identified as *ikweli* and *okuenu*. *Ikweli* exemplified the "I don't care" disposition—they were the sassy mamas with an attitude. *Okuenu* translated literally as "high or blazing fire." The *okuenu* and *ikweli* could care less; they were brazen and had an in-your-face attitude. In other words, *fa walu anya* (they did not listen to reason). Perhaps the *ikweli* and *okuenu* in fact needed to draw attention to themselves in a way that had not been necessary during an earlier time in order to appropriately capitalize on their sexual labors in a highly competitive colonial market.

During this time, Nsukka people also called prostitutes *akwuna*, which was an adaptation of the southern Igbo term *akwunakwuna*. In its original context, the word referred to a town in the Obubra Division of Calabarland, where such women were believed to have originated.[52] Benedict B. B. Naanen argues that by 1948 the town of Akunakuna had acquired such a reputation for prostitution that a colonial officer reported that the name had become "the household term for harlot throughout Nigeria and to a large extent . . . the Gold Coast."[53]

Okada is the most contemporary word for prostitute and calls to mind the ubiquitous motorcycles that have replaced taxicabs in most parts of Nigeria. The term *okada* dates from the late 1980s, a rough period in the economic life of Nigeria when motorcycles emerged as cheap alternatives to expensive taxicabs. In Nsukka, a prostitute is currently called *okada* because one hops on her as one hops on the motorcycle—hastily.[54] With "modernity"—especially in fast-paced urban areas—the indigenous institution in which *adanas, okuenus, ikwelis,* and *mgbotos* performed a wide range of services (cooking, conversation, and so forth) has evolved into its present form. Now it is a service that allows clients only enough time to hop on and off the *okada* hastily. This contemporary usage is, however, beyond the scope of this study.

The prostitute *oge mgbapu Ahebi* was constructed as a free woman. Indeed, "free woman" was the English term the Nsukka Igbo used to describe sex workers. When one attempts to deconstruct this word, two variables emerge: how Nsukka prostitutes viewed themselves and how Nsukka society viewed them. In Nsukka, the free woman was perceived as autonomous, independent, assertive, daring, bold—in other words, *o walu anya*. In this context, prostitutes were viewed with a degree of deference and possibly admiration. The free woman was not marginalized by society; she asserted herself and exercised a degree of power. Members of society realized that the services that the *adana, okuenu, ikweli,* and *mgboto* performed were an essential part of societal life. One collaborator explained that the *adana's* home was well known to all villagers and was a place where men could "unwind and relax." In fact, she suggested that other women in the village looked at the *adana* with some admiration because *adanas* seemed to be the only ones able to forge friendships with the men of the village.[55] Society's apparent lack of ambivalence toward this trade could be explained by its affirmation of a woman's right to control and use her body as she pleased before marriage. One saying expresses this affirmation: *Nwa mgboto kponu di, kponu oyi ya na mboro be nneya* (If a woman does not have a husband or a boyfriend, she will have to become a friend to her mother's second bed).

In the Nsukka institutions of *mgboto, ikweli, adana,* and *okuenu,* unlike their Western counterpart, there was a notable absence of the male pimp who exploited and degraded his "girls." The *mgboto, ikweli, adana,* or *okuenu* maintained control of her body and finances and decided what services to offer (or not offer) a client. She was engaged not in the servicing of men but in an assertion of her fundamental right and freedom to do whatever she desired with her own body. The discourse thus departs from Western arguments about sexuality and morality, victimization and exploitation, to focus on questions of power and agency, choice, and being in control. We will see, though, that Igbo sex workers who migrated out of rural Igboland into urban areas—many of which were non-Igbo-speaking—found themselves increasingly dependent on and in many cases completely subject to the whims and fancies of controlling and oftentimes abusive madams.

From what I have been able to gather, prostitution was not constructed in Igalaland in the same way as it was in Nsukka Division. In fact, there is little evidence to suggest that there was a comfortable relationship between Igala citizens and prostitutes *oge mgbapu Ahebi* or thereafter. Women in Igalaland were not like their northern Igbo counterparts, free to do as they wished with their bodies before marriage. In fact, Igala society instituted powerful prohibitions to ensure a woman's sexual morality and chastity before marriage, including rituals in which a bride-to-be had to swear before an oracle that she had in fact been chaste. The belief was that if she had not been, she would surely die.[56] Another ritual allowed parents to plant an important deity (*eboji*) on the heads of their daughters to keep any temptation at bay that might visit them or entice them to part ways with their virginity.[57] The presence of these rituals, as Mallam Umonu articulates, speaks volumes about the fact that it was unacceptable for Igala women or girls to express—let alone enjoy—their sexuality during the precolonial era: "Prostitution was not welcome in . . . Igalaland. So, whoever practiced it did so in secret. Nobody openly identified herself as a prostitute. . . . But, I am not suggesting that Igala women . . . did not practice prostitution. They did and still do, but it is not pronounced, nor is it a welcome development. Our people and our tradition frown upon it, but yet human beings being what we are, indulge in it secretly."[58]

Although prostitution was not an accepted practice in Igala country *oge mgbapu Ahebi,* concubinage was, and Igala men were encouraged (and in fact expected) to keep as many concubines (*enajas*) as they could afford.[59] In the words of one oral history collaborator: "Apart from your wife, a person's person [or *enaja*] is a lady you have some nice with. She gives you something at her place, plays with you. . . . Yes, Igala men have concubines."[60] Although this Igala collaborator gushed about the desirability of such unions, it is worth noting that the words "person's person" do not suggest an equal liaison. If anything, the construction is indicative of a relationship in which the male lover perhaps "owns" his *enaja* and her services for extended periods of time.[61] This extended ownership of female sexual and other labors by one man would not a relationship between a prostitute and a client make. A client does not own a prostitute, except perhaps for a restricted amount of time—"short-time" or "whole night"[62]—during which the client rents the prostitute's services. If we understand prostitution in this way, the Igala practice of concubinage could be viewed as akin to sex work. Both are institutions in which women are maintained by male lovers who present them with cash for services rendered. However, to suggest a congruence between sex work and concubinage would be considered sacrilegious because the Igala failed to see the *enaja* in that way.

Constructed negativities surrounding sex workers notwithstanding, my oral history collaborators did point to organized prostitution as being practiced both inside and outside Igalaland *oge mgbapu Ahebi*.[63] They believed that the vast majority of Igala-born prostitutes during this time worked in faraway places[64] such as Maiduguri, Kano, and Kaduna (incidentally, towns that were predominately Muslim).[65] These Nigerian towns—like Akunakuna—provided sex workers with the opportunity to work anonymously and then return home with enough money to make their mark by building houses and making other capital investments.[66] As for the prostitutes who worked in Igalaland *oge mgbapu Ahebi*, they were (interestingly enough) constructed as outsiders (primarily women from the Nsukka area of northern Igboland) who had "run away" from home, much like Ahebi had, to find solace in work that gave them immediate financial gratification.[67]

The words for prostitutes that were used in Igalaland were varied and, like the words for their counterparts in Nsukka Division, seemed to have evolved over time. *Oge mgbapu Ahebi*, prostitutes were known by Igala, Yoruba, Hausa, and Igbo words, perhaps capturing the multi-ethnic composition of the women who worked in the Igala urban sex industry.[68] The Igala words for prostitute included *ajoko*[69] or *eji-ako*, which literally translated into thief (*eji*) and husband (*oko*),[70] thus meaning "stealing somebody's husband." A prostitute in this construction was looked upon as a thief who stole what belonged to someone else. The Igala term *ama-ajoko* was a derivative of *ajoko* (stealing someone's husband) and was used in the same way.[71] The Igala also used the word *ajabutabu* (a woman that goes about with men). They saw the *ajabutabu* as irresponsible and for all intents and purposes a "homeless" person.[72] "Homelessness" in this context does not mean someone who cannot afford a home; it means a person who chooses to jump from home to home and bed to bed. Another term that was used was *ajojere* (someone who steals the legs of a man). The Igala people have a saying that "the penis is between the legs." Therefore, when a woman "steals" a man's penis, she also steals his legs.[73] The term could also be used to refer to a married woman who sneaks out "with her legs" to have illicit sex. She is said to steal (that which is between the legs of a man) with (that which is between) her own legs, not with her hands.[74]

The Igala place name Ayangba has survived in Nigerian Pidgin English as *ayangba,* a term for a prostitute or loose woman.[75] It seems very probable that *ayangba,* like the Calabar-derived term *akwunakwuna,* was a word used for prostitutes *oge mgbapu Ahebi.* A flourishing city during the colonial times, Ayangba, as discussed earlier, boasted a large oil mill and open-air market as well as a large community of European expatriates. It is conceivable that the town attracted sex workers from all over Nigeria to service the sexual appetites of the migrants who flocked to the town to earn a living. Even today, certain towns in Nigeria are known for the large number of prostitutes in their environs. One such town, Benin City, has the unenviable position of exporting more prostitutes to various European vicinities than any other Nigerian locality.[76] Perhaps Ayangba was where Ahebi learned the art of seduction, the art of "stealing one's husband," from masters of the trade.

The Yoruba call the prostitute or loose woman *ashawo,* another term that prostitutes were known by in Igalaland *oge mgbapu Ahebi.*[77] In its literal sense, the word means "someone who provides services in exchange for money" or "someone who breaks money," that is, a money changer.[78] The *ashawo* provided sex in exchange for money and would often break large bills to provide change for clients when requested.

The Igala also referred to sex workers by the Hausa name for a professional prostitute, *karuwa.*[79] Among the Hausa of northern Nigeria, the word was used pejoratively as an epithet to mean "a person (especially a woman) who sleeps around," "one who carried out illegitimate sex," or "a profligate person."[80] Just as this language implied, the prostitute in Igalaland slept around and was perceived as someone with extremely low moral standards.

The Igbo term used for prostitute in Igala country *oge mgbapu Ahebi* was *agalacha*[81]—literally "someone will lick" or "someone will be licked." When translated in the context of sexual intercourse and/or prostitution, that someone becomes the client, who "licks" and pleases the prostitute with his tongue, as would be expected during the act of oral sex, or receives fellatio from the prostitute. Prostitutes in Igalaland were also known, just as their Nsukka counterparts were, by the Igbo terms *nwa mgboto*[82] (a young person who goes naked or strips naked easily), and *akwunakwuna.*[83]

The diversity of Igala, Igbo, Yoruba, and Hausa names used to refer to prostitutes in Igala country speaks volumes about the ethnic origins of the women who practiced as prostitutes in Nigerian cities in colonial times. It seems certain that colonialism—with the construction of railways and the expansion of existing roadways—would have afforded women far and wide access to mobility to greener pastures that might not have been easily attainable during precolonial times.

There were basically two categories of Igala prostitutes who made their living as sex workers *oge mgbapu Ahebi*. First, there were professional prostitutes (these would include the *ajoko*, the *ajabutabu*, the *ayangba*, the *ashawo*, and the *karuwa*)—women who operated from hotels and brothels and established themselves as permanent workers. These prostitutes gave the owners of the hotels from which they operated a cut of their income.[84]

The second category of prostitutes practicing *oge mgbapu Ahebi* operated from their homes. For the most part these women were widows, although some were married women who exchanged sex for money. These particular prostitutes, *ajojere*, were also constructed as free women. Free not because women were allowed to do as they wished with their bodies (a marked difference between this institution and its Nsukka counterpart), but because most of them were said to have lost their husbands in death, hence realizing the "freedom" to engage in paid sex.[85] Furthermore, as in the Nsukka institution and the *enaja* institution, some of these prostitutes developed long-standing relationships with their male clients. The sex worker could have children for a male "friend" and eventually hope to marry him. He in turn would be expected to provide money for the support of his lover and their children. Some male clients even built homes for their prostitute girlfriends.[86]

Oge mgbapu Ahebi, two hotels were especially known for organized prostitution in Idah. These were the Premier Hotel (situated near the present-day National Electric Power Authority building at Idah) and the Cool Spot Hotel (situated where the Victory Church is now located). These hotels were allegedly constructed by Igbo men in the early 1900s and were patronized by men of all economic backgrounds.[87]

The story of a 30-year-old Igala prostitute named "Blessing," who works at the Cliff Motel, near the Police Station Junction in Idah, supports many of the contentions of my Igala oral history collaborators about the nature of prostitution in Igalaland *oge mgbapu Ahebi*. It focuses on the ethnic origins of the female workers who made their living selling sex for money and brings to the fore the fact that most Igala prostitutes combined sex work with other types of paid labor—including trading (as Ahebi was known to have done), farming, and, in the case of Blessing, hairdressing. Here are excerpts from a 2008 interview with Blessing:

Q. What is the usual price you collect from customers?

A. [laughs and giggles] Well, for "short-time," I get more than 500 naira. At times I collect 1,000 naira or 1,500 naira for "short-time." For a whole night, I charge 5,000, 4,000, or 3,000 naira.

Q. Do you have a madam for this job?

A. No, I work alone. What's my business with a madam?

Q. But are there prostitutes that have madams?

A. I don't know.

Q. Is there a place at Idah here in the form of a brothel?

A. Yes, you can find one at Burial Ground Road. That is the only one I know. You pay and enter. I don't know if it is cheap or not.

Q. I thought you ought to know.

A. But what would I go there to do? It is mainly Igbo people that are there. I don't have friends there. What is my concern with Igbo people? There are no Igala girls there.

Q. Are there some older women, some of whom may have lost their husbands that partake [take part] in this business?

A. Yes. That is at Burial Ground Road.

Q. Do these women provide sex and food too?

A. I don't know oh!

Q. Do prostitutes work in restaurants and eateries too?

A. Yes! Plenty of them!

Q. Are salesgirls also involved?

A. I am not certain.

Q. Have you been married before?

A. Yes, I was married. My husband is late.

Q. Do you have children?

A. Yes, I have two.

Q. Are you the one feeding [taking care of] them?

A. Yes.

Q. Is that why you are doing this prostitution?

A. Yes. They are in school. One just began school. The other
is in secondary school. They school in Idah here—one boy
and one girl. The boy is in secondary school. The girl is still
small.

Q. As you are out this late at night, who is with them?

A. My people [family] are there.

Q Are your people aware you do this job?

A. No! They are not aware. I work at the salon in the afternoon. My salon is at Opata.[88]

Blessing, a prostitute working in Idah about a century after Ahebi would
have, corroborates a number of facts about the nature of sex work *oge
mgbapu Ahebi*. First, some prostitutes in Igalaland worked out of hotels
(a fact confirmed by the presence of at least two hotels providing such
services *oge mgbapu Ahebi*);[89] second, other prostitutes combined sex
work with other trades (as Ahebi did);[90] third, a sizeable number of prostitutes practicing in Igalaland were Igbo (another fact that was supported
and corroborated by the evidence my oral history collaborators provided
and Ahebi's experience);[91] fourth, Igala women often became prostitutes
as a result of being widowed;[92] and fifth, Igbo women in Ahebi's day as
well as the present day, work out of brothels where sexual services, food,
and conversation are traded.[93]

Although the oral evidence available to us about Ahebi's involvement
in prostitution in Igalaland is scarce, I hope this discussion of the nature
of prostitution in Igbo and Igalaland *oge mgbapu Ahebi* and after sheds
some light on what the institution might have been like when Ahebi
practiced it. It also illustrates some of the choices Ahebi might have made
about how or how not to use her body during her time in exile.

Ahebi the Trader

> Explaining her ceaseless foraging for food the
> hen said, "I begin the day gathering food for
> my *chi*, then I gather for my *eke*, and by the
> time I gather for myself, it is night."[94]

In addition to her mother tongue (Igbo), Ahebi learned to speak
many languages, including Igala, Nupe, and Pidgin English, during her
years in exile. Although it is conceivable that she learned these languages

through her interactions with clients as a sex worker, it is equally possible
that she acquired these languages through trade, another activity that
we know she engaged in while she was exiled in Igala. Trade was one of
the most important economic activities in colonial Igalaland. The area
boasted a network of markets that linked numerous areas within and
outside the kingdom. The Ejule and Afor Gam-Gam markets were particularly well known *oge mgbapu Ahebi,* and the Ejule market was located
in a town where Ahebi lived. These markets were held on the four Igala
market days (Afor, Eke, Ukwo, and Ede). The confluence of the Niger,
Benue, and Anambra rivers created natural highways that traders took
advantage of *oge mgbapu Ahebi.* In fact, as early as the fifteenth century
the Igala were engaged in active trade with other groups along the Niger,
as well as with the Igbo, Hausa, Bini, and Nupe. They were also said
to have traded with people as far away as Calabar and with Europeans
along the Atlantic coast.[95] Oral evidence indicates that Ahebi used trade
networks such as the Ejule market while she lived in Igala.[96]

What is not clear is whether Ahebi practiced sex work concurrently
with trading or whether she was able to expand her trading interests by
channeling the proceeds gathered from her work as a prostitute into
marketing. Whatever the case, in time Ahebi became an astute businesswoman. She first traded in *okanwu* (potash), then palm oil and kola nut
and, at some point, horses.[97]

Oge mgbapu Ahebi, Igala women typically engaged in palm oil production, the preparation of special beers, trading, and farming.[98] In the
years of Ahebi's sojourn in Igala country, a ban (*ekpe enabe*) was placed
on the harvesting of palm fruits during specified periods in order to
allow the fruits to mature and ripen. When the ban was lifted, a time
known as *ekpe elaba,* Igala women would commission their men to har-
vest the palm fruits for them. The processing of palm fruits into oil *oge
mgbapu Ahebi* was entirely the preserve of Igala women, however. This
time-consuming project involved stripping and boiling the fruit until it
was soft, then pounding it into a pulp in a mortar and adding water as
it was pounded until the oil rose to the surface. The women would then
skim the oil off and separate the fiber from the nuts.[99] Evidence indicates
that Ahebi participated in this industry.[100]

Brewing was also the preserve of Igala women, who prepared two
different types of beer: *opito* and *bulukutu, oge mgbapu Ahebi. Opito* was
made out of guinea-corn, and *bulukutu* was made out of maize or mil-
let. In time, however, *opito* disappeared from the market, having been
replaced by another indigenous brew variously called *ote una* (fire wine)

or *kanyi-kanyi* (push-me-I-push-you).[101] The oral evidence available to us does not specifically indicate that Ahebi participated in beer brewing, but she certainly could have, because prostitutes practicing in both Igbo and Igalaland were known to offer various brews to their clientele to put them in the mood for sex *oge mgbapu Ahebi*.

Igala women controlled the bulk of petty buying and selling in Igalaland.[102] They traded in palm oil, *aikpele* (*Irvingia;* i.e., *ogbono*), *ugba* (*Pentaclethra macrophylla bentham;* i.e., "oil bean"), *egusi* (*Colocynthis citrullus lanatus;* i.e., "melon seeds"), and many processed foods such as *akara* (bean cakes), corn pap, *opito* and *bulukutu* beer, pounded yams, rice, beans, and *eji-agbo* (bambara groundnut; i.e., *okpa*).[103] We know that Ahebi engaged in petty trade. Perhaps she traded in some of these items during her time of exile.

Ahebi eventually made her mark as a horse trader. She was said to have accumulated enough stock to have made trips from Igalaland to the horse-trading center of Nkwo Ibagwa in Nsukka Division to sell horses. In fact, at the height of her trading career, Ahebi Ugbabe was one of the most affluent traders in the Igala-Igbo borderland area.[104] Given the level of her involvement in the horse trade, it is likely that Ahebi was familiar with the lucrative Uzo-Anyinya (i.e., the horse route that was controlled by Ibagwa-Ani middlemen and extended into Igalaland).[105]

Ahebi's success in trade and sex work enabled her to acquire economic power and political clout that was uncommon for individual women in precolonial Igbo or Igalaland. Moreover, her profession as a sex worker put her in touch with a number of prominent citizens, including some British colonialists[106] and Attah-Igala (the king of Igalaland),[107] whose power extended into northern Igboland.[108] She channeled some of her money into the purchase of "slaves," including Nweke, a female "slave," and Onuche, a male "slave" she bought from Ibara.[109] She later acquired many more "slaves" when she returned to Nsukka Division, including Stephen, who became her trusted confidant and adopted son.

During her sojourn in Igalaland, Ahebi dabbled in *ogwu* and *igwo ogwu*—traditional medicine and the performance of making this medicine. *Ogwu* was believed to have the power to inflict good or evil. As such there was good and bad medicine. Good medicine could bring good fortune, protect clients, cure ailments, and ward off enemies and evil spirits. Bad medicine, (*ajo ogwu*), on the other hand, had the potential to inflict psychological or bodily harm on individuals. The Igbo psyche accepted—and in fact encouraged—the making and use of good medicine. However, there was no place in society for *ajo ogwu*, which evolved through co-opting the rights and freedoms of other individuals within the community. From all indications, Ahebi Ugbabe initially became involved in the use of good medicine, partly in an attempt to ward off some of the more damning condemnations of the goddess she had rejected and partly to protect her from anyone who might attempt to do her harm.[110] She committed to the occult for another reason: to obtain the extra-human powers that would eventually lead her from success to success.[111] In the next chapter, we will see how her participation in the making and use of bad medicine would contribute to her eventual ostracism from the society of her birth.

Oge Otikpo / During the Time of the Destroyer: The Coming of Government in the Person of the White Man

All of this activity was happening against the backdrop of an over-whelming colonial invasion. By the turn of the twentieth century, the British colonial government had launched a series of military and police attacks that were aimed at subjugating the people of eastern Nigeria and bringing them under European rule. However, the penetration of the colony that would eventually be known as Nigeria had occurred earlier. Starting around 1851, the Nigerian hinterland was invaded and con-quered by the British in a process that would last over half a century. The invaders had revealed a vast territory in Nigeria as rich in raw materials as it was militarily weak.[112] The colonizers justified their military assault by citing a "moral obligation"[113] to rid Nigeria of the evils of the imagined practice of human sacrifice and to establish legitimate trade. Therefore, the British began setting up trading stations in strategic centers along the banks of the River Niger. Ultimately, however, these assaults were designed to colonize the inland communities and bring them under British rule.

During the time that Ahebi was in exile, the colonials had success-fully conquered Igalaland, bringing this large expanse of land under their newly created political entity of Okwoga Division. From this van-tage point, they launched more punitive patrols that penetrated further into the Igbo interior. Starting from the first month of 1909 until 1920, the British mounted a series of patrols and attacks on the Enugu-Ezike area—an expanse that they planned to administer together with the already-conquered Igala areas under the newly constituted Okwoga Division.[114] The British justified these actions under the guise of a noble motivation—the abolition of the domestic slave trade.[115] The success of their punitive patrols were, however, dependent upon the accessibility of classified information, available only to the indigenes—information that would allow the British invaders access to community roads and dirt paths through which they could infiltrate the lands they wished to conquer.

Ahebi Ugbabe, having traversed these roadways as well as several of the footpaths in question more times than once during her exile in Igalaland, would have been well placed to serve as such an informant to the British. But did she? Here is what we know. Ahebi Ugbabe definitely accompanied the British invaders into Umuida and Ogrute. However, what is not so clear is whether theirs was a chance meeting or whether Ahebi entered the region with the British in a calculated effort to punish her people and right a wrong done her many years before.

Perhaps the clearest confirmation of Ahebi's agency can be gleaned from archival evidence. In his report on the peoples of Enugu-Ezike, V. K. Johnson confirmed that Ahebi Ugbabe had collaborated with the British by showing them the routes to take in order to conquer her people.[116] It is certainly conceivable that Ahebi Ugbabe—who was herself a candidate for cult dedication—would wish to see domestic "slavery" eradicated. Ahebi's act of betrayal could also be interpreted as a cold rejection of a culture that not only attempted to punish her for the crimes of her father but also forced her into exile, where she endured rape and a life of prostitution.

As for her motivation, Abraham O. Eya of Amufie, Enugu-Ezike, provides a plausible explanation for Ahebi's actions. He suggests that Ahebi accompanied the British back to Enugu-Ezike with the understanding and assurance that they would stamp out domestic "slavery" in her town. Eya's wisdom was documented in a 1977 interview with Christopher Uchechukwu Omeje, in which he observed: "Ahebi Ugbabe Ayibi . . . brought the white man to stop the slave trade in Enugu-Ezike. The Hausa soldiers who accompanied the white man lived at Ekposhi."[117]

But what would have brought about the meeting between colonized and colonizer? It is conceivable that the prostitute Ahebi, who was said to have had sexual interactions with the Attah-Igala, met the British colonizers through her profession.[118] The colonials were said to have given her a helmet, which she wore as a crown, as a gift for services rendered (see the photograph of her nephew holding this helmet in Figure 1.7 and of the helmet itself in Figure 3.1).

Lessons Learned: The Lives and Times of Princesses Inikpi and Oma Idoko of Igalaland

We can only hypothesize about where Ahebi might have gotten her ideas about individualized female leadership. Her own people, the Igbo, did not have any form of individual leadership. Theirs was an egalitarian gerontocracy that bestowed leadership on a group of elders. Because Ahebi's most important formative years were spent in exile in Igalaland, it would not be far fetched to suggest that she was influenced by the people she spent this time with. In the last sections of this chapter, I will present the lives and times of two important princesses who would have been prominent figures in the transmission and recall of indigenous knowledge during the time Ahebi lived in Igalaland, princesses whom a young Ahebi might have emulated. But first, let us briefly revisit the history of another influential woman, Attah-Ebulejonu, whose life choices might also have influenced Ahebi in profound ways.

Attah-Ebulejonu was an extraordinary woman, and Ahebi undoubtedly was exposed to the oral traditions about her while she lived in Igala country. Ebule's was not only a well known story but one that was (and continues to be) passed down from generation to generation in Igalaland. It is possible, as I have hypothesized earlier, that Ahebi's performance of social and political status by assuming the praise-name Agamega (female leopard) and donning leopard court attire was done in honor of Attah-Ebulejonu's half-human, half-leopard father, Attah-Abutu Eje. However, to suggest that that was all Ahebi took away from that story would be inaccurate. Attah-Ebulejonu's story would have had more far-reaching consequences for Ahebi's life than just leopard dress and borrowed praise-names. What Attah-Ebulejonu's story would have done for a young Ahebi would have been to allow her the permission to fantasize about the possibility of one day becoming a female leader and king.

Two other women that Ahebi probably heard about and who may have also had a profound influence on the impressionable teenager were the princesses Inikpi and Oma Idoko, who, like Attah-Ebule, have been immortalized in the oral histories of the people of Igalaland.

Princess Inikpi was born to Attah-Ayegba Oma-Idoko during the last quarter of the seventeenth century. Attah-Ayegba was the king who was said to have defined the external and internal boundaries of the Igala kingdom and to have created the title system around which the kingdom evolved. During Ayegba's reign, the Igala moved to free themselves from the yoke of the Jukun kingdom. Thus, sometime in the last decade of the seventeenth century, when the Jukun king, the *aku,* sent his emissaries to collect their annual tribute from the Igala kingdom, the Igala people filled the *aku's* containers with stones and dung and sent his messengers back with a warning that they would no longer pay tribute to the

Jukun. On receiving this news, the *aku* was enraged and decided to teach Ayegba and his Igala kingdom a lesson: The Jukun declared war.[119]

Because the Jukun kingdom was the stronger of the two, Igala defeat seemed like a foregone conclusion. In an attempt to circumvent this assumed reality, Attah-Ayegba consulted a diviner,[120] who revealed that if the Igala kingdom wished to win the war, Attah-Ayegba would have to sacrifice the child he loved the most, his beloved daughter Inikpi, to the gods. A shaken Ayegba kept this chilling prophecy to himself and did nothing. Soon enough, his daughter Inikpi heard rumors that her father had visited a diviner and wanted to know what the diviner had revealed. A stoic Ayegba refused to breathe a word of the prophecy to his daughter. However, the *attah* had underestimated his daughter's persistence. Princess Inikpi grilled his closest confidantes and anyone she suspected would know what the diviner had revealed. She soon found out, and her action was as brave as it was swift. The princess ordered that a large hole be dug near the bank of the confluence of the Niger and Benue rivers. It took the workers several hours to dig the pit as big as Inikpi had instructed. Then, to the horror of her subjects, Princess Inikpi descended into the hole, accompanied by nine of her slaves. She called out to the workers to cover the hole tightly with earth. Princess Inikpi had been buried alive.[121]

Another woman from the Igala royal family was offered the opportunity to safeguard the Igala kingdom from the Jukun on the instruction of the same diviner or cleric. Princess Oma Idoko was a relative of Attah-Ayegba. Details about Oma Idoko's history are sketchy, but we know that she would not give herself willingly to be sacrificed and that she was forcibly buried alive.[122]

The diviner or cleric was also said to have prepared a medicine that was cast into the Inachallo River. Soon the report came that many of the Jukun enemy troops, who had eaten fish from that river, had died of food poisoning.[123] To the Igala, the food poisoning was in keeping with the prophecy of the diviner that they would defeat their enemy if they offered Inikpi and Oma Idoko as sacrifices to the gods. The weakened Jukun army was easily defeated.

Because of the courage and selflessness young Princess Inikpi demonstrated, her people elevated her to the rank of a goddess. She presently occupies the special space of chief intermediary between the Igala and their Great God, Ojo. A deified Inikpi has also been constructed as the protector of all Igala—a merciful mother who safeguards and intercedes on behalf of her children in time of trouble. She is also considered

FIGURE 2.1. Oshidadama, priest of the Oma Idoko Shrine, standing by the Inachallo River, Idah, Kogi State. *Photograph by Nwando Achebe, July 2007.*

FIGURE 2.2. Statue of Princess Inikpi, Idah Market, Kogi State. *Photograph by Nwando Achebe, July 2007.*

FIGURE 2.3. Statue of Princess Oma Idoko, Idah, Kogi State.
Photograph by Nwando Achebe, July 2007.

a goddess of fertility and is believed to grant children to barren Igala women. Each year during Ocho, the Igala kingdom's most important festival, the *attah* and his senior chiefs offer sacrifices at Princess Inikpi's shrine.[124] Today her statue stands at the Idah marketplace, near the confluence of the Niger and Benue rivers, marking the spot where Inikpi gave her life for the victory of her people.[125] Oma Idoko was also deified and immortalized with a statue to be worshipped by future generations of Igala indigenes in appreciation for the gift of survival she gave them.[126]

Princess Inikpi's influence continued to be felt long after Ahebi's life. In 1953, one of Igala's most memorable kings, Attah-Ameh Oboni, was ousted from his throne and forced into exile by the governor of the Northern Region because he allegedly ordered human sacrifice to be carried out in Princess Inikpi's honor during the year's Ocho festival.[127]

Perhaps Ahebi could relate to and appreciate the nobility of Princess Inikpi, a woman who felt compelled by oracular decree to sacrifice herself for the good of her people; her own Enugu-Ezike people had attempted to force her to sacrifice herself in marriage to a deity for the crimes of her father. Or perhaps Ahebi could relate to the injustice of another sacrifice, the ritual murder of Princess Oma Idoko at the hands of a people who were supposed to love, care for, and protect her. It appears that Ahebi might have transformed these oppressive and sexist events into a powerful statement of female agency when she performed a ceremony during which she was symbolically "buried" while she was alive in the mid-1940s. This peculiar occurrence, which was recalled by the Enugu-Ezike people as *ikwa onwe ya na ndu*, was a performance of gendered power that her people had never before witnessed, nor have they seen it since. (For more about this event, see chapter 5.) The statement that female King Ahebi Ugbabe was making was that she expected to be mourned and thus escorted to the world of the ancestors with pomp and pageantry, and she insisted that her funeral rites, rituals, and ceremonies be performed under her supervision and in her presence. An empty coffin was buried in her stead.

We know that Ahebi armed herself with protective medicine that not only shielded her from her enemies but also kept her supernaturally powerful. It is conceivable that another reason that Ahebi might have become involved with the occult was because of a determination not to allow what happened to either princess to happen to her. Moreover, the important relationships she cultivated with both the British colonials and the Igala kingship reveal a determination to protect her interests before all else. It was those relationships that allowed her to evolve the performance of the female masculinities of female headman, female warrant chief, female king, and full man. But these transformations would not happen overnight.

In the next chapter, I explore the circumstances that led up to Ahebi's return to Enugu-Ezike and the result of that return. I will discuss the tense relationship between Ahebi and the male elders of Enugu-Ezike. I will also analyze her relationship with the British, for it was that relationship that facilitated two of her four gendered performances—the transformations into female headman and female warrant chief. The chapter will also give me the opportunity to revisit Ahebi's relationship with Attah-Obaje of Igalaland, who crowned her female king. It will also examine the day-to-day running of the community under female headman and warrant chief Ahebi, concentrating on the types of cases she adjudicated and her use of bad medicine (*ajo ogwu*) to remain supernaturally powerful.

THREE

Performing Masculinities: Homecoming— and She Becomes a Man, ca. 1916–1930

Oge Otikpo / During the Time of the Destroyer: The Creation and Consolidation of a New Government

By 1914, most of Igbo country had been subjugated by the British. It would take until 1920, though, to bring the expanse of land in the northernmost corner of Igboland effectively under British control. In chapter 2 we saw how the British relied on intelligence information provided by members of the groups they were attempting to conquer. Ahebi Ugbabe was one such informant. She revealed the routes the British could use to reach and conquer Enugu-Ezike. Even so, the British appropriation of Nigerian land did not occur easily or peacefully. On the contrary, the peoples of the Nigerian hinterland fought valiantly against the British invaders in military confrontations that sometimes stretched out over several years. Human beings were seized, compounds were burned, villages were razed to the ground. The peoples of Nsukka Division vividly recall the destruction of Ekwegbe, Ohodo, Opi, and Ede-Oballa by Colonel Trenchard, who was working under the command of Captain R. M. Heron, who had strict orders to teach the peoples of Nsukka Division a lesson for not willingly providing food and water to his Niger-Cross River Expedition troops in 1908. His actions earned Trenchard the name Otikpo (The Destroyer) and his dreaded commanding officer Heron the name Akpoko (Pepper).[1]

The result of these battles was the annexation of the Igbo interior— a surrender in which the defeated "natives" were forced to relinquish their guns in a process collectively remembered as *oge ntiji egbe* (the time that the guns were destroyed). During the Aro Expedition (1901–1902), the policy of the British protectorate, the government of the soon-to-be colony, was to demand the surrender of one gun for every four houses.[2] This policy backfired in political terms; in the words of the British patrol officer, Major Gallway: "The practice of calling chiefs to meetings and then seizing them and of calling in guns to mark and then destroying them has resulted in a general distrust of the government and its policy."[3] Out of fear of injury or worse, death, Igbo people were forced to bring out their guns and stockpile them in front of the commanding British patrol officer, who reduced the arms stashes to burned rubble.[4]

Oge otikpo, Igbo communities were connected—often through the marketplace—by vibrant communication networks that conveyed gossip, rumor, and news. News of the destruction of guns and communities by the British during their so-called pacification (more appropriately, hammering) of Nigeria would have traveled freely throughout Igboland. It was, therefore, not surprising that certain villages would, out of fear of retaliation, choose to "befriend" the colonial invaders and present them with gifts. One such community was the Enugu-Ezike village of Amufie. Eighteen-year-old Abraham Eya was one of the Amufie delegates sent to appease the British soldiers who were camped at Umu-Ogbu-Ekposhi, Enugu-Ezike. There he met Ahebi Ugbabe, who was in the company of one or more of the British invaders. Although Eya incorrectly identified Ahebi as a slave girl who was sold to Idah and then Nupe, he provides an indigenous eyewitness account of her relationship with the British:

> Before the British came here, our people had heard stories about them and the strange guns they used at Obukpa. With that gun they had stopped the war between Ibagwa and Obukpa. We called that gun *akpara.*
>
> When they came here, I was small but I was among those who carried gifts to welcome them at [Umu-Ogbu-]Ekposhi, where they first camped. A Nupe man, Aduku [who would later become warrant chief], was the man who led us to them. Aduku was a trader. . . . It was Aduku who advised us to collect gifts and welcome them. Our people collected yams, chickens, eggs and other food items.
>
> All the members of the elders['] council were to appoint a delegate each for carrying the gifts to the British at [Umu-Ogbu-]Ekposhi. [Umu-Ogbu-]Ekposhi was a fierce battlefield and all the people did not like to go to the strange men there. My father being a member of the elders['] council had no other person to appoint but me. I was about 18 years. About thirty of us went.
>
> When we went there, they were many, about 600 in number. They lived in small tents. When we reached, one man called Mr. Nwambala came out to meet us. There was a lady called Ahebi. She was a slave girl sold away by her people [Umuida people] to Idah. From Idah she was sold to Nupe where she found favor with the soldiers and followed them back to her home. Only these were the Igbo element[s] in the whole lot of people. Others were Hausas.[5]

The annexation of Nigerian land was the first step in the British colonial enterprise. They also needed to control or, better yet, supplant the indigenous institutions that regulated the life of the colonized. This is where the genius or debacle (depending on who one asks) of indirect rule reared its ugly head. On paper, indirect rule was a system by which the British would rule the people of Nigeria through their indigenous institutions. The system was promulgated because it was cheap. However, the reality of indirect rule was often far different from the plan. In the noncentralized communities of Eastern Nigeria, pieces of paper—"warrants"—were issued to men who agreed to assume the role of the "native head" of their communities; they were called "warrant chiefs." This institution had begun in 1891. However, it would take another few years for the first legislation to be put into practice under Sir Ralph Moor's watch (1896–1903). After 1903, the system became revolutionized in the hands of Lord Frederick Lugard, who had been charged with amalgamating Northern and Southern Nigeria. From that point on, the institution of warrant chief as it existed in Eastern Nigeria was a fusion of the principles and practices that were already in place in Northern Nigeria and had been deemed successful by early British colonists.[6] It was against this backdrop that Ahebi Ugbabe emerged out of exile in Igala and traveled into Nsukka Division to be made headman and then warrant chief by the new British colonials.

Whether Ahebi collaborated with the British in order to help them subjugate her people or for the more noble motive of suppressing the trade in slaves, by the mid-1910s, Ahebi Ugbabe had returned home to her people. In the words of one oral history collaborator: "You know, when Ahebi returned newly it was not joyfully accepted that their lost child had returned. She was dreaded but the people were afraid to say anything because the British Administration had already come."[7]

Immediately following her return to Enugu-Ezike, Ahebi allied herself with the political elite. Her linguistic skills gave her access to the leading Igala and Nupe people,[8] who dominated most parts of Nsukka, and to the British colonial officers working in the area. Ahebi Ugbabe, who knew Pidgin English, was the only person in her village who could communicate with the British. She wasted no time; she quickly cultivated a relationship with them and began acting as an intermediary between her people and the new colonial masters.

Performing Masculinities, Phase 1: Ahebi Ugbabe's Transformation into Female Headman

Ever ambitious and talented, Ahebi recognized in the British new opportunities for political power and for gendered transformations that had not previously existed in the precolonial Nsukka order. Within a few months of her return to Enugu-Ezike, she was able to expel Ugwu Okegwu, the aged (and increasingly incompetent) British government–recognized headman. Ugwu did not speak English, Pidgin English, or Igala and consequently had very limited political influence. This was the first in a series of gendered transformations into distinct female masculinities that Ahebi Ugbabe performed in her ultimate quest to attain full manhood within the context of competing indigenous (i.e. Igbo) and alien (i.e., Igala, and British) orders.

Ugwu Okegwu was an Igbo man the British had appointed to be the head of the community. In Nsukka political culture, the symbolic heads of the community were the *onyishis umunwoke* (the oldest men in the village) and the *onyishis umunwanyi* (the oldest women in the village). These positions were not wholly political in nature; they were also religious, signifying the ritual discernment of the recognized heads. According to A. E. Afigbo, "To be a lineage head one needed not political ability, but free descent, reputation for moral rectitude and generally the right age."[9] M. M. Green put it like this: "[The lineage heads] might exercise certain political functions but basically they were there in virtue of their position in the kinship system."[10]

However, British colonials often did not see eye to eye with the community-recognized *onyishi umunwoke* and as a general rule excluded Igbo women altogether from governmental matters and leadership positions.[11] Moreover, many of these *onyishis* declined the advances of the British when they approached them with leadership positions, offering younger men to occupy these positions in their stead.[12] The British consequently appointed agreeable males, usually "strong and audacious young men"[13] who would readily follow their instructions and could thus be molded into stooges. The time-honored Igbo ideals of respectability, such as title taking, honor, and age were not factors in these appointments. These so-called indigenous headmen would come to realize powers that were much too individualized and autocratic for Igbo sensibilities.

In colonial Enugu-Ezike, each of the thirty-three villages was divided into wards and each village had a headman who controlled these wards. The headmen were the ultimate agents who carried out the orders of the alien government. With the cooperation of the government-appointed court messengers, they arrested criminals, served summons, and conscripted forced labor under the Roads and Creeks Ordinance. The government headman also followed his male warrant chief to court whenever it was his chief's turn to sit as a member of the Native Court. Headmen also gathered carriers for their chiefs, saw to the maintenance of colonial rest houses, and ensured that all touring British government officers were well provided for.[14] These jobs were unpopular, and they required the forced conscription of young men. As a result, the headmen earned an unfavorable reputation within the communities they "headed."

If the services of the Igbo headmen were not appreciated by the indigenous population, the reverse was the case when it came to the British. The new colonials recognized their headmen by according them the privilege of performing social class and status by wearing special caps with the insignia of the British crown. This practice was started at Ikot Ekpene by District Commissioner Reginald Hargrove, who gave fez caps with metal engravings of the British crown to all warrant chiefs and headmen who performed their duties well. This created, according to Afigbo, "a new hierarchy of status in society"[15] or in my own estimation, a new class of "big men," whose rank in society was intricately linked not to the performance of traditional markers of manhood and achievement (e.g., title taking, induction into the masquerade cult, warrior abilities), but to a new, easier, and, most important, heightened colonial one.[16] Moreover, the flashy and expensive imported fez cap replaced indigenous insignias of class, *owu ana eyi n'ukwu* (threads that are tied to the ankles), which were significant items of dress even though they were understated and inexpensive. The *red* fez cap was said to have been introduced as a distinguisher of titled status in Igboland by Igwe Amobi I of Ogidi, a first-generation Igbo warrant chief, who wanted to differentiate and elevate his special class of appointed chiefs from other titled men during his autocratic reign.[17] A new upper class of "big men" occasioned by colonial meddling was thus born in Eastern Nigeria. Now, ambitious and successful young Igbo men could hope to elevate their standing in society by becoming capped headmen. Moreover, these headmen could dream of one day stepping into the shoes of their masters (i.e., the warrant chiefs), thus realizing an enhanced performance of social and political status that was particularly appealing to many of them.[18]

I was unable to uncover much information about Ahebi Ugbabe the headman. The colonial record is silent on this. Oral history collaborators, however, provide more insight. They remember that Ahebi was a female headman and recall the factors that led up to her installment, but not much else: "She was initially made the headman [by the British]. That was usually the first designation or title. Whoever was made headman was recognized as the traditional or customary chief at that time.

A person becomes recognized or designated as such before he receives his warrant as a chief."[19]

The absence of knowledge about Ahebi's induction into the office of headman is understandable. It speaks volumes about how indigenous memory is constructed, highlighting the fact that society typically remembers only that which it deems worth remembering. In this instance, local memory seems to have subordinated Ahebi's short-lived position as female headman (she could not have performed the female masculinity of headman for more than eighteen months) to the longer lasting, more distinguishable recollection of a greater *ife di egwu* (thing of great incredulity), the performance of the enhanced female masculinity of female warrant chief—a point that was so well remembered that it changed the ordering of collective indigenous memory in these Igbo parts.

Here is what oral history collaborators remember: One collaborator notes that Ugwu Okegwu was implicated in a murder and that the colonial government relieved him of his post.[20] Others, however, recall that because Ugwu Okegwu was old and therefore ill-equipped to deal with the rigors of the post and because Ahebi knew Okegwu well (Ugwu Okegwu was said to have given Ahebi the land on which she built her palace), she agreed to step in and represent the headman, who did not speak or write Pidgin English, whenever he needed her to.[21] According to these sources, the British got to know her as she performed these duties and soon replaced Ugwu Okegwu with the more competent and energetic Ahebi. Fabian Azegba of Umuida, Enugu-Ezike, although mistakenly referring to Ugwu Okegwu as customary court judge (he was not customary court judge; he was the headman who accompanied the customary court judge or warrant chief to court) corroborates these details, adding that Ahebi served as Ugwu Okegwu's translator.

> When the white man came to Umuida, Ahebi accompanied them back to Umuida. The person that was the [headman][22] then was one Ugwu Okegwu. He is the one who owned the land where Ahebi built her house. Ugwu Okegwu had been going to court [i.e., accompanying the warrant chief] when the white man came. . . . Ugwu Okegwu was however a farmer and was therefore not interested in going to court all the time. So Ahebi used to go in his place. All of a sudden the British decided that Ugwu Okegwu would no longer be a [headman] because he was irregular. The last day that he went the white man threw his praise-singers out and they said that Ahebi would now be the [headman].[23]

These scenarios seem plausible and fit neatly into my overall narrative, especially when one considers the detail (confirmed by both colonial and indigenous knowledge) that Ahebi had already made contact with the colonials during their patrols of the area. It is no wonder, therefore, that the new British masters favored her for the posts of headman and, subsequently, warrant chief. In fact, the British presented Ahebi with a helmet—which she wore as her crown—in appreciation of the help she gave them during their patrol of the area. The helmet (see figure 3.1) seems to be an early-twentieth-century French *gendarmerie à cheval* (a French mounted policeman),[24] adding another interesting dimension of British "regifting" to King Ahebi's story.

However, in appointing Ahebi headman, the British had introduced a radical change in both Igbo and colonial British political cultures. Elevating a woman to high political office was not a departure in the context of the norms of precolonial Igbo political life, which allowed women significant power as members of the *otu umuada* (the daughters of the lineage who served as the supreme court of arbitration in society). Nevertheless, Ahebi's induction was an undeniably significant departure from the way that the British had historically handled indigenous governance in their African colonies. Ahebi Ugbabe became the only female in all of colonial Nigeria and arguably, British Africa, to fill these offices. Moreover, for the British to put in place an individual who represented such a radical departure from their normative political culture, they must have seen qualities in Ahebi that inspired their confidence in her.

One need not search far to discover what these qualities were. The British identified her as being loyal, intelligent, and sensible—qualities that far exceeded those of any of their British-appointed indigenous male functionaries. W. H. Lloyd and L. A. C. Helbert corroborate this perspective in a series of notes, observations really, in which they comment on the warrant chiefs of Nsukka Division during their tenure as district officers in the area. In separate entries on Ahebi Ugbabe, entitled "AHEBI (Female) (ENUGU EZEKE) [*sic*] (UMUIDAH) [*sic*]" that were entered during the period 1922 to 1931, District Officer Lloyd and, presumably, L. A. C. Helbert[25] had this to say:

> A lady of influence & power. Loyal & controls her quarter well, though owing to her loyalty [to the British] her people assaulted her and drove her out of the town during the patrol. She is intelligent & of a quiet disposition. When she does speak, it is usually to the point, & sensible. She gets on well with the chiefs and her reasoning in the native court is sound. . . . WHL 5/8/22. . . .

FIGURE 3.1. King Ahebi's helmet/crown, Umuida, Enugu-Ezike.
Photograph by Nwando Achebe, November 1996.

> She . . . stands out in court above most of the Enugu Ezeke
> [*sic*] chiefs. She has far more intelligence than the men. [Illegible
> initials] 23.6.31.[26]

In his 1934 intelligence report on the peoples of Enugu-Ezike, V. K.
Johnson confirmed Lloyd and Helbert's assessment of Ahebi:
"Undoubtedly she was and is an outstanding woman."[27]

One need only juxtapose these observations with Lloyd's remarks
about other male warrant chiefs in Nsukka Division to understand why
the British chose Ahebi. Of Chief Ogiginma of Obukpa, he had this to
say: "Old, weak, & a useless nonentity. Has no power & is absolutely in
the hands of the Awha [titled men] Members. At present has practically
no following with the exception of his own family."[28] Chief Eze Ibegwa
of Nsukka did not fare any better in Lloyd's estimation: "Untrustworthy
& lazy & quarrelsome. Has a certain amount of power in his quarter,
but has to be kept up to it, needs watching. Has been ill and very little
in evidence during the past year."[29] And here is what Lloyd wrote about
Eze Nwaibu of Imilike:

> Very weak. Has practically no say in the town. Was reported on
> as giving no help during recent patrol. Implicated in corruption

of witnesses in connexion with case of extortion brought against OBOZO court clerk and messengers: has done his utmost to spoil the case & succeeded. A nasty person & has a large amount of low cunning. He requires watching, is none too popular in his town & tries to gain control by charging the elders in court with the idea of getting them fined. He usually succeeds, but on looking into the cases there is usually no foundation to his charges & decisions are quashed.[30]

Finally, concerning Chief Agada, a warrant chief who served in the same court as Ahebi, Lloyd wrote: "Timid, with very little authority beyond the backing of his warrant. Tries to get his people along to native court & in consequence they bring up false charges against him periodically."[31] In the estimation of the British, Ahebi Ugbabe was the most qualified person—male or female—to perform the job of warrant chief.

Performing Masculinities, Phase 2: Ahebi's Transformation into a Female Warrant Chief

In October 1918, the British formed the Native Court of Enugu-Ezike. They chose three principal court members. Ahebi Ugbabe had served the British well as government headman. Thus, it was hardly surprising that Ahebi became the only woman in all of colonial Nigeria to be chosen to sit as a member of the Native Court as warrant chief. She was described by District Officer V. K. Johnson as "a female of strong Igala tendencies" who was "allowed to sit as [a] member of the Council in recognition of [her] past services."[32]

The other principal court members were Aduku, the "ambitious and powerful Nupe," and Ayiogu-ede, the "brother of the Atama Uguaka of Amube."[33] To this mix, the British added Atama Omeke of Obaike, Ona-Okochie of Onitsha,[34] Onoja Wyidu of Umu Agama, Ugu Annya Waonu of Abuibeje, Abugo Onogu of Umuopu,[35] Okoro Eze of Amuobu,[36] Agada of Aiji,[37] Apoko of Amara,[38] and Urarama-Asaba of Ogrute.[39]

The possession of a warrant, according to A. E. Afigbo, "meant political and economic power" as well as "status and achievement."[40] It was typically bestowed on a man who had a smattering of book knowledge or who had previously apprenticed as a headman.[41] Except for her biological sex, Ahebi Ugbabe had proven qualifications in both areas. It was not uncommon for a woman to transform herself into a man—or a man into a woman—in precolonial Igboland.[42] However, this gendered modification into the female masculinity of female warrant chief, much like her transformation into female headman, was not sanctioned by indigenous culture or sensibilities but rather by an encroaching foreign one—the British. Ahebi was consequently sustained in this station as a result of the backing of a force that had proven itself stronger than the indigenous one that it had unceremoniously replaced. Her position, wrote V. K. Johnson "is a peculiar one and is not likely to recur."[43] So peculiar, in fact, was her induction as warrant chief that each time Ahebi was referred to in colonial documentation, the letter "*f*" in parenthesis (for female) followed her name.

Warrant Chief Ahebi Ugbabe versus the Male Traditional Ruling Elite: The Origin of a Conflict

Once Ahebi Ugbabe was made warrant chief, a divide developed between her and the male elders of Enugu-Ezike. A nodding acquaintance with the political system that existed in the town before Ahebi's return will help explain the root of these hostilities.

Like elsewhere in Nsukka Division, there were essentially two political constituencies operating in Enugu-Ezike—the human and the spiritual. The spiritual arm of government was more powerful; in this political realm, leadership belonged to unseen spirits and human beings merely served to interpret the will of the gods. The unseen spirits who got their power from a relationship with the divine world included Ezechitoke, the Creator God who was neither male nor female; the lesser gods and goddesses who were personifications of natural phenomena; masked spirits; and the ancestors. The masked spirits or masquerades were the dead who had come back to life in the day-to-day existence of community. They constituted a decidedly male secret society and served as controllers and enforcers of community laws and ideals. Moreover, the masquerade cult was the institution that separated biological men from biological women and ordinary men from full men. In chapter 5, we will see that when Ahebi Ugbabe brought out a masked spirit called Ekpe Ahebi—thus performing an overt masculinity—her society ostracized her; and the act ultimately led to her downfall.[44]

The human political constituency had no central authority. Its system of government was a rule by elders. Power and authority were divided between men and women in what has been described as a dual-sex political system in which each sex managed its own affairs. The dual-sex nature of this political system allowed for a harmonious yet efficient and effective division of labor.[45]

Enugu-Ezike was divided into units that included the biological family, the extended family, the kindred, and the quarter. The nucleus of the government was the male and female council (*ndi oha* and *otu umuada*), which were composed of the male and female heads of kindreds and grades of titled officials, who wielded executive powers. Political authority lay in the hands of the oldest person in each unit, namely the *onyishi umunwoke* and the *onyishi umunwanyi,* who were assisted by other elders and titled officials.[46] This precolonial system was gerontocratic and community-based and recognized and upheld the views of the group rather than those of the individual.

The male ruling elite did not want to have any part in Ahebi's autocratic cross-gender political ascent. However, they found that they had no choice in the matter because the British stood firmly behind Ahebi, thus excluding them from the day-to-day running and decision making of state. In the words of one oral history collaborator:

> When the British came, they removed power and authority from [the *ndi oha*] and imposed [men] we did not know [their] background and from where [they] came on us. We were also made to take orders from a woman! Our people did not for one day like the warrant chiefs, but because they were backed by people with stronger weapons, there was nothing we could do . . . [but] subject ourselves to their rule.[47]

Wilfred Ogara, one of Ahebi's surrogate sons, put it like this:

> The British dealt directly with Ahebi, often ignoring the *onyishis* in the process. If the British wanted to pass on information to the villagers, it was through Ahebi that they would go. Ahebi acted as a middleman between the villagers and the British. If someone were accused of criminal activity, Ahebi would be the one to confirm it for the British. Ahebi was very sincere to the British. She helped the Europeans to understand our culture and rule.[48]

Moreover, cases that previously went to the *onyishi* council were now decided before Chief Ahebi: "When cases were tried, Ahebi did not travel to the *onyishi's* residence because she was king. The *onyishi* did not go to Ahebi's palace either. . . . However if a person committed a crime, Ahebi usually charged him or her to court for the appropriate action to be taken against the person."[49] Another oral history collaborator put it like this: "Before Ahebi became [warrant] chief and king all cases were decided at the place of the *onyishi.* Yes, she usurped the powers of the [male] elders."[50]

Day-to-Day Government:
The Workings of a Female Warrant Chief

Let us now turn our attention to the actual day-to-day operation of government under Warrant Chief Ahebi Ugbabe. According to A. E. Afigbo,

> The Warrant Chief system was synonymous with the Native Court system in the Eastern Provinces. . . . Whatever position of influence, responsibility and power which Warrant Chiefs enjoyed in this era derived from their possession of the warrant which made them members of the Native Court. Even if they functioned as executive authorities in their different villages, they did so as members of the Native Court, which really was the local government body.[51]

The Native Courts Proclamation of 1900 distinguished two categories of native courts in colonial Nigeria: the minor courts and the native councils. The minor courts were lower courts that were presided over by a native authority, preferably a local chief, whereas the native councils were presided over by political officers and were located at district headquarters. Before the Native Courts Proclamation of 1900, European officers sat as presidents of the native councils. After the proclamation was passed, however, the British District Office had the right to appoint a warrant chief to act as president of the native council—a practice that practically all district officers followed. To make sure that each community used the native court system, the British made it illegal for any "native" that was not in their employ to adjudicate cases.[52] This meant that cases could no longer be tried in the traditional manner at the homes of the oldest men and women in the community.

Each time the native council convened, it had a president, who presided over the session; a vice-president, who was seldom identified in colonial documentation as such but who assisted the president nonetheless; and four other bench members, one of whom was specifically summoned to represent the village or area in which the dispute that was being adjudicated had arisen.[53] The minor court had a president who was elected quarterly by the members of its bench.

Minor courts and native councils exercised different jurisdictions. Minor courts could award damages of no more than £25 in cases related to debt and damages not greater than £50 in inheritance cases. Native councils could judge inheritance cases in which damages of up to £200 could be granted. Land cases were typically handled by both courts, and each had the jurisdiction to adjudicate criminal cases, such as petty assault or disobedience to the lawful orders of a headman, warrant chief, or the like.[54] In fact, several warrant chiefs availed themselves of the services of the native courts in order to right real or imagined abuses of their subjects. On January 1, 1928, for instance, Chief Ezeasogwa Adjogwu of Ugbene took twenty-seven members of his community to the Native Court of Nkpologu, Nsukka Division, on the grounds that they "disobey[ed] the lawful order of their chief by refusing to do work in the public service one week ago." Twenty-three out of the twenty-seven defendants were found guilty and fined 10 shillings each or two weeks of hard labor. Five of the accused were found not guilty and discharged.[55] Eighteen days later, Oebobe of Uburu brought sixteen members of his community to the same native court on the same charge of "disobeying the lawful order of their chief by refusing to do work in the public service four days ago." Unfortunately, the judgment for that case is forever lost to us, because the page on which the judgment was entered had been torn out of the criminal casebook.[56]

Chief Ahebi Ugbabe brought at least two cases to native courts in 1922 that are worth discussing.[57] She brought the first case before the Enugu-Ezike Court on July 26, 1922. The case details Ahebi's accusation that one of her servants, Ezenweke, who was in charge of fetching water for her, had put medicine (*ogwu*),[58] in her water pot in order to harm her. Below is the case as recorded in the judgment book, complete with the testimony of witnesses who allegedly saw Ezenweke poison Chief Ahebi's water pot.

> CASE No 134
> Ahebe [*sic*] (f) of Umuida
>   VERSUS
> Ezenweke of Umuida
> CHARGE: Using drugs with intent to harm complt on or about
>   two weeks ago.
> PLEA: not guilty
>
> Complt Ahebe (f) S.[worn]S.[tates] I am a native of Umuida,
>   I came from court last 18/7/22, my boys informed me that
>   accused brought a water and put medicine in the water in
>   the pot to harm me. My boys showed me the medicine and
>   also arrested accused to wait until I return from Court, a
>   cry was made when the medicine was brought and old men
>   came & saw the medicine.

1st Witness Ugwu Azagba S.S. I am a native of Umuida, I was
    present when accused brought water in a pot, accd was put-
    ting the said water inside a pot, I was standing near accused
    with a lid of the pot, I saw a medicine dropped into the
    other pot where the water was put in. I asked accused what
    is that which dropped in the pot; accused said it is only grass
    from the water. I said it is not grass, I went and brought
    light to see it and it was medicine, the reason I went for
    light is because it was in the room. I am brother[59] to Chief
    Ahebi & I live with her. I was standing with Ugwunwana
    when accused was putting water in the pot.

No question from accused.

Question by court [:] was any other person present besides
    Ugwunwana?
Ans: Other boys were outside.

2nd Witness Ugwunwana S.S. I am a native of Umuida and
    brother to Ahebe (f) I live with her in her house. I was
    present when accused brought water in absence of Ahebe.
    Ugwuazagba was present when the water was brought, I
    told Ugwuazagba to find a pot to put in the water, a pot
    was found and accused was putting the water from his pot
    to Ahebi's own, a medicine dropped from accused pot to
    Ahebi's own. Ugwuazagba told accused what was it that
    dropped inside the pot, in a very short time a fire was
    brought then found it was medicine. Accused said he was
    accused of the putting the medicine to the water, a cry was
    made & all family came to see the medicine, accused was
    arrested until Ahebe came home from court.

Accused Ezenweke States: I am a native of Umuida, the quarter
    of Umuida has it in turns to get water for Ahebe. I took
    water to Ahebe and was told my pot was too small, the
    water was put to other pot and I went for the 2nd time and
    got the water which alas was put in another pot. I came
    out from the room after putting the water, Ugwuazagba
    asked me what is that fell in the water, I said where was
    that place the thing fell; Ugwuazagba put hand in the water
    and afterwards went to find light and when he brought the
    light came back and said he saw medicine in my water just
    put into the pot. I did not make any medicine nor put the

medicine in question to harm complt. Ahebe is my sister,[60] I serve her Juju for her. I do not see any reason to put any medicine to hurt Ahebi. The same pot was the place I put my two pots of water. I planted grand nut [sic] for Ahebe and I do all what I can to please her, she is my sister. I had before begged Ahebe not to allow her boys to come to my house that in case any one reports me to her she might said [sic] Anachuna to call me. The boys continually come to my house. I have no witness, I was alone to go for water.

JUDGMENT
Finding accused not guilty, Case dismissed on special oath. One year allowed to clear from the oath.[61]

Chief Olijo presdt his X mark
Witness to mark R.A. Erokwu
C.[lerk] N.[ative] C.[ourt] 26/7/22[62]

The second case was brought before the court on August 3, 1922. This time Chief Ahebi brought a relative, one Ugwu Nwape, into court for stealing one of her fowls four days earlier. Ahebi told the court that she brought him in so she would not be accused of settling criminal cases on her own.[63] The colonial criminal judgment book records the essentials of the case as follows:

Meeting held in Enugu Ezeke [sic] 3/8/22
Chief Olijo of Ihakpu   presdt
Members: Chief Atama Omeke
Chief Onoja Wyidu
Chief Ahebe [sic] (f)

CASE NO 125
Ahebi (f) of Umuida
    VERSUS
Ugwu Nwape of Umuida
CHARGE: Stealing one fowl value 1/-property of Ahebi (f) of
    Umuida 4 days ago.
PLEA: not guilty

Chief Ahebi sworn States: accused is my relative, he was running
    after his fowl and killed mine, I took action as theft but
    found out that it was by mistake he killed my own fowl. I
    brought the matter in court because if I did not report it,
    the court will consider that I settle a criminal case.

Accused Ugwu Nwape States: I am a native of Umuida and
related to complt. I have nothing to add to her statement. I
killed the fowl by mistake when running after my own fowl.

JUDGMENT
Finding accused not guilty

Chief Olijo prsdt his X mk
Witness to mkr R. A. Erokwu
C.N.C. 3/8/22[64]

Although the native courts were supposed to be guided by native law
and custom, in practice they often were not. From an indigenous point
of view, the rulings of the native courts of Nkpologu and Enugu-Ezike
are good examples of what could be deemed uninformed judgments or,
worse still, outright miscarriages of justice.

In the first two cases, the decision to fine the guilty work-deserting
males 10 shillings each or two weeks' hard labor, although perhaps justified, was not rooted in indigenous justice. In precolonial Enugu-Ezike,
communal work was performed by groups of young men known as
nteghuna or *asata*. The *nteghuna* were the "right hand men of the 'ohas'
[male council]"[65] and assisted them at council meetings; the *asata* were
the police of the community, official executioners, and administers of
the sasswood ordeal (I will return to this point later). If a member of
the *nteghuna* or *asata* failed to perform the communal work assigned to
him, he would be fined by the leader of his group and the fine would
be divided by all members of the organization. Typically, the fine would
amount to no more than two or three rods or a chicken. However, in a
case where the accused had been deemed unyielding, the Omabe masked
spirit would be summoned to appropriate all valuable property belong-
ing to the accused slacker.[66] Thus, although 10 shillings or two weeks'
hard labor might at first sight seem justified, this new British justice
actually paled in comparison to the justice meted out by supernatural
forces in precolonial society, which not only put fear in the hearts and
minds of the guilty but ensured that they would never again fall short
of societal expectations.

Igbo law and justice would also have handled the investigation and
punishment differently in the case where Ahebi accused her servant of
poisoning her water pot. Typically, disputes that arose in a family were
handled by that family. However, if the wronged was not satisfied by the
way the case was handled, they had the right to appeal to the *onyishi* of
the extended family and, if necessary, the *onyishi* of the village council. If

the complainant decided to take his or her case to the village council, he or she would have to take a pot of palm wine to the *onyishi* when asking that the case be heard by him and his council. If there was insufficient evidence to reach a decision after the case had been heard, the accused would be ordered to produce an oath for the accuser to swear that would support the veracity of his or her accusation. Another method of justice that could be invoked was calling in the Omabe spirit, which would intimidate the accused into being truthful. *Ohas* could also place an evil medicine (*ajo ogwu*) on the family of the accused that would do harm to family members if he or she was guilty. Conversely, if an individual was caught red-handed, as in the case of Ezenweke, the offender would be dealt with on the spot. A trial by ordeal would be the only test administered.[67] V. K. Johnson details what a trial by ordeal involved:

> The victim [would be] bound hand and foot and brought by the company of "asatas" before the onyeisi [*sic*] and ohas of the village. The accused would be asked to admit his guilt. If he refused, sasswood [would be] handed to him by one of the nteghuna. If he lived he was adjudged innocent, if he died his body [would be] thrown into the "bush of evil[,]" there to be devoured by the vultures.

Johnson continues: "As a matter of fact this simple expedient very often worked out justly. An innocent man would probably quaff the cup to the dregs and promptly vomit, whereas the guilty would sip of it hesitantly and die."[68]

When we examine the ways that indigenous justice handled cases, it is clear that the case of Ezenweke would not have found its way to any court system—familial or communal—in the precolonial era because he had been caught red-handed. Once the alarm had been raised and the elders had gathered, a trial by sasswood would have been administered immediately, and because Ezenweke claimed that he was innocent of the charge, he presumably would have survived the ordeal. Indigenous justice would not have allowed him one year to ponder the accusation.

Native courts could also bring cases against individuals in their communities. For instance, the Native Court of Nkpologu brought a case against Odokha-Aguluyar of Abi on January 18, 1928. The charge was "refusing to attend court in Criminal Case No 226 of 21/12/27." The accused was found guilty, but no punishment was recorded.[69]

There was another unofficial category of court in colonial Nsukka Division. These were courts held in the palaces of given warrant chiefs. Ahebi Ugbabe had such a court in her homestead in which she judged cases outside the purview of the colonial government. I will have more to say about this in chapter 4.

Each native court had at least one clerk who prepared lists of all the cases that came before the courts. The clerks also summoned members to attend court sessions. Each court had a judgment book in which the clerk recorded all the sessions; the dates of the sessions; the names of the president, vice-president, and ordinary members who presided over each case; and the names and towns of origin of the witnesses who were called to testify.[70] Each judgment was signed by the president or the vice-president (if the president was absent). Because of their illiteracy, the presidents and vice-presidents usually made a mark (the letter "X") before the clerk, who served as witness.

Bringing cases before the courts was expensive. In cases where there was only one defendant and one plaintiff, each summons cost two shillings. This would increase to three shillings and sixpence for cases that had more than one defendant or plaintiff. It cost individuals one shilling to summon a witness and sixpence for each hour taken to serve the summons.

Vice-presidents of native councils and presidents of minor courts were paid ten shillings a day. Members of ordinary courts received five shillings each. Warrant chiefs were paid for traveling long distances to hear cases. They would receive a special fee for sitting in judgment of cases that they had to walk more than an hour to hear. They received an additional sixpence for each extra half-hour they walked for a total not to exceed five shillings.[71]

To ensure that native courts functioned effectively, each had its own treasury, which derived its revenue from court fines and fees. Monies from these Native Court treasuries were used to build link roads, which connected one village to the next, as well as rest houses for chiefs and headmen. Court clerks and messengers also got their salaries from this treasury. The warrant chiefs got their sitting fees from this same pot of money.[72]

A warrant chief of Ahebi's stature did not walk anywhere. Each time Chief Ahebi went to court she put on a performance of her status by being carried on a hammock by four hefty men to the sounds of *egwu okanga* (okanga music). *Egwu okanga* was one of the oldest and most prestigious traditional musical forms in Enugu-Ezike and was performed by and for men of substance in the community. One of the verses composed and performed by her male court musicians related in song her comings and goings to and from court as well as what would happen to that unfortunate soul who refused to carry the female chief in ceremonial pomp and majesty. Called "Ivu ada anyi ga ada, Ahebi," it compares carrying Ahebi to the mastered skill of the African dung beetle, that little creature no longer than seven to nine millimeters that is known to carry much more than its weight in soil and manure. The song tells us that the weight a dung beetle carries does not weigh it down. It infers that Ahebi's weight cannot and will not weigh her carriers down. The lyrical celebration of the dung beetle's weight could also be an allusion to its weight in responsibilities, for the dung beetle helps improve the soil by enhancing its structure, adding nutrients, and supporting the growth of forage. When gathered in great numbers, these beetles also protect livestock (such as cattle, goats, and sheep) by eating and removing their droppings, thus displacing the pests and flies that would have made a home in the dung. Like the African dung beetle, Ahebi's carriers provide an essential service to the community when they carry the female chief.

"Ivu ada anyi ga ada, Ahebi" also celebrates the fact that Chief Ahebi is carried shoulder high and warns that if she is not carried in this way, she will persecute those responsible. It challenges her carriers, court musicians, and subjects to keep singing songs in her praise, chanting in melodious harmony that Chief Ahebi not only acts like a man, she behaves like a man, she is *indeed* a man. Moreover, the song proclaims that Ahebi is not just any ordinary man—she is a man who confers with a lion. The message of the song is clear: do not cross her!

> The dung beetle's load does not weigh the dung beetle down
> The dung beetle's load does not weigh the dung beetle down
> Ahebi
> Then, Ahebi is being carried along
> Ugbabe Ahebi Ohom Eguru
>
> The dung beetle's load does not weigh it down
> Ahebi Ugbabe is being carried shoulder high
> Truly
> You will be persecuted if you don't carry the king
> You will be punished if you don't carry the king
> Because she is Ahebi Ugbabe
> The woman who acts like a man
>
> Keep chorusing . . . The dung beetle's dung
>
> Ugbabe Ahebi Ohom Eguru
> Ogwurute Ezocha Ugwuoji

Elugwu Ezikoba Okoro Owo
Grandma, oome Nwonu Nwishida
Ugbabe Oome Ohom Eguru

The king has been propped up
The king is on her way to court
The king is through with the court proceedings and is on her way home
You will be prosecuted if you don't carry the king
You will be persecuted if you don't carry the king

A woman behaves like a man
Ahebi Ugbabe bought udoro
Ahebi, the king that confers with the lion
Ugbabe Ahebi
Ugbabe Ahebi

Oome Eguru Elechi
Is she not Ahebi Ugbabe
Odobo gbiye egwu
Odobo gbiye egwu.[73]

As warrant chief, Ahebi presided over numerous cases. She also served as a witness in at least two cases.[74] Criminal case No. 170 was brought before the Enugu-Ezike Native Council on October 6, 1922. Ahebi served as president of the court. In this case, Iyida of Isigwu accused Ali Nwoji Oyi of Umuopu of stealing two of his goats on or about October 3, 1922. Oyi pleaded not guilty, claiming that four different individuals gave him the goats to care for. Ahebi's court found him guilty and sentenced him to one year in prison. The transcript follows:

CASE NO. 170
Iyida of Isigwu
    VERSUS
Ali Nwoji Oyi of Umuopu

CHARGE: Stealing two goats property of Iyida of Isigwu on or
    about 3/10/22
    PLEA: not guilty

Complt Iyida Sworn States: I am a native of Isigwu, thieves came
    to my house and cut hole through to my house and stole
    two goats of mine. I followed the thief's feet & reached to
    accused, he had my goats in his hand & I took them from

Ivu Ada Gi Anyi Gi Ada

EXAMPLE 3.1. "Ivu Ada Anyi ga Ada, Ahebi." *Prepared by Joe Davey.*

him & caught him. It was night about cock crow. My son Onu was with me to catch accused.

Witness Onu Sworn States: I followed the print of thief's feet with my father Iyida, we caught accused with our stolen goat. We took the goats & accused to the court.

Accused Ali Nwojioyi States: I am a native of Umuopu, I was given the goats by Azagba for protection. One Ugwuanyi Osayi, Eze Nwona and Ogili Osayi are they who gave me

Ivu Ada Gi Anyi Gi Ada (continued)

EXAMPLE 3.1. continued

the goats on the road to be cared for them. I was taking the goats back to above persons when complt saw me & caught me with above goats. I was arrested & taken to the Court.

Question by Crt: when you were caught did you tell complt the goats were given you by Azagba & others?

Ans: Yes, I said so that was why I had a struggle with complt for taking the goats from me.

Q. Was any one present when the goats were given you?

Ans: No I was alone when the goats were given me.

JUDGMENT

Finding accused guilty, sentence to (1) one year P.[rison] H.[ard]
    L.[abor] Chief Ahebe [*sic*] (f) prsdt her X mark

Witness to mark R.A. Erokwu C.N.C. 6/10/22
Prison warrant 388817[75]

The next suit is one of the only cases in which Ahebi's own voice is
heard as a witness against the accused in a case that she did not bring to
court herself.[76] Tried in 1930, shortly after the abolition of the institution of warrant chief (at least on paper),[77] the case was presided over by
President Ugu-Ugwu of the Native Council of Enugu-Ezike. The case,
which had formerly been heard as a civil case, was a land dispute between
Abugu and Ezenwonojah, both of Umuida. Chief Ahebi testified that
she had intervened earlier in the case (which was under her jurisdiction),
instructing the accused to "buy palm wine and beg the *ohas* to assist
him" in carrying out the orders of the *onyishi* and the court. She also
testified that the accused had refused to obey her order. The specifics of
the litigation appear below:

Native Council Enugu-Ezike
Reg ND 139/30
CASE NO 59
Abugu of Umuida
    VERS
Ezenwonojah of Umuida

CHARGE: Failing to comply with order of Court in civil case NO
    34/30 of 13/3/30
PLEA: not guilty

Pros Abugu S/S. I am Abugu and a brother of the accused, I can-
    not disobey the order of the oyishi [*sic*], accused refuse to
    remove his house as order of court & the onyishi hence the
    action. The case where accused was given above order was
    heard about 2 months ago.

Witness Ugu Nwape, Idoko Owaya, Abugu Eze, and 40 others.

Ugu Nwape S/S. I am speaking for my father Apeh the onyishi
    of Umuonu, q[ua]rt[er], also am speaking on behalf of
    others behind me. Accused was ordered to leave the land
    when case was heard in court. See civil case No 34/30. He
    has not left the land hence we all took the above action.
    There is no doubt, accused still live on the land today.

> Accused Ezenwonojah S/S/ I am Ezenwonojah of Umuida, after
> the court case, I went home, on my way going home, I saw
> the pros and other, they were passing orders that none of our
> qrt should help me to carry my house from the land in ques-
> tion. I then went to clear other place where I shall remove
> the house. The chief agree to see that the house is removed
> & then I reported to the C.[lerk of the] N.[ative] C[ourt]
> who advised me to take action in court. I then took above
> action in civil case NO 55.

> Chief Ahebe [*sic*] states: I am chief Ahebe and a native of
> Umuida, the parties in this case are under my control. I told
> accd to buy palm wine and beg the ohas to assist him in
> removing the house thus carry out order of our oyishi [*sic*]
> and court, but he refused to do so.

> JUDGMENT.
> Finding accused guilty, sentence to fine (£3) three pounds or (3)
> months impr. Accused must remove remove [*sic*] his house
> as ordered by the court & to pay cost.
> Ugu-Ugwu pres. his X mark
> Witness to mark R. A. Erokwu
> C.N.C
> 5/5/30[78]

During Ahebi's tenure as warrant chief, she presided over numerous
cases, including cases that involved accusations of adultery, theft, refusing to obey a lawful order, the killing of twins, and the illegal felling
of trees. The vast majority of the cases brought before Ahebi were debt
and damages cases as well as divorce, adultery, and dowry hearings.[79]
In all cases, she handed down judgments in accordance with the laws
prescribed by the British colonial government. As discussed above, the
British wrote these laws to mimic the law and justice of the indigenous
people. In practice, however, British laws did not mimic indigenous
justice. Litigants found that they had no option but to accept the judgment handed down by the only legal court of jurisdiction operating in
the new colonial world that they were living in.

    The animal theft case provides an interesting example for the pur-
poses of comparing the old and new law systems. The accused claimed to
have been given the goats by four different people, none of whom were
present to testify. It is hardly surprising that Ahebi and her court decided

in favor of the plaintiff, who was able to corroborate his version of events with a number of witnesses. The judgment of one year in prison with hard labor might seem harsh, but it was not nearly as severe as the punishment that would have been meted out for a similar crime during the precolonial era. Before the British arrived, the crime of stealing was a grave one in Nsukka Division, and punishment varied according to the nature of the article(s) stolen, whether or not the theft had been committed within the kin group, and whether the thief had committed a similar crime before. Livestock theft was particularly abhorred and could be punished by death, especially if the thief was caught in the act of committing the crime, as Nwojioyi had been. If the thief was not caught in the act, he or she might be adorned with broken utensils and snail shells—symbols of the atrocious deed—and paraded in the marketplace and the community at large to the demoralizing derision of his peers. In the days of the slave trade, unrepentant thieves could be sold into slavery and might eventually end up on the West African coast.[80]

The land case in which Chief Ahebi testified for the prosecution is worth examining as well. Although the issue of the rightful owner of the land simmered at the surface, the case was not about determining rightful ownership—that had already been decided in a civil court. This case was more about upholding the lower court's ruling. Ezenwonojah was charged with "failing to comply with the order of the court" in a civil case. Ahebi's testimony was taken to bolster the case against the accused; she bore witness to the fact that the accused had failed to vacate the land and move his house. The ruling of the native council upholding the removal of Ezenwonojah's house from the land seemed just and in keeping with colonial ideas of justice. However, the indigenous justice system might have responded differently. If two parties had a dispute about land boundaries, the matter would be referred to the *onyishi* and his council. Both parties would be called upon to swear oaths that their claims were just. Or a diviner could be called upon to decide the case by supernatural means. The diviner would ask each party to present him with an object from the area that they believed was the real limit of their land. With these objects the spiritualist would perform rituals that would reveal to him which of the two was speaking the truth. It was not uncommon for a diviner to indicate that both were wrong and then reveal the "true boundary."[81] In precolonial justice, land cases seldom stretched out over time. They were decided swiftly and with the attention to detail that such important cases deserved. Either oaths would be sworn on the spot or a seer would be brought in to sniff out the truth. In either case, the introduction of the supernatural reflected the seriousness of land cases in Igboland.[82]

Forced Labor and Taxation: Two Indictments against Chief Ahebi

Several factors fueled the distrust of the peoples of Enugu-Ezike in Chief Ahebi Ugbabe. These included her use of forced labor to build the Ahebi Ugbabe Road and her involvement in the collection of taxes (*utuku*). *Oge Ahebi,* most roads constructed in Enugu-Ezike were link roads built by the community. Under the 1903 Roads and Creeks (Rivers) Proclamation, it became mandatory for every able-bodied man and woman to provide free labor to the administration.[83] The warrant chiefs under the direction of the District Office executed this ordinance. The chiefs took advantage of this decree and converted part of the labor force into their own private workforce. Defaulters were often fined, and the warrant chiefs were known to keep this money for themselves. In the second half of the 1920s, Chief Ahebi Ugbabe took advantage of her office to use this forced labor to build the Ahebi Ugbabe Road, which connected her birth town, Umuida, to her mother's village of Unadu.[84]

Oge Ahebi, the warrant chiefs, under order of the British Colonial Office, also managed the collection of taxes. In Enugu-Ezike, the job of determining how many people lived in the community fell into Ahebi's hands. The British needed this count in order to know who was eligible to be taxed. Chief Ugbabe ingeniously instituted what the villagers remember as the "palm kernel census"—the counting of heads by way of a palm kernel. Every person had to bring in one palm kernel to Ahebi's office. According to former councilor Fabian Azegba,

> *Oge Ahebi,* anything that the government was involved in, Ahebi was in charge [of]. [During] the first tax registration she told all the men[85] [in the community] to bring a palm kernel and put it in a bag, since the White people did not know how many taxable adults were in the area. All this was done under Ahebi. Ahebi organized this.[86]

To say that the people of Enugu-Ezike were unhappy with the census would be an understatement. The Igbo people did not believe that human beings should ever be counted, and this belief informed many sayings about what might happen to individuals who allowed themselves to be counted like animals. So not only were they unhappy, they blamed Ahebi for making the count possible. Moreover, the Igbo people did not feel that the British had any right to demand money as payment for

FIGURE 3.2. Ahebi Ugbabe Road, Umuida, Enugu-Ezike.
Photograph by Nwando Achebe, November 1996.

what they deemed was already theirs. Although the institution of taxation in these Nsukka parts did not have as brutal an outcome as it did in southern Igboland, where the women made war (*ogu umunwanyi*) on the colonial government, the people nonetheless registered their displeasure with Ahebi and the process that she had instituted, a resentment that would eventually build to an explosion.

The Coronation of a Female King:
Phase 3 of Ahebi's Gendered Transformation

Enjoying the fruits of her position as warrant chief was not enough for the ambitious Ahebi Ugbabe. Over the next few years, she mounted a vigorous campaign to become *eze* (king) to further cement her position in government and society. In the centralized kingdom of Igala discussed in the last chapter, we saw how female kingship was an exceedingly rare phenomenon; the kingdom had recognized only one female king since its inception. In noncentralized egalitarian societies, there was no King Ebulejonu equivalent. The nature of these societies did not allow *any* individual to assume such power. Thus, Ahebi broke new ground by introducing and imposing an autocratic form of individualized—and masculinized—authority in the office of king. Moreover, Ahebi's title was bestowed on her not because of her relationship with a man—that is, as a queen who was the wife of a king—but in her own right as a woman who had effectively transformed herself into a man. Nowhere has this gendered transformation more dramatically been illustrated than in V. K. Johnson's 1934 "Intelligence Report on People of Enugu-Ezike, Nsukka Division, Onitsha Province" in which he distinguished King Ahebi Ugbabe as "the 'chieftainess [who] had to . . . become a man,' and as such she has been regarded ever since."[87]

Ahebi had performed effectively as female headman and was performing just as well as female warrant chief (at least as far as the British were concerned). Now she would be introducing her third—and arguably most powerful—performance yet: the female masculinity of a female king. This time her gendered transformation, although it was sanctioned by Igbo society in principle, was performed and realized through her associations with Igala. Astute as always, Ahebi was able to ingeniously engineer and redefine the male political institution of *attah* (i.e., Igala paramount king) into a supreme female masculinized and Igbonized sovereign who espoused British and Igala ideals of rank and hierarchy rather than Nsukka Igbo standards of gerontocracy, merit, and respectability. In other words, her performance of the female masculinity of female king was an attempt to transport a uniquely Igala system of political leadership—the Attah-Igala—into Igboland. This Igala kingship, unlike its Igbo counterpart (the Igbo had an *eze nri,* who was primarily a spiritual leader), was "more concerned with notions of rank and hierarchy than with notions of individual achievement."[88]

Ahebi Ugbabe's return to Idah, Igalaland, was far different from her first. The journey, filled with pomp and pageantry, was undertaken for her coronation. Although both Igbo and Igala oral history collaborators are unable to date the event in exact historical time, the incident is remembered as having occurred in the second half of the 1920s. In the estimation of indigenous Igbo and Igala oral historians, this was *oge Attah-Obaje;* that is, during the reign of Attah-Obaje. *Oge Attah-Obaje,* Nsukka kingship was bequeathed by the *attah* of Idah and all *ezes* were obliged to make a ceremonial pilgrimage to Igalaland.[89] It should be noted, however, that the Nsukka kingship that was typically bequeathed by the Attah-Igala was in reality the *title* of *eze,* which was merely suggestive of an elevation of status (as would be the case of any Igbo title), not ideas of centralized kingship or the autocratic leadership of an entire group. C. K. Meek rejects the notion "that the Eze of any of the communities of Nsukka Division was ever so autocratic that he could disregard the other titled officials and heads of kindreds, who were his coadjutors.

And in some communities the Eze (or Ezes, for there maybe more than one) was not even the leading personage."[90] In contrast, the kingship that Ahebi Ugbabe was performing and introducing was not the *title* of king but the *autocratic office* of king.

Members of Attah Aliyu Obaje's retinue provide the details of this coronation. As noted above, the Attah-Igala who made Ahebi king was Attah-Obaje (who reigned 1926–1945), the father of the present Attah Aliyu Obaje.[91] A progressive king, he appears to have embraced the values of an earlier Igala generation, which, several centuries before, had crowned the kingdom's first and only female king, Ebulejonu. Perhaps the decision to crown Ahebi Ugbabe was not as revolutionary as it might have seemed at first glance. After all, Ahebi was not from Igalaland, and she would never rule there. Whatever informed his thinking, Attah-Obaje initiated Ahebi into the sacred throne of the *attah*. The large red beaded kingship cap (*olu mada*) was placed on King Ahebi's head. She was also presented with the Igala kingship horsetail and instructed to never again shake a person's hand. As king she would raise her horsetail in greeting in place of a handshake. The reason behind this taboo was to protect her from possible enemies who might try to poison her.[92] King Ahebi's neck and wrists were decorated with *etiri* beads, and Attah-Obaje gave her a black fowl to sacrifice to her *chi,* or personal god, when she returned to Enugu-Ezike. Finally, Attah-Obaje presented the *okah* (staff of male kingship) to Ahebi and perforated her ears, in keeping with the tradition begun after King Ebulejonu's death.[93] He gave her the praise-name Iyi Ebule, after Attah-Ebulejonu, and instructed that from that day on she be saluted by the names *Onye te* and *Adebu Attah*.[94]

After her coronation was performed, Ahebi returned from Idah, *okah* in hand, dressed in Igala chieftaincy regalia (*agwogwu*)[95] and riding on horseback. She was accompanied by a huge entourage of musicians and dancers who played and sang songs that affirmed and celebrated her kingship. Also with her were numerous *attah* officials (*olodi attah*) who carried guns that frightened the villagers. Great feasting and celebrating continued for days on end.

The songs performed by the musicians were called *ikorodo.* In pre-colonial Nsukka Division, *ikorodo* music was performed only on sacred occasions to accompany masked spirits and their male initiates. The *ikorodo* songs performed to celebrate Ahebi's kingship situated her gendered transformation in extrahuman and spiritual terms. One song proclaimed Ahebi as "*omeh oto nelue anyu!*" ("a pit that swallowed the axe!") and further stated that "*onyenye eyigi onwuruchi ma abugu Ahebi nwa Onu*"

FIGURE 3.3. Odogo, original part of the palace of the *attah*-Igala (oldest surviving portion), Idah, Kogi State. *Photograph by Nwando Achebe, July 2007.*

FIGURE 3.4. King Ahebi's regalia of office, Umuida, Enugu-Ezike. *Photograph by Nwando Achebe, November 1996.*

("no woman wears *owuruchi* except Ahebi, daughter of Onu.") These lyrics clearly attribute nonhuman proportions to Ahebi Ugbabe's power by claiming that she had been endowed with a physical strength that was greater than an axe—for only that which is greater than an axe can swallow the axe! Additionally, the song's reference to *onwuruchi*—a beautiful and expensive Igala robe that was patterned after the Igala Ekwe masquerade (an exclusive and secret male society) and was worn exclusively by affluent men and men of distinction—introduces a spiritual element to her transformation.

However, not everyone in Enugu-Ezike was pleased by these events. According to one oral history collaborator: "On getting home, Ahebi declared that she was king. . . . This turn of events surprised the Enugu-Ezike people. Throwing their hands up in defeatist resignation, the people wondered how an ordinary woman who had gone astray could return from Idah and become their king."[96]

The Igbo have a saying: *idi otutu bu ugwu eze* (a king has added strength and honor when his subjects are many). They also believe that *ora nwe eze* (the community owns the king). None of these sentiments were realized in Ahebi's case, however, as it became obvious that a group of detractors had surfaced. A song composed by one of Ahebi's official musicians confirmed this. The song, "Isi na Ahebi abugu eze, gaje mijamaru Idah,"[97] a catchy tune with explicit lyrics, challenged anyone who insisted that Ahebi was not the king to go and have it out with the Attah-Obaje of Idah, who had made her king:[98]

> Aha n'Idah ha n'Idah came from Idah. . . . Eeee
> Ahebi Nwonu Nwishida. . . . Eeee
> If you say that Ezike is not a king. . . . Eeee
> If you say that Ezike Idoko is not a king. . . . Eeee
> Come let's go to Idah and ask. . . . Eeee
> If you say that Ahebi is not king. . . . Eeee
> Go and find out from Idah. . . . Eeee
> If you say that Ahebi is not king. . . . Eeee
> Aha n'Idah ha n'Idah came from Idah. . . . Eeee
> Ugbabe Ahebi Ohom Eguru has sojourned in the spirit world. . . . Eeee
>
> The spirits have put Ezike inside ogelegele. . . . Eeee
> If you dispute Ezike Idoko's royalty. . . . Eeee
> If you contest Ahebi Ugbabe's royalty. . . . Eeee
> Aha n'Idah ha n'Idah came from Idah. . . . Eeee
> The spirits have put Ezike inside ogelegele. . . . Eeee
> Ahebi Ugbabe has sojourned in the spirit world. . . . Eeee

If you contest Ahebi's royalty proceed to Idah and make inquiries.
. . . Eeee
Ahebi Ugbabe won the coronation/crown from Idah. . . . Eeee
Ugbabe Ahebi Ohom Eguru came from Idah. . . . Eeee
If you dispute Ahebi's crown. . . . Eeee
Ezike has won the crown. . . . Eeee
The spirits have put Ezike inside ogelegele. . . . Eeee
If you doubt Ahebi's crown. . . . Eeee
That Ugbabe Ahebi is not a king. . . . Eeee

The child of Mkpume Nwiberyi o o. . . . Eeee
The child of Mkpume Nwiberyi o o. . . . Eeee
The child of Mkpume Nwiberyi o o. . . . Eeee
The child of Mkpume Nwiberyi o o. . . . Eeee
If you contest Ezike Idoko's crown. . . . Eeee
If you contest Ahebi Ugbabe's crown. . . . Eeee
Aha n'Idah na n'Idah went and knew Idah. . . . Eeee

The hunter saw a monkey, ducked, and picked up his gun. . . . Eeee
The hunter saw a monkey, ducked, and picked up his gun. . . . Eeee
The hunter saw a monkey, ducked, and picked up his gun. . . . Eeee
The crocodile may seem tailless, but when it lashes you with its tail,
it will burrow deep down your skin. . . . Eeee
The crocodile may seem tailless, but when it lashes you with its tail,
it will burrow deep down your skin. . . . Eeee
If you doubt Ezike's crown, come let's go to inquire from Idah people.
. . . Eeee
If you contest Ahebi Ugbabe's crown. . . . Eeee

Any educated person who steals should be sentenced to life
imprisonment. . . . Eeee
Any educated person who steals should be sentenced to life
imprisonment. . . . Eeee
Any educated person who steals should be sentenced to life
imprisonment. . . . Eeee
Ahebi Ugbabe has gone. . . . Eeee
If you contest Ahebi's crown. . . . Eeee
If you contest Ahebi Ugbabe's crown. . . . Eeee [99]

"Isi na Ahebi abugu eze, gaje mijamaru Idah" is sprinkled with many
metaphorical phrases that point to the glories of Ahebi. She is the hunter,
the crocodile, the spirit who is capable of subduing any opposition from

Isi Na Ahebi Abugu Eze, Gaje Mijamaru Idah

Unknown

EXAMPLE 3.2. "Isi na Ahebi Abugu Eze, Gaje Mijamaru Idah." *Prepared by Joe Davey.*

Isi Na Ahebi Abugu Eze, Gaje Mijamaru Idah *(continued)*

EXAMPLE 3.2. continued

EXAMPLE 3.2. continued

Isi Na Ahebi Abugu Eze, Gaje Mijamaru Idah *(continued)*

EXAMPLE 3.2. continued

her community. The first line of the song is difficult to interpret. "Aha n'Idah ha n'Idah" literally translates into "the name" (presumably Ahebi's kingship name) "in Idah" is "as big as Idah"—that huge centralized kingdom whose power was felt as far as Nsukka Division in the late seventeenth to early eighteenth centuries. A few lines later, the song tells about Ezike, the founding father of Enugu-Ezike: "If you say that Ezike is not king, come let's go to Idah to ask." In the song, the names Ahebi and Ezike are used interchangeably, likening Ahebi to the founding father, Ezike, who was said to have come from Idah. The line "Ugbabe Ahebi Ohom Eguru has sojourned in the spirit world" likens Ahebi's kingship to a sojourn into the unseen and awe-inspiring spirit world. In other words,

Ahebi has not only been to the spirit world, she has come back with an understanding of that world—something that distances her from mere mortals who can never claim knowledge of the supernatural. Later in the song Ahebi is praised as "the child of Mkpume" (i.e., the child of stone). Ahebi is that stone, she is unbreakable, totally uncrackable. The line "the hunter saw a monkey, ducked, and picked up his gun" is also worth examining. The hunter is Ahebi, who sees the monkey—a representation of Ahebi's rebellious society—and picks up her gun, with which she stalks her prey. The image is one of the proficient hunter who is capable of defending herself against the nuisance of the prey. The message is clear: Ahebi can more than defend herself against anyone in her community. This line may just as well be likening Ahebi to the Enugu-Ezike ancestor hunter Ezike, who killed his elephant prey at Amube. Ahebi is also the crocodile that seems tailless but can nevertheless "lash you with its tail" and "burrow deep [into] your skin"; the song is warning that no one had better offend her. The lines that declare in repeated harmony that "any educated person who steals should be sentenced to life imprisonment!" warn the knowledgeable not to try and "steal" what is Ahebi's. In other words, do not attempt to "steal" or challenge Ahebi's kingship, because if you do, you are liable to be sentenced to life imprisonment.

Ahebi easily quelled whatever resistance to her kingship existed, and the people of Enugu-Ezike were forced to recognize Ahebi Ugbabe as king, largely because Attah-Obaje and the European invaders stood firmly behind her coronation and legitimacy as king.[100]

The Birth and Nurturing of a Mythical Ahebi Ugbabe

Ahebi Ugbabe went out of her way to acquire a reputation as an all-powerful, no-nonsense, and fearsome ruler. She did this to guarantee her place as warrant chief and king, sparing no expense in achieving this end. First, she had a team of medicine men who were charged with concocting potions designed to keep her supernaturally powerful and mysterious. She had medicine men coming in to see her from Edem, Inyi, Okpo, and other places. One of Ahebi's personal medicine men was Amana Abojili. He was a member of the Akumabi ruling house, which is a branch of Aju Amacho (the royal house) of Idah.[101] A well-known and powerful occultist, Amana created a small god (*adalo*) with the powerful ritual plant (*ebo*) that Ahebi used to protect herself. *Adalo* was believed to protect against everything, including witchcraft. Three times a year, Amana would visit Ahebi, and he was said to concoct a bad medicine that had the ability to seize people's souls. This would be used to keep Ahebi supernaturally powerful and extend her fortunes. The medicine man carried this bad medicine shaped like an *ukwa* (breadfruit) pod around town and then planted it in an open space (*igbu aja*). It was believed that life would be sucked out of whatever unlucky soul encountered the medicine. This "life force" would be used to keep Ahebi supernaturally powerful and extend her fortunes. People were so afraid of this medicine man that when he visited, all the villagers in Ahebi's town hid in their homes until he left.

There was another medicine man, Onoja Atamaka, who came from Akpotoland to cure King Ahebi of all that ailed her. He too was said to usurp the well-being of other people in order to make Ahebi well. In the words of Oliefi Ugwu-Ogili: "At the time [Ahebi] was sick and aging, there was a medicine man who was treating her sickness. His name was Onoja Atamaka, an Akpoto man. He was her herbal doctor. Anytime she was sick, Onoja came and she recovered her heath and another person died in place of Ahebi."[102]

The villagers also alleged that Ahebi had a live cock buried on her grounds. From time to time, they would hear haunting sounds of drumming followed immediately by the chilling sounds of a cock crowing from within Ahebi's grounds. Enough people claimed to have heard this terrible crow to put fear into the hearts of her subjects. Ahebi kept other types of medicine in her palace grounds. Indeed, the retinue of medicine men that were attached to her palace consulted with one another to produce medicine for her. Ezenweke of Umuida was one of those men; recall that when Ahebi took him to court on the charge of attempting to poison her water pot, he pointed out that he could not have dropped medicine into Chief Ahebi's pot because, among other things, he was one of the people who looked after Ahebi's house *juju*.[103]

It was also rumored that Ahebi could have no lovers—that any man who spent a night with her would have to be killed. In fact, people claimed to know of an unfortunate man or two who had suffered this fate. Did this actually mean that Ahebi as king did not have any lovers? I would think not. Moreover, evidence presented in chapter 4 suggests that Ahebi most likely engaged in sexual relations with Attah-Obaje, king of Igalaland. The construction of this rumor (by society), in my view, speaks more to the discretion that was expected of her kingly office than to a lack of sexual engagement on her part.

Ahebi soon developed a reputation as a greatly feared ruler, the *agamega* (the "female leopard").[104] In its original context, the title *agamega* was bestowed only on male kings and chieftains. In Igalaland, the king was believed to be transformed into a lion or leopard after death. Ahebi

Ugbabe's other praise-names included *oyiodo* and *igwonyi*, both of which mean "[girl]friend of the great Odo masquerade." *Oyiodo* and *igwonyi* were titles conferred only on very exceptional women; that is, women who had in effect transformed themselves into men, as Ahebi had. Her other praise-name was Ogbu Efi (the killer of cows). This title was conferred only on extraordinary men. Its female equivalent was Oji Efi, a name that Ahebi would most likely have shrugged her shoulders at, because she no longer considered herself a gendered woman. Ogbu Anyinya (the killer of horses) was another one of her praise-names. It also was conferred only on exceptional men. Finally, the greatest of her praise-names was Ogbu Abo (the killer of both cows and horses). Very few men had ever taken this title. Ahebi had clearly dramatized her social, political, and economic distinction in the performance of title-taking.

Whenever King Ahebi made an appearance, her presence would be performed by a professional flute blower and drum beater. Her personal crier would then bellow: "*Adebu Attah, Adebu Attah,*" dramatizing for all to hear Ahebi's gendered transformation into the female masculinity of king. Ahebi was carried everywhere she went on a beautiful hammock by four hefty men from the different villages that made up her village group. Apart from a remarkable warrant chief here and there, the only other dignitaries carried in this manner *oge Ahebi* were the British district officers.[105] This performance was done to the glorious sounds of *egwu okanga*—songs of tribute and admiration belted out by her male praise-singers and musicians.

A mixed entourage of men and women attended to her every whim and fancy. Ahebi's feet, it was rumored, never touched the ground. In fact, no one had ever seen Ahebi walk anywhere, not even in her palace grounds.[106] All of these legends were perpetuated to further her mystique. King Ahebi's use of *ajo ogwu*, as well as rumor, gossip, and innuendo had worked ingeniously.

Chapter 4 is "Inside King Ahebi's Palace." Reconstructed primarily through oral history, it provides a glimpse into the day-to-day private life of this remarkable warrant chief and king. It will explore the ordering of her palace grounds, a self-sufficient city of sorts, and the lives of the people who called King Ahebi's palace home. With the aid of a fine artist, I will reconstruct what her palace grounds must have looked like when she was alive. The chapter will end with a discussion of King Ahebi's Palace School and the events that led to the departure of her third palace teacher, Mr. Jacob Elam.

FOUR

Inside King Ahebi's Palace, ca. 1916–1948

The Palace Grounds

King Ahebi's palace grounds were large. The palace was a gated community of sorts, with a market, a court, a prison, a school, a "retraining" house, a masquerade house, animal stables, several residential homes, guest houses, and a brothel. Samuel Apeh, a retired army sergeant and one of the pupils who attended King Ahebi's palace school, equated the extent of Ahebi's palace grounds to several football (soccer) fields or plots of land: "What is a [football] field? It was way bigger than a field. It was more than 20 plots [of land]. In fact, it was uncountable. It was really vast oh! It was about 28 or 30 plots [of land]."[1] Ahebi Ugbabe acquired much of this land by force. As warrant chief and king, she would simply point to a piece of land she wanted to have, and the owners of the property would "gift" it to her.[2]

The grounds were enclosed. The palace had a dwarf mud wall on the inside. On the outside, "the part facing Umuareji [another village] was a fence covered with palm fronds, *ekarika.*"[3] A substance called *okikpa* was added to the fence to prevent it from crumbling.

A market named after King Ahebi—Nkwo Ahebi (or Nkwo Chief)—was located within the palace grounds at the present site of the Ahebi Primary School. It served as Umuida's main market, providing all sorts of goods and services for the citizenry of Enugu-Ezike.

King Ahebi's personal palace court, where she judged cases away from the prying eyes of the colonial government, was located at the front of the palace grounds, directly inside its inner mud wall (see Figure 4.1).

King Ahebi's animal stables were located inside the inner wall. She reared numerous cows and goats, and her chickens were housed in a chicken coop.[4] Every morning the palace men collected grasses to feed these animals, which were allowed to roam freely in the section of the grounds set aside for them. Samuel Apeh observed: "King Ahebi had many, many, big cows, goats and chickens. They stayed in a house at her palace. They would wander around, and at the end of the day, they would come back to their houses."[5]

FIGURE 4.1. Surviving wall of King Ahebi's court, Umuida, Enugu-Ezike. *Photograph by Nwando Achebe, November 1996.*

Tucked away in one corner of her palace was the masquerade house (*ulomma*). King Ahebi's Ekpe Ahebi masquerade emerged from the *ulomma*. Some oral history collaborators suggested that the great Omabe masked spirit also came out of Ahebi's masquerade house,[6] which I think unlikely.[7] Of King Ahebi's *ulomma*, Alice Akogu had this to say: "In this masquerade house, King Ahebi kept everything. Women were not allowed to enter it. No woman ever entered there."[8] The *ulomma* was also used as a storage facility. Akogu continues: "Any time food was to be cooked and she was at home, Nnenne went into the *ulomma* to bring out the food items to be cooked. No woman ever entered there."[9] The *ulomma* structure highlighted the gendered nature of space within Ahebi's palace grounds.

Between the palm-frond fence and the dwarf mud wall, the palace farm was situated on both sides of King Ahebi's palace court. This farm was one of numerous farmlands spread all throughout Nsukka Division and beyond that King Ahebi owned. The palace farm workers planted *ede* (cocoyam), groundnuts, cassava, *ekpei,* and corn: "Yes, there was space for farming [in her palace]. She planted crops like cocoyam and *ekpei.* All the men who lived in the palace worked King Ahebi's palace farm."[10]

The main crop that King Ahebi's farmers—freeborn and "slave"—planted on her other farmlands was the male crop, yam. Yam was the king of crops and anyone who possessed these tubers was considered wealthy. Ahebi owned over twelve barns of yams (*oba ji iri na abua*).[11] As she did in her palace farms, she had her farmers interplant female crops (e.g., cocoyams, groundnuts, and corn) with her yams. All able-bodied men in Umuida and the surrounding communities—Akpaturu, Ogrute, Ogene, and Umuadogwu—were obligated to work on King Ahebi's farmlands in rotation. The *agogo* gong was used to call the people to work. King Ahebi had farms in Akpanya (Igalaland), where there was a lot of land, as well as in Unadu. She also had farmland in Ayokpa and Okpe (Igalaland).

Ogbu Nwa Obeta was King Ahebi's head farmer. Other farmers who worked for the female king included Stephen Ahebi, Onoja Nwa Onuche, Ukweze Omada, Ezeja Nwiyi, and Eze Nwa Obeta. King Ahebi's farmers were notorious for taking the law into their hands when they worked outside Umuida, and they always went unpunished. Alice Akogu shared a story about how Ahebi's workers would go into the marketplace at Unadu when they farmed there and raid it for whatever they wanted to eat: "One day Ahebi's workers went into Afor Unadu to raid for what to eat on the farm. Tobacco was taken from the Akpoto people. Each of Ahebi's workers stole as much as he wanted on that day. Nobody dared question the workmen. If they saw groundnut or other farm items, they snatched them from the sellers for their use."[12]

There were numerous residential homes on King Ahebi's palace grounds. There were so many houses that every man who lived there had his own *obu* (man's house) and each married woman had her own house. Men who had multiple wives accommodated them in different homes. No two wives had to share living space on King Ahebi's grounds. The majority of the homes on the palace grounds had roofs thatched with grass; about ten of them had zinc roofs.[13] According to Oliefi Ugwu-Ogili, the zinc-roofed houses were reserved for people whom King Ahebi considered special:

> Onoja lived in a zinc house. Onuche Ahebi lived in one. Stephen had a zinc house, Atabo, her [great] grandson had another. These are the [people] I remember that lived in those zinc houses. . . . The zinc houses surrounded Ahebi's own personal house. King Ahebi's residence was at the center of those special zinc houses.[14]

The abode that King Ahebi slept in was different from the stone house where she received her visitors (see Figure 4.2). Her sleeping

FIGURE 4.2. Stone building for King Ahebi's visitors, Umuida, Enugu-Ezike. Built in 1938. *Photograph by Nwando Achebe, November 1996.*

FIGURE 4.3. Artist's impression of King Ahebi's visitors' house and other structures. *Chinedu Chukwurah, July 2007.*

quarters was one of the big zinc houses. Little virgin girls slept in the same room with Ahebi. Their presence demonstrated that space in Ahebi's palace was gendered. Neither teenage girls nor women were allowed to sleep anywhere in the vicinity of Ahebi's dwelling space. This was because King Ahebi observed certain taboos, including the belief that menstrual blood was contaminating.[15] King Ahebi slept on a special raffia bed located on one side of the house, and the virgin girls slept on bamboo floor mats on the other side of the house. Ahebi's niece, Nwoyeja Obeta (Felicia Ugwu Agbedo), was one of the girls who slept with her. She remembers having to empty out King Ahebi's urinal each morning: "[King Ahebi] urinated into an earthen bowl, *akere,* and we the children emptied it in rotation every morning."[16]

At the back of the zinc quarters were long dwellings "which looked like school buildings,"[17] and this was where the other palace residents— and there were many of them—were housed. Two of the palace residents had known Ahebi in Igalaland and had accompanied her when she returned to Enugu-Ezike. Ahebi returned from Idah with a stand-in "husband" (*onye nkuchi*), Alasha (Alhassan), who lived in the palace. He was not a husband in the true sense of the word; he was simply a man that Ahebi used as a protector. King Ahebi also came home with another man named Olaka. Nwoyeja Obeta described him as "an old man." "He was becoming older when I knew him. He came down with Nnenne Ahebi from Igalaland. Olaka followed her home."[18]

Other men and women lived in King Ahebi's palace as well, each occupying a separate house on the grounds. There was Anekwu Ahebi, who had two wives, one of whom was Amee Nwoji. Onuche Ahebi lived there, too. Like Ankewu, he had two wives. His first wife was Nwada Amedu Iyamu; his second was Okpete Omeh. King Ahebi's adopted "slave" son, Stephen Ahebi, and his ten wives were other inhabitants. So was Ugwu Ibudu, "the man with the disfigured hand."[19] Ugwu Ibudu had no wife. Eze Ibagwu, a laborer from Ibagwu Iheaka, and Ezeja Nwa Ugwunengwu, from Obukpa, lived with King Ahebi as well. So did Ogara Nwa Oriefi and his two wives, Ocheboja and Nwomaja Ogara. Omeje Aneke, another Obukpa native, lived in King Ahebi's palace. According to Nwoyeja Obeta, Omeje was one of Ahebi's most loyal servants: "Omeje . . . was obedient and served King Ahebi well. So she trusted him with all things, including her money. Omeje even married a wife at our place but the woman bore him no child."[20]

In July 2007, I had an artist, Chinedu Chukwurah, sit with a number of people who knew and lived with King Ahebi and sketch from their recollections what her palace looked like *oge Ahebi.*[21] Figure 4.4 is the artist's composite sketch.

A Measure of a Person Can Be Gauged by the Company She Keeps

> [Around] 1938, we hadn't started school then.
> [Ahebi's palace] was the center of attraction.
> This is where we met our first European.
> This is where we first saw a bicycle, an old
> [European] man with a bicycle. The whole
> village was following him and it was magical.
> They called it *anyinya igwe. Anyinya* means
> horse, but this was a metal horse.[22]
>
> —*Samuel Apeh, retired army sergeant
> and pupil at Ahebi's palace school*

King Ahebi's palace was the showpiece of town. According to Oliefi Ugwu-Ogili, "There is no part of Igboland, and beyond, which people did not travel from to visit Ahebi at her palace—all great people of substance."[23] As king, Ahebi received guests and dignitaries, including European district officers and workers who passed through town, several policemen, and at least two Attah-Igalas—Attah-Obaje and Attah-Ameh:

> I know two *attahs* who came to King Ahebi's palace—the first one, and the other who succeeded him after his death. One was fair in complexion, tall and huge. The first one was dark in complexion and huge. Obaje Ocheji was [the first] one, and Ameh Obonyi was the other *attah.*[24]

Attah-Obaje visited King Ahebi several times during her reign. On each occasion, he showed up with a large entourage of court musicians, workers, and cooks: "Each time Attah-Igala visited, he was accompanied by his court musicians—those who played *okeregwu* [a kind of musical instrument], those who played or beat the *okanga* [drums], and his *okakach* men—all accompanied him."[25] He also came bearing gifts. Some were showpieces that the community had never seen before: "One day he brought one kind of live animal. I have forgotten its name. Oh yes, its name is *odum* [hyena]. He also brought a live lion with him during one of his visits to the palace. He brought it to the chief's palace."[26]

FIGURE 4.4. Artist's impression of King Ahebi's palace grounds. *Chinedu Chukwurah, July 2007.*

FIGURE 4.5. Artist's impression of the wooden gateway to King Ahebi's palace. *Chinedu Chukwurah, July 2007.*

Nwoyeja Obeta remembers him bringing foodstuffs: "The *attah* of Idah was Ahebi's friend. I was very young then. Whenever the *attah* visited her, he brought gifts in separate vehicles. The gifts included *ikerike* [salt], *okp-eye* [a spice], and *ogbono*."[27] Likewise, Alice Akogu remembers him bringing many large bags of dry fish known as *onu nkita* (literally, "the mouth of a dog"), which "could only be cut to pieces with an axe." His carriers packed them into large basins and carried them on their heads.[28]

Attah-Obaje visited on alternating years, and when he did, the children would run away because they were afraid of him: "The Attah-Igala used to visit Nnenne on alternate years. I know this. . . . I ran away each time I saw him because nobody had courage to stay when he visited."[29] Obeta also alluded to a sexual relationship that might have occurred between King Ahebi and Attah-Obaje during his trips: "Nnenne used to take all her clothes off except for a little piece of cloth when the *attah* was around. . . . Everybody disappeared when they sat together. Both of them spoke Igala. The language was difficult to understand or to learn. Ahebi did not tell us how she came to know the *attah*."[30] When an *attah* was leaving, King Ahebi would reciprocate his generosity with gifts of her own. To each of the two *attahs,* she gave a cow and kola nuts. She also gave a goat to each member of the *attah*'s entourage.[31]

The question of what kind of sexuality that would be appropriate for a female king such as Ahebi is an important one that bears exploration. It seems certain that Ahebi engaged in sex with King Obaje while in exile in Idah (see chapter 2). She also—as Nwoyeja Obeta's oral history suggested—seems to have had sexual relations with him when he visited her in Enugu-Ezike. King Ahebi also engaged in sexual relations with one or more European colonialists.[32] Therefore, it is safe to surmise that her people would have constructed an appropriate sexual liaison for a king such as she as one that would involve sex with big men of distinction, such as kings and Europeans. In this positioning, her people might have viewed King Ahebi's sexual encounters as another performance of social status in which the female king engaged in sex with men of her caliber. This is not to suggest that Ahebi might not have engaged in sex with commoner men, but I suspect that she would have been extremely guarded about such liaisons.

Some of the policemen who frequented King Ahebi's palace did so to strategize with the female king about law and order concerns in Umuida. Others did so to take advantage of the sexual services provided by King Ahebi's prostitutes. According to Fabian Azegba, Ahebi's "slave son" Stephen arranged liaisons between policemen and prostitutes: "*Oge*

Ahebi, the police would come to Ahebi's house and demand women
for their sexual gratification. . . . The person who arranged this was
Stephen."[33]

King Ahebi's "Slaves," Workers, and *Gago*

So that her palace grounds would function smoothly and efficiently,
King Ahebi bought and kept human "slaves,"[34] including Onojo Nwa
Onuche, Onuche Ahebi, Ogbu Ahebi, Ugwu Ibudu, Ogbodo Nwa
Ahebi, Ogbodo Nwa Anekwu Ahebi, Omeje Aleke, Michael Ahebi,
Rufus Ahebi, Nweke Ahebi, and Stephen Ahebi. She bought Onuche
and Nweke Ahebi in Igalaland. The mere presence of these "slaves" was
a performance of social, political, and economic status and prestige by
visibly demonstrating the number of human beings she could afford to
accumulate. Her "slaves" did heavy manual labor and helped work her
fields.

King Ahebi had a labor force of women whose husbands had
brought them to her to be disciplined (a point that will be discussed
later). Every week or so, these women would rub red mortar and soil
from Itchi town (which had a rich red tone to it) on the homes in King
Ahebi's palace, paying particular attention to the king's private dwellings. They would decorate the buildings with intricate designs called *uli,*
which the women made by applying dye to the walls with twigs. When
the walls were completed, each building looked revitalized and smooth
and had a reddish tint.

One of King Ahebi's special "slaves" was Stephen Ahebi. She trusted
him and treated him as a son. Stephen saw to the ordering of her palace
grounds. It was he who was charged with digging up, cleaning, and
counting her money, as his wife, Alice Akogu, related:

> Ahebi Ugbabe was very rich. On the day her money was placed under
> the sun, it was my husband, Stephen Ahebi, and Omeje Aneke who
> did it. Omeje Aneke was the man who followed her everywhere and
> with whom she went to court. . . . [My husband Stephen] and Omeje
> Aneke sunned Ahebi's money on mats spread at the back of the house.
> They dug out the red coins from the ground to sun. . . . I saw *ochibu
> adu* [large plates] for the first time in her palace. They were all filled
> with Ahebi's money. Bitter lemon juice was used to wash the coins
> before being spread on the mats. When the money was dry, it was
> packed back into the containers and buried again in the soil. The
> calabash containers were known as *mbodo.*[35]

King Ahebi was generous with cash. Alice Akogu continues: "From the cashbox on which Ahebi rested her feet, she would remove her feet so that my husband could collect all the money he needed."[36]

Because King Ahebi was so taken with Stephen, she married ten wives for him, including Obeta Nwa Omeje (Stephen's first wife), Alice Akogu (his second wife), Amina (his third wife), Oyima Ugwu, Anweke, Bessie, Agnes, Oyibo Ome, and Owaja Ossai.[37] As discussed in chapter 1, *oge Ahebi,* wealthy Igbo women were known to perform masculinities and social, political, and economic status by marrying wives for themselves, for their husbands (if they were married), and for their sons. In the words of Stephen's second wife, Alice:

> My husband had many women in the palace to choose from. Every day he promised to wed a woman and she became his wife. He had control of the clothes, money, women, and everything in the palace. I was not his first wife. We were very well cared for by Ahebi. Obeta Nwa Omeje was his senior wife. I was his second wife. Amina was the third, Oyima Ugwu, Anweke were his other wives. I always quarreled with Obeta Nwa Omeje because she always caused disputes between herself and Amina, Bessie, Agnes, Oyibo Ome, Obeta Nwa Omeje, Anweke—all were my husband's wives.[38]

Stephen regarded King Ahebi as his mother and did not think that she was anything but that until after her death in 1948, when he heard whispers that he was in fact her "slave." A devastated Stephen began the task of searching for his birth family and home. Alice Akogu related to me, in heart-wrenching tones, several decades after the fact, the events that led up to Stephen's discovery of who he really was:

> Some Ogrute people knew about my husband's history—that my husband was from Ofante. It happened that a young boy [from Akpotoland] visited my husband when they were children. It so happened that the people of Ofanteland kidnapped the little boy and sold him into slavery. The boy's kinsmen came to make war on my husband's people and the Ofante people decided to make restitution for the kidnapped boy. My husband was [the person] given to the Akpoto people in place of their son. They took my husband to sell at our place, Umuida.[39] He was taken to Ugwu Okegwu to buy. Ugwu Okegwu sent him to Nnenne Ahebi who had the problem of not having any sons. Ahebi bought him. People who knew this history and who knew that my husband's relatives were still at Ofante came after Ahebi had died to reveal the secret to me.[40]

When King Ahebi was alive, people held their tongues about Stephen's origins out of fear. Alice continues:

> [After King Ahebi's death] I was at home nursing a baby, as usual, when others were busy buying and selling at the market. Nwoye Ugwuanyi came to me and told me that Nwoye Ujah informed her that Stephen was from Ofante. When Stephen returned I told him everything. Nwoye told me that the annual Manyu festival of Isiugwu people, a village close to Aji in Enugu-Ezike, was coming up in a few days time and that if Stephen attended he could meet his blood relatives.
>
> I am now telling you why he came home to this place [Ofanteland]. He left on horseback and went to Isiugwu. When he arrived, the people in fear inquired where he came from. He said that he came from Opi, to deceive them. After some time, he narrated his story. The person he was speaking to was his uncle—of the same parents as his own mother. His uncle let out a cry, and this embarrassed [Stephen]. All the Ofante people present gathered when the alarm was raised. Two of Stephen's brothers were still alive then. They ran to Ofante. When they got there, they shouted that Stephen was [their son], Akogu Inyamu. They had seen and recognized him at Isiugwu. Stephen's mother and father, you see, had given him the name Akogu Inyamu, but Stephen was his baptismal name. So it was. I have told you the story of how we returned to this place, Ofante.
>
> When they were grabbing things at Umuida, Stephen did not care. No matter how poor one's mother or father is, one always gravitates to one's parents, even if one's father is but ashes. That was why Stephen came back to his fatherland. He was not worse off for returning.[41]

King Ahebi had a *gago* force (palace police officers and errand men) of at least seventy. Some of her *gago* included Ogbu Nwa Obeta, who was married to Oriefi Azegba, Omeje Aneka, Ibagwa Nwa Ogara, Enekpo, Attah Aboh, and Onuche. Ugwu Ibudu, "the man with the disfigured hand," was her chief policeman and disciplinarian. He was charged with buying palm wine each day for palace entertainment. So much palm wine was purchased that a special storehouse had to be built in the palace for it. According to Alice Akogu, Ibudu's right hand had been disfigured by the heavy *echi* (a rod, which was Igbo money at the time) that he carried every day that he went to buy palm wine.[42]

The *gago* became a notorious vigilante group. According to Fabian Azegba, "Anytime Ugwu Ibudu or the *gago* came to your house; you knew that you were in trouble."[43] *The gago* were also corrupt and could be bought. Samuel Apeh noted:

FIGURE 4.6. Alice Akogu (formerly Ahebi) standing by the gravestone of her husband, Stephen Akogu (formerly Ahebi), Ofante, Kogi State. *Photograph by Nwando Achebe, October 1998.*

> If the *gago* came to your house because you went contrary to Ahebi's rules, you had to settle them. If you were stubborn and did not settle them, they would tie a rope around your waist and drag you to King Ahebi's palace. When you were brought to Ahebi's court to speak, you wouldn't even stand up while they were questioning you, you would kneel down during the process and if you looked at them with your eyes squinted, they would slap you.[44]

The district officer of Nsukka Division, W. H. Lloyd, writing on July 10, 1924, acknowledged the notoriety of this group of young men, the havoc that they wreaked, and the fact that their exploits had caused friction between King Ahebi and her people: "[Ahebi] [i]s not in favour with her people at the moment, owing to the fact that she keeps a number of boys & hangers on (they say about 70) who refuse to do any work with the quarter & play havoc generally in her name. Have turned them all out & hope things will settle down again."[45]

The Women's Sanctuary and Retraining School at King Ahebi's Palace

Ahebi's palace also served as a sanctuary for runaway women whose husbands abused them. These women sought refuge in Ahebi's palace and refused to return to their husbands.[46] King Ahebi Ugbabe married some of the women who decided to stay, such as Nwoye Ugwuanyi and Omada Nwa Areji, and thus became their female husband. Another way that Ahebi would acquire wives was through the unscrupulous services of some of her servants (ndi iboyi), including Ogbodo Nwa Anekwu and Michael Ahebi, who were notorious for harassing and kidnapping men's wives for themselves and their master. The majority of the wives and concubines bore children for Ahebi. For these marriages to be considered legitimate, Ahebi had to perform all marriage rites—particularly the payment of child-price—in the names of the women. These performances of marriage rites—which effectively transformed Ahebi into the female masculinities of female husband and father—elevated her standing in society. The marriages could be interpreted as the female king performing a type of economic and social class and status that was akin to the status that men who were married to more than one wife attained. These unions were desirable for King Ahebi because they demonstrated that her path (ama) or (male) house (obu) was not closed; they allowed a generation of Ahebi name-bearers to be born. But how could Ahebi create/invent descendents through these woman-to-woman marriages? She did so by relying on the services of male sperm donors, who, having befriended her wives, would be encouraged to consummate the relationships, thus enabling Ahebi's wives to bear children in the name of their female king. What was in it for the wives? Some of them were runaways or abused women. In Ahebi's home they found compassion, protection, and comfort. Also, as wives to a female husband, they could express their sexuality in ways that wives involved in woman-to-male relationships could not. In essence, they were like prostitutes oge mgbapu Ahebi, in that they were able to have as many sexual partners as they pleased. And their marriage to a female husband legitimized these sexual pleasures.

The performance of marriage rites between a female husband and wife did not constitute a lesbian relationship, though. Female husbands and their wives never shared a bed or any other intimate sexual space. Ahebi's wives found sexual fulfillment and comfort in the arms and beds of their male lovers, while Ahebi herself engaged in sexual activity with big men that confirmed and enhanced her status and perhaps had discreet sex with male commoners. Thus, the relationship between King Ahebi and her wives was a one of companionship, a close friendship, such as best girlfriends might have.[47]

Some of Ahebi's wives, especially the beautiful ones, were encouraged to service the physical needs of the king's important male visitors, such as the Attah-Igala, British colonial officers, and Nigerian policemen who visited Ahebi's palace. Thus, Ahebi served as *nne mgboto, nne okuenu,* or *nne ikweli* (as a mother of a prostitute or as a madam). Nwoyeja Obeta described this part of palace life:

> King Ahebi ceased to be a prostitute when she became king because all the other women [who did not marry Ahebi or her "sons"] were prostitutes and mixed freely with men in the palace. . . . The houses for the prostitutes were arranged along on a line [she draws a line on the ground on left]. The houses where men lived were arranged on the other line [she draws another line on the right].[48]

One of the major attractions for women at Ahebi's palace was her retraining school for disobedient or unruly wives. The services provided in this school were not free. On the contrary, husbands seeking retraining for their wives had to present gifts of kola nuts, chickens, goats, and wine to King Ahebi so their wives would be allowed to stay. According to Fabian Azegba,

> Ahebi was a disciplinarian. Husbands who were not happy with the behavior of their wives took them to Ahebi's house so that Ahebi could discipline them. When they got there, Ahebi would put them to hard work. *Oge Ahebi,* any woman who was told that she was going to Ahebi's house for punishment was never happy because of the kind of work she would be forced to do. Husbands were the ones who took their wives there.[49]

Retraining in Ahebi's palace meant physical punishment and beatings:

> If a stubborn or badly behaved wife was sent to her palace for discipline, the woman became changed within a short time. After some severe beatings and subjection to serious manual work or labor, the mischievous woman became a changed wife. Men whose wives misbehaved sent their wives to Ahebi for retraining, after which time the woman would plead to be allowed to go back to her husband.[50]

Other badly behaved women fared better. Some women were co-opted into the palace workforce as cooks. They did not cook for the female king, but they did cook for all the other residents of the palace, as Alice Akogu noted: "If a badly behaved woman was sent to the palace and such a woman could cook well and King Ahebi liked her, she was instructed to cook for the men in the palace. Such a woman cooked and ate and became fat, to the astonishment of her husband, whose intention was to punish his wife at Ahebi's palace."[51]

It was from these reformed women that King Ahebi married wives for her relatives. Nwoyeja Obeta spoke about how her mother came to live in Ahebi's palace: "Ahebi . . . was already a chief when she married my mother for my father, her brother. My mother was already big when she quarreled with her first husband and so she was sent to Ahebi for retraining. [My mother] did not tell me the nature of their disagreement. She had no child for that man [the first husband]."[52]

Some of the women whose behavior changed became dear to Ahebi, and she eventually married them to her "sons," solidifying her social status and reputation by performing these marriages.

> Whenever the women's true husbands, that is, the men who sent their wives to be disciplined, came, they were repaid [by King Ahebi] the bride-price [indicating the termination of the marriage]. . . . She married some women for herself, of course. This means that she paid the usual bride-price on each woman she decided to marry or for the men who served her. For my father, she married Nwoye Ugwanye, who was Barna's [Barnabas's] mother; and Omada Nwa Areji from Itchi, who was my own mother. Any of the women she paid bride-price for ceased to be free [i.e., prostitutes] in the palace and became married women.[53]

Women remained in King Ahebi's palace as long as *obi siri fa ike*[54] (they remained difficult). Money was refunded to the husbands of those women whose hearts had softened and thus had been married in Ahebi's palace. From time to time, Ahebi interviewed the women. She would wear her "crown" (the helmet the British gave her) during these interrogative performances. If King Ahebi determined that the women were now prepared to live in peace and harmony with their husbands, she would release them. The husbands would have to reimburse her for all monies spent on their maintenance (and more). If, however, she determined that they were not ready to change, the women remained in her palace as free women (prostitutes).

A father could send a bad or disobedient son to stay at Ahebi's palace for retraining as well. When this happened, Ugwu Ibudu was responsible for their discipline. "He caned people with his left hand because his right hand was disfigured," Nwoyeja Obeta told me.[55]

A Day in the Life of King Ahebi

At first cockcrow, King Ahebi awakened and had a bath. She did not bathe herself: she was bathed by young virgin bath maids who were related to her. One of my collaborators, Nwoyeja Obeta, served Ahebi in this capacity when she was very young. It was her duty to sponge Ahebi's entire body with imported soap and then rinse her with warm water:

> I remember that I prepared warm water and helped to bathe King Ahebi each time she was preparing to go to court. No grown-up woman [i.e., sexually active woman] ever assisted her in taking a bath. I did this because of my blood relationship with her. Any other girl of my age could not have done it, if she were not related to her by blood as I was. . . . She had an area marked out for her to bathe.[56]

Another one of King Ahebi's young nieces, Oyima Obeta Nwa Ugbabe, scrubbed her back.

After she had bathed, King Ahebi sat in her personal residence listening to the *okanga* drums that were beaten by her male court musicians in her honor. As soon as she stepped out into public view, the *okanga* drummers greeted and saluted her with continuous chanting until she waved them to stop. They would great her: "*Adebu Attah . . . Adeeeeeebu, Adebu Attah*," performing in praise the multiplicity of female masculinities King Ahebi had acquired until late in the morning.

In addition to her bath maids, Ahebi Ugbabe had many female attendants who performed a variety of duties and roles. Some of the women served as cooks and took turns catering for the people who lived at the palace. However, as Alice Akogu noted, only virgin girls could prepare food that was to be eaten by King Ahebi: "Adults were not allowed to cook for Ahebi. After she came back from Idah as king she instructed that virgin girls only, *ndi gba oto* [literally, girls that went naked,] could cook for her from then on. Grown-up women or sexually active adolescents could no longer cook for her. . . . I was one of the girls who cooked for her."[57] Oyibo Anekwu, Oyima Obeta Alice Abugu, Omada Ogbu, Anweke Onaja, and Oyodu Urama were some of the other virgin girls who cooked King Ahebi's food. Nwoyeja Obeta explained the rationale behind this:

> Little girls, virgin girls only, cooked King Ahebi's food. Only young girls cooked for her because it was one of her sacred rules. Any girl who defiles herself, that is, a girl who has ever had sexual relations with a man, ceases to cook for King Ahebi. The reason? Whoever has moved with the *attah* is no small person. Is it a small thing to go with the *attah*? No particular person cooked for her. Any of us, the little children who were given food, did the cooking at any particular time. No cook was brought or employed. After all, any person brought will have to

Figure 4.7. Artist's impression of King Ahebi sitting on her throne. *Chinedu Chukwurah, July 2007.*

leave the moment she became a woman. It was a sacred rule because of her kingship. Do you hear me? . . . [Having virgins cook for her] was a mark of respect and honor due to her as king.[58]

King Ahebi seemed to have brought this prohibition back from Igalaland, where her counterpart, the Attah-Igala, observed this restriction as well. The reason for the prohibition was the assumption that menstrual blood would pollute the food.

Whenever King Ahebi's food was ready to eat, the virgin girls had to sound a warning to let her know that it was ready:

> We took it to Okpeke [the palace crier] to sound our notice four times before we could take the food inside to her. Not all people were allowed to see her eat. Only her children [meaning her relatives] could see her when she ate. The rest of the people in her palace ate the general food cooked by the female residents of the palace.[59]

A gong was beaten to invite the men and women of the palace to eat. Whoever failed to heed the call of the gong missed his or her ration.

King Ahebi liked pounded yams served with specially prepared soup that contained coiled, smoked fish of exceptional taste bought from Nsukka:

> We cooked what she ordered. At times we prepared yams and beans cooked together. I know how I cooked her food to her taste. At times I cooked *utara okpa* [i.e., *okpa fufu*] for her; the soup was always different and special. [The soup was special because] we used *okpeye azu* [a special spice mixed with fish] and meat in such a special blending that it made the soup taste differently and the best. You only needed to be near the palace to hear the wonderful smell with your nose. King Ahebi ate her food in a breakable plate. After eating the little she needed, she invited us her children to eat. We knelt down in turns to receive lumps of food from her.[60]

King Ahebi was not choosy about the foods she ate (*oda aso nni*). She ate all types of foods cooked with lots of fish, meat, and spices. As she ate, she washed her food down with palm wine, which she drank from a special buffalo horn.[61] Alice Akogu provided details about how the food was prepared:

> *Jiapa* [meaning *aribo*], she ate it. It was well cooked, well mixed with *okpa*, well mixed and prepared. I did the mixing and turning and I also cooked it. . . . Ogbu Nwa Obeta was the man who pounded yams for her. Any day Ogbu was not around and yams needed to be pounded,

I did the pounding. I pounded it. . . . [Chuckles to herself in remembrance.] Ah, you reminded me, I am old.[62]

The *okpeye* [spices] used in cooking King Ahebi's food were never bought at the market; they were specially prepared at the palace. Oyodu Urama was one of the few women who knew how to make it. In Alice Akogu's words: "That *okpeye*, ah, it was special oh."[63]

Because of the large number of people living in the palace, King Ahebi had to buy food in large quantities:

> Nnenne brought food ingredients in large quantities. She brought salt in large, large, sacks. *Okpeye* was cooked and prepared by over six people at a time. Her palm-oil processing was a big business, producing about nine tins of palm oil at any particular process. She had many things in large quantities. Water pots for drinking water were so many that they covered a large part of her compound.[64]

King Ahebi owned many beautiful and expensive clothes and jewels: "She had a box filled with *aka* (beads) and leopard teeth called *eze* or *eze agu*. The year we all went to Umuokpu, we, the palace women who were closest to Ahebi, had the first choice [of her jewels], and after us, the rest of the palace women collected what they wore."[65] King Ahebi's clothing was supplied by a trader who bought his materials from the famous Onitsha Market.[66] Her clothing was unique, which was important to the female king:

> Eze Nwa Iyida Ogbo from Amufie sold clothes to King Ahebi. He usually sold his merchandise at Afor Unadu. However, each time he returned from Onitsha market, he brought his one-of-a-kind clothes for Nnenne to buy. . . . The times that Eze stayed [in the palace] to sell to King Ahebi, he was given wine, meat, and food in sufficient quantities to eat. When he stayed to sell and eat in the palace, he would go home at the close of the market day without reaching the general market. So it was.[67]

Other women were charged with the duty of plaiting Ahebi Ugbabe's hair. Her hair was always extravagantly braided in styles that were original and were not to be copied by members of her community. Alice Akogu plaited her hair. So did Orie Nwa Adejo, Oyima Obeta Nwa Ugbabe, and Anekwe.[68]

King Ahebi's hairdos were influenced by the hairstyles of the Igala women with whom she lived during her exile. Alice Akogu remembered that she often had a female attendant braid currency into each part of her hair: "She wore a heavy Igala hairstyle on her head, which was made out of a combination of natural and artificial materials. I used to make her hair. She also plaited money into her hair when going to court. Yes, oh, she did."[69] Oyima Obeta Nwa Ugbabe also reminisced about the hairdos that Ahebi wore:

> Yes, this type of your hairstyle [points to my hairdo, which was braided back in cornrows], I used to plait her hair then. We would plait it, tie it at the ends, and then let it drop on her back. Thread was not used *oge Ahebi,* only *isi aka.* After her hair was made, on the days that she would go to court, she would put on her crown [the helmet] and be carried to her palace court.[70]

The lavish selection of food that King Ahebi ate represented a performance of social, economic, and political class, for only one as wealthy as a female king could afford to eat the way that she did. The preparation of Ahebi's meals was informed by restrictions imposed by the Igala throne on how food for kings should be cooked. By adopting these same taboos, Ahebi was not only performing status, she was reenacting her gendered transformation into the female masculinity of king. Moreover, her choice of exquisite one-of-a-kind hairstyles with money braided in and expensive clothing further solidified her visual performance of big man status.

The Performance of Justice in Chief Ahebi's Palace Court

As discussed in chapter 3, all legal cases in British Nigeria were supposed to be taken to the minor courts or native councils. As warrant chief, King Ahebi had served as president and member of the Native Council of Enugu-Ezike since 1918. Like other warrant chiefs of her time, she turned her palace into a private court. There she could adjudicate cases away from the eyes of the European administration and its numerous rules that governed the arbitration of "native" law. She was also able to settle cases for profit and invariably did away with the "assistance" of the court clerk, who registered all case proceedings and decisions and had been deemed indispensable by British colonial administrators.

All types of cases were settled in King Ahebi's palace court. If a man maltreated his wife or was a thief, he could be tried there. If he was convicted, he could be locked up in the palace prison. King Ahebi also heard cases involving land, debt, and adultery and cases where plaintiffs accused defendants of using the occult to meddle in people's lives. Here is Nwoyeja Obeta's memory:

> Nnenne heard many types of cases. She heard cases between wives
> and their husbands. If after the judgment was handed down, the man
> decided to abandon his wife, then the woman joined the many "free"
> women in the palace until her husband had a change of heart. If he
> didn't, she just stayed there.[71]

King Ahebi's court allowed her to perform her social, political, and economic status. The outcome of many cases also served her goal of filling
her palace with more bodies.

Oliefi Ugwu-Ogili further commented on the types of cases brought
before King Ahebi in her role as warrant chief: "All types of disputes were
judged there—cases between husbands and wives, cases between family
relatives. . . . People brought cases from near and distant places. Even
cases of people who fought were judged there also."[72]

However, bringing cases before King Ahebi was costly. Plaintiffs
who wished to have their cases heard at her court had to present gifts
of wine, money, yams, chickens, goats, and other offerings to the court;
this was the same as offering gifts to Ahebi herself. Defendants also had
to present gifts of all sorts of items to the court in order to be allowed
to respond to a summons. Often the value of the gifts the defendant
was required to bring far exceeded the value of those required of the
plaintiff. Once the gifts had been presented by both the plaintiff and the
defendant, a date was set for the hearing.

King Ahebi's court did not meet every day. Special days were set
aside for hearings. At the court, litigants were allowed to present witnesses and the sessions were open to the entire community. In the words
of Oliefi Ugwu-Ogili, "Witnesses were there and observers were allowed
in the court. It was never done in secret. The hall was always filled with
people. No one was prevented from observing the proceedings."[73]

King Ahebi sat on the court as chief arbitrator, looking every inch
the part. According to Alice Akogu: "On the days of a court session,
Chief Ahebi dressed up, looking like a leopard."[74] This, perhaps, was
her attempt to bring the authority of Igala leopard symbolism to her
palace court. She also wore her helmet/crown to augment her intimi-
dating gaze. In her posture and her attire, King Ahebi performed both
female masculinities and high status on court days for the benefit of all
gathered.

Chief Ahebi did not judge cases on her own. She was assisted by
other adjudicators, including Ezegwu Idoko, Ojobo Nwaiyoke Ugwu,
Ugwu Okegwu (Ahebi's predecessor as headman), and Aji Ugwu:

When King Ahebi sat in judgment, she was assisted by Ezegwu Idoko, who stayed by her side. Ojobo Nwaiyoke Ugwu was also there. They conferred with Ahebi and reached a conclusion before any judgment was delivered. I do not remember the names of others who sat in judgment with Ahebi. All the judges were Enugu-Ezike people. They were all men; no woman was included.[75]

King Ahebi's "Children"

In this section, I present first-person narratives from a group of individuals who lived with King Ahebi and regarded her as their mother. They reminisced about life *oge Ahebi,* relating what it was like to live and grow up in King Ahebi's palace and attend the palace school. First, Wilfred Ogara, who grew up in Ahebi's palace and was one of Ahebi's adopted sons. He told me his story in 1996.

I grew up in Ahebi's palace. My father died when I was so tender, and so one of the sons of Ahebi remarried my mother. This was around 1932. . . . My mother was a palm produce seller and through her proceeds, she eventually raised enough money for my education. At that time, a tin of palm oil cost sixpence. . . .

The influence of Ahebi's children enabled me to start schooling, particularly Stephen and Onoja, who both were attending a Catholic school called St. Joseph's Primary School. It is now a secondary school, but it was not *oge Ahebi.* While Stephen was in class 5, Onoja[76] was in class 2. We continued to live at Ahebi's palace, going to school there.

I started to be influenced by people who were coming to Ahebi's palace, mostly policemen, and those people liked me very much because I was handsome that time and I was so clean. I was going to school through Ahebi's period of reign, so the history I shall give you is the real one. . . . Whatever you want, I will supply you. I will start around 1935, when I knew something. By 1935, the C[hurch] M[issionary] S[ociety] arrived in our area through the influence of Ahebi and established a primary school in the land. By that time I was in infant 3.[77] You go from infant 3 to class 1. I failed my exams to class 1. My teacher couldn't understand why I failed, so he wrote to the headmaster at Nsukka to take me. The headmaster at Nsukka told me that if it was God's will, we will start class 1 at Nsukka. This was in 1937.

I read class 1 in Nsukka in 1937. I was admitted to do class 1 at the CMS school. At that time our headmaster was Stephen Ume from Ude-Abia, while my teacher was Vincent Ajaelo from Achi. In 1942, I was admitted to St. Peters, Enugu, where I wrote my standard

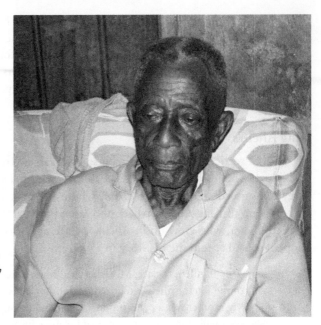

FIGURE 4.8.
Wilfred Ogara,
Umuida, Enugu-
Ezike. *Photograph
by Nwando
Achebe,
November 1996.*

6 examinations. At the end of our examination, one of the teachers who came from Nsukka named Felix Adugu took my colleagues and I to the barracks for sightseeing. After observing the parade exercise, I was excited and subsequently decided to join the army. This was in February 1942.

I was conscripted after being interviewed. . . . I went to the army headquarters in Nsukka and the official there took a good look at me and said that I was too handsome and clean, and [I was] underage. So they decided to send me to Zaria [northern Nigeria] to attend a training center for three months. After three months I passed my exam and I was given a uniform and became a soldier. I was paid for the three months that I spent there, a little over 4 pounds. I brought home this money to my brother. I then went to residential training for six months. After training, I was sent to Gold Coast and from there to Southeast Asia, to Burma. There were no planes then, we went by sea. We did not know what was happening. Fifteenth June 1945[78] they told us that the war was over. I was in group 8. We got back to Lagos on June 14, 1947.[79]

When I went to Umuida in July 2007, I visited Wilfred Ogara's home, only to learn that he had passed away some years earlier. His widow and grandson, however, received Mr. Erobike Eze and me graciously.

FIGURE 4.9.
Simeon Nweke,
Umuida,
Enugu-Ezike.
*Photograph by
Nwando Achebe,
November 1996.*

SIMEON NWEKE

Simeon Nweke was Wilfred's classmate and also attended King
Ahebi's palace school:

> I was born in early 1919. I was in my mother's stomach during the bad
> part of the influenza, but as it was getting better, I was born. When
> the British invaders came, round 1921 or 1922,[80] my parents brought
> me here [Umuida] to hide.
>
> I have a standard 6 diploma. I started school in 1936. I was in
> elementary school for three years. In 1939, I was about to start my class
> 1 and we did not have any money for me to do this. In 1940, I started
> my class 1. Infant school was in Ahebi's palace school at Umuida.

Class[es] 1 and 2 were in Nsukka, and I was there between 1941 and 1945 at the boarding school.

In those days, anyone who passed 6 would be a teacher, but I did not pass. So I went to live with the pastor of the CMS church so that I could attend some more school and retake my exams at the end of the year. I lived under the personage of the missionary Rev. G. P. Bernard at Nsukka as a gardener. In 1947, I was sent to Awka College, Awka, under something called "rural activity" to do farming.

In 1950, I came back to Umuida and was chosen to represent my people at the council. When I worked in the council, we were able to build three schools. I was [on] the council for twenty-three years.[81]

I went to Simeon Nweke's home in July 2007, only to learn that he was too ill to receive visitors. His wife, however, graciously received us and took my monetary gift in to him on his sickbed. When she came out, she acknowledged that he remembered me from eleven years earlier and was very appreciative of the gift.[82]

BARNABAS OBETA NWA UGBABE

In 1996, when I asked Barnabas Obeta (see an image of him in Figure 1.7), Ahebi's oldest surviving relative, to tell me about his aunt, his first words were "Nnenne was a woman who later became a man." He then talked about himself:

My name is Barnabas Obeta. . . . My father and Ahebi are from the same parents. After the death of Ahebi, my father inherited the crown [actually a helmet, but Ahebi wore it as a crown], however, with the death of my father, I inherited it. The crown [helmet] and other inherited items including her *aka* beads, are the property of the entire family including generations unborn. However, women are exempt from ownership, because they usually marry outside their villages. This happens to the present day.

When I was a little boy, *oge Ahebi,* I was the person responsible for bringing grass for Ahebi's cows. I continued this until I grew up and got married. This was while Ahebi was still alive. I reared cows for Ahebi. Do you hear me? However, with the death of Nnenne Ahebi, I inherited her property. All the property you see around here was owned by Ahebi, including the land.

With the death of my father, I am now in charge. I, however, own this jointly with the entire family. When I die, someone else will take charge. Presently, I am *okpara* [the eldest] Ugbabe and so, am in control of the ancestral shrine. When I was still young, I never envisaged reaching my present stature in the family lineage. In fact, it still seems strange to me, but it is the will of God that I should inherit Ahebi Ugbabe's property.[83]

In a subsequent interview two years later, Barnabas Obeta talked about attending King Ahebi's palace school:

> Stephen Ahebi was a native of Ofante. He stayed in Nnenne's house. From there he went to school, and then to the army, after which he came back to Nnenne. Onoja Nwa Onuche, whose father was a native of Nta, lived at Nnenne's house. While there, he went to school, and after that he joined the army. Later he returned. So, when they were going to school I was a small boy. I schooled at Ahebi['s] palace school. All these people from Ofante, Akpoto, and other places—all the people who came from various places took Ahebi to be their mother. They prevented us, the original children of the family, from being well educated.[84]

I interviewed Barnabas Obeta six times during my field research—in 1996, 1998, and 2007. Each time I visited with him, he received me well; on one occasion he fed my research guide, Erobike Eze, our driver, and I lunch. However, he never failed to demand as much money as he could from me. The only time I heard him speak English was in 1996, when he exclaimed in exasperated response to my plea that I did not have any more money to give him because I was merely a college student: "You got money, money, money, money. Give me money!" During that trip I had to pay him one sum of money to bring out King Ahebi's kingship relics so that I could see them and another sum so that I could photograph them. When I visited in 2007, he showed me his leaking roof and indicated that it needed fixing. He also instructed his sister, Oyima Obeta Nwa Ugbabe, not to provide me with too much information when I was interviewing her so that I could "bring more money." Nevertheless, Barnabas was a pleasant (albeit somewhat difficult and demanding) oral history collaborator.

OYIMA OBETA NWA UGBABE

Oyima Obeta Nwa Ugbabe is Ahebi's oldest surviving niece. (See an image of her in Figure 1.8.) I spent time with her in 1996, 1998, and 2007. She talked about the joys and pressures of growing up King Ahebi's niece, her failed marriages, and her regret, much like that of her

older brother, Barnabas, that she did not get to go to school—a failure
that she blamed on her aunt. Below are excerpts of a conversation with
her in July 2007:

> My name is Oyima Obeta Nwa Ugbabe. I was baptized Rosaline Obeta
> Nwa Ugbabe. Ahebi was my father's mother.[85] She brought me up. My
> father was Obeta Nwa Ugbabe. . . . This person [points to Barnabas]
> and I, are of the same father and mother, but the other person, Uroko,
> is our half-brother, because he is of a different mother. What prevented
> Uroko from coming? [she asks Barnabas.] He will be coming [she
> speaks to herself; however, Uroko does not join us]. What I am saying
> is this: My mother[86] was a great ruler, she was a king. Ahebi Ugbabe
> was coronated by the Attah-Idah. She wore wrist bands as a mark of
> her coronation as a king. That road [pointing] which extends from
> Nsukka, through Ogrute, through Umuida through Odigru down to
> Idah was built by Ahebi Ugbabe. She built the road when she was alive.
> That was my mother.
>
> When my bride-price was paid, Nnenne received it. My grand-
> father said that I was completely her own and she owned everything
> that was paid for my marriage. She bought the goods which were
> traditionally needed for me to establish my new home as a wife.[87] She
> cared for me until she died. I lived in harmony with her.
>
> When I lived in Nnenne's palace as her daughter, I wanted to go
> to school, but she said no. She was the first person to establish a school
> in Enugu-Ezike area. She did not allow me to go to school because I
> cooked her food. She would not eat food prepared by others who were
> not close to her.[88] Because of this, I was not sent to school to become
> educated. She thought she was doing me a favor, but now, it is a dis-
> advantage to me. If I had been educated then, I could have attained a
> height where I could get my people employed in government establish-
> ments. Just as I did not go to school, this person Barnabas [points] did
> not go to school also. I remember when we were small, a white man
> came for this person [points to Barnabas] to take him to be educated.
> Ahebi objected, contending that if Barnabas was taken away, nobody
> would make fire for Onoja [Barnabas's father], her son. We had every
> opportunity to be educated but Nnenne Ahebi refused. We did not
> know that life would change for us. If she had known that life could
> change this way,[89] she would have allowed us to be educated.
>
> I was married to a first, second, and so on [waves her finger round
> in circles] husbands. I did not assume the prestige of Ahebi's daughter
> in my relations with people who married me. I was always patient with
> them. But when they failed to please me, I rejected each of them as

they came. While they were interested in marrying Ahebi's daughter, I did not live in some of the men's houses. The first man who married me, he was not caring and loving. One day Nnenne Ahebi asked me to go to my husband's place. I told her that I was not going. I refused to go. I told her that I was not going to marry the man. I did not like him. She sent for him to come, so that we could state our cases. He came. We stated the grievances we had before every member of the palace—servants and all—as was the practice. Cases were brought up and judged before everybody. Nothing was hidden. Whoever was guilty was told that by Ahebi in the presence of everyone. The name of that my husband was Azegba. I did not live with him as husband and wife and we did not consummate the relationship.

Throughout the times I was married to various men, I was a virgin. People just wanted to be my husband, one after another, because I was Ahebi Ugbabe's daughter. The man for whom I later delivered children, he's dead now, took my virginity. I decided to break our marriage because the children I had with him died, all of them. At the break of that marriage, we stated our cases as usual and because the judgment was against me, my former husband was repaid the *echi* (money) he paid to marry me. King Ahebi said that her daughter was not a trouble seeker. I stayed with Nnenne Ahebi until I married again.

The man who married me much later was Mathias Ozioko. I have a child for him even now. My mother Ahebi had died before this marriage. I was still very young when Nnenne Ahebi died. The name of that husband that I had when our children were dying was Amedu Nwa Ugwuanyi from Umuareji. There I gave birth to four children and none survived. The man was not bad to me as husband. I loved him and he loved me, but I left him because of the way our children died.[90]

NWOYEJA OBETA

Nwoyeja Obeta (Felicia Ugwu Agbedo) was another one of King Ahebi's nieces. She not only lived with Ahebi but was one of her virgin bath maids and cooks. She also slept in King Ahebi's bedroom and emptied out her urinal. I visited with Nwoyeja in 1998; below are excerpts from our conversation:

When I was living with Ahebi I was called Nwoyeja Obeta. Obetaja Ugbabe and Ahebi Ugbabe were born of the same parents and Obetaja was my father. My baptismal name is Felicia. Now I am known as Felicia Ugwu Agbedo. Ugwu Agbedo is my husband's name. Ahebi had other relations born by their father, but not of the same mother. They included Onoja Ugbabe whose mother came from Umuareji.

. . . Ahebi took me as her daughter. Apart from non-blood relations who called her mother, there were other blood relations who lived in her palace as her children. They included Oyima Obeta and Barna[bas] Obeta. All other small ones were born after she has died. On Onoja Ugbabe's side, the older ones among them are not living anymore. What remains of them are grandchildren.[91] . . .

My functions in the palace? I did not do much except cook her food when she asked me to. She also sent me on other errands. . . . She was not harsh to me but sent me on such errands a mother would her daughter. I was lazy! Ah, and she always reminded me in jokes that I was lazy. [She chuckles.] She did not assign to me tasks that could hurt me. Yes oh, she loved me and did not want me to suffer. The child who responds cheerfully and promptly to the demands and messages of elders is loved by the elders.

My bride-price was paid to her, and she bought items to send me to my husband's house. She did not collect any money from my husband until she was sure I had a child for him. That was four months after my first child was born. My first child was male, but he is dead.[92]

When I visited Enugu-Ezike in July 2007 and asked after Nwoyeja Obeta, her niece, Mrs. Uwakwe Ezejah, told me that she had passed away the year before. I was extremely saddened by this news, because when I first met Nwoyeja Obeta in 1998, she had been extremely hospitable to a student researcher she did not know. She was the first to have shared memories of the private world of King Ahebi's palace with me. She spent several hours singing, dancing, and cooking me one of the tastiest meals that I have ever had. I am thankful that I was able to meet this great storyteller. May her soul rest in peace.

BARNABAS AKOGU

Barnabas Akogu (formerly Ahebi), the first son of King Ahebi's "slave" son Stephen, was born a few years before Ahebi's death. He is a tailor by profession. I visited with him and his family in Ofante, Kogi State, on several occasions during the period 1998 to 2007. This particular interview was conducted in his tailor shed, located at one of the Ofante marketplaces, in 2007:

My name is Barnabas Akogu. . . . I was born on December 30, 1942. How do I know this? I know this because it is written on my baptismal certificate. King Ahebi died in 1948. . . . Barnabas is my bap-

FIGURE 4.10. Barnabas Akogu (formerly Ahebi) standing by the gravestone of his father, Stephen Akogu (formerly Ahebi), Ofante, Kogi State. *Photograph by Nwando Achebe, October 1998.*

tismal name, but my Igbo name is Akogu. When we lived at Ahebi's palace, I used to enter her *obu*, where it was said that women were not authorized to enter. From her house, we went to school at Nkwo Iyida. But first, I went to King Ahebi's palace school. At the time that I am telling you, I was in the infant class. After the infant classes, we were promoted to the next class, primary or class 1. After my class 1, King Ahebi died. Yes, we first went to prima [primer class], then we entered infant; after infant, we entered class 1. It was after class 1 that she died and from then we did not go to school again. After some stay [at Umuida], we returned to our village [Ofante] here.[93]

The Ahebi Palace School and the Culmination of a Village Conflict

In 1930, roughly ten years after the British administration was instituted, the Roman Catholic Mission arrived in Enugu-Ezike.[94] Mr. L. A. C. Helbert, the district officer, a staunch Catholic, encouraged all his warrant chiefs to embrace this denomination of Christianity and establish schools where reading, writing, and arithmetic would be taught. In the beginning, mission schools were established in the homes of the warrant chiefs. Ahebi Ugbabe set up such a school in her palace.[95] In many ways, King Ahebi was ahead of her time, a modernizer. Ahebi's palace school was coeducational; it admitted and trained girl children at a time when it was unusual for them to be educated. King Ahebi's niece, Nwoyeja, was one such student. She continued her education until she got married:

> I went a bit to school, Ahebi's palace school, which was a CMS school. It happened that I became married to a non-Christian. I prayed that he would allow me continue going to school, but he refused. I even begged him to allow me go to church, but he refused. When I was with Nnenne [Ahebi], I was going to school.[96]

Once young girls were admitted, they went through the same rigorous curriculum as the boys, studying side by side with them through the primer class and infants 1, 2, and 3. This was in sharp contrast to the education provided in the mission schools *oge Ahebi,* where the instruction of girls was geared toward activities that would prepare them for marriage, such as cooking, sewing, and home economics.[97]

In addition, King Ahebi did not distinguish between the free and the bound in her schools. Thus, the first generation of students to attend Ahebi's palace school included a mix of freeborn and "slave" children. They included Vincent Aji Okegwu, Stephen Ahebi, Ogara Ahebi, Wilfred Ogara, Simeon Nweke, Godwin Aji Okegwu,[98] Samuel and Daniel Apeh, and Nwoyeja Obeta. Samuel Apeh, Fabian Azegba, and Barnabas Akogu followed these pioneers.

The teachers who taught in King Ahebi's palace school also came from diverse backgrounds. The school's first instructor, Philip Uba, was originally from Okigwe, as was its second teacher, Felix Nsofor. Samuel Apeh remembers this teacher even though he had not started attending the palace school at the time: "[The second teacher was] Mr. Nsofor. But you know I hadn't started school then. I used to follow Omabe."[99] Subsequent teachers also came from different locales. Jacob Elam came from nearby Aku, and his successor, Samuel Nwume, came from Awka. Vincent Ozoh, from neighboring Ovoko, taught at the palace school during the period 1945 to 1948. Samuel Nwume held a special place in the heart of one of King Ahebi's first pupils: "We used to be happy to see Mr. Nwume. I will never forget his name because he wanted to marry me. [Chuckles.] . . . When that teacher came to marry me, Ahebi refused because I was too small to marry. She believed that people would say that she sold me; after all, she lacked for nothing."[100] Samuel Apeh remembered the man who taught him: "Our teacher was Vincent Ozoh from Ovoko."[101]

The book used for instruction at the palace school was one of the first Igbo primers, which was published in 1904.[102] Called *Akwukwo Ogugu Ibo (Azu Ndu), Azu Ndu* for short, it was compiled by the Society for Promoting Christian Knowledge under the aegis of the CMS. *Akwukwo Ogugu Ibo* means "Book of Igbo Readings"; *Azu Ndu* can mean "Fresh Fish," "Live Fish," or "Back of Life," depending on what tonal inflection is placed on the word "*azu*." This book in a green cover was a basic text for beginners, intended to teach youngsters the new Igbo alphabet and how to spell simple Igbo words. Such publications were the result of the first efforts of missionaries to study the language, phonology, and grammar of the people they were working among as well as a way to help their workers learn how to communicate in the Igbo language. These efforts produced books of sorted and compiled word lists that subsequently evolved into children's texts.[103] Samuel Apeh recalls learning from these:

> They used to teach us *A B GB D*. . . . They used to teach us with *Azu Ndu. Azu Ndu* was very, very, interesting. . . . Yes, *oge Ahebi* they used to teach us about the alphabets. But you know that the Anglican and Catholic alphabets were not the same. The Anglican *N* had an intonation on top, while the Catholic didn't. Even the *O* had an intonation on the top and the bottom too. We started as Catholics at King Ahebi's palace infant school. So when we went to the Anglican school, they took us back to the whole alphabet learning again. That was standard 1.[104]

The teachers also taught children how to count and do simple arithmetic: "We used to write 1, 2, 3, etc. We wrote on slate. Everyone had their own slate. Do you know slate? It was very beautiful to write on that slate. We used to write with something that looked like a pencil."[105]

School instruction at the palace school started at 8 AM; classes were dismissed at 1 PM:

> We used shadows as clocks then. We would watch our shadows to know what time it was. When it was 1 o'clock, our teacher, Vincent Ozoh, would make a mark on the slate. Then the following day, when he outlined the same mark, we would know that it was time to go.[106]

Galilee, Sweet Galilee

Unknown

EXAMPLE 4.1. "Galilee Sweet Galilee." *Prepared by Joe Davey.*

Apeh continued: "[Our teachers] used to tell us lots of stories. They used to teach us how to sing." They taught their students a number of Christian songs including "Galilee Sweet Galilee."[107]

The youngsters at the Ahebi Palace School were also taught the song "Talitha Koum!" in religious studies. According to the Book of Mark, the daughter of the synagogue ruler, Jairus, died before Jesus could reach her. Mourners had already gathered, "crying and wailing loudly." Even so, Jesus was said to have called out to her in Aramaic "Talitha Koum!"—"Little girl, I say to you, get up!" And she did.[108] The words to the sweet melody went like this:

> *Talitha koum* [Little Girl, I Say to You, Get Up!]
> Little girl
> I tell you to get up!
> In a little while open [your eyes] up![109]

At the end of the school day, the students sang "Oge Ezuwo, Anyi ga Ana" [The Time Is Up, We Will Go][110] with enthusiasm:

> The time is up, we will go
> The time is up, we will go
> Thank you to our teachers who have taught us
> We will go home so that we can help
> Our mothers and fathers with the work at home.[111]

The students at the palace school particularly enjoyed recess, which they looked forward to with the excitement of children who had been introduced to sweets for the first time. Samuel Apeh reminisces: "Ah, recess, recess, recess [smiles broadly as he remembers]. We used to play games: running, high jump, wrestling."[112]

Talitha Koum

Unknown

EXAMPLE 4.2. "Talitha Koum!" *Prepared by Joe Davey.*

During the Christmas session, the children, like all Christian young-sters of the time, got into the Christmas spirit by playing dress-up for money:[113] "We children had a special meeting that we called *shapara*. During Christmas [time], we would wear special clothes and go and greet Ahebi. When we got to her palace, she would give us plenty of money. She used to be very happy to see us."[114]

Oge Ezuwo, Anyi Ga Ana

Unknown

EXAMPLE 4.3. "Oge Ezuwo, Anyi ga Ana." *Prepared by Joe Davey.*

But all would not remain well at the palace school. A conflict arose between King Ahebi and the community during the tenure of the school's third teacher, Jacob Elam. On July 20, 2007, I interviewed Jacob Elam's wife, Madam Rose Elam, in Aku. Although she was unable to provide information about the conflict, the ailing Madam Elam was most hospitable about sharing recollections of the time when her deceased husband had served Ahebi:

> Mama *deje* [greetings]

Mama speaks:

> *Deje, Ala* [greetings]. I am not healthy. My head [she cradles her head in both hands]. For this reason I asked this girl [gestures toward her granddaughter] to check these drugs [points to a number of capsules lying on a nearby table] so that I may take them. I do not know whether my problem is typhoid. I suffered from it sometime before and became ill again. [Pauses.] I do not know whether I can remember all he [Jacob Elam] told me. He said that he lived in Ahebi Ugbabe's place. Let me think . . . *Eh, heh.* . . . He was a teacher there and Ahebi paid them five shillings at the end of the month. I asked him whether the five shillings was enough for his feeding. He said that it was enough. He said that Ahebi regarded all of them as her children because she invited all of them each time she was about to do certain things. He did not go to work regularly, but at the end of the month she paid him full salary. He said that he did not stay very long there.[115]

The reason that Jacob Elam "did not stay very long there" was because he had naïvely attempted to boost the extremely poor enrollment at the palace school without first discussing his plans with Ahebi. Mr. Elam, who had already spent a few months teaching, decided to introduce himself to the elders of Umuida. The elders informed Jacob that attendance was low because he had disregarded tradition. If he came to teach the whole of Umuida, his school should not be in Ahebi's palace but at the home of the oldest man in Ogrute, Abugu Aina, according to custom. The teacher therefore moved into Abugu Aina's house. A slighted Ahebi called in the police, who rounded up all the elders involved and threw them in the Nsukka prison for three days. She then sent word to the district officer's interpreter, Ishmael, who found a replacement teacher, Samuel Nwume. In the words of one of Ahebi's students: "Three days later a man called Samuel Nwume introduced him-

FIGURE 4.11.
Jacob Elam
shortly after his
stint as a teacher
at Ahebi's palace
school early
to mid-1930s.
*Photograph cour-
tesy of Madame
Alice Elam, Aku,
Enugu State.*

self as our new teacher. We all welcomed him and were able to continue
with our schooling."[116] Mr. Nwume was sent by the Church Missionary
Society, and thus, Ahebi and her followers became Anglican.[117]

In chapter 5, I examine the conflict between King Ahebi and the
male elders of her community—a conflict that was instigated by the
departure of her third palace teacher, Jacob Elam, and would lead to the
community's abandonment of the Nkwo Ahebi or Nkwo Chief marketplace. "The final insult" occurred with the procurement or seizure—
depending on what side of the masquerade dance one was seated—of
King Ahebi's masked spirit, Ekpe Ahebi. "Mastering Masculinities" is
about the diminishing of King Ahebi's power.

FIVE

Mastering Masculinities: Ekpe Ahebi Masquerade—the Final Insult, ca. 1931–1948

The underlying reason that the elders encouraged schoolteacher Jacob Elam to move out of Ahebi's palace was that they had had enough of her antics and abuses. It was not simply that Ahebi had eroded the traditional leadership of male elders by transforming herself into a British-sanctioned and imposed headman and warrant chief and then into an Igala-imposed female king; she had also abused her political power. The indigenous political elite were particularly troubled by the autocratic practices of Ahebi Ugbabe that constituted unthinkable violations against social mores, such as refusing to consult with the elders, using forced labor, receiving bribes, and forcibly taking away men's wives.

The final straw, however, was when the ambitious Ahebi, perhaps in her quest to achieve full manhood, invaded the last and ultimate sanctuary of men: she created and brought out a masked spirit, Ekpe Ahebi. Patterned after the Igala kingdom's fiercest masked spirit, Ekwe, it was the most beautiful masquerade Enugu-Ezike villagers had ever seen.[1] The lyrics of one of Ekpe Ahebi's outing songs remind us of this fact: "No matter how beautiful or well built that a person is; that person cannot in any way compare to Ekpe." Oshageri Azegbo, a professional musician, added: "Ekpe's beauty was legendary. It was used as a yardstick for measuring village beauty."[2] Wilfred Ogara, Ahebi's adopted son, explained why her action enraged the elders: "The male elders felt that Ahebi was getting out of hand. She was the only woman to *ever* bring out a masquerade. An abomination had been committed. Masquerades belonged to men."[3]

In Enugu-Ezike, the masquerade society is called *umu-mma* ([male] children of the masked spirit). According to tradition, the origin of the *mma* (masked spirit) can be traced back to *oge gbo gbo* (the beginning of time), when the first humans settled in Enugu-Ezike. Masquerades were said to have been instituted in order to keep in check the insatiable desire of some individuals to acquire more than their fair share of authority and wealth. It was the desire to limit the acquisition of too much authority that encouraged Igbo people to surround themselves with powerful

FIGURE 5.1. Ekwe masquerade, no date. *Photograph courtesy of the Palace of the Attah-Igala, Idah, Kogi State.*

prohibitions[4] and cautionary sayings, which culminated in a strange combination of power and lack of power.[5] As one proverb says, "If you want to be a king; you can be a king in your own mother's backyard." In other words, the Igbo were adamant that no individual should be able to overgovern (*oke ochichi*) their community. Ahebi had done this, and her people were ready to take action.

King Ahebi's society checked the accumulation of too much wealth in a different way. The *mma* tradition informs us that a dispute arose among the first inhabitants of Enugu-Ezike over the distribution of land. One settler who had been unfairly attacked by another felt that the only way to prevent this offender from usurping his land was to construct a strange being whose presence, he hoped, would scare his enemy away. Thus, he went into his *obu* (man's house) and covered himself from head to toe with raffia and similar materials. He then emerged from the *obu*, cane in hand, and chased the offending man, who ran away in fear. Because his ruse had succeeded, the man decided thereafter to use this terrifying being, which he had since named *mma*, as his private police guard; in other words, to perform social control.[6] This was the beginning of the decidedly male institution of the *mma* secret society in Enugu-Ezike.

Another tradition highlights the use of the masked spirit by Enugu-Ezike against an enemy society during a war that also took place *oge gbo gbo*. An Umuida man was said to have turned himself into a leopard during the confrontation between his village and Unadu. As soon as the man/leopard leapt into the battlefield, the Unadu warriors fled in fear.[7] The masked man in leopard form thus enabled the town of Umuida, Enugu-Ezike, to gain an advantage in the battle.

In his groundbreaking study *The Peoples of Southern Nigeria*, A. Talbot describes the significance of the masked spirit in Igboland: "[The *mma*] are supposed to be the dead returned to earth to assure their families of their safe arrival and happiness in the spirit-land. No women are ever allowed to be members, and, as a rule, these regard the [masquerade] society with the utmost dread."[8] A. O. Onyeneke lends further insight into the significance of this cultural practice: "The masquerade serves the special function of differentiating the male and the female in Igbo society. Everywhere it is the exclusive function of the male, while the female[s] are always excluded even where a female character is portrayed in the masking. . . . The social definition of a man therefore is the ability to control a masquerade."[9]

The Igbo expectation about the relationship of women to masked spirits is clear. However, they distinguish between categories of male associations with masquerades as well. In Igbo sensibilities, the *umu-mma* (masquerade secret society) is the institution that separates full men (i.e., biological men who have been initiated into the *umu-mma*) from uninitiated men and women. It is forbidden for any individual who is born female (i.e., a biological woman or a gender-transformed or masculinized (wo)man, including female husbands, female fathers, female sons, and, in Ahebi's case, female warrant chiefs and female kings) to control a masked spirit in Igboland. Moreover, it is forbidden for uninitiated biological men to control masked spirits. Biological women (again, including gender-transformed women) and uninitiated biological men were supposed to run away at the sight of a mask; if they claimed knowledge of what was behind the mask—in essence, if they claimed that they had seen the mask in its nakedness—they would have committed an abomination against the mask. Thus, although Ahebi Ugbabe had effectively transformed herself into the British and Igala female masculinities of headman, warrant chief, and king, as far as Igbo society was concerned, she could neither create nor control a masked spirit, nor could she view a masquerade in its nakedness (*ikpo ifu mma*) because she was biologically female. Ahebi's attempt to realize and humanize the aspiration of her symbolic kingship praise-song "Ahebi Ugbabe Is the Odo Masquerade" consequently met with severe opposition from Enugu-Ezike full men. In addition, her actions were considered to have caused the total desecration of the Ekpe Ahebi masked spirit because no woman or uninitiated man could ever invoke the performance of an ancestral spirit. This, in essence, was Ahebi's crime.

The people of Nsukka Division, however, allowed exceptional post-menopausal Igbo (wo)men[10] to have a special relationship with masked spirits—they could be *oyimas* (female friends of Omabe) or *oyiodos* (female friends of Odo). These (wo)men were believed to have been divinely chosen by the masquerades to serve as their helpers. Unlike ordinary women, they could go into the sacred field (*agu*) of Omabe and Odo and talk to the masquerades during the homecoming preparation of these masked spirits. They sacrificed and prepared special foods for Omabe and Odo, their masked spirit boyfriends. They also were privileged to dance for their spirit friends in the village square (*otobo*). It was the *oyima* or *oyiodo* who had the extraordinary right to stop or start an Omabe and Odo performance by placing their hands or legs on one of the masked spirit's musical instruments. Only titled men who had sacrificed a horse to Omabe and Odo enjoyed this same privilege. In some Nsukka communities only one *oyima* and *oyiodo* existed, and she was always the oldest (wo)man in the lineage.[11] In other communities, the *oyiodo* housed Odo's dress and the masked spirit could not appear until the old woman had "seen" him and declared in a loud voice, "I have seen Odo." However, this "seeing" was limited to viewing the masquerade in its clothed form, not in its nakedness. Only members of the *umu-mma* secret society could see the unclothed masquerade.

Although relatively young, King Ahebi had already become a girl-friend of Omabe, a reality revealed in the title of *oyima* that she took. From the evidence available to us, it would appear that the people of Enugu-Ezike did not register any feelings of dissent about Ahebi's acquisition of the title at a young age. In fact, they seemed to have—knowingly or unknowingly—celebrated it. However, as far as these same people were concerned, being an *oyima* was very different from attempting to become a full man. It was this performance of viewing the masked spirit in its unmasked form or nakedness, more than any other, that led to King Ahebi's downfall.

To understand the gravity of Ahebi's offense, one must consider the special space that the masked spirit filled in Igboland. As discussed in chapter 3, the real rulers of Igbo towns were the spirits. One such spirit was the masquerade, of which there were two types: *mma otutu* (day, or visible, masked spirits) and *mma anyasi* (night, or invisible, masked spirits). The *mma otutu* were overwhelmingly female, they were visually pleasing, and they functioned primarily as entertainment, whereas night masquerades were used to enforce *omenani* (the law of the land). These masked spirits (excluding the entertainment spirits) functioned as agents of social control (i.e., as police guards and law enforcement agents),[12] were used during warfare and hunting, and functioned as integral parts of the legal system as the spiritual supreme court of arbitration.

War masquerades were used to dramatize masculine strength and were some of the most powerful and dangerous masked spirits in Enugu-Ezike. Their features were terrifying and tended to take the form of dangerous animals. Masks in animal form were also used during hunting expeditions to hide the human identity of the hunter, enabling him to enter the territory of dangerous animals without being harmed.

There were also wonder-making masquerades, who could increase or decrease in size or change their shape. These performances were managed by elderly men steeped in the mysteries of the occult. One such masquerade was Ozibo, which appeared on the rare occasion of an *onyishi*'s passing. It honored the dead, crying and sending praises to them in the spirit world. Ozibo also celebrated the achievement of the dead in song. Women were strongly prohibited from appearing when this masked spirit was out, for it was believed that if a woman crossed Ozibo's shadow, she would die.[13]

Membership in the masquerade society was restricted to initiated males over the age of 15. Younger boys could not be initiated, for it was believed that they could not withstand the ordeal initiates had to undergo before they could be entrusted with the secrets of the mask. There were two phases of initiation (*ikpo ifu mma*). During the preparatory first phase, initiates were taught songs that cautioned against participating in abominable acts. As the initiates sang, they were expected to "wet an ant hole." "Wetting an ant hole" called for the initiate to completely cover himself in mud. The action meant that the initiate was preparing himself for the unmasking of a masquerade or to be masked himself. He was then subjected to vigorous interrogation and flogging—measures meant to build character and test the endurance of the would-be initiate, who would be disqualified if he showed any sign of weakness. The second phase involved another round of flogging by a masquerade that invited each initiate to pass between its legs. As the initiate attempted to crawl through the masquerade's widely spread legs, he would receive a severe lashing. Then came the all-important unmasking of the spirit, whose identity the new initiate would keep secret from all members of the larger society, including his blood relatives.[14]

Performing the Ultimate Masculinity: Ekpe Ahebi's Outing and Confiscation

King Ahebi was able to communicate her modification into the absolute Igbo masculinity of full man by staging performances of her Ekpe masquerade dance—performances that she would thrust upon her society. When Ahebi appeared with her Ekpe masquerade, the music that accompanied the (wo)man and the spirit were adaptations of traditional Igbo rhythms—war and night masquerade songs—that were constructed as male, thus cementing for all King Ahebi's gendered performances of masculinity, both within the natural physical world (as a great warrior) and in the supernatural world of powerful male masked spirits.

The music that accompanied Ahebi's Ekpe affirmed this female king's identity as a (wo)man who had become an initiated man—a (wo)man who had seen the masked spirit in its nakedness and had not only become a full man, but a full man who could control all men. The lyrics of Ekpe Ahebi's song—*Ahebi Ugbabe onu, Odo neji mmadu, onye neli mmadu, ologi ologi agboo* (Ahebi Ugbabe is a pit, an Odo masquerade that catches men, a pit that swallows men, a pit that swallows men totally)—not only dramatized King Ahebi's gendered transformation into a female masquerade, it also performed Ahebi's female masculinity in spiritual terms, thereby setting her apart from mere male mortals (whom we are told that she "catches and swallows totally"). The lyric takes on added meaning when one understands that men in Nsukka Division traditionally used the Odo masked spirit as an instrument to control female behavior. Therefore, Ahebi located her gendered transformation in terms of a preexisting Igbo male institution that she had effectively negotiated into a masculinized but uniquely biologically female mechanism and threatened to use it to control male behavior.

Another one of Ekpe's outing songs, which concerned social protocols that governed who was entitled to bring out a masked spirit, breathed meaning into the tension between Enugu-Ezike elders and Ahebi. In the song, the elders are called morons for daring to question King Ahebi's authority to own a masked spirit. The song further proclaims that Ahebi uses heavy rain to kill. In other words, it would be foolhardy for any individual to question the female king's authority. Another line of the song challenges "those who have nose but without snuff bottle to just wait for Ekpe's arrival." Every human has a nose, but it takes a hardened human, a man of substance, to be able to *ikpo utaba* (literally, "call on" or beckon the tobacco and "peg" the substance in his nostrils)—a motion that shook the strongest of bodies to their core. Even so, the song warned in a veiled threat that that person of substance should be afraid of Ekpe Ahebi's arrival: "Just wait for Ekpe's arrival." The singers then proudly declare that "Ekpe is Ahebi's child." In other words, Ahebi was bigger than Ekpe. She was the mother of Ekpe. And as the Igbo are bound to remind us, Nneka (mother) is supreme. Therefore, as Ekpe's mother, Ahebi was declaring her preeminence over the masked spirit—an assertion that was both bold and daring because spirits in Igboland were always constructed as superior to human beings. The song then pointed out—perhaps in an attempt to further cement Ahebi's greater-than-spirit persona—that it was from King Ahebi's house that Ekpe originated. The song was telling its listeners that Ekpe dresses and undresses in the female king's house, the significance of which places Ahebi firmly within the realm of full manhood, for it is only in the house of a full man that a masked spirit would dress and undress. The song finally tells "those who opposed Ahebi's masquerade's outing" not to worry themselves with details beyond their control, for "Ahebi's masquerade is already on its way":

A o wee lee lee . . . A o wee lee lee
A o wee lee lee . . . A o wee lee lee
That they use heavy rain to kill. . . . A o wee lee lee
A o wee lee lee . . . A o wee lee lee
That they use heavy rain to kill. . . . A o wee lee lee

Descendants of Nwonu Nwoome Nwishida use heavy rain to kill.
. . . A o wee lee lee
Ahebi Ugbabe uses heavy rain to kill. . . . A o wee lee lee
Those that have nose but without snuff bottle. . . . A o wee lee lee

Those who insisted that Ahebi will not succeed. . . . A o wee lee lee
When they have nose but without snuff bottle. . . . A o wee lee lee

Wait for the Ekpe's arrival. . . . A o wee lee lee
Just await Ekpe's arrival. . . . A o wee lee lee
That is Ugbabe, Ahebi's child. . . . A o wee lee lee
Ugbabe Ohom Eguru Elechi. . . . A o wee lee lee
Descendants of Nwoome Nwonu Nwishida. . . . A o wee lee lee

Those who have nose but without snuff bottle. . . . A o wee lee lee
Where are those morons? . . . A o wee lee lee
Those who opposed Ahebi's masquerade's outing. . . . A o wee lee lee
But Ahebi's masquerade is already on its way. . . . A o wee lee lee
No matter how beautiful you are, you are still not comparable to Ekpe.
. . . A o wee lee lee
No matter how well built, you are not Ekpe. . . . A o wee lee lee
Ekpe originated from Ahebi Ugbabe's home. . . . A o wee lee lee
Those who have nose but without a snuff bottle. . . . A o wee lee lee
Ahebi Ugbabe uses heavy rain to kill. . . . A o wee lee lee
Those who have nose but without a snuff bottle. . . . A o wee lee lee

Will you be as rich as Ahebi? . . . A o wee lee lee
Will you be as wise as Ahebi? . . . A o wee lee lee
Those who have nose but lack a snuff bottle. . . . A o wee lee lee
Those who have nose but lack a snuff bottle. . . . A o wee lee lee
Those who have nose but lack a snuff bottle. . . . A o wee lee lee
Those who have eyes but are blind. . . . A o wee lee lee
Ugbabe Ohom Eguru Elechi. . . . A o wee lee lee

The poverty of the wretched is no hindrance to his verbal assaults.
. . . A o wee lee lee
The poverty of the wretched is no hindrance to his verbal assaults.
. . . A o wee lee lee
Ahebi Ugbabe has actually arrived. . . . A o wee lee lee
Wait for Ekpe. . . . A o wee lee lee
If you are beautiful, you are not Ekpe. . . . A o wee lee lee
If you are well built, you are not Ekpe. . . . A o wee lee lee[15]

In Enugu-Ezike it was customary for a masked spirit to be "brought
out." This performance symbolized the introduction of the masked spirit
to the community and normally took place during a festive ceremony
held at the *onyishi*'s compound specifically for this purpose. The highlight of the ceremony was when each masquerade in attendance paid
tribute to the *onyishi* and his council of elders (*ndi oha*). At the time of

A Owo Lee Leele

Unknown

EXAMPLE 5.1. "A Owo Lee Leele." *Prepared by Joe Davey.*

EXAMPLE 5.1. continued

A Owo Lee Leele *(continued)*

EXAMPLE 5.1. continued

Ekpe's outing, Apeh Azegba was the *onyishi* and was the luminary who received the community's masquerades.

On the day in question, sometime in 1939,[16] all the masked spirits in Ogurte gathered at the *onyishi's* compound. Separately, they emerged and took center stage. Each masquerade first performed a short opening sequence—pieces in which they presented themselves to the people and then greeted each elder councilman by his praise-name—then danced up to the *onyishi* and curtseyed before him as a mark of respect. This process was repeated by each of the masked spirits in attendance, to the delight of the people gathered. Soon it was the turn of Ahebi's masked spirit, Ekpe, to pay tribute to Apeh Azegba. The people who accompanied the masquerade were Obeta Nwaonowu, Itodo Abu, Ogbu Nwaukwaba, and Omeje Njoga.[17] Amos Abugu describes what transpired:

> As Ahebi approached with her masquerade to pay tribute to Apeh
> Azegba, he welcomed them. In Ogurte, the oldest man has a sacred cap

of office called *ishi eso,* which he wore only on very special occasions. Everyone in Ogurte knew to avoid any form of confrontation with the *onyishi* when he was wearing this cap. As soon as Ahebi and her Ekpe approached Azegba, he put on his *ishi eso.* Ahebi Ugbabe brought out kola nuts and offered them to Azegba, explaining that her masquerade had come to pay its respects. Azegba remained silent for a time, shook his head, and then beseeched his ancestors to pretend not to have heard the abomination that had been uttered from Ahebi's lips—after all, women were NEVER allowed to own masquerades in Igboland. He then spoke directly to Ahebi. "Do you not know our culture?" He did not even wait for her to respond, but instead beckoned his cronies to escort Ahebi's Ekpe to the backyard—and there it remained, never to be seen again.[18]

The indigenous leadership of male elders and full men had finally acted, and the message was clear. Ahebi Ugbabe's impertinence and performance of exaggerated female masculinities, which stemmed from her total disregard of Enugu-Ezike restrictions on gendered constructions and transformations, would no longer be tolerated.

Ahebi Ugbabe versus Enugu-Ezike: The Court Trial and Betrayal of the British

Ahebi Ugbabe, spoiling for a fight, immediately ordered Apeh Azegba and his council of male elders to court. The case was so extraordinary and unprecedented that it had to be taken to the resident's office in Onitsha. After he heard the case, the resident pronounced his ruling: Ahebi Ugbabe did not have the right to create or "bring out" a masquerade because she was a woman. He then instructed the villagers to repay Ahebi whatever money she had used to acquire the masked spirit and keep the masquerade.

This decision of the court revealed the duplicity of the British colonials. They had proven that they were not trustworthy. They had used Ahebi's knowledge of the geography of Enugu-Ezike to conquer and subjugate her people and then patted her on the back by presenting her with the positions of headman and warrant chief. They had also superficially supported her during squabbles with individual members of her community. But when it *really* counted, the British betrayed her in the worst possible way. For all intents and purposes, the British no longer needed Ahebi's services and loyalty because they had already gained a foothold in Enugu-Ezike. Politically, the institution of warrant chief had been abolished about ten years earlier, following the 1929 *ogu umu-nwanyi*, or Igbo women's war, and Ahebi's services in that office were no longer needed. In fact, the British had transferred leadership rights to a group of eight judges and were themselves taking a much more active role in the administering of justice. Economically, through its partici-pation in the palm oil trade, the town of Enugu-Ezike had essentially become, according to Elizabeth Isichei a "dependent monoculture, con-tributing one of the many commodities needed by industrial Europe."[19] Added to that, the colonial government's articulated aim of maintain-ing law and order in its Nigerian colony meant that its on-the-ground administrators would first and foremost spend their limited resources in suppressing conflicts between Igbo groups.[20] It seems clear that sup-pressing the squabble between Ahebi and members of the Enugu-Ezike male elite fell into this overall British aim.

Moreover, the action of the male elders had shown the British that Ahebi was not as invincible as she once seemed. She seemed to have lost the loyalty of a good portion of her subjects, which could prove disastrous for the continued success of indirect rule in Enugu-Ezike. Therefore, it could be argued that the court decision of the British was a superficial endorsement of community values in an attempt to con-nect with a group of male elders whose influence they had previously disregarded and underestimated. It also appears that the British resident viewed Ahebi's action as overstepping her "native" authority as govern-ment-appointed chief, thus alienating her subjects.[21]

As soon as the resident instructed that Ahebi relinquish her Ekpe masquerade to her community, her influence lessened and her image as superhuman and untouchable unraveled. The people of Enugu-Ezike stopped attending Chief Ahebi's court. They also stopped marketing at Nkwo Ahebi. They relocated it to its present space (on the Ahebi Ugbabe main road) and renamed it Nkwo Iyida (Nkwo of Umuida). It is worth noting that the motivating force behind the relocation was Abugu Aina, the same elder who orchestrated the departure of Ahebi Ugbabe's palace teacher, Jacob Elam. Aina, it would appear, was prepared to con-tinue his obsessive quest to destroy Ahebi for as long as he could.[22]

Thus, after many years, the male elders triumphed in their battle against the autocratic rule of King Ahebi. Detractors immediately com-posed songs that sought to humiliate and ridicule her. One such song, "Ahebi akpogo ifu mma woo ogbodu," stated that Ahebi Ugbabe (the gendered transformed [wo]man) had been initiated into the masquerade cult only to be stripped of all the rights and privileges due initiates and had accordingly become an ordinary woman.

Ahebi Akporo Ifu Mma Woo Ogbodu

Unknown

EXAMPLE 5.2. "Ahebi Akpogo Ifu Mma Woo Ogbodu." *Prepared by Joe Davey.*

Ahebi got initiated into mmanwu cult and became a moron.
. . . E-e-oo Eee
Ahebi got initiated into mmanwu cult and became a moron.
. . . E-e-oo Eee
Ahebi got initiated into mmanwu cult and became a moron.
. . . E-e-oo Eee

Ahebi Akporo Ifu Mma Woo Ogbodu *(continued)*

EXAMPLE 5.2. continued

> Is she not the one called Ahebi Ugbabe? . . . E-e-oo Eee
> Ahebi Nwoome Nwonu Nwishida. . . . E-e-oo Eee
> Ahebi got initiated and turned into a moron. . . . E-e-oo Eee
> Ahebi got initiated and turned into a moron. . . . E-e-oo Eee
> A masquerade does not visit a woman. . . . E-e-oo Eee
> Ahebi got initiated and turned into a woman. . . . E-e-oo Eee
>
> Those who made this claim. . . . E-e-oo Eee
> Is it not Ahebi Ugbabe's kindred? . . . E-e-oo Eee
> Ahebi got initiated and turned into a moron. . . . E-e-oo Eee
> That is Ugbabe Ahebi Ohom Eguru. . . . E-e-oo Eee
> Ugbabe Ahebi Ohom Eguru Elechi. . . . E-e-oo Eee
>
> Ahebi got initiated and turned into a moron. . . . E-e-oo Eee
> Ahebi got initiated and turned into a moron. . . . E-e-oo Eee
> Ahebi got initiated and turned into a moron. . . . E-e-oo Eee
> Ahebi got initiated and turned into a moron. . . . E-e-oo Eee
> Ahebi got initiated and turned into a moron. . . . E-e-oo Eee
> Ahebi Ugbabe Ahebi Ohom Eguru. . . . E-e-oo Eee
> Ahebi Ugbabe Ahebi Ohom Eguru. . . . E-e-oo Eee[23]

Although she remained powerful until she died in 1948, King Ahebi never fully recovered from the ruling of the British resident. The 1940s consequently would have been a mixed bag for her. While oral history is mostly silent about exactly how Ahebi lived in the years following the community's confiscation of her Ekpe masquerade, we can hypothesize about her later life from the evidence that is available to us. It seems clear that King Ahebi no longer attended the British courts as warrant chief, since cases tried after 1930 in Nsukka Division were presided over by British colonial officers.[24] Moreover, the November 1929 *ogu umun-wanyi* (women's war) had effectively led to the abolition of the warrant chief position in colonial Nigeria. We also already know that the people of Enugu-Ezike stopped attending Ahebi's palace court. Therefore, she most likely would not have had any avenue to serve as judge after 1939. Nonetheless, her life would not have been all bad. We can surmise that, apart from her palace court no longer functioning, the rest of King Ahebi's palace would have remained relatively unchanged. The female king still would have had a support base of "slaves" and workers who would have run her palace grounds and cultivated her numerous farmlands. We are able to come to this conclusion because only a female king of great wealth could have performed her status in the way that Ahebi was about to in an *ikwa onwe ya na ndu* ceremony.

Ikwa Onwe Ya Na Ndu—King Ahebi's Burial While She Was Still Living

Though King Ahebi's performance of her burial rights while she was still alive (*ikwa onwe ya na ndu*) was empowering, she had a more immediate reason for her action: Ahebi did not trust that her society would accord her a befitting burial.[25] The ritual or, better put, performance of burying oneself while still alive was not like anything that Enugu-Ezike people had ever seen. As suggested in chapter 2, it is possible that King Ahebi adapted this ritual from the example of two Igala princesses, Inikpi and Oma Idoko, who had been buried alive centuries before. The difference was that Ahebi had succeeded in transforming an act that disempowered the princesses—albeit for the common good of the community—into an empowering performance in which she, Ahebi, female king extraordinaire, would guarantee herself a place in the world of ancestors. For the Igbo believed that if a person was not buried properly, that person would not join the world of ancestors but would instead wander the earth as an evil spirit. Therefore, it was Ahebi's intention to perform her own burial rites in such a magnificent manner that her society would never forget that an incredible being such as herself had lived.

On the day of her *ikwa onwe ya na ndu* funeral, which occurred a few years before her actual death in May 1948, gunshots were sounded throughout the village. Alice Akogu reported that the gunmen were enveloped in so much smoke from the gunfire that they could not see themselves: "On the day of the funeral, guns were shot. It [the shooting] was done on Eke day, at the shrine of Akporisa Enugu-Ezike, which is out of bounds to ordinary people. The guns sounded so much that the gunmen could not see themselves because of the smoke that the guns raised."[26]

As was customary during the interment of an important man, cows and horses were sacrificed in King Ahebi's honor. Alice Akogu remembered that "back at home [i.e., in Ahebi's palace], at night, the number of cows and goats killed were uncountable. Nnenne Ahebi asked the people to do, when she still lived, whatever they would have offered to her when she was dead because she wanted to see it while she lived."[27] But she went much further than societal expectations. To perform her status and wealth, she not only sacrificed numerous animals in her own honor but she had each one of her relatives sacrifice an animal which she supplied to them as well. She also gave a number of cows to Ogrute in compensation so it would close its market, Eke Ogrute—something that had never before been done. To further impress the spectators, she offered up sacrifices for herself in the name of inanimate objects. Her niece, Nwoyeja Obeta, elaborates on these offerings, the closing of the village market, and the ceremony itself:

> During Nnenne's funeral-while-she-was-living—yes, she did it—we even did the *igba echi* ceremony for that purpose. . . . We her daughters and others dressed well and wore ceremonial *echi* [rods used as money *oge Ahebi*]. We marched with all those cows and horses to Eke market in Ogrute. Nnenne gave a number of cows to the entire Ogrute— *ikpoye afia* or *igbuye Eke*—so that the market would be closed. People started to salute us *okpome Eke* [people who stopped the Eke market from functioning]. Those of us who wore *echi* included Oyima, Oyibo Anekwu, Ikeje, and I, who were her daughters. All other people dressed in one piece of cloth on the funeral day, including all members of her wider or extended family. . . . She even bought cows and offered one to the mortar which was used for processing her palm produce; and [she] offered another cow to her cooking pots! Yes, nothing was too small for Nnenne to sacrifice both cows and horses to.[28]

Ahebi instructed the *umuada* (the [association of the] daughters of the land), who would collectively spend a night at their natal village only when a clansperson died, "to come and stay as usual for her funeral-while-she-lived, and they did. The ceremonial eight large bamboo mats were brought for the *umuada* to sit and sleep on."[29] Alice Akogu continues:

> Nnenne sent word to inform her mother's and grandmother's people at Unadu and Obukpa respectively [of her symbolic passing]. They

brought a goat each. She notified the *odinala* [literally, "it is in the land," but meaning "the owners of the land"] people that her kin had gathered to mourn her. The money which was given to her by guests during her *ikwa onwe ya na ndu* funeral filled a box larger than the one she used to place her feet on and from which my husband [Stephen] used to take money several times—the box that I told you was buried in the ground. As you know, during funerals people bring cash, goats, chickens. . . . Nnenne wanted people to do so while she was still living, so that she could see all that was hers. After she saw all of the merrymaking around her, she relaxed, she was satisfied.[30]

Because King Ahebi "died" a gendered man, she was buried as a man, not as a woman. Alice Akogu continues:

Ufie instrument, which was used when a titled man dies, was brought to the funeral at Nnenne's request. She ordered that no woman should carry her *oba* [symbolic representation of the property of the dead that indicates the severing of ties with the living]. It was instead carried by a man because Nnenne was a man. The name of the man who carried her *oba* was Ameh Nwa Adojo. *Obonyi* [a musical ritual group that played when a mighty and gallant man had died in battle] was played at the ceremony.[31]

King Ahebi's *ikwa onwe ya na ndu* funeral was attended by Attah-Ameh as well as several European officers and "native" police: "When King Ahebi 'died,' the white men sent in policemen, and the *attah* sent in his guards to keep watch, for fear that human beings would be sacrificed as offerings to King Ahebi during her burial."[32] Attah-Ameh presented Ahebi with a cock whose blood was dropped into the female king's eyes before she was symbolically buried. He also offered a he-goat and ram as a sacrifice to the "dead" Ahebi.

At the end of her symbolic burial ceremony, King Ahebi presented one horse to her grandmother's people in Obukpa and another to the people of her mother's town, Unadu. She also gave a cow and a horse to her father's people and another horse to the *odinala* people, after which she was said to have been satisfied. Alice Akogu explains further, supporting Nwoyeja Obeta's assertion that no one and nothing was too small to receive a sacrificial animal from King Ahebi:

To her mortar, where her food was pounded, she dedicated a cow. We, the wives of her sons, and her own wives were given a horse each. I cannot remember all. To her Ojobe people [a meeting of men], one of whom was Apeh Nwomah, she also gave a cow. That Apeh Nwomah, whenever he came to the Ojobe meeting when my mother-in-law was alive, at his arrival Nnenne's songsters would sing: "*Nwa Eze rigide na Omaranga ncho. Eze Nwaeze rigide na Omaranga ncho. Ahebi Ogbu efi ngi gbugide na omarangi ncho*" [Prince eat, for you lack nothing. Son of king, eat or enjoy for you have enough. Ahebi the cow killer you enjoy (or you eat) for you lack nothing]. As the songsters sang, the Ojobe people would pour money on him. Yes [smiling in remembrance], his name was Apeh Nwaomah. It was to this man that Ahebi gave a cow during her funeral. She gave a horse to us. To her pillow on her bed she offered a cow. Do you hear what I am saying? She gave a cow to her pillow. You can never finish telling what Ahebi did. She said that the reason she did that ceremony while she was still living was because Stephen had joined the army, and she feared that there would be no befitting ceremony when she died if Stephen died a soldier. And so it was.[33]

Burial songs were sung during and after King Ahebi's *ikwa onwe ya na ndu* ceremony. These songs were performed by the female king's official musicians and sounded until the early hours of the morning. One such song, "Igba naana eee," called on the souls of the departed (*igba naana*), who were believed to come to the burial site of a great personality, to accompany the soul of the departed to the spirit world. In the words of professional musician Oshageri Azegbo: "Because *igba naana* are invisible, it is our belief that as soon as somebody gives up his ghost, the disembodied souls will come and accompany the dead man's spirit back home from where he came."[34] In the song, the various spirits announce that they are coming to escort the newly departed home. They reveal the names of individuals who have just died—Ahebi included—and confirm that these newly materialized souls know that *igba naana* are coming for them. In other words, the new souls realize that their journey as human beings has come to an end and that they are about to embark upon a new, profound, and uncharted journey as spirits in the world of the ancestors. Below are the words and melody to "Igba naana eee," the song that was performed in King Ahebi's honor:

Igba naana eee . . . Igba naana
Anana Omada knows we shall come. . . . Igba naana
Anana Omada knows that we will come. . . . Igba naana
Ahebi Ugbabe knows that we will come. . . . Igba naana
Ahebi Ugbabe knows that we will come. . . . Igba naana
Anana Omada that powered Oja. . . . Igba naana
Anana Omada knows that we will come. . . . Igba naana
Anana Omada knows that we will come. . . . Igba naana

Anana Omada that powdered Oja. . . . Igba naana
Anana Omada that powdered Oja. . . . Igba naana
Ahebi powdered Oja. . . . Igba naana
And Onyeke powdered Oja. . . . Igba naana
And Onyeke did wear the ring. . . . Igba naana
And Ahebi Ugbabe powdered Oja. . . . Igba naana

Mba Anana knows that we will come. . . . Igba naana
Ahebi Ugbabe powdered Oja. . . . Igba naana
Ugbabe Ahebi Ohom Eguru Elechi. . . . Igba naana
We shall go after the king's burial. . . . Igba naana
We shall go once the king is buried. . . . Igba naana
We shall go once the king is buried. . . . Igba naana
And the king herself will still go. . . . Igba naana
And the king herself will still go. . . . Igba naana
Ahebi Ugbabe has gone to Ogwugwu. . . . Igba naana
Gone to Ogwugwu, the spirit world. . . . Igba naana
Ugbabe Ahebi . . . Igba naana
Ugbabe Ohom Eguru Elechi . . . Igba naana
Ahebi Nwonu Nwoome Nwishida . . . Igba naana
Nwoome Nwonu Nwishida will go. . . . Igba naana
Ahebi Ugbabe knows that we will go. . . . Igba naana
And after our stay on earth, we shall die. . . . Igba naana
Keep chorusing Igba naana. . . . Igba naana
Keep chorusing Igba naana. . . . Igba naana
Keep chorusing Igba naana. . . . Igba naana
Keep chorusing Igba naana. . . . Igba naana
Omada Omeje Agama Ugbabe . . . Igba naana
    gba naana knows that we will come. . . . Igba naana
Nwagada Ahebi . . . Igba naana
Ebi knows that we will come. . . . Igba naana
And after our sojourn on earth, we will go. . . . Igba naana

Abugu Odobo hails from Okido Ogiriyi. . . . Igba naana
Abugu Odobo hails from Okido Ogiriyi. . . . Igba naana
And Ebi knows that we are visitors. . . . Igba naana
Eze nwa Abugu shine. . . . Igba naana
Keep chorusing. . . . Igba naana
Keep chorusing. . . . Igba naana
Keep chorusing. . . . Igba naana
Keep chorusing. . . . Igba naana
Omada Omeje Agama Obara Ugbabe . . . Igba naana

Our prince knows that we are all visitors. . . . Igba naana
Our prince knows that we are all visitors. . . . Igba naana
Our prince knows that we are all visitors. . . . Igba naana[35]

Another song that was played during Ahebi's symbolic burial was "Onye agbala niya uta" [Let no one shoot the arrow], a song that implored the people gathered not to shoot an arrow because Ahebi had turned into a woodpecker. The song affirmed King Ahebi's death and said that there was no need to shoot the woodpecker because the woodpecker (i.e., Ahebi) was already dead. The woodpecker should be allowed to perch in peace, it said. In other words, the soul of Ahebi should be allowed to rest in peace.

Let no one shoot the arrow, let no one shoot. . . . Let no one shoot
Ahebi Ugbabe has turned into a perched woodpecker. . . .
Let no one shoot
The king is buried, the king departs. . . . Let no one shoot
Ugbabe Ahebi has turned into a perched woodpecker. . . .
Let no one shoot
If she perches, let her perch. . . . Let no one shoot
Ahebi Ugbabe. . . . Let no one shoot
Ugbabe Ahebi Ohom Eguru. . . . Let no one shoot

Ohom Eguru Elechi. . . . Let no one shoot
Nwoome Nwonu Nwishida. . . . Let no one shoot
Ahebi Ukpabi Ndeke Elechi. . . . Let no one shoot

Ahebi Ugbabe has turned into a perched woodpecker. . . .
Let no one shoot
If she perches, let her perch. . . . Let no one shoot
Because of Ahebi Ugbabe. . . . Let no one shoot

A masculine woman has turned into a perched woodpecker.
. . . Let no one shoot
Ahebi Ugbabe has turned into a perched woodpecker. . . .
Let no one shoot
If she perches, let her perch. . . . Let no one shoot
Ugbabe Ahebi Ohom Eguru Elechi. . . . Let no one shoot
Ugbabe Nwonu Nwoome Nwishida. . . . Let no one shoot
Ugbabe Ukpabi Ndeke Elechi. . . . Let no one shoot
Nwa Ukpabi Ndeke Elechi. . . . Let no one shoot
Nwoome Nwaryoli. . . . Let no one shoot

Ahebi Ugbabe has turned into a perched woodpecker. . . .
Let no one shoot

Igba Naana Eee, Igba Nana

Unknown

EXAMPLE 5.3. "Igba Nnaana." *Prepared by Joe Davey.*

Igba Naana Eee, Igba Nana *(continued)*

EXAMPLE 5.3. continued

EXAMPLE 5.3. continued

A woman that behaves like a man. . . . Let no one shoot
If she perches, let her perch. . . . Let no one shoot
Ahebi Ugbabe was crowned king during dry season. . . .
Let no one shoot
The next morning witnessed heavy downpour. . . . Let no one shoot
Ugbabe Ahebi Ohom. . . . Let no one shoot
Ugbabe Ahebi Ohom Eguru Elechi. . . . Let no one shoot
Ahebi has gone forever. . . . Let no one shoot

Whoever has wine should bring it now. . . . Let no one shoot
Whoever has kola should bring it. . . . Let no one shoot
Because the king has gone. . . . Let no one shoot
Those with money should come forward. . . . Let no one shoot
Because Ahebi Ugbabe is gone. . . . Let no one shoot

Ahebi has turned into woodpecker. . . . Let no one shoot
Ahebi has turned into woodpecker. . . . Let no one shoot
If she perches, let her perch. . . . Let no one shoot
Ugbabe Ahebi Ohom . . . Let no one shoot
Ugbabe Ahebi Ohom . . . Let no one shoot
Ugbabe Ahebi Ohom . . . Let no one shoot
Ahebi Ugbabe was crowned king during dry season. . . .
Let no one shoot
She was the person crowned at Idah. . . . Let no one shoot
Ahebi has perched. . . . Let no one shoot
She has transformed into a perched woodpecker. . . . Let no one shoot
Therefore, if she perches, let her perch. . . . Let no one shoot [36]

Ahebi Ugbabe's actual death in May 1948 took the residents of Enugu-Ezike by surprise, because in the words of one collaborator, "nobody knew that King Ahebi was actually mortal and could die."[37] Her real burial ceremony was tame in comparison to the one that had come before it. King Ahebi was buried quietly on her palace grounds. She did not even have a headstone.

In the *Mmechi* (Conclusion), I will explore the real and mythical Ahebi Ugbabe and look at how the idea of Ahebi has been perpetuated in present-day Enugu-Ezike. I will explain about a modern-day Ahebi Ugbabe medicine that has been elevated to a deity. I will also look at conversations about who Ahebi was and what she stood for. To this end, I will present and analyze portions of interviews conducted with the principal, teachers, and students of the Ahebi Primary School. Each of these sources will enable me to present information about how Ahebi is remembered, theorized, and fantasized about in Enugu-Ezike today.

Onye Agbala Niya Uta, Onye Agbala Niya Uta

Unknown

EXAMPLE 5.4. "Onye Agbala Niya Uta." *Prepared by Joe Davey.*

Onye Agbala Niya Uta, Onye Agbala Niya Uta *(continued)*

EXAMPLE 5.4. continued

Mmechi / THE CONCLUSION:

Ahebi Today—the Works That We Do
Are the Things By Which We Are Remembered

The Ahebi Primary School: Reflections on a 1996 Visit

It was a relatively cold day that harmattan morning of November 23, 1996. Being a Saturday, the Ahebi Primary School was closed. However, the trip to Umuida enabled me to take a self-guided tour of the layout of the elementary school named after the female king I was researching.

From my vantage point on Ahebi Ugbabe Road, I could see the large school, with its three spacious classroom buildings that could feasibly house four or five different classes, or so I thought. When I walked into one of the buildings,[1] however, I was surprised to see that there were no walls separating the classrooms and that the building that I had just entered held far more than several classrooms. Its front and back walls had a pair of makeshift chalkboards (in reality they were squares of black paint applied to the center of each wall). The side walls had four additional squares painted on them, numbering six chalkboards in all—in my estimation, six separate classrooms.

I had been assured by Mr. Samuel Ezeja, a teacher from Enugu-Ezike whom I had met a few days earlier,[2] that he would be happy to accompany me to the school the following Monday. That way, he said, I would have a chance to speak with the headmaster. Monday turned out to be as cold a day as the preceding Saturday. As soon as we arrived at the school, we were ushered into the headmaster's office. Mr. Michael Idoko was a slender man of dark complexion who appeared to be about 60 years old. He received Mr. Ezeja and I well: "You are welcome. We shall help you out of your problems. We shall give you any information you need. If I fail to give you, I will send you down to someone who will do better."[3] The headmaster paused and then continued, introducing himself to me in the third person: "Michael Idoko is an aborigine. I grew up here. I schooled here and eventually I became the headmaster, the present headmaster of this school. I didn't know Ahebi myself because I was too young when she died. But many people told me stories about her."[4] Headmaster Idoko then offered me a chair and talked with me about Ahebi Ugbabe for ninety minutes.

Afterward, Mr. Idoko allowed us to visit the school's classrooms, but he warned us that the students of Ahebi Primary School actually knew very little about the female king whose name their school bore. As we walked from classroom to classroom, we were disheartened to see how uninformed the children were about King Ahebi. But even more disturbing was the fact that their teachers did not seem to know much more.

The first class that we walked into was Primary 6A. It was one of four streams of grade six in the school. As soon as we entered the classroom, the class prefect[5] knocked five times on his desk, and all the members of the class rose to their feet. "Good morning, visitors," the students chanted in unison. "Good morning students," Headmaster Idoko, Mr. Ezeja, and I responded. Mr. Ezeja asked "How are you?" to which the students, still standing, responded, "We are fine."[6]

I found myself operating the camcorder—a brand-new gadget I had purchased especially for this research trip. Mr. Ezeja served as impromptu interviewer. I had not planned to seek information from the teachers and pupils of the Ahebi Primary School, but the questions easily fell into place. He posed his first question to the teacher, Osagwa: "Please tell us all you know about Ahebi. Have you been teaching these children about the king whom this school was named after?" The teacher fidgeted nervously with his chalk and then responded, "The only thing I have told them is that Ahebi is the founder of this school. I do not know much." Mr. Ezeja then turned to one of the students: "Do you know about Ahebi Ugbabe?" The male student, still standing, nodded. Mr. Ezeja continued: "Who then is Ahebi Ugbabe?" Male student: "She was a king who was female."[7] To a female student in the same class, Mr. Ezeja inquired: "Do you know where Ahebi Ugbabe lived?" The female student, also standing, responded: "Yes." Mr. Ezeja continued: "Where did she live?" Pointing in the direction of the surviving portion of King Ahebi's palace, she said, "At the back of our school." Mr. Ezeja followed this pattern of questioning as we moved from classroom to classroom.

The next classroom we walked into was Primary 6C. "Good morning, visitors," the students said in unison. "Good morning students," Mr. Ezeja, the headmaster, and I responded. Having witnessed the greeting ritual in the first classroom, I now joined Mr. Ezeja in asking, "How are you?" to which the students responded, again in unison, "We are well." Mr. Ezeja asked the teacher: "Can you tell us how you know Ahebi?" The teacher responded: "I was told by my father that Ahebi was once a very prominent king in this area. She participated in settling cases. And I learned that she was the person who founded this school in 1954." The headmaster interjected the correction, "1934." Mr. Ezeja, continuing with his self-appointed job of interviewer, asked: "Could you please do well in inculcating this knowledge to these very children? [The teacher nodded in agreement.] Okay, good. And again you know that in social studies, it is nice that the children who attend the school that is named after Ahebi should know much about Ahebi, so that when they graduate, they can write much about Ahebi. [Pause.] Thank you very much."

Some students were studying underneath a mango tree in the school's large courtyard. This, we were told, was Primary 6B. They were studying outside because there was not enough room for all the classes in the cement buildings. Their teacher was Mr. Samuel Ene. Mr. Ezeja inquired of Mr. Ene: "This is Ahebi Primary School, you know. What do you know about Ahebi?" "I know very little about her because I was too tender in age when she was king." Mr. Ezeja, undeterred by the teacher's response, continued: "Okay, have you been teaching these children much about Ahebi from what you learned about her in social studies and civics? That is, performed your civic duty for the students to know about the person who this school was named after?"[8] Before Mr. Ene could answer, the headmaster interjected, "We are in the 1st term." Headmaster Idoko then unleashed his frustration with the Nigerian federal government, which, he said, had promised to turn the Ahebi Primary School into a model school but had not made good on its promise.

The last class that we visited was Primary 6D, whose teacher was Mr. Christopher Asogwa. The students greeted us as usual and Mr. Ezeja commenced with interviewing the teacher: "Are you a[n] [Umuida] native?" "No," the teacher responded. "Have you heard about Ahebi?" Mr. Asogwa responded, "All I know is that in the olden days she was the chief of this place. She achieved so many things and that is why they named the school after her." Mr. Ezeja asked, "Okay, before coming to this place had you read in any social studies or history books about Ahebi Ugbabe?" Mr. Asogwa said, "No." As in the classes before, Mr. Ezeja's next question had to do with teaching about Ahebi: "Have you been teaching these children here about Ahebi? [Have you been teaching them] all they are supposed to know about this paramount chief?" Teacher Asogwa responded: "Well, I teach them the much that I know." Mr. Ezeja continued: "Are you suggesting that a book about Ahebi should be developed to enable you teach about her?" The teacher responded: "Yes, it is necessary." Headmaster Idoko elaborated: "Yes, I think that efforts should be geared toward writing a book so that people will know much about Ahebi Ugbabe, especially the children that go here. They go to Ahebi Primary School and they do not know much about the woman who made it possible to establish this very school."

Indeed, not much else was known about the woman whose name the Ahebi Primary School bore, except for the fact that Ahebi had ruled as *eze* and the belief of many that there was a cock buried within the grounds of her palace that crowed every midnight. It is my hope that this book will fill that need.

The year I visited the Ahebi Primary School was also the year I first met Barnabas Nwa Ugbabe Obeta, Ahebi's oldest surviving nephew, who lived not far from the school named after his aunt. I visited him several times during the fifteen-plus years I spent researching the life and world of King Ahebi. During our initial meeting, Barnabas showed me some of King Ahebi's surviving kingship relics and talked to me about how the paraphernalia is used by Umuida people in the present day: "In our community," he said, "anyone that buys a horse will come and collect this crown [helmet], and when returning it, he will bring along with it ten tubers of yam, four gallons of palm wine and ₦200.00. All these items together with the money are given to me as a mark of respect as the oldest [surviving] person [of Ahebi's lineage]."[9]

The people of Enugu-Ezike, it would appear, have found in King Ahebi's paraphernalia a modern-day way to perform social and economic status and wealth. Barnabas Obeta, for his own part, had found in Ahebi's inheritance a way to make money on the side. To my knowledge, King Ahebi's kingship relics are still being loaned out, at exorbitant amounts, to Umuida citizens to use for adornment during festive occasions.

A Legacy of Fear

The belief that there is a live cock that crows from within the grounds of King Ahebi's palace has also survived to the present day. I first heard mumblings about this cock during my pre-dissertation trip in 1996. I heard about it again in 1998, during a second research trip. When I returned to Umuida almost ten years later in 2007, the villagers of Umuida and beyond still told the same story. According to the villagers, it was because of this cock that the only surviving building—the visitors' house—in King Ahebi's palace had been abandoned. A number of collaborators had informed me that the administration of the Ahebi Primary School had attempted to put King Ahebi's visitors' house (which remains a surprisingly strong building) to good use by making it available as an accommodation for the school's out-of-town teachers. However, these teachers claimed that they had heard the terrible cock crow and had immediately moved out of the house for fear that harm would come to them. It is for this reason that this only surviving portion of King Ahebi's palace has been abandoned and has fallen into disuse. Its only semblance of life is graffiti drawings etched on its interior walls.

In fact, so strong was the fear of the danger that would befall any inhabitant of the house that my Umuida collaborators expressed unguarded awe and admiration for a young female researcher who they believed was, in fact, a little bit like King Ahebi (i.e., fearless). My elevation to the rank of an Ahebi was realized because I had on several occasions entered the building in question to take pictures. "Were you not afraid of what might happen to you?" the villagers inquired each time. Flattering comparisons to King Ahebi notwithstanding, I must confess that I was never in the building or on her palace grounds at twelve midnight, the crowing hour. Therefore, it is impossible for me to speculate as to whether or not a bird actually does crow from within the palace grounds.

One fact of which I am certain is the need to preserve what has survived of King Ahebi's palace as well as her relics. To that end, I have been in talks with the leaders of the Umuida community as well as community representatives in the local and national government, and I hope that in the near future we will be able to not only salvage this particular building but also return King Ahebi's palace grounds to their former splendor. The site could serve as a tourist attraction and the people of Umuida could use the revenue from this historical reconstruction to fund projects to maintain community roads and provide electricity and pipe-borne water for all residents. Perhaps they could even rebuild the Ahebi Primary School into a model school, as the Nigerian federal government had promised. The Umuida elite with whom I am engaged seem excited about these prospects, and I hope that we will be able to raise the funds necessary to make it a reality.

The Deification of a Legend

On July 14, 2007, my research guide, Erobike Eze, and I found ourselves *be ikwu nne Ahebi* (in Ahebi's mother's town) in Unadu. We had been to this town nine years earlier, when we interviewed Bernard Ameh, the great-great-grandson of King Ahebi. Mr. Ameh had graciously loaned me, a stranger student researcher, family heirlooms—five photographs of King Ahebi's now-deceased biological descendants (see Figures 1.2, 1.3, and 1.4). At the time, I had promised to take the photographs with me to my family photographer, Mike Photos, whose shop was located at the Egede market just outside the limits of the university town, Nsukka, where I had grown up. I was certain that I could trust the copying of such aged treasures to the owner of the shop, who happened to be a native of my own hometown of Ogidi, in Anambra State.

I later learned from Bernard that his decision to loan me the artifacts had caused him several sleepless nights. Even before the four-day loan period had expired, he had begun to question the decision to trust his only family heirlooms to a complete stranger. What if the woman with the one-year-old daughter walked away with his photographs? He had heard of people ("some White man and his White wife"[10]—from where, his Umuida relatives were not certain) who a few years earlier had made away with several of King Ahebi's relics of office, never to return them.[11] I did return as promised four days later with Mr. Ameh's pictures in hand—actually in better shape than I had borrowed them, because Mike had taken it upon himself to clean the pictures and the frames in which they had been placed. I handed back the photographs to a visibly relieved Bernard, who was not afraid to admit just how thoroughly family and friends had rebuked him for his decision.

Hence, on July 14, 2007, Erobike Eze and I wanted to find Mr. Ameh and present him with a bottle of whiskey as a measure of our appreciation and to let him know that I was now working on a full-length biography of his cherished relative. After nine years, neither of us could remember the convoluted pathways that led to his home in the interior of town. Instead, we found Utubi, a loud and boisterous medicine man, who had concocted an Ahebi Ugbabe medicine for himself and the community. Over the years, this medicine had been elevated by society into a goddess. Thus, in death, Ahebi Ugbabe had not only joined the world of spirits as an ancestor but had assumed the rank of a much more powerful god. And her sojourn into the immortal unseen world, it would appear, had been realized as a result of matrifocal expression. The Igbo adage *Nneka* (mother is supreme) had truly come to fruition in the elevation of Ahebi into a supernatural deity that was not merely respected but was worshipped with sacrifices.

As a result, my narrative of how Ahebi is remembered today cannot be complete without a discussion of my encounter with Ahebi Ugbabe the goddess. My introduction to goddess Ahebi occurred in the company of her human intermediary, Priest Utubi, who was in charge of the Ahebi shrine, a mud enclosure situated on the right side of his Unadu compound. With exaggerated tones Utubi loudly chanted incantations to goddess Ahebi. He then emerged from the shrine, marched into a room behind where I was sitting, and emerged with a gourd that was filled to the brim with an unidentifiable liquid. No sooner had he emerged than he again disappeared into Goddess Ahebi's shrine, chanting and spraying libation as he went. I was not allowed near or into the shrine. The reason for this, I was told, was that the priest did not want to break one of the goddess's most powerful taboos. Goddess Ahebi, like most deities in Nsukka Division, deemed menstrual blood unclean, a pollutant.[12] What I found most remarkable about this encounter was not Goddess Ahebi's abhorrence of menstruation but rather the fact that Priest Utubi, acting on the goddess's behalf, was able to discern my condition by simply looking at me. Priest Utubi claimed to have been informed of this fact by Goddess Ahebi. Suffice it to say that I was indeed in my menstrual period and had not revealed this fact to any of my companions. The modern-day Ahebi Ugbabe divinity was thus proved to be a seer and a revealer of the unknown. I would later find out from her priest that she took this responsibility seriously and was consulted and worshipped by many—near and far—in time of need.[13]

Ahebi is also remembered in several sayings and songs performed in Enugu-Ezike today. One need not search long to hear references to her weighty ways. It is not uncommon to hear Umuida people admonishing prideful behavior: "You are being carried on a hammock, are you Ahebi?" They also evoke Ahebi's memory in their community's determination that no single individual, male or female, would ever be allowed to rule them again: "We will not allow another woman [or man] to ever rule us like Ahebi did."[14] Other sayings that have survived speak to Ahebi's modification into a man: "Ahebi Ugbabe was the woman who became a man," and "Ahebi Ugbabe was the woman who was crowned a king." King Ahebi's Ekpe masquerade has become the yardstick by which beautiful women are measured in Umuida today: "You are beautiful, but not as beautiful as Ahebi's Ekpe." Ahebi has become the benchmark by which affluence is determined: "No woman wears *onwuruchi* except Ahebi, daughter of Onu."[15]

Sayings have survived that speak of King Ahebi's honor as well as her dishonor. One such saying, a lyric from one of her praise songs, recalls the female king's physical strength, describing it as greater than that of an axe. It declares: "Ahebi is a pit that swallowed the axe!" Another lyric that states that Ahebi is "a pit, an Odo masquerade that catches men, a pit that swallows men, a pit that swallows men totally" conjures up the image of a strong female who not only controls males but destroys them completely. But of course, the elders are quick to point out that Ahebi was an aberration of sorts, a female deviant who operated *oge gbo* (a long time ago) and that present-day society would never tolerate another attempt to challenge manliness in all of its expressions. Other Ahebi-inspired sayings call attention to the futility of attempting to go beyond the contours of accepted gendered transformations in society: "*Ahebi kpolu ifu mma woo obodu*" (Ahebi was allowed to view the masked spirit in its nakedness, only to become an ordinary person, a useless person), thus reminding us of society's ability to rein in behavior that it deems unacceptable. But perhaps most important are the physical reminders of Ahebi's presence—the Ahebi Ugbabe Road and the Ahebi Primary School—that stand as testaments to Ahebi's prowess in the Enugu-Ezike world.

By Way of Concluding . . .

During an era when women were marginalized politically across Africa, Ahebi Ugbabe's story presents an unrivaled portrait of one (wo)man's power and agency in the face of a rapidly changing British colonial landscape. It contributes a great deal to our understanding of continuity and change in Igbo gendered politics and to our knowledge about competing and overlapping definitions and constructions of female masculinities and manhood in colonial Nsukka Division. *The Female King of Colonial Nigeria* is also about the production, framing, and interpretation of knowledge about gender in Africa.

In the course of her journey through life, Ahebi Ugbabe asserted her fundamental right as a gendered Igbo actor to perform multiple female masculinities. She was able to negotiate her life first within the historical context of British colonialism and (later) Igala ascendancy in ways that extended, altered, and attempted to challenge in fundamental ways the preexisting Nsukka gender ideals that governed the extent to which a woman could become a man. However, when this extraordinary woman attempted to achieve acceptance and full manhood in the ultimate sanctuary of full Igbo men, she was immediately reined in by indigenous gerontocratic male authority, revealing Igbo society's resolve about the extent to which female gendered transformations would be allowed to materialize.

Let us examine in greater detail the historical conditions/context that unintentionally allowed Ahebi the space to alter and extend her gendered identity. In colonial Igbo country, the British invaders initially sought to create conditions that would recognize and celebrate the so-called native authority of Igbo male elders. Thus, they instituted the office of headman, superficially patterned after the indigenous role of the *onyishi umunwoke* (the oldest man in the community). The appointed Igbo elders soon became junior partners in the political processes of colonialism in their districts. However, by the 1920s, a time when colonial rule was consolidating its hold in Igboland, the British switched their loyalties and began to privilege male youth. It is valuable to visualize this modification in broader terms. It would appear that the British sought out male youth whom they believed would be much more amenable and energetic than their aged predecessors and as a result would be more likely to accept their instructions. Once selected, the young Igbo men were empowered with warrants of office, which served to elevate and celebrate youth while pushing aside age and respectability, traditional determinants of power and authority in Nsukka.

Although Ahebi Ugbabe was born a woman, she was able to tap into the British obsession with youth. She was young, beautiful, loyal, and dependable, and, most important, she had proven herself to be an invaluable asset in the consolidation of British rule in Enugu-Ezike. Evidence suggests that Ahebi not only worked to satisfy the sexual appetites of the British colonials but she also revealed the routes by which the British could conquer her people. Her linguistic skills further cemented her connection with the British, because she was the only person in Umuida who could communicate with and relay British objectives to colonized Enugu-Ezike citizens.

One could argue that by embracing a highly masculinized form of colonial leadership (i.e., headman), Ahebi Ugbabe sought to redefine the preexisting indigenous role of *onyishi umunwanyi* (the oldest woman in the community), a dignitary who existed side by side with the Onyishi Umunwoke and who was already constructed as male in Nsukka consciousness. However, in this indigenous gendered system, age, respectability, and achievement were prerequisites for this type of gendered transformation into an "honorary man." Ahebi Ugbabe, who did not possess any of the determinants of Nsukka leadership, was nevertheless able to perform social and political status by tapping into the British colonials' privileging of youth and transform herself into young female headman. This ingenious gender and age negotiation set the stage for Ahebi's British-sustained transformation into female warrant chief.

Ahebi's triumph in transforming herself into a warrant chief in 1918 revealed not only her extraordinary abilities but also her exceptional gift for inventing and reinventing herself within the new and viable context of British colonial rule. Like the headman position that she so ingeniously modified to fit her needs, Ahebi Ugbabe was able to streamline British ideals of male youthfulness in leadership and assume the office of warrant chief as an already transformed female man. In fact, Ahebi Ugbabe was the only (wo)man to hold this office in all of colonial Nigeria. In becoming a female headman and warrant chief, Ahebi Ugbabe essentially redefined, expanded upon, and evolved a role that already existed in Nsukka (*onyishi umunwanyi*) while adapting individualized and youth-based British masculinities within the context of indirect rule. She subsequently turned to the Igala constitution to uphold the third in a series of gendered performances—a successful quest to become female king.

When Ahebi created and brought out a masked spirit in her attempt to realize full manhood within the Enugu-Ezike indigenous context, full men and members of the Enugu-Ezike male gerontocratic elite immediately reined her in. Their message was clear: "*ochichi Ahebi agafego oke*" (Ahebi was governing too much). She had crossed beyond the limits of acceptable female behavior. In a series of reprisals, her society obtained retribution for her objectionable conduct. First, the male elders took away her palace teacher, Jacob Elam. Then they seized her Ekpe Ahebi masquerade. As a consequence of the fallout from the confiscation of the masked spirit, the community stopped attending King Ahebi's palace court. They also closed down Nkwo Ahebi (or Nkwo Chief), the daily market held in King Ahebi's honor. But their most crushing blow was taking away her masked spirit. In this action, the male elders in essence took away Ahebi's spiritually based masculinized powers, thus symbolically forcing her to re-transform into a woman. Moreover, the British government's decision to stand behind the Enugu-Ezike male elders established that they too were unwilling to defend such unprecedented deviant behavior on the part of a (fe)male junior partner in "native" government.

Ultimately, Enugu-Ezike full men as well as its male gerontocratic elite succeeded in stripping King Ahebi of most of her political clout. In the end, she was forced to perform her burial rites while she was still alive (*ikwa onwe ya na ndu*) because she did not trust that her society would accord her a befitting burial. *Omenani* (laws that guide and order group relationships in Igbo society) thus proved victorious in its struggle against excessive and inordinate female ambition.

Select Criminal and Civil Cases in Nsukka
Division in which Ahebi Participated, 1918–1930

Oge Ahebi, there were five native court areas in Nsukka Division. These were Adani Native Court, Eha Amufu Native Court, Obollo Native Court, Opi Native Court, and Ahebi's own Enugu-Ezike Native Court. The earliest cases to go before the native courts in Nsukka Division occurred in 1911.

All cases brought before the native courts in Nsukka Division are documented in civil and criminal judgment books, civil judgment books, criminal judgment books, Native Cause books, and Native Court general note books, which are housed at the National Archives of Nigeria, Enugu, NAE. Each civil and criminal judgment book contains transcripts of about 300 cases. These judgment books cover the period starting 1911–1922. Each civil judgment book also contains transcripts of about 300 individual cases. These judgment books cover the period starting 1912–1946. Like the other judgment books, the criminal judgment books contain the transcripts of about 300 individual cases. These judgment books cover the period starting 1913–1954. The Native Court cause books are divided into civil and criminal books. Each cause book contains compilations, in index form, of all cases heard in Nsukka Division from 1934 to 1946. The Native Court general note books contain short notes of specific cases heard from 1923 to 1933.

During my fieldwork, I first consulted all civil and criminal judgment books, civil judgment books, criminal judgment books, Native Court cause books, and Native Court general note books covering the period starting 1918–1930 that were available (during the Nigerian/Biafran Civil War, numerous documents at the Nigerian National Archives, Enugu were destroyed). The period represented the time when Chief Ahebi was active either as president or member of the Native Court. I collected and photocopied all cases in which Chief Ahebi was active as president or member. I also collected and photocopied all cases in which Chief Ahebi was called in as a plaintiff or witness. Since the warrant chief institution was abolished on paper in 1929, my 1930 cut-off point represented the "official" end of the warrant chief institution. However, cases were still brought before the Nsukka Division Native Courts until 1954. These post-1930 cases were presided over by European colonialists. The case that had initially propelled my search (Ahebi taking her community to court over the confiscation of her Ekpe masquerade) would have, in my estimation taken place after 1939, and before King Ahebi's *ikwa onwe nya na ndu* ceremony. I thus conducted an additional review of all cases that appeared before the Nsukka Division native courts up to 1946.

In total I consulted the only time-relevant civil and criminal judgment book at the archive,[1] seventy-two criminal judgment books,[2] twenty-seven civil judgment books,[3] four Native Court criminal cause books,[4] five Native Court civil cause books,[5] and one Native Court general note book.[6]

1. Civil and Criminal Cases in Nsukka Division Native Courts in Which Ahebi Participated, 1918–1930

CIVIL CASES			
Member	President	Plaintiff	Witness
50	43	0	2

CRIMINAL CASES			
Member	President	Plaintiff	Witness
27	7	2	1

TOTAL CASES
132

2. Categories of Civil Cases in Nsukka Division Native Courts in Which Ahebi Participated, 1918–1930

DEBT DAMAGES		DISTURB-ING THE PEACE		DIVORCE AND ADULTERY		DOWRY		PAWNAGE		LAND DISPUTE		TOTAL CASES
M[1]	P[2]	M	P	M	P	M	P	M	P	M	P	
24	14	3	4	13	7	2	15	2	1	8	4	97

Notes
1. Member
2. President

3. Categories of Criminal Cases in Nsukka Division Native Courts in Which Ahebi Participated, 1918–1930

CONTEMPT/ CIVIL DISOBE-DIENCE		DEBT		THEFT/ FALSE REPRE-SENTA-TION		ASSAULT		LAND DISPUTE		POISON		WRONG-FUL ARREST		TOTAL CASES
M[1]	P[2]	M	P	M	P	M	P	M	P	M	P	M	P	
1/7	0/1	1	0	5/1	1/1	8	2	3	0	0	1	1	0	33

Notes
1. Member
2. President

From these two tables, we can see that from 1918 to 1930, Chief Ahebi oversaw an almost equal number of debt and damages (38 cases) cases as divorce, adultery, and dowry cases (37 cases). The tables also tell us that Ahebi participated in many more civil cases (97) than criminal cases (33) during the same time period.

4. Criminal Cases in Which Ahebi Participated as a Member of the Nsukka Division Native Court, 1918–1930

CASE NO.	CATEGORY	RULING	AHEBI'S ROLE VIS-À-VIS THE NATIVE COUNCIL
56/21	Debt	Defendant guilty	Member
165/21	Contempt	Defendant guilty	Member
174/21	Theft/forced imprisonment	Defendant guilty	Member
82/21	Civil disobedience	Defendant guilty	Member
85/21	Theft	Defendant guilty	Member
87/21	Theft	Defendants not guilty	Member
91/21	Assault	Defendant guilty	Member
89/21	Land dispute	Data missing	Member
102/21	Theft	Defendant guilty	Member
101/21	Civil disobedience	Defendant guilty	Member
106/21	Civil disobedience	Defendant guilty	Member
108/21	Land dispute	Data missing	Member
101/22	Assault	Defendant guilty	Member
102/22	Theft/	Defendant guilty	Member
104/22	False representation	Defendant not guilty	Member
107/22	Assault	Case dismissed	Member
110/22	Theft	Defendant guilty	Member
114/22	Land dispute	Defendant guilty	Member
120/22	Assault	Defendant guilty	Member
121/22	Assault	Defendant not guilty	Member
125/22	Theft	Defendant not guilty	Plaintiff
128/22	Civil disobedience	Defendant guilty	Member
132/22	Assault	Defendant not guilty	Member
134/22	Assault with poison	Defendant not guilty	Plaintiff
139/22	Assault	Defendant guilty	Member

CASE NO.	CATEGORY	RULING	AHEBI'S ROLE VIS-À-VIS THE NATIVE COUNCIL
160/22	Wrongful arrest	Defendant not guilty; wrongful arrest	Member
159/22	Civil disobedience	Data missing	Member
164/22	Assault	Defendant guilty	Member
169/22	Assault	Defendant guilty	President
170/22	Theft	Defendant guilty	President
142/22	Civil disobedience	Case withdrawn	President
167–68/22	Assault with poison	Defendant not guilty	President
171/22	False representation	Defendant guilty	President
172/22	Theft	Defendant guilty	President
164/21	Civil disobedience	Defendant guilty	President
59/30	Contempt	Defendant guilty	Testified against defendant

5. Civil Cases in Which Ahebi Participated as a
Member of Nsukka Division Native Court, 1918–1930

CASE NO.	CATEGORY	FINDING	AHEBI'S ROLE ON NATIVE COUNCIL
31/22	Divorce or adultery	For plaintiff	Member
33/22	Land dispute	For plaintiff	Member
32/22	Debt damages; divorce or adultery; theft	Not Guilty. Case dismissed.	Member
53/22	Debt damages	For plaintiff	Member
66/22	Disturbing the peace; divorce or adultery	For plaintiff	Member
67/22	Pawnage[1]	For plaintiff	Member
62/22	Land dispute	For plaintiff	Member
70/22	Divorce or adultery	For plaintiff	Member
69/22	Debt damages	For plaintiff	Member
75	Disturbing the peace	For defendants. Case dismissed.	Member
84/22	Divorce or adultery	For plaintiff	Member
94/22	Divorce or adultery	For plaintiff	Member
100/22	Land dispute	Case adjourned	Member
106/22	Land dispute	For plaintiff	Member
38/22	Debt damages	For plaintiff	President
68/22	Land	Settled[2]	President
110/22	Dowry	For plaintiff	President
107/22	Dowry	For defendant	President
113/22	Dowry	For plaintiff	President
111/22	Dowry	For plaintiff	President
117/22	Dowry	Data incomplete	President
114/22	Dowry	For plaintiff	President
115/22	Debt damages	For defendant	President
116/22	Dowry	For defendant	President
121/22	Dowry	For plaintiff	President

CASE NO.	CATEGORY	FINDING	AHEBI'S ROLE ON NATIVE COUNCIL
80/22	Debt damages	Dismissed	President
101/22	Land dispute	Dismissed	President
123/22	Divorce or adultery	Settled out of court	President
127/22	Debt damages	For plaintiff	President
126/22	Debt damages	For plaintiff	President
112/22	Dowry	For plaintiff	President
130/22	Divorce or adultery	For defendant	President
128/22	Debt damages	For plaintiff	President
124/22	Debt damages	Settled out of court	President
129/22	Divorce or adultery	For defendant	President
132/22	Divorce or adultery	For defendant	President
125/22	Dowry	For defendant	President
131/22	Disturbing the peace	For defendant	President
134/22	Divorce or adultery	For plaintiff	President
140/22	Debt damages	For plaintiff	President
139/22	Divorce or adultery	For defendant	President
89, 90, 91, 92/22	Land dispute	For plaintiff	President
97, 98, 99/22	Land dispute	For defendant	President
133/22	Dowry	For plaintiff	President
137/22	Debt damages	For plaintiff	President
138/22	Disturbing the peace	For plaintiff	President
142/22	Debt damages	For plaintiff	President
145/22	Divorce or adultery	For plaintiff	President
143/22	Disturbing the peace	For plaintiff	President
144/22	Disturbing the peace	For defendant	President
61, 61/23	Land dispute	For defendant	Member
79, 78/23	Land dispute	For Plaintiff	Member

CASE NO.	CATEGORY	FINDING	AHEBI'S ROLE ON NATIVE COUNCIL
80/24	Disturbing the peace	For defendant	Witness
1226/23 and 3/24	Debt damages	For plaintiff	Member
99/24	Land Dispute	For plaintiff	Member
112/24	Debt damages	For defendant	President
150/24	Debt damages	For plaintiff	President
154/24	Debt damages	Settled	President
155/24	Debt damages	Settled	President
177/24	Dowry	For plaintiff	President
180/24	Dowry	For plaintiff	President
181/24	Dowry	For plaintiff	President
174/24	Dowry; pawnage	For plaintiff	President
66/24	Theft	Defendant to swear an oath	Witness
185/24	Dowry	For defendant	Member
250/24	Divorce or adultery	For defendant	Member
237/24	Debt damages	Data incomplete	Witness
246/24	Debt damages	For defendant	Member
271/24	Debt damages	For defendant	Member
250	Debt damages; dowry	For plaintiff	Member
258	Land	Data incomplete	Member
291	Dowry	For plaintiff	Member
284	Debt damages; divorce, adultery	For plaintiff	Member
306	Debt damages	For plaintiff	Member
282/24	Dowry	Struck	Member
257/24	Divorce or adultery	Struck	Member
228/24	Debt damages	Struck	Member

CASE NO.	CATEGORY	FINDING	AHEBI'S ROLE ON NATIVE COUNCIL
210/24	Dowry	Struck	Member
156/24	Debt damages; dowry	Struck	Member
149/24	Divorce or adultery	Struck	Member
123/24	Pawnage	Struck	Member
314/24	Divorce or adultery	For plaintiff	Member
310/24	Debt damages	For plaintiff	Member
356/24	Debt damages	For plaintiff	Member
363/24	Divorce or adultery	For defendant	Member
342, 343/24 (reopened)	Divorce or adultery; pawnage	For defendant	Member
368/24	Disturbing the peace	Dismissed	Member
373/24	Debt damages	For plaintiff	Member
378/24	Debt damages	For plaintiff	Member
37524	Debt damages; disturbing the peace	For plaintiff	Member
374/24	Debt damages	Dismissed	Member
392/24	Debt damages	For plaintiff	Member
397/24	Debt damages	For defendant	Member
366/24	Debt damages	Settled	Member
372/24	Debt damages	Settled	Member
318/24	Debt damages	Struck	Member
329/24	Debt damages	Struck	Member
330/24	Debt damages	Struck	Member

Notes

1. In pawnage, a person is pawned to repay a debt. It is a form of "slavery."

2. "Settled" (as opposed to "settled out of court") means that the warrant chiefs made a determination on their own and did not find for either party.

GLOSSARY OF CHRONOLOGICAL TERMS

One of the contributions of this book to history is its adoption of a uniquely African system of dating—a system that privileges periods of time and not particular dates. When possible, however, I have used traditional chronological methods of dating as well. Listed below are some of the terms I have used in this book to date history:

interwar period: a period of great fighting between Nsukka communities to secure more land for themselves that occurred primarily during the seventeenth century, intensifying during and after the abolition of the slave trade.

mgbapu Ahebi: "Ahebi's flight." In this biography, I use the phrase *oge mgbapu Ahebi* to delineate the period of time roughly from 1895 to 1916, when Ahebi ran away from home to Igalaland. The word *mgbapu* means "running away" or "taking flight." It is used to describe the action of a person running away from their home and community.

oge: "during the time of"

oge Ahebi: "during the time of Ahebi." This term is used to represent the time of Ahebi's life after she was made female headman, female warrant chief, and coronated female king—events that were so incredulous that they changed the way that history was recalled in Enugu-Ezike. That collective memory privileges an overidentification with everything Ahebi during these periods. According to Gregorian calendar dating, this period would commence around 1916–1917 and end after King Ahebi's death in 1948.

oge Attah-Obaje: during the reign of Attah-Obaje, 1926–1945.

oge gbo gbo: "the early, early times" or "a long, long time ago." I use the phrase to refer to the periods of time that were many centuries ago, such as in the time of creation

oge gbo: "during the early days" or "a long time ago."

oge ntiji egbe: "the time that the guns were destroyed." During the annexation of the Igbo interior, the defeated "natives" were forced out of fear of injury or death to bring out their guns and stockpile them in front of the commanding British patrol officer, who took immense pleasure in reducing the stashes before him to burned rubble.

oge nwatakili: the time of childhood.

oge oso Omabe: during the run of the Omabe masquerade, which occurred once every two years and symbolized the return of the dead to life. Omabe was the most powerful masked spirit in Enugu-Ezike. The masquerade played a role in the arenas of political leadership and organization; it was part of the executive-legislative process and was actively used as an agent of social control.

oge otikpo: "during the time of the destroyer," the language the Enugu-Ezike people used to refer to the colonial government. I use the phrase specifically to denote the early colonial period, the period of pacification and consolidation of territory under the British.

The vast majority of the words on this list are Igbo; I indicate which ones are not in parentheses. Many of the titles (and other words) used in Nsukka Division are ancient and borrow from neighboring dialects; thus, the literal meanings are not always apparent.

Afo: the third day of the week in both Igbo and Igala

attah (Igala): literally, "father," king

attama (Igala): literally, "lord of many," priest

be ikwu nne Ahebi: the town where Ahebi's mother was born

chi: a personal spirit that protects and guides a person throughout life

dibias: medicine men

Ede (Igala): the second day of week

ego nwanyi: bride-price or as used in this biography, child-price.

Eke: the first day of the Igbo week and the fourth day of the Igala week

ewo (Igala): goat

ewu (Igbo): goat

fulu efu: got lost

Gabaidu: the *attah*'s praise-name; the respectful way to address the *attah*

ife di egwu: thing of great incredulity

Igba afa: to seek out the divine; to divine the root of their problems

igberema: a person dedicated to a deity in a marriage-type relationship as a living sacrifice

Igbo enwe eze: the Igbo have no kings

igo mma ogo: becoming the in-law of a deity; a type of spiritual "slavery" in which the individual is tied to a deity in a marriage-type relationship

igu afa: act or performance of naming

ikpo: "to call" somebody or something or "to peg" something to the ground

nkowa: the introduction

nkwado: the preparation

Nkwo: the fourth day of the Igbo week

nna anyi: our father

nnenne: literally "my mother's mother," but the term is not often used to refer to that relationship; it is instead used as a pet name, a name that a mother often bestows on a favorite daughter or a niece on an aunt

nwada: daughter [of the lineage]

nwatakili walu anya: a difficult and conceited girl or boy who does not listen to reason

o be taa na o chie: if things begin to get better today (i.e., immediately) or (even better) if identified problems are solved today, that would be sufficient

o gbapu: he or she took flight

ogba afas or *ndi ogba afa:* diviners

ogu umunwanyi: war of the women

oje gba afa: to trace the origin of ill fortunes; sought out the expertise of a diviner

okanga: *okanga* drums are two ended drums made out of rare animal skin, and played only by men; *egwu okanga* is one of the oldest and most prestigious traditional musical forms in Enugu-Ezike and was performed by and for men of substance in the community.

omenani: literally that which the goddess Ani says is right or wrong; the law of the land

onye elugwu: the hill dweller

onye obia: visitor or guest

onyishi: oldest man in the community

Otikpo: the destroyer

Oye: the second day of the week

umu: children of

umunna: the children of a common forefather

umunne: the children of one mother

umunne na ununna: the children of a common forefather and the children of one mother

utaba: snuff

walu anya: a wayward person

NOTES

Ekene / Acknowledgments

1. After the publication of my first book, *Farmers, Traders, Warriors, and Kings: Female Power and Authority in Northern Igboland, 1900–1960* (Portsmouth, N.H.: Heinemann, 2005), Professor A. E. Afigbo wrote the following e-mail message to me: "Dear Nwando, Greetings. First this mail comes to wish you A Happy and Prosperous 2006. I am sure it will see you and your affairs to greater and still greater heights; [i]n the second place I would like you to know that I have now had a detailed look at your book on women in Nsukka. Not only did I find it interesting, I also found it elucidating. I can see that scholars have already put it in the pigeonhole for gender studies. Perhaps you went into the study to make a contribution in that field. There is no doubt that that ambition was more than fully achieved. From my perspective, however, its special merit lies in the field of Igbo Studies. Long after gender studies would have followed similar intellectual fashions into the garbage heap of History as another passing cliché, your book will continue to stand out as one of the few works which bring out how women actually lived their lives in Igbo society. This is not because you gave Igbo women voice as Professor Ekechi suggested, but because you made manifest the voice they have always had. You highlighted a reality that had always been there but which many before you were unable to see or highlight. Congratulations!!" A. E. Afigbo, e-mail correspondence, January 2, 2006.

Nkwado / The Preparation

1. C. K. Meek, *Law and Authority in a Nigeria Tribe: A Study of Indirect Rule* (London: Oxford University Press, 1937), 158.

2. In a recent conversation, Claire Robertson brought to my attention the existence of a Kikuyu woman chief, Wangu wa Makeni, whom the British recognized as chief in 1901. Wangu was said to have passed away in 1936. As chief she was particularly emphatic about education and farming and helped establish the Church Missionary Society in her area. She was never referred to as warrant chief, however, nor did she seem to have the range of responsibilities—for instance, she did not sit in judgment of cases as a member or president of a court—that the British-imposed warrant chief Ahebi did. Therefore, Wangu sounds more like a British-recognized headwoman. Many thanks to Claire Robertson for this information. Claire Robertson, telephone conversation with author, October 5, 2009. See also Evelyn K. Mungia and Joy Awori, eds., *Kenya Women Reflections* (Nairobi: Lear Publishing Company, 1984), viii–x.

3. See Judith Halberstam, *Female Masculinity* (Durham, N.C.: Duke University Press, 1998).

4. Ibid., xi.

5. Ibid., 4.

6. For more on this, see Nwando Achebe, "'And She Became a Man': King Ahebi Ugbabe in the History of Enugu-Ezike, Northern Igboland, 1880–1948," in *Men and Masculinities in Modern Africa*, ed. Stephan F. Miescher and Lisa A. Lindsay (Portsmouth, N.H.: Heinemann, 2003), 52–68.

7. See Judith Butler, *Gender Trouble: Feminism and the Subversion of Identity* (New York: Routledge, 1990); as well as Judith Butler, "Performative Acts and Gender Constitution: An Essay in Phenomenology and Feminist Theory," in *Performing Feminisms: Feminist Critical Theory and Theatre*, ed. Sue-Ellen Case (Baltimore, Md.: Johns Hopkins University Press, 1990), 270–282.

8. See Paulla A. Ebron, *Performing Africa* (Princeton, N.J.: Princeton University Press, 2002). Lisa A. Lindsey has also adapted the concept in *Working with Gender: Wage Labor and Social Change in Southwestern Nigeria* (Portsmouth, N.H.: Heinemann, 2003).

9. See Stephan Miescher, *Making Men in Ghana* (Bloomington: Indiana University Press, 2005) for a Ghana case study of this.

10. For Mandinka (Gambia) and Asante (Ghana) case studies, see Paulla A. Ebron, "Constituting Subjects through Performative Arts," in which she argues that gender is both "self-consciously and unself-consciously" performed and suggests that the notion of performativity of gender can illuminate our knowledge about social class, the "possibilities of development projects and global economic inequities." In *Africa After Gender,* ed. Catherine M. Cole, Takyiwaa Manuh, and Stephan F. Miescher (Bloomington: Indiana University Press, 2007), 171–190.

11. Male femininities can also be performed in Igboland, making men into female priestesses. For more on this, see Nwando Achebe, "'[T]he Real Rulers of [Nsukka] Town[s] are the Ancestors or Spirits . . . ': Understanding the Female Principle in Igbo Religion," in *Igbos in the Atlantic World*, ed. Toyin Falola and Matt Childs (Bloomington: Indiana University Press, forthcoming).

12. M. F. Smith, *Baba of Karo: A Woman of the Muslim Hausa* (London: Faber and Faber, Ltd. 1954).

13. It is interesting to note that even though *Baba of Karo* begins around 1890 and spans six decades, it largely ignores this important period in the history of Northern Nigeria because of the author's overconcentration on family matters such as marriages, divorces, births, and deaths.

14. See Margaret Strobel, *Muslim Women of Mombasa, 1890–1975* (New Haven, Conn.: Yale University Press, 1979); and Margaret Strobel and Sarah Mirza, *Three Swahili Women: Life Histories of Mombasa* (Bloomington: Indiana University Press, 1989).

15. Strobel and Mirza, *Three Swahili Women,* 3.

16. Jean Davison, *Voices of Mutira: Lives of Rural Gikuyu Women* (Boulder, Colo.: Lynne Rienner Publishers, 1989).

17. Marjorie Shostak, *Nisa: The Life and Words of a !Kung Woman* (New York: Vintage, 1981).

18. Belinda Bozzoli, *Women of Phokeng: Consciousness, Life Strategy, and Migrancy in South Africa, 1900–1983* (Portsmouth, N.H.: Heinemann, 1991).

19. Claire Robertson, *Sharing the Same Bowl: A Socioeconomic History of Women and Class in Accra, Ghana* (Ann Arbor: University of Michigan Press, 1990). Berida Ndambuki and Claire Robertson's *We Only Come Here to Struggle: Stories from Berida's Life* (Bloomington: Indiana University Press, 2000), is also worth mentioning. A treatment that straddles the gray area between autobiography and biography, it tells the story of Nairobi trader, Berida, documenting the trails of tribulations of her everyday life.

20. Marcia Wright, *Strategies of Slaves and Women: Life-Stories from East/Central Africa* (London: James Currey, 1993).

21. Patricia C. Romero, *Profiles in Diversity: Women in the New South Africa* (East Lansing: Michigan State University Press, 1998).

22. Clifton Crais and Pamela Schully, *Sara Baartman and the Hottentot Venus: A Ghost Story and a Biography* (Princeton, N.J.: Princeton University Press, 2008); and Rachel Holmes, *African Queen: The Real Life of the Hottentot Venus* (New York: Random House, 2007).

23. Wambui Otieno, *Mau Mau's Daughter: A Life History* (Boulder, Colo.: Lynne Rienner Publishers, 1998).

24. Mamphela Ramphele, *Across Boundaries: The Journey of a South African Woman Leader* (New York: The Feminist Press of CUNY, 1999).

25. Cheryl Johnson-Odim and Nina Mba, *For Women and the Nation: Funmilayo Ransome-Kuti of Nigeria* (Urbana: University of Illinois Press, 1997).

26. Susan Geiger, *TANU Women: Gender and Culture in the Making of Tanganyikan Nationalism, 1955–1965* (Portsmouth, N.H.: Heinemann, 1997).

27. Adelaide M. Cromwell, *An African Victorian Feminist: The Life and Times of Adelaide Smith Casely Hayford, 1868–1960* (Washington, D.C.: Howard University Press, 1992).

28. Of the numerous studies on Winnie Mandela, *Winnie Mandela: Part of My Soul Went with Him* (New York: W. W. Norton & Company, 1985) is the only narrative that Mandela wrote.

29. Wangari Maathi, *Unbowed: A Memoir* (New York: Vintage, 2007).

30. See Nwando Achebe, "The Day I 'Met' Ahebi Ugbabe, *Female* King of Enugu-Ezike, Nigeria," *Journal of Women's History* 21, no. 4 (Winter 2009): 134–137.

31. The working title for my dissertation at this point was "Farmers, Traders, Warriors and Wives: Women in Northern Igboland, 1900–1960."

32. My revised dissertation became *Farmers, Traders, Warriors, and Kings: Female Power and Authority in Northern Igboland, 1900–1960*. I argue that one only tells part of the history if one focuses exclusively on the human physical realm. In order to tell the complete history of Igbo women one must focus on both the human and spiritual realms, hence my adoption of the term "female principle" to encompass all female activity in Igboland.

33. V. K. Johnson, "Intelligence Report on the People of Enugu-Ezike, Nsukka Division, Onitsha Province" paragraph 22, OP 1071 ONDIST 12/1/709, National Archives of Nigeria, Enugu (hereafter NAE). See also paragraphs 25 and 26 for more information about King Ahebi.

34. A. E. Afigbo, "Women in Nigerian History," in *Women in Nigerian Economy*, ed. Martin O. Ijere (Enugu, Nigeria: Acena Publishers, 1991), 35–36. See also a three-line reference to her in A. E. Afigbo, "Igbo Women, Colonialism and Socio-Economic Change," paper presented at the Seminar on Igbo Women in Socio-Economic Change, Better Life Program for Rural Women, Imo State Wing, Owerri, and Institute of African Studies, University of Nigeria, Nsukka, April 3–5, 1990, 3.

35. In my work, I used oral history to uncover Igbo and Igala people's voices and generate new insights about their experiences of themselves. I created spaces in which Igbo and Igala women and men felt safe to make serious contributions instead of assuming passive roles in the investigative procedure. The process was indeed

collaborative (hence my use of the term collaborator or oral history collaborator), encouraging a true exchange of ideas and experiences based on mutual respect, support, and accountability. For more on this, see "Nwando Achebe—Daughter, Wife, and Guest—A Researcher at the Crossroads," *Journal of Women's History* 14, no. 3 (Autumn 2002): 9–31.

36. Abodo Nwa Idoko was in his mid-80s; therefore I used the expression *nna anyi* as a sign of respect.

37. Abodo Nwa Idoko, interview with author, Ikpamodo, Enugu-Ezike, Anambra (now Enugu) State, Nigeria, September 26, 1998. The vast majority of the interviews conducted were in Igbo. I transcribed this and all other translations of the Igbo interviews.

38. In my translation of this conversation from Igbo to English, I adopted some decidedly Nigerian idioms. Nigerians use the term "wonderful" to express incredulity and "you have tried" to express the fact that one has done very well.

39. Abodo Nwa Idoko, interview (1998).

40. See chapter 2 for a discussion of *mgbapu Ahebi*.

41. In his chapter "The Dialogue between Academic and Community History in Nigeria," E. J. Alagoa confronts similar issues of community silence occasioned by the community's need to project a particular history, an official history. It deals with contestations arising between himself and members of that community's association, with whom he had teamed up to write the history. Alagoa attempts to answer the question "How can the scholar remain faithful to professional canon of objectivity while maintaining a discourse responsible to local needs and demands?" In *African Words, African Voices: Critical Practices in Oral History,* ed. Luise White, Stephan F. Miescher, and David William Cohen (Bloomington: Indiana University Press, 2001), 91–102.

42. In "Lives, Histories, and Sites of Recollection," Tamara Giles-Vernick describes her unsuccessful early attempts to elicit information from her Mpiemu-speaking subjects. She had to rethink and expand her approach to gathering information to include a constellation of "sites of recollection" (an agricultural field, a "site" of burial), all of which invoked historical memory. See Tamara Giles-Vernick, "Lives, Histories, and Sites of Recollection," in *African Words, African Voices: Critical Practices in Oral History,* ed. Luise White, Stephan F. Miescher, and David William Cohen (Bloomington: Indiana University Press, 2001), 194–213.

43. Boniface Abugu, interview with author, tape recording, Umuida, Enugu-Ezike, Enugu State, Nigeria, October 4, 1998.

44. For more about the relationship between the indigenous researcher and her community of research, see Achebe, "Nwando Achebe—Daughter, Wife, and Guest"; and Chi-Chi Undie, "My Father's Daughter: Becoming a 'Real' Anthropologist among the Ubang of Southeast Nigeria," *Anthropology Matters* 9, no. 1 (2007): 1–9.

45. For the first time in my fifteen years of experience in fieldwork research, I was forced to use the services of an interpreter because I had no knowledge of the Igala language. The experience made me appreciate the importance of being able to understand everything that was being said. Many times I felt lost, as though I could not properly ask follow-up questions; moreover, I was not sure that the translator was providing translations of everything that was being said. In fact, many times I had the unsettling feeling that he was simply summarizing information, something that I attempted to counter by having another Igala person do the transcriptions.

46. Gabaidu is the Attah's praise-name. It is the respectful way to address the *attah*. Mr. Ocheni suggested that I address Attah Obaje in this way.

47. Nwando Achebe, handwritten copy of letter to the *attah*, rough copy, research notes, July 5, 2007.

48. I asked for clarification on whether Ahebi was coronated king or queen, and I was assured that she was in fact made king. I discuss the historical precedent that would explain this coronation in chapter 2.

49. Stephanie Newell, *The Forger's Tale: The Search for Odeziaku* (Athens: Ohio University Press, 2006), 10.

50. The rich literature on homosexuality in Africa includes the following studies: Marc Epprecht, *Unspoken Fact: A History of Homosexualities in Africa* (Zimbabwe: GALZ, 2008); Marc Epprecht, *Heterosexual Africa? The History of an Idea from the Age of Exploration to the Age of AIDS* (Athens: Ohio University Press, 2008); Mark Gevisser and Edwin Cameron, eds., *Defiant Desire: Gay and Lesbian Lives in South Africa* (New York: Routledge, 1995); William J. Spurlin, *Imperialism within the Margins: Queer Representation and the Politics of Culture in Southern Africa* (New York: Palgrave Macmillan, 2006); Neville Hoad, *African Intimacies: Race, Homosexuality, and Globalization* (Minneapolis: University of Minnesota Press, 2007); Will Roscoe and Stephen O. Murray, *Boy-Wives and Female Husbands: Studies of African Homosexualities* (New York: Palgrave Macmillan, 2001).

51. Filomina Chioma Steady, "An Investigative Framework for Gender Research in Africa in the New Millennium," in *African Gender Scholarship: Concepts, Methodologies, and Paradigms,* ed. Signe Arnfred, Bibi Bakare-Yusuf, and Edward Waswa Kisiang'ani (Dakar, Senegal: CODESIRA, 2004), 50.

52. I have spoken about my audience in some of my other works. I will not bore my readers by rehashing those arguments. Suffice it to say, however, that I write for several audiences, but my primary audience is the people who own the stories I am telling. For more on this, see Achebe, "Nwando Achebe—Daughter, Wife, and Guest"; and Nwando Achebe, *Farmers, Traders, Warriors, and Kings: Female Power and Authority in Northern Igboland, 1900–1960* (Portsmouth, N.H.: Heinemann, 2005), 1–22.

53. For more on this, see Nwando Achebe and Bridget Teboh, "Dialoguing Women," in *Africa After Gender?* ed. Catherine M. Cole, Stephan F. Miescher, and Takyiwaa Manuh (Bloomington: Indiana University Press, 2007), 91–113. See also Achebe, *Farmers, Traders, Warriors and Kings,* 28–29.

54. Christie Chinwe Achebe, Achebe House, Bard College, Annandale-on-Hudson, N.Y., handwritten communication with author, December 22, 2008.

55. A. E. Afigbo, "Oral Tradition and the History of Segmentary Societies," *History in Africa* 12 (1985): 4–5.

56. Oliefi Ugwu-Ogili, interview with author, digital voice recording, Umuida, Enugu-Ezike, Enugu State, Nigeria, July 13, 2007.

57. Augustine Abutu, interview with author, digital voice recording, Unadu, Enugu State, Nigeria, July 15, 2007.

58. See *Mmechi* /The Conclusion for a discussion of my encounter with Utubi.

59. Like many young men and women who lived with Ahebi, Utubi addresses her as his mother, a sign of respect.

60. Priest Utubi, a.k.a. Francis Idoko, interview with author, digital voice recording, Unadu, Enugu State, Nigeria, July 14, 2007.

61. Attah-Obaje is either referred to as Attah-Obaje Ocheje or Attah-Obaje. They are the same person. For ease of understanding, in my own writing I will refer to him as simply Attah-Obaje.

62. Alice Akogu (formerly Ahebi), interview with author, digital voice recording. Ofante, Kogi State, Nigeria, October 5, 1998.

63. J. S. Boston, *The Igala Kingdom* (Ibadan: Nigerian Institute of Social and Economic Research and Oxford University Press, 1968), 57; "Genealogy of Attah Kingship," in *The Golden Jubilee Celebration of the Enthronement of His Royal Majesty Alhaji Aliyu O. Obaje* (Lagos: Attah Igala and Chancellor, University of Lagos, n.d.), 19; P. E. Okwoli, *The History of the Fifty Years Reign of the Attah Igala, Alhaji Aliyu Ocheja Obaje, 1956–2006* (Enugu, Nigeria: Snaap Press, 2006), 38; Yusufu Etu, *Igala History in Questions and Answers* (Jos, Nigeria: New Concepts Incorporated Book House, 2001), 33.

64. See earlier discussion of my interaction with the present Attah Aliyu Obaje and my interview with the sister of the Attah-Obaje (senior). I also benefited from the "official" history of the Igala kingdom, which was commissioned by Attah Aliyu Obaje; at least two members of the Igala monarchy consulted that document on my behalf.

65. "Genealogy of Attah Kingship," 19; Okwoli, *The History of the Fifty Years Reign,* 39; Etu, *Igala History in Questions and Answers,* 33.

66. Prince Idakwo Ameh Oboni, *Ameh the Great* (Ibadan: Intec Printers, 1989), 124; Gertrude Ojochide Onogu, "The Place of Princess Inikpi in the Igala Traditional Belief System of Kogi State" (Diploma, University of Nigeria, Nsukka, 1996), 37.

67. In the next chapter, I lay out the periodization that I have used throughout this book. Much like my first book, it follows conceptualizations of time from an indigenous point of view.

68. The Native Court cause books are divided into civil and criminal books. Each is a compilation, in index form, of all cases heard in Nsukka Division during the period 1923–1933.

69. These books contain short notes of specific cases heard from 1923 to 1933.

70. These include Native Court Criminal Cause Books 17/1/1, 17/1/2, 17/1/4, 17/1/5 and 17/1/6 (covering the years 1934–1946), Nsukka Protectorate Criminal Court Book 17/1/3 (covering the years 1936–1943), and Native Court Civil Cause Books 18/1/1, 18/1/2, 18/1/3, 18/1/4, 18/1/5, 18/1/6, and 18/1/7 (covering the years 1925–1945).

71. The five court areas in Nsukka Division were Adani Native Court, Eha Amufu Native Court, Obolo Native Court, Opi Native Court, and Ahebi's own Enugu-Ezike Native Court.

72. The totals represented all criminal and civil case judgment books in Nsukka Division. The judgment books that were relevant to my study covered the years 1917–1954, the period when Ahebi was warrant chief, up to a few years after her death.

73. These are Criminal Judgment Book 1925–26, NSUDIV 14/1/67; Criminal Judgment Book 1925–30, NSUDIV 14/1/68; Criminal Judgment Book 1928, NSUDIV 14/1/77; Criminal Judgment Book 1929, NSUDIV 14/1/79; Criminal Judgment Book 1929–30, NSUDIV 14/1/80; Criminal Judgment Book 1929–30, NSUDIV 14/1/81; Criminal Judgment Book 1937–43, NSUDIV 14/1/87. All in NAE.

74. Criminal Judgment Book 1943–54, NSUDIV 14/1/88; Civil Judgment Book 1923–29, NSUDIV 16/1/24; and Civil Judgment Book 1926–27, NSUDIV 16/1/28. Both in NAE.

Nkowa / The Introduction

1. J. Barmby, "Intelligence Report on the Villages of Ukehe, Onyoho, Ochima, Ikolo, Aku, Ohebe, Umuna, Ngalakpu, Umunku and Idoha, Nsukka Division," 5, OP 1029 ONPROF 8/1/4724, 1934, NAE.

2. Ibid., 5.

3. In fact, one can argue that the nuclear family does not really exist in Igboland. The basic family structure is the extended family—a husband, a wife, their children, and their grown children's spouses and their children as well as the original couples' siblings and cousins. I use the term "family" in this book to delineate both the rare nuclear family and the more common extended family.

4. C. K. Meek, *An Ethnographical Report on the Peoples of Nsukka Division—Onitsha Province* (Enugu: Government Printer, 1930), 5–6, paragraph 15.

5. C. K. Meek, *Law and Authority in a Nigeria Tribe: A Study of Indirect Rule* (London: Oxford University Press, 1937), 88.

6. Ibid., 89.

7. The interwar period refers to the period of great fighting between Nsukka communities to secure more land for themselves. It occurred primarily during the seventeenth century, intensifying during and after the abolition of the slave trade.

8. See Sylviane A. Diouf, "Introduction," in Diouf, *Fighting the Slave Trade: West African Strategies* (Athens: Ohio University Press, 2003), ix–xxvii.

9. See Nwando Achebe, *Farmers, Traders, Warriors, and Kings: Female Power and Authority in Northern Igboland, 1900–1960* (Portsmouth, N.H.: Heinemann Social History Series, 2005), 54–80; Nwando Achebe, "*Igo Mma Ogo:* The Adoro Goddess, Her Wives and Challengers—Influences on the Reconstruction of Alor-Uno, Northern Igboland, 1890–1994," *Journal of Women's History* 14, no. 4 (Winter 2003): 83–104; and Nwando Achebe, "When Deities Marry: Indigenous 'Slave' Systems Expanding and Metamorphosing in the Igbo Hinterland," in *African Systems of Slavery*, ed. Stephanie Beswick and Jay Spaulding (Lawrenceville, N.J.: African World Press, 2010), 105–133.

10. In my writing, I put the term "slave" in quotes, because the institution of slavery in Igboland was so much more benign than its New World counterpart. Achebe, "*Igo Mma Ogo*" and Achebe, "When Deities Marry" delve into the "slave"/master relationship as it exists in Nsukka Division.

11. For more about colonialism as a gendered and gendering process, see Nancy Rose Hunt, Tessie P. Liu, and Jean Quataert, eds., *Gendered Colonialisms in African History* (Malden, Mass.: Blackwell Publishers, 1997); and Catherine M. Cole, Takyiwaa Manuh, and Stephan F. Miescher, eds., *Africa After Gender?* (Bloomington: Indiana University Press, 2007); Oyèrónké Oyewùmí, ed., *African Gender Studies: A Reader* (New York: Palgrave Macmillan, 2005); Andrea Cornwall, ed., *Readings in Gender in Africa* (Bloomington: Indiana University Press, 2005); Jean Allman, Susan Geiger, and Nakanyike Musisi, eds., *Women in African Colonial Histories* (Bloomington: Indiana University Press, 2002); and Dorothy L. Hodgson and Sheryl A. McCurdy, eds., *"Wicked Women" and the Reconfiguration of Gender in Africa* (Portsmouth, N.H.: Heinemann, 2001).

12. See Nwando Achebe, "Murder in Ochima: Priestess Mgbafor-Ezira, Nwachukwu and the Circumstances Leading Up to the Death of Major G. L. D.

Rewcastle," in *Emergent Themes and Methods in African Studies: Essays in Honor of Adiele Eberechukwu Afigbo,* ed. Toyin Falola and Adam Paddock (New Jersey: African World Press, 2008), 249–279.

13. See Ifi Amadiume, *Male Daughters, Female Husbands: Gender and Sex in an African Society* (London: Zed Books, 1987).

14. For more on male priestesses, see Nwando Achebe, "'[T]he Real Rulers of [Nsukka] Town[s] are the Ancestors or Spirits . . . ': Understanding the Female Principle in Igbo Religion," in *Igbos in the Atlantic World,* ed. Toyin Falola and Matt Childs (Bloomington: Indiana University Press, forthcoming).

15. The Igbo are surrounded by the Edo, the Igala, the Ibibio, the Ijaw, and the Idoma—nations that all have kingship institutions.

16. Let me note here that the Igbo did have the title *eze,* which was merely a title without any of the autocratic-type individualized power that real kings had in kingship systems. They also had a religious king (*eze nri*) who had more prohibitions levied on him than normal citizens. For instance, he was not allowed to eat or sleep outside his compound and he was forced to plant his own yams. Leaders in Igbo society were therefore merely symbols of communal power and authority. What was more, they were bound by an unwritten constitutional framework called *omenani* (taboos and observances), which imposed checks and balances on a leader's power. For more on this, see T. Uzodinma Nwala, *Igbo Philosophy* (Lagos, Nigeria: Literamed Publications, 1985), 172; and Ikenna Nzimiro, *Chieftaincy and Politics in Four Niger States* (London: Frank Cass, 1970), xvi and 253. Evidence was also gathered from Chinua Achebe, telephone conversation with author, October 13, 1999.

17. Wilfred Ogara, interview with author, tape recording, Umuida, Enugu-Ezike, Enugu State, November 25, 1996; Amos Abugu, interview with author, tape recording, Umuida, Enugu-Ezike, Enugu State, October 4, 1998; Boniface Abugu, interview with author, tape recording, Umuida, Enugu-Ezike, Enugu State, October 4, 1998.

18. See Nwando Achebe, "'And She Became a Man': King Ahebi Ugbabe in the History of Enugu-Ezike, Northern Igboland, 1880–1948," in *Men and Masculinities in Modern Africa,* ed. Stephan F. Miescher and Lisa A. Lindsay (Portsmouth, N.H.: Heinemann, 2003), 61–63; and Achebe, *Farmers, Traders, Warriors and Kings,* 213–215.

19. A. O. Onyeneke, *The Dead among the Living: Masquerades in Igbo Society* (Nimo, Nigeria: Holy Ghost Congregation, Province of Nigeria, and Asele Institute, 1987), 78.

20. For various discussions on men's roles in masquerade cults in West Africa, see Jean M. Borgatti, "Okpella Masking Traditions," *African Arts* 9, no. 4 (July 1976): 24–33, 90–91; Polly Richards, "Masques Dogons in a Changing World," *African Arts* 38, no. 4 (Winter 2005): 46–93; Elisabeth L. Cameron, "Men Portraying Women: Representations in African Masks," *African Arts* 31, no. 2 (Spring 1998): 72–79; and Frances Harding, "To Present the Self in a Special Way: Disguise and Display in Tiv Kwagh-hir Performance," *African Arts* 31 (Winter 1998): 56–67.

21. *Oge* in Igbo language means "during the time of." *Oge Ahebi* means "during the time of Ahebi." This phrase will be used to indicate the time of Ahebi's life, especially after her appointment as female headman and female chief and her coronation as female king. According to the Gregorian calendar, this period would commence around 1916–1917 and end after King Ahebi's death in 1948.

22. *Oge gbo gbo* translates into "the early, early times" or, put differently, "a long, long time ago." This phrase will be used in reference to the periods of time that were a long time ago, such as in the time of creation.

23. *Oge otikpo* will be used to denote the time during the colonial period. Specifically, it translates into "during the time of the destroyer." The "destroyer" was what the Enugu-Ezike people called the colonial government. This phrase will be used specifically to denote the early colonial period—the period of pacification and consolidation of territory under the British.

24. The history of census taking in Nigeria is a long and interesting one. The first census was taken in Lagos, Nigeria, in 1866; the next one was in 1869. Beginning in 1871, Nigerian censuses were taken every ten years until 1931. The 1881, 1891, 1911, 1921, and 1931 censuses occurred *oge Ahebi*. However, the 1881, 1891, and 1901 censuses were limited to the Colony of Lagos; the census did not cover the entire region until the amalgamation of Lagos with Southern Nigeria. The first national census was taken in 1911. World War II interrupted the census counts, but they restarted in 1952–1953 and were taken every ten years thereafter. See Femi Mimiko, "Census in Nigeria: The Politics and the Imperative of Depoliticization," *African and Asian Studies* 5, no. 1 (2006): 10; and P. K. Makinwa-Adebusoye, "History and Growth of the Nigerian Census," president's address delivered at the 7th Annual Conference of the Population Association of Nigeria, University of Lagos, Lagos, December 6–10, 1988.

25. "Nigerian Census of 1911, Okwoga Division, J. Watt, Esquire, Officer in Charge," available at www.nigerianstat.gov.ng/1911_census_archive/00002809.xls (retrieved February 15, 2008).

26. V. K. Johnson, "Intelligence Report on the People of Enugu-Ezike, Nsukka Division, Onitsha Province," 3, paragraph 12, OP 1071 ONDIST 12/1/709 1934, NAE.

27. Michael Idoko, interview with author, tape recording, Umuida, Enugu-Ezike, Enugu State, November 25, 1996.

28. Ibid.; Samuel Ezeja interview with author, tape recording, Umuida, Enugu-Ezike, Enugu State, November 25, 1996; Bernard Ameh interview with author, tape recording, Unadu, Enugu-Ezike, Enugu State, September 29, 1998; Fabian Azegba interview with author, tape recording, Umuida, Enugu-Ezike, Enugu State, October 2, 1998; Amos Abugu interview (1998); Boniface Abugu interview (1998).

29. W. H. Lloyd, "Annual Report on the Onitsha Province for the Year 1934," 40, paragraph 9, CO 583/204/BOX, The National Archives (hereafter TNA).

30. "Annual Report N[sukka] D[ivision]," 15, number 45, NS 795 NSUDIV 8/1/190 1937, NAE.

31. See Federal Office of Statistics, "Census District NO: 305302, Census District Name: Nsukka North," in *Population Census of Nigeria, 1963*, vol. 1, part 4, *Census of Population, Eastern Nigeria, 1963* (Lagos: Federal Census Office, [1964–1965?]), 132.

32. A. E. Okorafor, "The Population of the Nsukka Area," in *The Nsukka Environment,* ed. G. E. K. Ofomata (Enugu, Nigeria: Fourth Dimension Publishers, 1978), 123.

33. The word *umu* means "children of." Therefore *umuitodo* means "the children of Itodo."

34. Patrick Odo Agashi, "Pre-Colonial Warfare in Enugu-Ezike" (B.A. thesis, History Department, University of Nigeria, Nsukka, June 1979), 6; Gloria Nkeiru

Apeh, "The Traditional Oracle and Culture in Enugu-Ezike" (Diploma Programme/ Certificate, Department of Religion, University of Nigeria, Nsukka, 1997), 1.

35. In 1963, Umuida had a population of 8,328 people. The other village where Ahebi's clout was felt was Ogurte, which had a population of 1,071 in 1963. Federal Office of Statistics, "Census District NO: 305302, Census District Name: Nsukka North," in *Population Census of Nigeria, 1963,* vol. 1, part 4, *Census of Population, Eastern Nigeria, 1963* (Lagos: Federal Census Office, [1964–1965?]), 132.

36. The Akpoto people are described as "Iga[l]a-speaking [A]kpotos"; see J. R. Wilson-Haffenden, "Ethnological Notes on the Kwottos of Toto (Panda) District, Keffi Division, Benue Province, Northern Nigeria: Part I," *Journal of the Royal African Society* 26, no. 104 (July 1927): 368.

37. Johnson, "Intelligence Report on the People of Enugu-Ezike, Nsukka Division, Onitsha Province," 4, paragraph 13.

38. Ibid., 1, paragraph 1.

39. Ibid., 3, paragraph 9.

40. Ibid., 4, paragraph 14.

41. Agashi, "Pre-Colonial Warfare in Enugu-Ezike," 1.

42. Johnson, "Intelligence Report on the People of Enugu-Ezike, Nsukka Division, Onitsha Province," 2, paragraph 6, and 4, paragraph 14.

43. Ibid., 2, paragraph 6; Agashi, "Pre-Colonial Warfare in Enugu-Ezike," 2.

44. *Oba* is the title of the kings of Benin.

45. Many thanks to Chinua Achebe, who provided much of the information for the interpretations in this section. Chinua Achebe, telephone conversation with author, April 2, 2008; and Chinua Achebe, written communication with author, April 10, 2008.

46. Apeh, "The Traditional Oracle and Culture in Enugu-Ezike," 1–3.

47. *Attama* is an Igala word that means "lord of many" and is used to refer to a shrine priest.

48. Jecinta Nneka Abugu, "The Worship of [a] Deity: A Case Study of Enwe Deity in Ogrute, Enugu-Ezike" (Diploma Certificate in Religion, University of Nigeria, Nsukka, 1998), 3.

49. In some other renderings, the woman's name is recalled as Ikoji. See Apeh, "The Traditional Oracle and Culture in Enugu-Ezike," 2.

50. Agashi, "Pre-Colonial Warfare in Enugu-Ezike," 2–3; Abugu, "The Worship of [a] Deity," 2–3.

51. Apeh, "The Traditional Oracle and Culture in Enugu-Ezike," 1–3; Abugu, "The Worship of [a] Deity," 4.

52. John Nwachimereze Oriji, *Traditions of Igbo Origin: A Study of Pre-Colonial Population Movements in Africa* (New York: Peter Lang, 1994), 67.

53. An *onyishi* (the person who comes first) is the oldest man in a community.

54. Oriji, *Traditions of Igbo Origin,* 67; Abugu, "The Worship of [a] Deity," 4.

55. Stephen Belcher, *Epic Traditions of Africa* (Bloomington: Indiana University Press, 1999), 4.

56. Stephen Belcher, *African Myths of Origin* (London: Penguin Books, 2005), xii–xiii.

57. Belcher, *African Myths of Origin,* xv.

58. Ibid.

59. A. E. Afigbo, "Traditions of Igbo Origins: A Comment," *History in Africa* 10 (1983): 5.

60. Belcher, *African Myths of Origin,* xvii–xviii.

61. Ibid., xix.

62. A. E. Afigbo, "The Nsukka Communities from Earliest Times to 1951: An Introductory Survey," in *The Nsukka Environment,* ed. G. E. K. Ofomata (Enugu: Fourth Dimension Publishers, 1978), 29; Lawrence Offie Ocho, "Nsukka: The Meeting Point of Four Civilizations," *Okikpe* 3, no. 1 (1997): 68.

63. J. S. Boston, "The Hunter in Igala Legends of Origin," *Africa: Journal of the International African Institute* 14, no. 2 (April 1964): 118.

64. Afigbo, "Traditions of Igbo Origins," 10.

65. Ibid.; A. E. Afigbo, "Southern Nigeria, the Niger-Benue Confluence, and the Benue in the Precolonial Period: Some Issues of Historiography," *History in Africa* 24 (1997): 5.

66. Philip Adigwe Oguagha and Alex Ikechukwu Okpoko, *History and Ethno-archaeology in Eastern Nigeria: A Study of Igbo-Igala Relations with Special Reference to the Anambra Valley* (Cambridge Monographs in African Archaeology 7, BAR International Series 195, 1984), 14–15.

67. Ibid., 16–17.

68. Ibid., 17.

69. Many thanks to Harry Odamtten for providing some of the interpretative information for this section. Harry Odamtten, written communication with author, April 24, 2008.

70. Boston, "The Hunter in Igala Legends of Origin," 116.

71. Ibid., 124–125.

72. *Asadu* in its original Igala context is the title of the Igala king's councilor.

73. Amos Abugu interview (1998); Boniface Abugu interview (1998).

74. I will use the concepts of *amaechina* (may my path not be closed) and *obiechina* (may my [male] house not be closed) as interpretative models to analyze the Igbo institution of woman-to-woman and deity-to-woman marriage. See chapters 1, 2, and 6.

75. I have decided to adopt the past tense to speak of events that happened during Ahebi's time, even when those same events still happen today. This methodological approach forced the historian in me to consciously fight the temptation to write in the ubiquitous present, which would have introduced the element of ahistoricity to the biography.

76. G. T. Basden, *Niger Ibos: A Description of the Primitive Life, Customs and Animistic Beliefs, &c., of the Ibo Peoples of Nigeria by One Who, for Thirty-five Years, Enjoyed the Privilege of their Intimate Confidence and Friendship* (London: Frank Cass, 1966), 167.

77. There were, however, variances to this rule in which both parents could be called upon to name their children. See Amaury P. Talbot, *The Peoples of Southern Nigeria: A Sketch of Their History, Ethnology and Languages, with an Account of the 1921 Census,* 4 vols. (London: Oxford University Press, 1926), 2: 366.

78. Daryll Forde and G. I. Jones, *The Ibo and Ibibio-Speaking Peoples of Southwestern Nigeria* (London, 1950), 24; Basden, *Niger Ibos,* 174.

79. See G. T. Basden, *Among the Ibos of Nigeria: An Account of the Curious and Interesting Habits, Customs and Beliefs of a Little Known African People by One Who Has for Many Years Lived Amongst Them on Close and Intimate Terms* (London, 1921); Basden, *Niger Ibos;* Talbot, *The Peoples of Southern Nigeria;* Meek, *An Ethnographical Report on the Peoples of Nsukka Division,* Meek, *Law and Authority;* Forde and G. I. Jones, *The Ibo and Ibibio-Speaking People.*

80. Talbot, *The Peoples of Southern Nigeria,* 2: 367.

81. Ibid., 365.

82. Ibid., 366.

83. George Nnaemeka Oranekwu, *The Significant Role of Initiation in the Traditional Igbo Culture and Religion: An Inculturation Basis for Pastoral Catechesis of Christian Initiation* (Frankfurt: IKO-Verlag, 2004), 101–102.

84. Ibid., 101.

85. Ibid.

86. Meek, *Law and Authority,* 295.

87. Oranekwu, *The Significant Role of Initiation in the Traditional Igbo Culture and Religion,* 102.

88. Basden, *Niger Ibo,* 174.

89. Ik Ogbukagu, *Traditional Igbo Beliefs and Practices: A Study on the Culture and People of Adazi-Nnukwu* (Owerri, Nigeria: Novelty Industrial Enterprises, 1997), 217; Talbot, *The Peoples of Southern Nigeria,* 2:362; Basden, *Niger Ibo,* 174.

90. In Nsukka Division the Creator is called Ezechitoke (i.e., God; a combination of *eze* [king]; *chi* [spiritual force]; *toke* [sharer of all goodness, creator of all things]). Ezechitoke is neither male nor female but rather a very powerful force of both male and female principles.

ONE *Oge Nwatakili*

1. Apex Apeh, handwritten communication with research assistant Leonard Mbah, Department of History, University of Nigeria, Nsukka, February 13, 2008.

2. Oshageri Azegbo interviews with author, tape and video recording, Umuogbo Agu, Enugu-Ezike, Enugu State, Nigeria, November 19 and December 6, 1998; Barnabas Obeta interviews with author, tape recording, Umuida, Enugu-Ezike, Enugu State, Nigeria, November 25, 1996, October 2, 1998, and December 6, 1998; and Oyima Obeta Nwa Ugbabe, interview with author, tape recording, Umuida, Enugu-Ezike, Enugu State, Nigeria, October 2, 1998.

3. None of my collaborators were able to tell me exactly when Ahebi Ugbabe was born. However, using all the sources available to me, I was able to determine that Ahebi was most likely born during the last quarter of the nineteenth century. Here is the information we know for sure: Ahebi Ugbabe absconded to Igalaland when she was young. When we take into consideration the time she spent in Unadu and the fact that collaborators described her as already having breasts before she ran off to Igalaland, I would estimate her age to have been about 14 or 15 years when she left home. We also know that Ahebi was made warrant chief in 1918 and that prior to that she had lived in Igalaland for many years—long enough for her to gain a degree of economic and perhaps social clout. It would therefore not be reaching far to suggest that Ahebi Ugbabe spent between twenty and twenty-one years in Igalaland. That

would put her return to Enugu-Ezike at around 1916 and her age at return of about 36. If these estimates are correct, she was about 38 when she was made warrant chief in 1918. V. K. Johnson, "Intelligence Report on the People of Enugu-Ezike, Nsukka Division, Onitsha Province, 1934," 8, paragraph 22, OP 1071 ONDIST 12/1/709, NAE.

See also Nwando Achebe, *Farmers, Traders, Warriors, and Kings: Female Power and Authority in Northern Igboland, 1900–1960* (Portsmouth, N.H.: Heinemann, 2005), 200; Nwando Achebe, "'And She Became a Man': King Ahebi Ugbabe in the History of Enugu-Ezike, Northern Igboland, 1880–1948," in *Men and Masculinities in Modern Africa,* ed. Stephan F. Miescher and Lisa A. Lindsay (Portsmouth, N.H.: Heinemann, 2003), 52, 54.

4. Is it also possible that Ahebi's grandmother came from Obukpa, which is also in Nsukka Division. See Alice Akogu (formerly Ahebi), interview with author, tape recording, Ofante, Kogi State, Nigeria, October 5, 1998; Nwoyeja Obeta (Felicia Ugwu Agbedo), interview with author, tape recording, Umuida, Enugu-Ezike, Nigeria, October 4, 1998.

5. Oshageri Azegbo interviews (November 19 and December 6, 1998); Barnabas Obeta interviews (1996 and 1998); Oyima Obeta Nwa Ugbabe interview (1998).

6. P. E. Okwoli, interview with author, digital voice recording, Idah, Kogi State, Nigeria, July 7, 2007. See also P. E. Okwoli, "Igala Names: A Survey of Some Igala Names, Their Meanings, Relevance and Source," unpublished manuscript, 5. I also drew on information that P. E. Okwoli conveyed to Leonard Mbah in telephone conversations on February 5 and 6, 2008.

7. Ibrahim Omale, *Igala, Yesterday, Today and Tomorrow: A Developmental Perspective* (Lagos, Nigeria: Summit Press, 2001), 6.

8. P. E. Okwoli, telephone conversations with Leonard Mbah, February 5 and 6, 2008. *Owa,* on the other hand, is an Akpoto word for "age group." See Austin J. Shelton, *The Igbo-Igala Borderland: Religion and Social Control in Indigenous African Colonialism* (Albany: State University of New York Press, 1971), 269.

9. P. E. Okwoli interview (2007); P. M. Onekutu, Department of Igala, College of Education, Ankpa, Kogi State, Nigeria, handwritten communication with Leonard Mbah, February 3, 2008.

10. P. E. Okwoli interview (2007).

11. Erobike Eze, Trans Ekulu, Enugu, Enugu State, Nigeria, handwritten communication with author, July 20, 2008.

12. Apex Apeh (of Enugu-Ezike, Nigeria), Department of History, University of Nigeria, Nsukka, handwritten communication with Leonard Mbah, 2008; Amadi Nnaji, Department of Linguistics, University of Nigeria, handwritten communication with Leonard Mbah, February 3, 2008.

13. Barnabas Obeta interview (1998).

14. P. M. Onekutu, handwritten communication with Leonard Mbah, 2008.

15. Nwoyeja Obeta (Felicia Ugwu Agbedo) interview (1998).

16. See Ifi Amadiume, *Male Daughters, Female Husbands: Gender and Sex in an African Society* (London: Zed Books, 1987), 70.

17. Nwoyeja Obeta (Felicia Ugwu Agbedo) interview (1998); Barnabas Obeta interviews (1996 and 1998); Barnabas Obeta, interview with author, digital voice recording, Umuida, Enugu-Ezike, Nigeria, July 13, 2007; Oyima Obeta Nwa Ugbabe

interview (1998); Oyima Obeta Nwa Ugbabe, interview with author, digital voice recording, Umuida, Enugu-Ezike, Nigeria, July 13, 2007.

18. A female friend of a masked spirit was typically a postmenopausal woman who had "befriended" the spirit and was allowed to cook as well as do other duties around the spirit as needed. I say more on this in chapter 5.

19. See Achebe, *Farmers, Traders, Warriors, and Kings*, 25. I also gathered information about the Omabe masquerade from Apex Apeh of Enugu-Ezike, Nigeria, handwritten communication with Leonard Mbah, 2008.

20. Stephen S. Nwodo, "African Traditional Religion in Enugu-Ezike" (B.A. thesis, Department of Religion, University of Nigeria, Nsukka, 2001), 31.

21. P. E. Okwoli interview (2007); Apex Apeh, handwritten communication with Leonard Mbah, 2008.

22. In Ogbede, Nsukka, the name Oriefi is given to the tenth child of a woman because a cow is killed for a woman after she delivers her tenth child; Apex Apeh, handwritten communication with Leonard Mbah, 2008; Amadi Nnaji, handwritten communication with Leonard Mbah, 2008.

23. Apex Apeh, handwritten communication with Leonard Mbah, 2008; Amadi Nnaji, handwritten communication with Leonard Mbah, 2008.

24. Bedford Okpe, interview with author, digital voice recording, Lagos, Lagos State, Nigeria, July 23, 2007. The vast majority of my collaborators could not say whether or not Ahebi married Eze Nwa Ezema. However, in interviews, the following collaborators told me that she did: Bedford Okpe (2007); Bernard Ameh, interview with author, tape recording, Unadu, Enugu-Ezike, Enugu State, Nigeria, September 29, 1998; and Wilfred Ogara, interview with author, tape recording, Umuida, Enugu-Ezike, Enugu State, Nigeria, November 25, 1996.

25. Nwoyeja Obeta (Felicia Ugwu Agbedo) interview (1998).

26. Alice Akogu interview (1998). Madam Akogu reiterated that a rape may have occurred in a second interview almost ten years later; Alice Akogu, interview with author, digital voice recording, Ofante, Kogi State, Nigeria, July 11, 2007.

27. Bernard Ameh interview (1998); Wilfred Ogara interview (1996).

28. Prostitution as it was constructed in Igbo and Igalaland was not associated with the types of oppression women sex workers encountered elsewhere during the colonial era. For one, women in these parts never had a male pimp who controlled their wages and what they did. I will examine the institution in more detail in chapter 2. For more on this, see Nwando Achebe, "The Road to Italy: Nigerian Sex Workers at Home and Abroad," *Journal of Women's History* 15, no. 4 (Winter 2004): 177–184; and Nwando Achebe, "West Africa," in *The Encyclopedia of Prostitution and Sex Work*, 2 vols., ed. Melissa Hope Ditmore (Westport, Conn.: Greenwood, 2006), 2:532–536.

29. Bernard Ameh interview (1998).

30. Ibid.

31. Ibid.

32. P. M. Onekutu, handwritten communication with Leonard Mbah, 2008.

33. Nwoyeja Obeta (Felicia Ugwu Agbedo) interview (1998).

34. P. M. Onekutu, handwritten communication with Leonard Mbah, 2008.

35. Ibid.

36. The institution of *igwe* is a modern construct. In a noncentralized community such as Unadu, the *igwe* is a copy of a traditional "king" but without the overreaching power of a king.

37. The following oral history collaborators provided information in interviews that enabled me to reconstruct Ahebi Ugbabe's family tree: Ogbu Agashi, interview with author, tape recording, Enugu-Ezike, Enugu State, Nigeria, September 26, 1996; Oshageri Azegbo interviews (November 19 and December 6, 1998); Abodo Nwa Idoko, interview with author, tape recording, Ikpamodo, Enugu-Ezike, Enugu State, Nigeria, September 26, 1998; Boniface Abugu, interview with author, tape recording, Umuida, Enugu-Ezike, Enugu State, Nigeria, October 4, 1998; Ayogu Onu Odum, interview with author, tape recording, Umuida, Enugu-Ezike, Enugu State, Nigeria, September 29, 1998; Enwo Odo Nweze Nwaba, interview with author, tape recording, Umuida, Enugu-Ezike, Enugu State, Nigeria, September 29, 1998; Bernard Ameh interview (1998); Michael Idoko, interview with author, tape recording, Umuida, Enugu-Ezike, Enugu State, Nigeria, November 25, 1996; Alice Akogu interview (1998); Barnabas Obeta interviews (1996, 1998, and 2007); and Oyima Obeta Nwa Ugbabe interviews (1998 and 2007).

38. Alice Akogu interview (1998).

39. For more on *chi* in Igbo cosmology, see Damian U. Opata, *Essays on Igbo World View* (Enugu, Nigeria: AP Express, 1998), 152–155.

40. Onyishi Augustine Abutu, interview with author, digital recording, Unadu, Enugu State, Nigeria, July 15, 2007.

41. Alice Akogu interviews (1998 and 2007).

42. Alice Akogu interview (1998); Nwoyeja Obeta (Felicia Ugwu Agbedo) interview (1998), Barnabas Obeta interviews (1996 and 1998); Bernard Ameh interview (1998).

43. Ogbu Agashi interview (1996); Abodo Nwa Idoko interview (1998); Boniface Abugu interview (1998); Alice Akogu interview (1998); Nwoyeja Obeta (Felicia Ugwu Agbedo) interview (1998); Oshageri Azegbo interview (1998); Ayogu Onu Odum interview (1998); Barnabas Obeta interviews (1996, 1998, and 2007); Enwo Odo Nweze Nwaba interview (1998); Bernard Ameh interview (1998); Michael Idoko interview (1996); Wilfred Ogara interview (1996); Samuel Ezeja, interview with author, tape recording, Umuida, Enugu-Ezike, Enugu State, Nigeria, November 25, 1996; Fabian Azegba, interview with author, tape recording, Umuida, Enugu-Ezike, Enugu State, Nigeria, October 2, 1998; Uroke Nwa Iyida Oku (Raymond Iyida), interview with author, tape recording, Onitsha, Enugu-Ezike, Enugu State, Nigeria, September 28, 1998; Simeon Nweke, interview with author, tape recording, Umuida, Enugu-Ezike, Enugu State, Nigeria, November 26, 1996; Abugwu Eze Nwa Asanya, interview with author, tape recording, Umuida, Enugu-Ezike, Enugu State, Nigeria, September 29, 1998; Asanya Onu, interview with author, tape recording, Umuida, Enugu-Ezike, Enugu State, Nigeria, September 29, 1998; Chikere Abugwu, interview with author, tape recording, Umuida, Enugu-Ezike, Enugu State, Nigeria, September 29, 1998; Ogbu Nwa Abugwu Asenya Onu, interview with author, tape recording, Umuida, Enugu-Ezike, Enugu State, Nigeria, September 29, 1998; David Ugwuaku, interview with author, tape recording, Umuida, Enugu-Ezike, Enugu State, Nigeria, September 29, 1998; Jonathan Abugwu Asanya, interview with author, tape recording, Umuida, Enugu-Ezike, Enugu State, Nigeria, September 29, 1998; Fabian Omeke, interview with author, tape recording, Umuida, Enugu-Ezike, Enugu State, Nigeria, September 29, 1998; Michael Omeke Onasanya, interview with author, tape recording, Umuida, Enugu-Ezike, Enugu State, Nigeria, September 29, 1998; Fidelis Eze Nwonu Asanya, interview with author, tape recording, Umuida, Enugu-Ezike, Enugu State,

Nigeria, September 29, 1998; Oyima Obeta Nwa Ugbabe interview (1998); Ignatius Abugu, interview with author, tape recording, Imufu, Enugu-Ezike, Enugu State, Nigeria, September 28, 1998. I also drew on two interviews taken by Cyprian U. Agbedo and transcribed in his thesis, "Slavery and Slave Trade in Enugu-Ezike in the Pre-Colonial Period" (B.A. thesis, Department of History, University of Nigeria, Nsukka, 1979): interview with Ogbu Nwa Agashi Ogrute, Enugu-Ezike, Enugu State, Nigeria, July 22, 1978 (page 64); and interview with Onyeke Nwede, Ogrute, Enugu-Ezike, Enugu State, Nigeria, August 5, 1978 (page 73).

44. Enwo Nwa Odo Nweze Nwaba Osogwu, interview with author, tape recording, Umuida, Enugu-Ezike, Enugu State, Nigeria, September 29, 1998. See also Ogbu Nwa Agashi, interview with Cyprian U. Agbedo, Ogrute, Enugu-Ezike, Nigeria, July 22, 1978, in Agbedo, "Slavery and Slave Trade in Enugu-Ezike in the Pre-Colonial Period," 65.

45. A. E. Afigbo, "Women in Nigerian History," in *Women in Nigerian Economy*, ed. Martin O. Ijere (Enugu, Nigeria: Acena Publishers, 1991), 35.

46. Ibid., 40.

47. Samuel Ezeja interview (1996); Uroke Nwa Iyida Oku interview (1998); Simeon Nweke interview (1996);Wilfred Ogara interview (1996); Bernard Ameh interview (1998); Michael Idoko interview (1996); Barnabas Obeta interviews (1996 and 1998); Alice Akogu interviews (1998 and 2007); Abodo Nwa Idoko interview (1998); Ogbu Agashi interview (1996); Nwoyeja Obeta (Felicia Ugwu Agbedo) interview (1998); Boniface Abugu interview (1998); Oyima Obeta Nwa Ugbabe interview (1998); Ignatius Abugu interview (1998); Josiah Ogbonna, interview with author, tape recording, Nkofi Edem, Enugu State, Nigeria, September 14, 1998; Selina Ugwuoke Adibuah, interview with author, tape recording, Trans Ekulu, Enugu, Enugu State, Nigeria, October 23, 1996. See also Agbedo, "Slavery and Slave Trade in Enugu-Ezike in the Pre-Colonial Period," 24; and Onyeke Nwede, interview with Cyprian U. Agbedo, in Agbedo, "Slavery and Slave Trade in Enugu-Ezike in the Pre-Colonial Period," 73.

48. A. E. Afigbo, interview with author, tape recording, Owerri, Imo State, Nigeria, October 3, 1996.

49. Ayogu Onu Odum interview (1998); Wilfred Ogara interview (1996); Samuel Ezeja interview (1996); Fabian Azegba interview (1998); Simeon Nweke interview (1996); Ignatius Abugu interview (1998); Ogbu Nwa Agashi, interview with Cyprian U. Agbedo, in Agbedo, "Slavery and Slave Trade in Enugu-Ezike in the Pre-Colonial Period," 65. See also P. O. Agashi, "Government at Nsukka, 1929–1979" (M.A. history project, Department of History, University of Nigeria, Nsukka, 1986), 17.

50. One collaborator maintained that Ahebi Ugbabe "had developed breasts" at the time. Because in those days women tended to mature a lot later than they do today, 13–14 years old is a conservative estimate. Abodo Nwa Idoko interview (1998).

51. Ibid.

52. Chinua Achebe, telephone conversation with author, April 4, 2008; Christie Chinwe Achebe, telephone conversation with author, April 4, 2008. See also Emefie Ikenga Metuh, *God and Man in African Religion* (London: Geoffrey Chapman, 1981),79; Edmund Ilogu, *Igbo Life and Thought* (Onitsha, Nigeria: University Publishing, 1985), 17; Emefie Ikenga Metuh, *African Religions in Western Conceptual*

Scheme: The Problem of Interpretation (Ibadan, Nigeria: Pastoral Institute, 1985), 161; Austin J. Shelton, "The Meaning and Method of Afa Divination among the Northern Nsukka Igbo," *American Anthropologist* 67, no. 6 (December 1965): 1442; G. E. Parrinder, *West African Religion* (London: Epworth Press, 1969), 152; and Francis Arinze, *Sacrifice in Igbo Religion* (Ibadan, Nigeria: Ibadan University Press, 1970), 63–64, 67.

53. Many thanks to Chinua Achebe for helping me work through these meanings. Chinua Achebe, telephone conversation, 2008.

54. Shelton, "The Meaning and Method of Afa Divination," 1444.

55. Pius Idoko, interview with author, tape recording, Imufu, Enugu-Ezike, Enugu State, Nigeria, November 23, 1996.

56. Pius Idoko interview (1996); Pius Idoko, interview with author, tape recording, Imufu, Enugu-Ezike, Enugu State, Nigeria, September 27, 1998.

57. Pius Idoko interview (1996). Onitsha and Benin City are approximately 118 kilometers from Enugu-Ezike.

58. Ibid.; Pius Idoko interview (1998).

59. Arinze, *Sacrifice in Ibo Religion*, 81–82.

60. Nsukka Division boasts a number of these *igberema* communities; I have written extensively about two such communities. See discussion of Efuru's *igberema* community in Achebe, *Farmers, Traders, Warriors, and Kings*, 71–77; and Achebe, "When Deities Marry."

61. The *obi* (or *obu*, as it was called in Nsukka Division), was the Igbo man's house. The philosophy of *obiechina* spoke to the Igbo person's absolute desire for children, but it was also about their desire for *male* children who would not change their family name but would carry it from generation to generation.

62. Abodo Nwa Idoko interview (1998).

63. Boniface Abugu interview (1998).

64. Abodo Nwa Idoko interview (1998); Oshageri Azegbo interview (November 19, 1998).

65. Boniface Abugu interview (1998).

66. Abodo Nwa Idoko interview (1998).

67. *O gbapu* literally means "she took flight." I will say more about this construction in chapter 2.

TWO *Mgbapu Ahebi*

1. Tom A. Miachi, "Introducing the Igala People," in *The Golden Jubilee Celebration of the Enthronement of His Royal Majesty Alhaji Aliyu O. Obaje* (Lagos: Attah Igala and Chancellor, University of Lagos, n.d.), 18.

2. Members of the Igala Ruling Council, including HRH Jacob Osheni Odiba (the Odom Ata-Igala), HRH Amodo D. Haruna (the Onuega/Egen-Ata-Igala), HRH Chief S. U. Amanabu (the O-Dekina Ata-Igala), HRH Chief Omolobu Ata (the Wada Omeje Igala), HRH Chief E. O. Musa (the Ohe-Omogboro Ata), HRH Chief Abdullahi O. Ocheje (the Ochi Ata), HRH Alahji Hayatu Amodu (the Nalogu Ata), HRH Chief Ada Edein (the Ekpa Ata), HRH Chief Nuru I. Ogaji (the Amana Ata Okwuaja Idah), and HRH Odo. C. Hajia Sabime (the Abalaka Iye Ata), group interview with Leonard Mbah and Winifred Nwaefido, tape recording, Attah-Igala's Palace, Idah, Kogi State, Nigeria, January 30, 2008; Mallam Umonu, interview with Leonard

Mbah and Winifred Nwaefido, tape recording, Idah, Kogi State, Nigeria, February 1, 2008.

3. Yusufu Etu, *Igala History in Questions and Answers* (Jos, Nigeria: New Concepts Incorporated Book House, 2001), 16; P. E. Okwoli interview with author, digital voice recording, Idah, Kogi State, Nigeria, July 7, 2007; P. E. Okwoli, interview with Leonard Mbah and Winifred Nwaefido, tape recording, Idah, Kogi State, Nigeria, January 30, 2008.

4. The Wukari tradition of Igala kingship origin is one of three traditions remembered today in Igalaland. The other two point to Benin and Yorubaland for their origins. See Paul Chike Dike, "Symbolism and Political Authority in the Igala Kingdom" (Ph.D. diss., University of Nigeria, Nsukka, 1977), 29.

5. Ibid., 28–29; P. E. Okwoli interview (2007).

6. P. E. Okwoli, *The History of the Fifty Years Reign of the Attah Igala, Alhaji Aliyu Ocheja Obaje, 1956–2006* (Enugu, Nigeria: Snaap Press, 2006), 335–336.

7. C. K. Meek, *Law and Authority in a Nigeria Tribe: A Study of Indirect Rule* (London: Oxford University Press, 1937), 158.

8. I have already discussed the place of the hunter in Igala traditions of origin in the *Nkowa* chapter. Information on Ebule and Acho was obtained from Dike, "Symbolism and Political Authority in the Igala Kingdom" 38; and P. E. Okwoli interview (2007).

9. Dike, "Symbolism and Political Authority," 35–39; P. E. Okwoli interview (2007); members of the Igala Ruling Council, including HRH Jacob Osheni Odiba (the Odom Ata Igala), HRH Amodo D. Haruna (the Onuega/Egen-Ata Igala), HRH Chief S. U. Amanabu (the O-Dekina Ata Igala), HRH Chief Omolobu Ata (the Wada Omeje Igala), HRH Chief E. O. Musa (the Ohe-Omogboro Ata), HRH Chief Abdullahi O. Ocheje (the Ochi Ata), HRH Alahji Hayatu Amodu (the Nalogu Ata), HRH Chief Ada Edein (the Ekpa Ata), HRH Chief Nuru I. Ogaji (the Amana Ata Okwuaja Idah), and HRH Odo. C. Hajia Sabime (the Abalaka Iye Ata), group interview (with Leonard Mbah and Winifred Nwaefido, 2008); Mallam Umonu interview (with Leonard Mbah and Winifred Nwaefido, 2008).

10. Prince Idakwo Ameh Oboni, *Ameh the Great* (Ibadan, Nigeria: Intec Printers, 1989), 59; Dike, "Symbolism and Political Authority in the Igala Kingdom" 39; Ahebi's ears were perforated several centuries later, after she was made female king by Attah-Obaje. See Oshageri Azegbo, interview with author, tape and video recording, Umuogbo Agu, Enugu-Ezike, Enugu State, Nigeria, November 19, 1998; Oshageri Azegbo, interview with author, tape and video recording, Umuogbo Agu, Enugu-Ezike, Enugu State, Nigeria, December 6, 1998.

11. *Programme of Events for the 50th Anniversary of the Enthronement of His Royal Majesty Alh. (Dr.) Aliyu O. Obaje, Attah Igala and Chancellor, University of Lagos,* 16. Brochure in author's possession.

12. Alice Akogu, interview with author, tape recording, Ofante, Kogi State, Nigeria, October 5, 1998; Alice Akogu, interview with author, digital voice recording, Ofante, Kogi State, Nigeria, July 11, 2007; Bedford Okpe, interview with author, digital voice recording, Lagos, Lagos Sate, Nigeria, July 23, 2007; Bernard Ameh, interview with author, tape recording, Unadu, Enugu-Ezike, Enugu State, Nigeria, September 29, 1998; Barnabas Obeta, interview with author, tape and video recording, Umuida, Enugu-Ezike, Enugu State, Nigeria, November 25, 1996; Barmabas Obeta,

interview with author, tape recording, Umuida, Enugu-Ezike, Enugu State, Nigeria, October 2, 1998; Oyima Obeta Nwa Ugbabe, interview with author, tape recording, Umuida, Enugu-Ezike, Enugu State, Nigeria, October 2, 1998; Oshageri Azegbo interviews (November 19 and December 6, 1998); Michael Idoko, interview with author, tape recording, Umuida, Enugu-Ezike, Enugu State, Nigeria, November 25, 1996; Wilfred Ogara, interview with author, tape recording, Umuida, Enugu-Ezike, Enugu State, Nigeria, November 25, 1996; Ogbu Agashi, interview with author, tape recording, Umuida, Enugu-Ezike, Enugu State, Nigeria, September 26, 1996.

13. A. E. Afigbo, "Oral Tradition and the History of Segmentary Societies," *History in Africa* 12 (1985): 4.

14. *Oge mgbapu Ahebi* means "in the time of Ahebi's flight." In this chapter, I will use the phrase to delineate the period of time (roughly 1895 to 1916) when Ahebi ran away from home to Igalaland—a period that corresponded with her twenty to twenty-one years in exile. The word *mgbapu* means "running away" or "taking flight." It is used to describe the action of one person running away from their home and community. The Igbo have a collective phrase, *igba oso,* which is used to explain the action of an entire community moving from one location to another—an action that communities take when they are in danger. For instance, the expression *oge ndi Igbo gbalu oso* has survived in Igbo consciousness to describe when Igbo people ran away from the non-Igbo-speaking areas of Nigeria (e.g., during the Nigerian/Biafran Civil War). Thanks to Chinua Achebe for his assistance in devising this indigenous periodization. Chinua Achebe, telephone conversations with author, September 4, 2008, and September 5, 2008.

15. The routes plotted below were charted using only "all-season roads." Some roads may have been impossible to navigate during the rainy season.

16. Chinua Achebe, *Things Fall Apart* (New York: Knopf, 1992), 115–116.

17. Ibid., 116–117.

18. The route maps in this chapter were constructed from several colonial political, geographical, and road maps of the region. The earliest plotted map that I could locate was an Igala road map drawn in the early twentieth century. The earliest Nigeria road map available to me was drawn in the early 1940s. While the 1940 map documents road networks during a period considerably later than Ahebi's journeys, I am comfortable using it to theorize about roads *oge mgbapu Ahebi* because Nigerian colonial roads for the most part were expanded out of existing precolonial roads. See S. A. Olanrewaju, "The Nigerian Road Transport System," in *Transport Systems in Nigeria,* ed. Toyin Falola and S. A. Olanrewaju (Syracuse, N.Y.: Maxwell School of Citizenship and Public Affairs, Syracuse University, 1986), 55–56; and Gilbert James Walker, *Traffic and Transport in Nigeria: The Example of an Underdeveloped Tropical Territory,* Research Series No. 27 (London: Colonial Office, 1959), 89.

19. Toyin Falola and G. O. Ogunremi, "Traditional, Nonmechanical Transport Systems," in *Transport Systems in Nigeria,* ed. Toyin Falola and S. A. Olanrewaju (Syracuse, N.Y.: Maxwell School of Citizenship and Public Affairs, Syracuse University, 1986), 18–23.

20. Walker, *Traffic and Transport in Nigeria,* 88. In Enugu-Ezike and Igalaland, the animal most often used was the horse.

21. Olanrewaju, "The Nigerian Road Transport System," 55–56; Walker, *Traffic and Transport in Nigeria,* 89.

22. Walker, *Traffic and Transport in Nigeria,* 89.

23. Olanrewaju, "The Nigerian Road Transport System," 56; see also E. K. Hawkins, *Road Transport in Nigeria: A Study of African Enterprise* (London: Oxford University Press, 1958), 16.

24. Olanrewaju, "The Nigerian Road Transport System," 53; see also Hawkins, *Road Transport in Nigeria,* 12.

25. This and other distances used in this chapter were calculated for me by Sarah J. AcMoody of Remote Sensing & GIS Research and Outreach Services, Michigan State University. Many thanks to her for providing these calculations and for preparing my maps.

26. The route maps were constructed from a variety of sources. Geocommunity provided Digital Chart of the World (DCW) data that served as the base roads layer for the maps. The DCW is an Environmental Systems Research Institute, Inc. (ESRI) product originally developed for the US Defense Mapping Agency (DMA) using DMA data. The DCW 1993 version at 1:1,000,000 scale was used. The DMA data sources are aeronautical charts, which emphasize landmarks important from flying altitudes.

Sarah AcMoody, the cartographer at Remote Sensing & GIS Research and Outreach Services at Michigan State University, compiled the maps based on DCW data and *Physical Map of Nigeria,* compiled, drawn, and reproduced by Director of Surveys, Nigeria, 1949, partially revised and reproduced by Director of Federal Surveys, Lagos, 1956 as well as a combination of period-specific printed maps, including maps of Igala Division from J. S. Boston, *The Igala Kingdom* (Ibadan: Oxford University Press, 1968), 2; "Nigeria in the 20th Century, Surrounding Regions, and Nsukka Division," from Nwando Achebe, *Farmers, Traders, Warriors and Kings,* pages 24, 30, and 31; and "Enugu-Ezike," and "Umuida (Enugu-Ezike) to Unadu," from Patrick Odo Agashi, "Pre-Colonial Warfare in Enugu-Ezike" (B.A. Research Project, History and Archeology Department, University of Nigeria, Nsukka, June 1979).

27. See also "Railroads, Roads and Navigable River Map," attachment to Walker, *Traffic and Transport in Nigeria.* Also helpful is Olanrewaju, "The Nigerian Road Transport System," 58; and Toyin Falola and Olanrewaju, "Traditional, Nonmechanical Transport Systems," 19, both in *Transport Systems in Nigeria,* ed. Toyin Falola and S. A. Olanrewaju (Syracuse, N.Y.: Maxwell School of Citizenship and Public Affairs, Syracuse University, 1986).

28. The town of Ankpa was the traditional seat of the *attah*'s powerful provincial governors. See Gertrude Ojochide Onogu, "The Place of Princess Inikpi in the Igala Traditional Belief System of Kogi State" (Diploma, University of Nigeria, Nsukka, September 1996), 6.

29. The colonial map does not indicate the name of the expanse between Adoru and Keffi.

30. We know that Ahebi traded in Ejule; see Alice Akogu interview (2007).

31. Wilfred Ogara interview (1996).

32. Onogu, "The Place of Princess Inikpi," 7.

33. Given the condition of the roads at the time, my assumption is that it would take her at least twelve minutes to walk one kilometer and that therefore it would take her a little over five hours to walk twenty-six kilometers. A lorry driver would not have been going more than 30 to 40 kilometers an hour.

34. Biodun Ogunyemi, "Knowledge and Perception of Child Sexual Abuse in Urban Nigeria: Some Evidence from a Community-Based Project," *African Journal of Reproductive Health* 4, no. 2 (October 2000): 3; Viktoria Perschler-Desai, "Childhood on the Market: Teenage Prostitution in Southern Africa," *African Security Review* 10, no. 4 (2001), available at http://www.iss.co.za/pubs/ASR/10No4/Perschler.html; M. Baral, I. Farley, M. Kiremire, and U. Sezgin, "Prostitution in Five Countries: Violence and Post-Traumatic Stress Disorder (South Africa, Thailand, Turkey, USA, Zambia)," *Feminism & Psychology* 8, no. 4 (1998): 405–426; B. M. Willis and B. S. Levy, "Child Prostitution: Global Health Burden, Research Needs, and Interventions," *Lancet* 359, no. 9315 (April 2002): 1417–1422. Studies in the Malaysian context also confirm the link between sexual abuse and child prostitution; see Z. M. Lukman, "Childhood Abuse among Children Involved in Prostitution in Malaysia," *The Social Sciences* 4, no. 6 (2009): 567–572. There are several U.S.-based studies available on this topic; they include N. D. Kellogg, T. J. Hoffman, and E. R. Taylor, "Early Sexual Experience among Pregnant and Parenting Adolescents," *Adolescence* 43 (1999): 293–303; J. G. Noll, P. K. Trickett, and F. W. Putnam, "A Prospective Investigation of the Impact of Childhood Sexual Abuse on the Development of Sexuality," *Journal of Consulting and Clinical Psychology* 71 (2003): 575–586; E. O. Paolucci, M. L. Genuis, and C. Violato, "A Meta-Analysis of the Published Research on the Effects of Child Sexual Abuse," *Journal of Psychology* 135 (2001): 17–36; and E. M. Saewyc, L. L. Magee, and S. E. Pettingall, "Teenage Pregnancy and Associated Risk Behavior among Sexually Abused Adolescents," *Perspectives on Sexual and Reproductive Health* 36, no. 3 (2004): 98–105.

35. The present Attah-Igala is Attah Aliyu Obaje, who has reigned for over fifty years. It was his father, Attah-Obaje (I), who made Ahebi king.

36. Evidence was gathered by the following collaborators to support the fact that Ahebi was a prostitute in Igalaland: Olu Oha Ogbu Agashi, interview with author, tape recording, Enugu-Ezike, Enugu State, Nigeria, September 26, 1996; Oshageri Azegbo interview (November 19, 1998); Chief Abodo Nwa Idoko, interview with author, tape recording, Ikpamodo, Enugu-Ezike, Enugu State, Nigeria, September 26, 1998; Boniface Abugu, interview with author, tape recording, Umuida, Enugu-Ezike, Enugu State, Nigeria, October 4, 1998; Ayogu Onu Odum, interview with author, tape recording, Umuida, Enugu-Ezike, Enugu State, Nigeria, September 29, 1998; Enwo Odo Nweze Nwaba, interview with author, tape recording, Umuida, Enugu-Ezike, Enugu State, Nigeria, September 29, 1998; Bernard Ameh interview (1998); Michael Idoko interview (1996); Alice Akogu interview (1998); Nwoyeja Obeta (Felicia Ugwu Agbedo), interview with author, tape recording, Umuida, Enugu-Ezike, Enugu State, Nigeria, October 4, 1998; Barnabas Obeta interviews (1996 and 1998); Wilfred Ogara interview (1996); Samuel Ezeja, interview with author, tape recording, Umuida, Enugu-Ezike, Enugu State, Nigeria, November 25, 1996; Fabian Azegba, interview with author, tape recording, Umuida, Enugu-Ezike, Enugu State, Nigeria, October 2, 1998; Uroke Nwa Iyida Oku (Raymond Iyida), interview with author, tape recording, Onitsha, Enugu-Ezike, Enugu State, Nigeria, September 28, 1998; Simeon Nweke, interview with author, tape recording, Umuida, Enugu-Ezike, Enugu State, Nigeria, November 26, 1996; Abugwu Eze Nwa Asanya, interview with author, tape recording, Umuida, Enugu-Ezike, Enugu State, Nigeria, September 29, 1998; Asanya Onu, interview with author, tape recording, Umuida, Enugu-Ezike, Enugu State,

Nigeria, September 29, 1998; Chikere Abugwu, interview with author, tape recording, Umuida, Enugu-Ezike, Enugu State, Nigeria, September 29, 1998; Ogbu Nwa Abugwu Asenya Onu, interview with author, tape recording, Umuida, Enugu-Ezike, Enugu State, Nigeria, September 29, 1998; David Ugwuaku, interview with author, tape recording, Umuida, Enugu-Ezike, Enugu State, Nigeria, September 29, 1998; Jonathan Abugwu Asanya, interview with author, tape recording, Umuida, Enugu-Ezike, Enugu State, Nigeria, September 29, 1998; Enwo Nwa Odo Nweze Nwaba Osogwu, interview with author, tape recording, Umuida, Enugu-Ezike, Enugu State, Nigeria, September 29, 1998; Fabian Omeke, interview with author, tape recording, Umuida, Enugu-Ezike, Enugu State, Nigeria, September 29, 1998; Michael Omeke Onasanya, interview with author, tape recording, Umuida, Enugu-Ezike, Enugu State, Nigeria, September 29, 1998; Fidelis Eze Nwonu Asanya, interview with author, tape recording, Umuida, Enugu-Ezike, Enugu State, Nigeria, September 29, 1998; Oyima Obeta Nwa Ugbabe interview (1998); Olu Oha Ignatius Abugu, Onyishi Imufu, interview with author, tape recording, Imufu, Enugu-Ezike, Enugu State, Nigeria, September 28, 1998. I also drew on two interviews with Cyprian U. Agbedo, both of which are transcribed and cited in his thesis, "Slavery and Slave Trade in Enugu-Ezike in the Pre-Colonial Period" (B.A. thesis, University of Nigeria, Nsukka, 1979): Ogbu Nwa Agashi, Ogrute, Enugu-Ezike, Anambra (now Enugu) State, Nigeria, July 22, 1978 (pages 64–65) and Onyeke Nwede, Ogrute, Enugu-Ezike, Anambra (now Enugu) State, Nigeria, August 5, 1978 (page 73); and on P. O. Agashi, "Government at Nsukka 1929–1979," (M.A. history thesis University of Nigeria, Nsukka, 1986), 17.

37. A European colonist that Ahebi most likely would have encountered was colonial officer S. W. Sproston, the district officer of the newly created Okogwa Division. He would have been instrumental in eventually securing a warrant chief position for her in Enugu-Ezike, which, at the time, was managed out of Okogwa Division.

38. Luise White, *The Comforts of Home, Prostitution in Colonial Nairobi* (Chicago: University of Chicago Press, 1990), 43. In Emmanuel Akyeampong's critical study of prostitution in the Gold Coast, he argues that even though prostitution as an institution emerged during the colonial period, the public women of precolonial Gold Coast formed formal sexual relationships with elite men. These public women were enslaved, though, not free. See Emmanuel Akyeampong, "Sexuality and Prostitution among the Akan of the Gold Coast, c. 1650–1950," *Past and Present* 156 (1997): 144–173. Other studies on prostitution in Africa include Carina Ray, "The Sex Trade in Colonial West Africa," *New African* 466 (October 2007): 80; Saheed Aderinto, "Prostitution: A Social Legacy of Colonialism in Nigeria," in *Nigeria's Urban History: Past and Present*, ed. Hakeem Ibikumle Tijani (Lanham, Md.: University of America Press, 2006), 75–98; Saheed Aderinto, "Demobilization and Repatriation of Undesirables: Prostitutes, Crime, Law and Reformers in Colonial Nigeria," in *Nigeria's Urban History: Past and Present*, ed. Hakeem Ibikumle Tijani (Lanham, Md.: University of America Press, 2006), 99–118; John K. Anarfi, *Female Migration and Prostitution in West Africa: The Case of Ghanaian Women in Côte d'Ivoire* (Accra: GTZ Regional AIDS Programme for West and Central Africa, 1995); and Maria Eugenia G. FaSanto, Do Espirito, and Gina D. Etheredge, "And Then I Became a Prostitute . . . Some Aspects of Prostitution and Brothel Prostitutes in Dakar, Senegal," *The Social Science Journal* 41 (2004): 137–146.

39. White, *The Comforts of Home.*

40. In my analysis of Nsukka Igbo and Igala prostitution, I use the concept of construction as a creation of a perceived social reality (of being single or free, for example) by a particular group.

41. Single girls and women in Nsukka Division were encouraged to explore and express their sexuality as they desired. In his chapter on marriage customs in Igboland, G. T. Basden suggests that both boys and girls were encouraged to express their sexuality in a playful manner before marriage. He wrote: "It is not an uncommon custom for boys and girls to cohabit as a 'game.'" G. T. Basden, *Niger Ibos: A Description of the Primitive Life, Customs and Animistic Beliefs, &c., of the Ibo Peoples of Nigeria by One Who, for Thirty-five Years, Enjoyed the Privilege of Their Intimate Confidence and Friendship* (London: Frank Cass, 1966), 214.

42. See "Table No. 19, Administration of [Indigenous] Law," in Amaury P. Talbot, *The Peoples of Southern Nigeria: A Sketch of Their History, Ethnology and Languages, with an Account of the 1921 Census,* vol. 3 (London: Oxford University Press, 1926) for the penalties imposed on a man who has sex with a married woman in Igboland. He could be forced to pay up to £15 as well as fines in livestock, especially cocks and goats and palm wine.

43. Benedict B. B. Naanen, "Itinerant Gold Mines: Prostitution in the Cross River Basin of Nigeria, 1930–1950," *African Studies Review* 34, no. 2 (September 1991): 64.

44. See Nwando Achebe, "The Road to Italy: Nigerian Sex Workers at Home and Abroad," *Journal of Women's History* 15, no. 4 (Winter 2004): 180.

45. Basden, *Niger Ibos,* 204.

46. Ibid.

47. In precolonial Igboland, girls and adolescents typically went naked save a few *jigida* beads worn around their waists.

48. This clause is borrowed from Luise White's important study (of the same name) of prostitution in colonial Nairobi.

49. These items, particularly the cigarettes, allow the historian to place the *adana* in historical time; cigarettes were not available until the colonial era.

50. These eateries also help place the *adana* during the colonial period and beyond.

51. Victoria Ugwoke, handwritten interview with author, Ikenga, Ogidi, Anambra State, Nigeria, September 24, 1999; Christopher Ezema, conversation with author, Ikenga, Ogidi, Anambra State, Nigeria, September 24, 1999.

52. Chinua Achebe, telephone conversation with author, March 28, 1999.

53. Naanen, "Itinerant Gold Mines," 60. It would also appear that a large number of Igbo women migrated back to Igboland from Akunakuna during the Nigerian/ Biafran Civil War, a detail that sheds light on how long these migrants tended to live away from home. Chinua Achebe, telephone conversation, 1999.

54. Obioma Nnaemeka, e-mail correspondence about terms and translations, April 3, 1999; Igwebueze Ugwuoke, interview with author, tape recording, Ihe Obukpa, Enugu State, Nigeria, November 6, 1996; Victoria Ugwoke, handwritten interview with author, September 24, 1999.

55. Victoria Ugwoke, handwritten interview with author, September 24, 1999; Erobike Eze, personal communication with author, Nsukka, Enugu State, Nigeria, September 26, 1998.

56. Members of the Igala Ruling Council, including HRH Jacob Osheni Odiba (the Odom Ata-Igala), HRH Amodo D. Haruna (the Onuega/Egen-Ata-Igala), HRH Chief S. U. Amanabu (the O-Dekina Ata-Igala), HRH Chief Omolobu Ata (the Wada Omeje Igala), HRH Chief E. O. Musa (the Ohe-Omogboro Ata), HRH Chief Abdullahi O. Ocheje (the Ochi Ata), HRH Alahji Hayatu Amodu (the Nalogu Ata), HRH Chief Ada Edein (the Ekpa Ata), HRH Chief Nuru I. Ogaji (the Amana Ata Okwuaja Idah), and HRH Odo. C. Hajia Sabime (the Abalaka Iye Ata), group interview (with Leonard Mbah and Winifred Nwaefido, 2008); Mallam Umonu interview (with Leonard Mbah and Winifred Nwaefido, 2008).

57. Mallam Umonu, P. E. Okwoli, and Ibrahim Omale each gave oral histories to Leonard Mbah and Winifred Nwaefido in 2008 about the deity *eboji* in Igalaland *oge mgbapu Ahebi:* Mallam Umonu interview (with Leonard Mbah and Winifred Nwaefido, 2008); P. E. Okwoli interview (with Leonard Mbah and Winifred Nwaefido, 2008); and Ibrahim Omale, interview with Leonard Mbah and Winifred Nwaefido, tape recording, Anyingba, Kogi State, Nigeria, February 2, 2008.

58. Mallam Umonu interview (with Leonard Mbah and Winifred Nwaefido, 2008).

59. Members of the Igala Ruling Council, including HRH Jacob Osheni Odiba (the Odom Ata-Igala), HRH Amodo D. Haruna (the Onuega/Egen-Ata-Igala), HRH Chief S. U. Amanabu (the O-Dekina Ata-Igala), HRH Chief Omolobu Ata (the Wada Omeje Igala), HRH Chief E. O. Musa (the Ohe-Omogboro Ata), HRH Chief Abdullahi O. Ocheje (the Ochi Ata), HRH Alahji Hayatu Amodu (the Nalogu Ata), HRH Chief Ada Edein (the Ekpa Ata), HRH Chief Nuru I. Ogaji (the Amana Ata Okwuaja Idah), and HRH Odo. C. Hajia Sabime (the Abalaka Iye Ata), group interview (with Leonard Mbah and Winifred Nwaefido, 2008); Mallam Umonu, interview (with Leonard Mbah and Winifred Nwaefido, 2008); P. E. Okwoli interview (with Leonard Mbah and Winifred Nwaefido, 2008); Lawrence Achimugu, interview with Leonard Mbah and Winifred Nwaefido, tape recording, Idah, Kogi State, Nigeria, January 28, 2008; Atukolo Obaka, interview with Leonard Mbah and Winifred Nwaefido, tape recording, Idah, Kogi State, Nigeria, February 7, 2008; and Grace Ajanigo Obaje (Akpata), interview with Leonard Mbah and Winifred Nwaefido, tape recording, Idah, Kogi State, Nigeria, February 7, 2008.

60. Ibrahim Omale, interview with Leonard Mbah and Winifred Nwaefido, tape recording, Idah, Kogi State, Nigeria, February 1, 2008.

61. For more on concubinage in other parts of West Africa, see Paul E. Lovejoy, "Concubinage and the Status of Women Slaves in Early Colonial Northern Nigeria," *Journal of African History* 29 (1988): 245–266; and Victor C. Uchendu, "Concubinage among Ngwa Igbo of Southern Nigeria," *Africa* 35, no. 2 (April 1965): 187–197. In the Sokoto Caliphate, according to Lovejoy, concubines were not constructed as free. They were considered enslaved to their masters. Among the Ngwa Igbo, concubines (*ikos*) were freeborn and consented to the sexual relationships that they developed.

62. Blessing (pseudonym), interview with Leonard Mbah, tape recording, Idah, Kogi State, Nigeria, January 29, 2008.

63. Lawrence Achimugu interview (with Leonard Mbah and Winifred Nwaefido, 2008); members of the Igala Ruling Council, including HRH Jacob Osheni Odiba (the Odom Ata-Igala), HRH Amodo D. Haruna (the Onuega/Egen-Ata-Igala), HRH Chief S. U. Amanabu (the O-Dekina Ata-Igala), HRH Chief Omolobu Ata (the

Wada Omeje Igala), HRH Chief E. O. Musa (the Ohe-Omogboro Ata), HRH Chief
Abdullahi O. Ocheje (the Ochi Ata), HRH Alahji Hayatu Amodu (the Nalogu Ata),
HRH Chief Ada Edein (the Ekpa Ata), HRH Chief Nuru I. Ogaji (the Amana Ata
Okwuaja Idah), and HRH Odo. C. Hajia Sabime (the Abalaka Iye Ata), group inter
view (with Leonard Mbah and Winifred Nwaefido, 2008); Mallam Umonu interview
(with Leonard Mbah and Winifred Nwaefido, 2008); Victor Akpan (Bassey), written
interview with Leonard Mbah and Winifred Nwaefido, Idah, Kogi State, Nigeria,
February 3, 2008; S. A. Ogah, interview with Leonard Mbah and Winifred Nwaefido,
tape recording, Idah, Kogi State, Nigeria, February 3, 2008; Theresa Etubi, interview
with Leonard Mbah and Winifred Nwaefido, tape recording, Idah, Kogi State,
Nigeria, February 3, 2008; Grace Ajanigo Obaje (Akpata) interview (with Leonard
Mbah and Winifred Nwaefido, 2008); Blessing interview (with Leonard Mbah, 2008);
Charity (pseudonym), interview with Leonard Mbah, tape recording, Idah, Kogi
State, Nigeria, February 1, 2008; Mohammed Balah Aliyu, interview with Leonard
Mbah and Winifred Nwaefido, tape recording, Idah, Kogi State, Nigeria, February 1,
2008; Pius Eje, interview with Leonard Mbah and Winifred Nwaefido, tape recording,
Sabongeri area of Idah, Kogi State, Nigeria, February 1, 2008; Ibrahim Omale inter-
view (with Leonard Mbah and Winifred Nwaefido, February 2, 2008).

64. Akyeampong's *Sexuality and Prostitution among the Akan of the Gold Coast*
supports the premise that the vast majority of prostitutes worked not in their region of
birth but outside it (i.e., in faraway places).

65. See Susan Geiger, *TANU Women: Gender and Culture in the Making of
Tanganyikan Nationalism, 1955–1965* (Portsmouth, N.H.: Heinemann, 1997), 34–36
for a discussion of prostitution in predominantly Muslim Tanganyika as well as Luise
White's study on prostitution in Nairobi, *The Comforts of Home.*

66. Pius Eje interview (with Leonard Mbah and Winifred Nwaefido, 2008).

67. P. E. Okwoli interview (with Leonard Mbah and Winifred Nwaefido, 2008);
Mohammed Balah Aliyu interview (with Leonard Mbah and Winifred Nwaefido,
2008); Ibrahim Omale interview (with Leonard Mbah and Winifred Nwaefido, 2008).

68. It is important to note that information about Igala prostitution was gathered
mainly from the Igala kingdom capital city Idah.

69. Lawrence Achimugu interview (with Leonard Mbah and Winifred Nwaefido,
2008); P. E. Okwoli interview (with Leonard Mbah and Winifred Nwaefido, 2008);
Blessing interview (with Leonard Mbah and Winifred Nwaefido, 2008); members of
the Igala Ruling Council, including HRH Jacob Osheni Odiba (the Odom Ata-Igala),
HRH Amodo D. Haruna (the Onuega/Egen-Ata-Igala), HRH Chief S. U. Amanabu
(the O-Dekina Ata-Igala), HRH Chief Omolobu Ata (the Wada Omeje Igala), HRH
Chief E. O. Musa (the Ohe-Omogboro Ata), HRH Chief Abdullahi O. Ocheje (the
Ochi Ata), HRH Alahji Hayatu Amodu (the Nalogu Ata), HRH Chief Ada Edein (the
Ekpa Ata), HRH Chief Nuru I. Ogaji (the Amana Ata Okwuaja Idah), and HRH Odo.
C. Hajia Sabime (the Abalaka Iye Ata), group interview (with Leonard Mbah and
Winifred Nwaefido, 2008); Pius Eje interview (with Leonard Mbah and Winifred
Nwaefido, 2008); Ibrahim Omale interview (with Leonard Mbah and Winifred
Nwaefido, 2008); S. A. Ogah interview (with Leonard Mbah and Winifred Nwaefido,
2008); Theresa Etubi interview (with Leonard Mbah and Winifred Nwaefido, 2008);
Atukolo Obaka interview (with Leonard Mbah and Winifred Nwaefido, 2008); Grace
Ajanigo Obaje (Akpata) interview (with Leonard Mbah and Winifred Nwaefido, 2008).

70. P. E. Okwoli interview (with Leonard Mbah and Winifred Nwaefido, 2008).

71. Mohammed Balah Aliyu interview (with Leonard Mbah and Winifred Nwaefido, 2008).

72. S. A. Ogah interview (with Leonard Mbah and Winifred Nwaefido, 2008).

73. Lawrence Achimugu interview (with Leonard Mbah and Winifred Nwaefido, 2008); P. E. Okwoli interview (with Leonard Mbah and Winifred Nwaefido, 2008).

74. Grace Ajanigo Obaje (Akpata) interview (with Leonard Mbah and Winifred Nwaefido, 2008).

75. See F. F. Ademola-Adeoye, "Language, Gender and Identity: A Social, Cultural and Psychological Study," available at http://www.staff.hum.ku.dk/smo/smo2/RC-News-vi-ni/Art-Lg-Gender.htm (retrieved May 16, 2008); "Nigerian Slangs," at http://www.nigeriancircle.com/forum/oencyclopedia.php (retrieved May 16, 2008).

76. See Achebe, "The Road to Italy," 177–184; and Nwando Achebe, "West Africa," in *The Encyclopedia of Prostitution and Sex Work*, 2 vols., ed. Melissa Hope Ditmore (Westport, Conn.: Greenwood, 2006), 2:532–536.

77. Blessing interview (with Leonard Mbah, 2008); members of the Igala Ruling Council, including HRH Jacob Osheni Odiba (the Odom Ata-Igala), HRH Amodo D. Haruna (the Onuega/Egen-Ata-Igala), HRH Chief S. U. Amanabu (the O-Dekina Ata-Igala), HRH Chief Omolobu Ata (the Wada Omeje Igala), HRH Chief E. O. Musa (the Ohe-Omogboro Ata), HRH Chief Abdullahi O. Ocheje (the Ochi Ata), HRH Alahji Hayatu Amodu (the Nalogu Ata), HRH Chief Ada Edein (the Ekpa Ata), HRH Chief Nuru I. Ogaji (the Amana Ata Okwuaja Idah), and HRH Odo. C. Hajia Sabime (the Abalaka Iye Ata), group interview (with Leonard Mbah and Winifred Nwaefido, 2008); Mohammed Balah Aliyu interview (with Leonard Mbah and Winifred Nwaefido, 2008); Ibrahim Omale interview (with Leonard Mbah and Winifred Nwaefido, 2008); Theresa Etubi interview (with Leonard Mbah and Winifred Nwaefido, 2008).

78. Many thanks to Folu Ogundimu for providing this Yoruba translation. Folu Ogundimu, conversation with the author, Lansing, Michigan, May 8, 2008.

79. P. E. Okwoli interview (with Leonard Mbah and Winifred Nwaefido, 2008); members of the Igala Ruling Council, including HRH Jacob Osheni Odiba (the Odom Ata-Igala), HRH Amodo D. Haruna (the Onuega/Egen-Ata-Igala), HRH Chief S. U. Amanabu (the O-Dekina Ata-Igala), HRH Chief Omolobu Ata (the Wada Omeje Igala), HRH Chief E. O. Musa (the Ohe-Omogboro Ata), HRH Chief Abdullahi O. Ocheje (the Ochi Ata), HRH Alahji Hayatu Amodu (the Nalogu Ata), HRH Chief Ada Edein (the Ekpa Ata), HRH Chief Nuru I. Ogaji (the Amana Ata Okwuaja Idah), and HRH Odo. C. Hajia Sabime (the Abalaka Iye Ata), group interview (with Leonard Mbah and Winifred Nwaefido, 2008).

80. Many thanks to Ibro Chekaraou for providing this Hausa translation; e-mail correspondence with author, May 8, 2008.

81. Ibrahim Omale interview (with Leonard Mbah and Winifred Nwaefido, 2008).

82. Grace Ajanigo Obaje (Akpata) interview (with Leonard Mbah and Winifred Nwaefido, 2008).

83. Mallam Umonu, interview (with Leonard Mbah and Winifred Nwaefido, 2008); Pius Eje, interview (with Leonard Mbah and Winifred Nwaefido, 2008); Victor Akpan, interview (with Leonard Mbah and Winifred Nwaefido, 2008); Grace Ajanigo Obaje, interview (with Leonard Mbah and Winifred Nwaefido, 2008).

84. Theresa Etubi interview (with Leonard Mbah and Winifred Nwaefido, 2008).

85. P. E. Okwoli interview (with Leonard Mbah and Winifred Nwaefido, 2008); Grace Ajanigo Obaje, interview (with Leonard Mbah and Winifred Nwaefido, 2008).

86. Mohammed Balah Aliyu interview (with Leonard Mbah and Winifred Nwaefido, 2008).

87. Pius Fje interview (with Leonard Mbah and Winifred Nwaefido, 2008).

88. Blessing interview (with Leonard Mbah, 2008).

89. Pius Eje interview (with Leonard Mbah and Winifred Nwaefido, 2008); Mallam Umonu, interview (with Leonard Mbah and Winifred Nwaefido, 2008); Mohammed Balah Aliyu, interview (with Leonard Mbah and Winifred Nwaefido, 2008); Victor Akpan, interview (with Leonard Mbah and Winifred Nwaefido, 2008); Grace Ajanigo Obaje, interview (with Leonard Mbah and Winifred Nwaefido, 2008).

90. P. E. Okwoli interview (with Leonard Mbah and Winifred Nwaefido, 2008); Ibrahim Omale interview (with Leonard Mbah and Winifred Nwaefido, 2008); Mallam Umonu interview (with Leonard Mbah and Winifred Nwaefido, 2008).

91. Mohammed Balah Aliyu interview (with Leonard Mbah and Winifred Nwaefido, 2008; Pius Eje interview (with Leonard Mbah and Winifred Nwaefido, 2008); Ibrahim Omale interview (with Leonard Mbah and Winifred Nwaefido, 2008); Victor Akpan interview (with Leonard Mbah and Winifred Nwaefido, 2008); Grace Ajanigo Obaje interview (with Leonard Mbah and Winifred Nwaefido, 2008).

92. P. E. Okwoli interview (with Leonard Mbah and Winifred Nwaefido, 2008); Grace Ajanigo Obaje interview (with Leonard Mbah and Winifred Nwaefido, 2008); Mohammed Balah Aliyu interview (with Leonard Mbah and Winifred Nwaefido, 2008).

93. Pius Eje interview (with Leonard Mbah and Winifred Nwaefido, 2008); Ibrahim Omale interview (with Leonard Mbah and Winifred Nwaefido, 2008).

94. *Chi* and *eke* refer to an individual's creator-spirit.

95. A. Edime, "The Rise and Fall of Igala State," *Nigerian Magazine* no. 80 (1974): 20.

96. Alice Akogu indicated that Ahebi did in fact trade at Ejule (interview, 2007). This fact was corroborated by Oyima Obeta Nwa Ugbabe in her 1998 interview.

97. Alice Akogu interviews (1998 and 2007).

98. Mallam Umonu interview (with Leonard Mbah and Winifred Nwaefido, 2008); Ibrahim Omale, "The Igala Woman," 1–27, unpublished ms., Department of Public Administration, Kogi State University, Anyigba, Kogi State, Nigeria.

99. Omale, "The Igala Woman," 6.

100. Alice Akogu interview (1998); Barnabas Obeta interviews (1996 and 1998); Ayogu Onu Odum interview (1998); Ogbu Nwa Abugwu Asenya Onu interview (1998); Oyima Obeta Nwa Ugbabe interview (1998); Bernard Ameh interview (1998); Nwoyeja Obeta (Felicia Ugwu Agbedo) interview (1998); Fabian Azegba interview (1998); Uroke Nwa Iyida Oku (Raymond Iyida) interview (1998); Michael Idoko interview (1996); Samuel Ezeja interview (1996).

101. Ibid., 15–16; Mallam Umonu interview (with Leonard Mbah and Winifred Nwaefido, 2008).

102. There is a rich literature on women's involvement in trade in West Africa. The following studies are worth mentioning: Polly Hill, "Markets in Africa," *The Journal of Modern African Studies* 1, no. 4 (December 1963): 441–453; B. W. Hodder and U. I. Ukwu, *Markets in West Africa: Studies of Markets and Trade among the Yoruba and Ibo*

(Ibadan: Ibadan University Press, 1969); E. Frances White, "Creole Women Traders in the Nineteenth Century," *International Journal of African Historical Studies* 14, no. 4 (1981): 626–642; Catherine VerEecke, "Muslim Women Traders of Northern Nigeria: Perspectives from the City of Yola," *Ethnology* 32, no. 3 (Summer 1993): 217–236; Claire C. Robertson, *Sharing the Same Bowl. A Socioeconomic History of Women and Class in Accra, Ghana* (Bloomington: Indiana University Press, 1984); Jane Turrittin, "Men, Women, and Market Trade in Rural Mali, West Africa," *Canadian Journal of African Studies* 22, no. 3 (Summer 1988): 583–604; Jane I. Guyer, "Women's Work in the Food Economy of the Cocoa Belt: A Comparison," *International Journal of African Historical Studies* 14, no. 2 (1981): 371–378; Gracia Clark, *Onions Are My Husband: Survival and Accumulation by West African Market Women* (Chicago: University of Chicago Press, 1994); and F. K. Ekechi, "Gender and Economic Power: The Case of Igbo Market Women in Eastern Nigeria," in *African Market Women and Economic Power: The Role of Women in African Economic Development*, ed. Bessie House-Midamba and Felix. K. Ekechi (Westport, Conn.: Greenwood Press, 1995), 41–57.

103. Omale, "The Igala Woman," 10.

104. Alice Akogu interviews (1998 and 2007); Barnabas Obeta interviews (1996 and 1998); Ayogu Onu Odum interview (1998); Ogbu Nwa Abugwu Asenya Onu interview (1998); Oyima Obeta Nwa Ugbabe interview (1998); Bernard Ameh interview (1998); Nwoyeja Obeta (Felicia Ugwu Agbedo) interview (1998); Fabian Azegba interview (1998); Uroke Nwa Iyida Oku (Raymond Iyida) interview (1998); Michael Idoko interview (1996); Samuel Ezeja interview (1996).

105. Ugwokeja Ozioko, interview with Aniemeka Michael Ugwu, Uzo Anyinya, Obukpa, Enugu State, Nigeria, October 10, 1983, in Aniemeka Michael Ugwu, "Some Aspects of Obukpa History before 1960" (B.A. thesis, Department of History, University of Nigeria, Nsukka, June 1984), 22; D. C. Ugwu, *This Is Obukpa: A History of Typical Ancient Igbo State* (Enugu, Nigeria: Fourth Foundation Publishers, 1987), vii, 5.

106. Abodo Nwa Idoko interview (1998); Boniface Abugu interview (1998); Ogbu Agashi interview (1996); Alice Akogu interview (1998); Nwoyeja Obeta (Felicia Ugwu Agbedo) interview (1998); Ayogu Onu Odum interview (1998); Barnabas Obeta interviews (1996 and 1998); Enwo Odo Nweze Nwaba interview (1998); Bernard Ameh interview (1998); Michael Idoko interview (1996); Ayogu Onu Odum interview (1998); Wilfred Ogara interview (1996); Samuel Ezeja interview (1996); Fabian Azegba interview (1998); Uroke Nwa Iyida Oku (Raymond Iyida) interview (1998); Simeon Nweke interview (1996); Abugwu Eze Nwa Asanya interview (1998); Asanya Onu interview (1998); Chikere Abugwu interview (1998); Ogbu Nwa Abugwu Asenya Onu interview (1998); David Ugwuaku interview (1998); Jonathan Abugwu Asanya interview (1998); Enwo Nwa Odo Nweze Nwaba Osogwu interview (1998); Fabian Omeke interview (1998); Michael Omeke Onasanya interview (1998); Fidelis Eze Nwonu Asanya interview (1998); Oyima Obeta Nwa Ugbabe interview (1998); Olu Oha Ignatius Abugu interview (1998); Ogbu Nwa Agashi interview, in Agbedo, "Slavery and Slave Trade," 65.

107. *Oge mgbapu Ahebi* there were four possible Attah-Igalas that Ahebi could have encountered. It is unlikely that Ahebi would have had any dealings with Attah-Amaja (1876–1900) or Attah-Ochejeonokpa (1901–1903), because she was quite young at the time they reigned. The *attahs* who were more likely to have interacted with her were Attah-Oboni (1905–1911) and Attah-Oguche Akpa (1911–1919). For more on the genealogy of Attah kingship, see *Programme of Events for the 50th Anniversary of the Enthronement of His Royal Majesty Alh. (Dr.) Aliyu O. Obaje*, 19.

108. Alice Akogu interviews (1998 and 2007); Barnabas Obeta interviews (1996 and 1998); Oyima Obeta Nwa Ugbabe interview (1998); Nwoyeja Obeta (Felicia Ugwu Agbedo) interview (1998); Simeon Nweke interview (1996); Abodo Nwa Idoko interview (1998); Fabian Azegba interview (1998); Adebo Peter Obalua, interview with author, digital voice recording, Ajeufo Palace, Idah, Kogi State, Nigeria, July 7, 2007.

109. Alice Akogu interviews (1998 and 2007).

110. Barnabas Obeta interviews (1996 and 1998); Boniface Abugu interview (1998); Fabian Azegba interview (1998); Abodo Nwa Idoko interview (1998); Wilfred Ogara interview (1996).

111. Evidence for Ahebi's participation in good and bad medicine and the reasons for this commitment were gathered from interviews with the following collaborators: Abodo Nwa Idoko (1998); Boniface Abugu (1998); Ogbu Agashi (1996); Alice Akogu (1998); Felicia Ugwu Agbedo (1998); Ayogu Onu Odum (1998); Barnabas Obeta (1996 and 1998); Enwo Odo Nweze Nwaba (1998); Bernard Ameh (1998); Michael Idoko (1996); Wilfred Ogara (1996); Samuel Ezeja (1996); Fabian Azegba (1998); Uroke Nwa Iyida Oku (1998); Simeon Nweke (1996); Abugwu Eze Nwa Asanya (1998); Asanya Onu (1998); Chikere Abugwu (1998); Ogbu Nwa Abugwu Asenya Onu (1998); David Ugwuaku (1998); Jonathan Abugwu Asanya (1998); Enwo Nwa Odo Nweze Nwaba Osogwu (1998); Fabian Omeke (1998); Michael Omeke Onasanya (1998); Fidelis Eze Nwonu Asanya (1998); Oyima Obeta Nwa Ugbabe (1998); and Olu Oha Ignatius Abugu (1998).

112. Several expeditions were launched against Nigerian communities, including the Yoruba, the Aro, the Ekumeku in the Asaba hinterland, and the Olokoro in Umuahia. For more on these attacks, see Johnson U. J. Asiegbu, *Nigeria and Its British Invaders, 1851–1920: A Thematic Documentary History* (Lagos: Nok Publishers International, 1984); and S. N. Nwabara, *Iboland: A Century of Contact with Britain, 1860–1960* (London: Hodder and Stoughton, 1977), unnumbered first and second pages of the preface, 79–96.

113. The Christian missionaries had been operating in Eastern Nigeria since 1841 and like the British colonialists labeled the area the "citadel of Satan"; Felix K. Ekechi, "The Holy Ghost Fathers in Eastern Nigeria, 1885–1920: Observations on Missionary Strategy," *African Studies Review* 15, no. 2 (September 1972): 237. They wasted no time in pioneering attacks against internal slavery, the killing of twins, and the activities of oracular institutions. The impact of three Niger expeditions—in 1841, 1854, and 1857—heralded what Ogbu Kalu has described as the dawn of a new economic, social, and religious reality in the lives of the Igbo. By 1857, a permanent Church Missionary Society mission had been established in Onitsha and the "scramble for souls" had begun. Much of this "good news" spread north to Enugu and south to Owerri under the direction of John Christopher Taylor, an Igbo from Sierra Leone. The phenomenal success of the Christian missionary enterprise owed part of its success to a close association with British colonialists who owned arms and the priority that missionaries placed upon education. See Ogbu Kalu, *The Embattled Gods: The Christianization of Igboland 1841–1991* (Lagos: Minaj Publishers, 1996), 80; and Edmund Ilogu, *Christianity and Ibo Culture* (Leiden: E. J. Brill, 1974), 56–60.

114. V. K. Johnson, "Intelligence Report on the People of Enugu-Ezike, Nsukka Division, Onitsha Province," paragraph 21, OP 1071 ONDIST 12/1/709, NAE.

115. It is interesting to note, however, that the concern of Europeans initially centered on the amelioration of the treatment of "slaves" rather than the immediate

eradication of slavery. In fact, some missionaries purchased "slaves" to use as domestic servants and as missionary workers and interpreters. See C. Ejizu, "Continuity and Discontinuity in Igbo Traditional Religion," in *The Gods in Retreat: Continuity and Change in African Religions,* ed. Emefie Ikenga Metuh (Enugu: Fourth Dimension Publishers, 1986), 145–148; Don Ohadike, "The Decline of Slavery among the Igbo People," in *The End of Slavery in Africa,* ed. Suzanne Miers and Richard Roberts, (Madison: University of Wisconsin Press, 1988), 443–450.

116. Johnson, "Intelligence Report on the People of Enugu-Ezike," paragraph 26.

117. Abraham Eya, Amufie, Enugu-Ezike, interview with Christopher Uchechukwu Omeje, October 29, 1977, in Omeje, "The Establishment of British Rule in the Old Nsukka Division" (B.A. thesis, History and Archaeology Special Project, University of Nigeria, Nsukka, 1978), 71.

118. Abodo Nwa Idoko interview (1998); Boniface Abugu interview (1998); Ogbu Agashi interview (1996); Alice Akogu interview (1998); Nwoyeja Obeta (Felicia Ugwu Agbedo) interview (1998); Ayogu Onu Odum interview (1998); Barnabas Obeta interviews (1996 and 1998); Enwo Odo Nweze Nwaba interview (1998); Bernard Ameh interview (1998); Michael Idoko interview (1996); Wilfred Ogara interview (1996); Samuel Ezeja interview (1996); Fabian Azegba interview (1998); Uroke Nwa Iyida Oku (Raymond Iyida) interview (1998); Simeon Nweke interview (1996); Abugwu Eze Nwa Asanya interview (1998); Asanya Onu interview (1998); Chikere Abugwu interview (1998); Ogbu Nwa Abugwu Asenya Onu interview (1998); David Ugwuaku interview (1998); Jonathan Abugwu Asanya interview (1998); Enwo Nwa Odo Nweze Nwaba Osogwu interview (1998); Fabian Omeke interview (1998); Michael Omeke Onasanya interview (1998); Fidelis Eze Nwonu Asanya interview (1998); Oyima Obeta Nwa Ugbabe interview (1998); Olu Oha Ignatius Abugu interview (1998).

119. Okwoli, *The History of the Fifty Years Reign of the Attah Igala,* 17; Yusufu Etu, *Igala History in Questions and Answers* (Jos, Nigeria: New Concepts Incorporated Book House, 2001), 21; J. S. Boston, *The Igala Kingdom* (Ibadan, Nigeria: Oxford University Press, 1968), 23; Onogu, "The Place of Princess Inikpi," 20–22.

120. Some tellings indicate that he consulted a Muslim cleric. See Okwoli, *The History of the Fifty Years Reign of the Attah Igala,* 17; Boston, *The Igala Kingdom,* 23.

121. Okwoli, *The History of the Fifty Years Reign of the Attah Igala,* 17; Boston, *The Igala Kingdom,* 23; Onogu, "The Place of Princess Inikpi," 20–23.

122. Okwoli, *The History of the Fifty Years Reign of the Attah Igala,* 17; Attama Oma Idoko Oshidadama, interview with author, digital voice recording, Agwa, Kogi State, Nigeria, July 7, 2007; P. E. Okwoli interview (2007); Idris Alaji, interview with author, digital voice recording, Bebejika, Kogi State, Nigeria, July 7, 2007; Elija Damasule, interview with author, digital voice recording, Attah-Igala's Palace, Idah, Kogi State, Nigeria, July 6, 2007; Adebo Peter Obalua interview (2007); Friday O. Ochenu, Attah-Igala's Palace, Idah, Kogi State, Nigeria, handwritten communication with author, July 5, 2007; members of the Igala Ruling Council, including HRH Jacob Osheni Odiba (the Odom Ata-Igala), HRH Amodo D. Haruna (the Onuega/ Egen-Ata-Igala), HRH Chief S. U. Amanabu (the O-Dekina Ata-Igala), HRH Chief Omolobu Ata (the Wada Omeje Igala), HRH Chief E. O. Musa (the Ohe-Omogboro Ata), HRH Chief Abdullahi O. Ocheje (the Ochi Ata), HRH Alahji Hayatu Amodu (the Nalogu Ata), HRH Chief Ada Edein (the Ekpa Ata), HRH Chief Nuru I. Ogaji (the Amana Ata Okwuaja Idah), and HRH Odo. C. Hajia Sabime (the Abalaka Iye Ata), group interview (with Leonard Mbah and Winifred Nwaefido, 2008).

123. Another version of this tradition claims that the soldiers were infected with cholera. See Okwoli, *The History of the Fifty Years Reign of the Attah Igala,* 17; Onogu, "The Place of Princess Inikpi," 22.

124. Oboni, *Ameh the Great,* 110; Onogu, "The Place of Princess Inikpi," 23.

125. Onogu, "The Place of Princess Inikpi," 23; P. E. Okwoli interview (with Leonard Mbah and Winifred Nwaefido, 2008); members of the Igala Ruling Council, including HRH Jacob Osheni Odiba (the Odom Ata Igala), HRH Amodo D. Haruna (the Onuega/Egen-Ata Igala), HRH Chief S. U. Amanabu (the O-Dekina Ata Igala), HRH Chief Omolobu Ata (the Wada Omeje Igala), HRH Chief E. O. Musa (the Ohe-Omogboro Ata), HRH Chief Abdullahi O. Ocheje (the Ochi Ata), HRH Alahji Hayatu Amodu (the Nalogu Ata), HRH Chief Ada Edein (the Ekpa Ata), HRH Chief Nuru I. Ogaji (the Amana Ata Okwuaja Idah), and HRH Odo. C. Hajia Sabime (the Abalaka Iye Ata), group interview (with Leonard Mbah and Winifred Nwaefido, 2008).

126. Oral information about Oma Idoko being elevated to a goddess was gathered in interviews with the following collaborators: Hajia Salime Abakwa, interview with Leonard Mbah and Winifred Nwaefido, tape recording, Idah, Kogi State, Nigeria, January 31, 2008; Elijah Damasule interview (2007); Agu Obaje, interview with author, digital voice recording, Attah's Palace, Idah, Kogi State, Nigeria, July 6, 2007; Adebo Peter Obalua interview (2007); Attama Oma Idoko Oshidadama interview (2007); Idris Alaji interview (2007); P. E. Okwoli interview (with Leonard Mbah and Winifred Nwaefido, 2008); members of the Igala Ruling Council, including HRH Jacob Osheni Odiba (the Odom Ata Igala), HRH Amodo D. Haruna (the Onuega/Egen-Ata Igala), HRH Chief S. U. Amanabu (the O-Dekina Ata Igala), HRH Chief Omolobu Ata (the Wada Omeje Igala), HRH Chief E. O. Musa (the Ohe-Omogboro Ata), HRH Chief Abdullahi O. Ocheje (the Ochi Ata), HRH Alahji Hayatu Amodu (the Nalogu Ata), HRH Chief Ada Edein (the Ekpa Ata), HRH Chief Nuru I. Ogaji (the Amana Ata Okwuaja Idah), and HRH Odo. C. Hajia Sabime (the Abalaka Iye Ata), group interview (with Leonard Mbah and Winifred Nwaefido, 2008).

127. Attah-Ameh Oboni later committed suicide in exile. See Oboni, *Ameh the Great,* 108–110, 124; Onogu, "The Place of Princess Inikpi," 37.

THREE Performing Masculinities

1. J. Barmby, "Intelligence Report on the Villages of Ede, Opi, Akwebe, Ohodo, Ozala and Lejja," 5, paragraph 10, EP 10862A CSE 1/85/5352, 1934, NAE; A. E. Afigbo, "Nsukka from Earliest Times to 1951," in *The Nsukka Environment,* ed. G. E. K. Ofomata (Enugu, Nigeria: Fourth Dimension Publishers, 1978), 34.

2. A. E. Afigbo, *The Warrant Chiefs: Indirect Rule in Southeastern Nigeria, 1891–1921* (Ibadan, Nigeria: Humanities Press, 1972), 68.

3. Major Gallway, quoted in Afigbo, *The Warrant Chiefs,* 69. Major Gallway's use of the word "chief" in this context is faulty: the Igbo people his infantry had conquered did not have village chiefs. This institution was introduced during the colonial period under the British.

4. For another study of British consolidation of power in Igboland, see Nwando Achebe, "'Ogidi Palaver': The 1914 Women's Market Protest," in *Nigerian Women in History, Culture and Development,* ed. Obioma Nnaemeka and Chima Korieh (New Jersey: Africa World Press), 49–76.

5. Abraham Eya, interview with Patrick Odo Agashi, Amufie, Enugu-Ezike, Anambra (now Enugu) State, Nigeria, August 15, 1978, in Patrick Odo Agashi, "Pre-Colonial Warfare in Enugu-Ezike" (B.A. thesis, University of Nigeria, Nsukka, June 1979), 75. In his transcription of Abraham Eya's interview, Agashi misspells the name of Nupe warrant chief Aduku as "Adukwu." I have corrected the spelling of his name in this excerpt. In the interest of consistency I will use this spelling (which I believe is the correct spelling of his name) in the rest of my book. The number 600 that Abraham Eya gives was not the number of British invaders present; it is the number of the Nigerian (mainly Hausa) troops that accompanied the British invaders.

6. Afigbo, *The Warrant Chiefs*, xi.

7. Boniface Abugu, interview with author, tape recording, Umuida, Enugu-Ezike, Enugu State, Nigeria, October 4, 1998. When asked why Ahebi was dreaded, Boniface Abugu explained that it was because she had run away from a decreed cult dedication and the deity she had refused was believed to be all-powerful. The people lived in fear that Ohe might release her wrath on the entire community.

8. We have already seen that Ahebi was in the company of Aduku, a Nupe man who was made warrant chief before Ahebi.

9. Afigbo, *The Warrant Chiefs*, 35.

10. M. M. Green, *Igbo Village Affairs* (New York: Frederick A. Praeger, 1947), 73.

11. Nwando Achebe, *Farmers, Traders, Warriors, and Kings: Female Power and Authority in Northern Igboland, 1900–1960* (Portsmouth, N.H.: Heinemann, 2005), 177–178; Kamene Okonjo, "The Dual-Sex Political System in Operation: Igbo Women and Community Politics in Midwestern Nigeria," in *Women in Africa: Studies in Social and Economic Change*, ed. N. J. Hafkin and Edna G. Bay (Stanford, Calif.: Stanford University Press, 1976), 55; Judith Van Allen, "'Sitting on a Man': Colonialism and the Lost Political Institutions of Igbo Women," *Canadian Journal of African Studies* 6 (1972): 171–172; Nina Mba, *Nigerian Women Mobilized: Women's Political Activity in Southern Nigeria, 1900–1965* (Berkeley: University of California Press, 1982), 38–39.

12. Afigbo, *The Warrant Chiefs*, 71.

13. Ibid., 104.

14. Ibid.

15. Ibid., 105.

16. For more on big men in colonial Africa, see Stephan F. Miescher and Lisa A. Lindsay, eds., *Men and Masculinities in Modern Africa* (Portsmouth, N.H.: Heinemann, 2003).

17. Chinua Achebe, telephone conversation with author, September 24, 2008. See also Nwando Achebe, "'Ogidi Palaver,'" 49–76.

18. Afigbo, *The Warrant Chiefs*, 105.

19. Abodo Nwa Idoko, interview with author, tape recording, Ikpamodo, Enugu-Ezike, Anambra (now Enugu) State, Nigeria, September 26, 1998.

20. Ogbu Agashi, interview with author, tape recording, Umuida, Enugu-Ezike, Anambra (now Enugu) State, Nigeria, September 26, 1996.

21. Simeon Nweke, interview with author, tape recording, Umuida, Enugu-Ezike, Anambra (now Enugu) State, Nigeria, November 25, 1996; Fabian Azegba, interview with author, tape recording, Umuida, Enugu-Ezike, Anambra (now Enugu) State, Nigeria, October 2, 1998; Okuti Ikorodo, interview with author, digital voice recording, Umuida, Enugu-Ezike, Enugu State, Nigeria, July 13, 2007.

22. I have taken the liberty of substituting in brackets the word "headman" each time Azegba incorrectly uses the term "customary court judge."

23. Fabian Azegba interview (1998).

24. Many thanks to Gordon Stewart; Mike Unsworth, History Librarian, Michigan State University; Peter Harrington, curator of the Anne S. K. Brown Military Collection in the John Hay Library, Brown University, Providence, Rhode Island; and Alfred Umhey, leading uniformologist from Europe, for their e-mail correspondence with me on October 2, 2008, about the helmet.

25. The initials are illegible in the archival sources, but we know that the district officer of Nsukka Division in 1931 was L. A. C. Helbert.

26. Native Court General Note Book, 1923–1927, 47, NSUDIV 25/1/5, NAE.

27. V. K. Johnson, "Intelligence Report on the People of Enugu-Ezike," paragraph 26, OP 1071 ONDIST 12/1/709, NAE.

28. Native Court General Note Book, 1923–1927, 2, NSUDIV 25/1/5, NAE.

29. Ibid.

30. Ibid., 5.

31. Ibid., 47.

32. Johnson, "Intelligence Report on Enugu-Ezike," paragraph 63.

33. Ibid., paragraph 28. Johnson's report informs us that Aduku of Amufie died on June 22, 1931.

34. Ona-Okochie died on December 24, 1932. Ibid.

35. Abugo Onogu died on July 6, 1928. Ibid.

36. Okoro Eze died on April 9, 1923. Ibid.

37. Agada died on January 1, 1923. Ibid.

38. Apoko died on April 4, 1923. Ibid.

49. Urarama-Asaba died in September 1922. Ibid.

40. Afigbo, *The Warrant Chiefs*, 174.

41. Ibid., 76.

42. See Nwando Achebe, "'[T]he Real Rulers of [Nsukka] Town[s] are the Ancestors or Spirits . . . ': Understanding the Female Principle in Igbo Religion," in *Igbos in the Atlantic World*, ed. Toyin Falola and Matt Childs (forthcoming) for a discussion of Igbo men who transformed themselves into male priestesses.

43. Johnson, "Intelligence Report on the People of Enugu-Ezike," paragraph 58.

44. The action of bringing out a masked spirit will be discussed in chapter 5.

45. For a detailed discussion of this system, see Achebe, *Farmers, Traders, Warriors, and Kings*, 162–173. See also Okonjo, "The Dual-Sex Political System in Operation," 47.

46. C. K. Meek, *Law and Authority in a Nigerian Tribe: A Study of Indirect Rule* (London: Oxford University Press, 1937), 148; Johnson, "Intelligence Report on the People of Enugu-Ezike," paragraphs 32–36; Samuel Ezeja, interview with author, tape recording, Umuida, Enugu-Ezike, Enugu State, Nigeria, November 25, 1996; Michael Idoko, interview with author, tape recording, Umuida, Enugu-Ezike, Enugu State, Nigeria, November 25, 1996.

47. Abraham Eya, interview with Christopher Uchechukwu Omeje, Amufie, Enugu-Ezike. Anambra (now Enugu) State, Nigeria, October 29, 1977, in Christopher Uchechukwu Omeje, "The Establishment of British Rule in the Old Nsukka Division" (B.A. thesis, University of Nigeria, Nsukka, 1978), 73.

48. Wilfred Ogara, interview with author, tape recording, Umuida, Enugu-Ezike, Anambra (now Enugu) State, Nigeria, November 25, 1996.

49. Ibid. Ahebi became king a few years after her induction as warrant chief and thereafter served her community in the capacity of both female warrant chief and king.

50. Barnabas Obeta, interview with author, tape recording, Umuida, Enugu-Ezike, Anambra (now Enugu) State, Nigeria, October 2, 1998.

51. Afigbo, *The Warrant Chiefs*, 37.

52. Ibid., 87–90.

53. A native council bench included a president, a vice-president, and four additional members, one of whom represented the village or district in which the dispute arose.

54. Afigbo, *The Warrant Chiefs*, 85.

55. Case No. 1, Criminal Judgment Books, 1928, 10–12, NSUDIV 14/1/76, NAE.

56. Criminal Judgment Books, 1928, illegibly numbered pages, NSUDIV 14/1/76, NAE.

57. See the appendix to this volume for charts showing the types of cases brought before the native courts in Nsukka Division during the period 1918–1930 and the judgments rendered.

58. As discussed in chapter 2, Igbo people believe that there is good and bad medicine. Good medicine (*ogwu*) is often curative, whereas bad medicine (*ajo ogwu*) is believed to have the power to do harm and kill.

59. The use of the word "brother" in this context does not refer to the biological state of being a brother. Rather, brotherhood in the Igbo sense could simply refer to a close relationship.

60. Similarly, the use of the word "sister" does not refer to the biological state of being siblings.

61. A special oath most likely means having the accused swear on an *ofo*. *Ofo* in Igboland is an emblem, a staff that represented the principle of peace and justice. Guiltless Igbo people evoke *ofo* in an action called *ijidelu mmadu ofo* that upheld the belief that an individual who has done no harm to another is innocent and therefore cannot be held accountable in any way, even if they have offended the said person. In this positioning, granting the accused one year to clear the oath represents the period that the community will keep vigil to see whether the accused falls sick or dies, because it is believed that if a guilty person swears on an *ofo*, s/he will surely die. For more on *ofo*, see Nwando Achebe, "When Deities Marry: Indigenous 'Slave' Systems Expanding and Metamorphosing in the Igbo Hinterland," in *African Systems of Slavery*, ed. Stephanie Beswick and Jay Spaulding (Trenton, N.J.: African World Press, 2010), 117.

62. Criminal Judgment Book, 1922, three illegibly numbered pages, NSUDIV 14/1/39, NAE.

63. See chapter 4 for more about Ahebi's personal palace court.

64. Case No. 125, Criminal Judgment Book, 1922, one illegibly numbered page, NSUDIV 14/1/39, NAE.

65. Johnson, "Intelligence Report on Enugu-Ezike," paragraph 48.

66. Ibid., paragraphs 70–71, 75–77.

67. Ibid., paragraphs 48–51. See also Meek, *Law and Authority*, 147.

68. Johnson, "Intelligence Report on Enugu-Ezike," paragraphs 78–79.

69. Case No. 226, Criminal Judgment Books, 1928, illegibly numbered pages, NSUDIV 14/1/76, NAE.

70. Afigbo, *The Warrant Chiefs*, 87.

71. Ibid., 87–88.

72. Ibid., 97.

73. "Ivu ada anyi ga ada, Ahebi" was twice performed by Oshageri Azegbo: tape and video recording, Umuogbo Agu, Enugu-Ezike, Enugu State, Nigeria, November 19, 1998; and tape and video recording, Umuogbo Agu, Enugu-Ezike, Enugu State, Nigeria, December 6, 1998. Translation by Dr. Chris U. Agbedo, Department of Linguistics University of Nigeria, Nsukka.

74. See table 1 in the appendix for an accounting of the criminal and civil cases in Nsukka Division native courts in which Ahebi participated as president, member, or witness, 1918–1930.

75. In a July 11, 1924 case, Chief Ahebi testified as a witness for the defense in a case against "one of her boys," Ogili of Umuida. In the case, the *ohas* seem to have struck a vindictive blow against Chief Ahebi owing to an unspecified dispute. They did this by levying a fine against Ahebi's "boy" for not having participated in public work for the past twelve years. Ahebi testified to the gang-up of the *ohas*, revealing that the men had sworn to effectively sever all ties with her and punish anybody who associated with her. The members of the court could not reach a decision immediately; they indicated that they would have to suspend the matter until the elders of Umuida were consulted. Civil Judgment Book, 1922–1924, 259–261, NSUDIV 16/1/23, NAE.

76. The institution of warrant chief in colonial Nigeria was abolished as a result of *ugu umunwanyi*—the (southern Igbo) women's war of 1929 in which southern Igbo women "made war" in order to call attention to a number of colonial policies that adversely affected their interests as women. They believed that the colonial government would institute direct taxation on them. They also held the colonial government responsible for the dramatic decline of palm-oil prices, which in fact was due to a world depression. Southern Igbo women were convinced that they were being cheated when the colonial government introduced an inspection of their produce and changed the method of purchase from measure to weight. The women were enraged at the persecutions, extortions, and corruption of the warrant chiefs and native court members. These factors, coupled with the fact that women felt disregarded and disrespected by the colonial officials, fueled the women's anger, presenting a need to put the British colonialists in order. At the end of the war, numerous government structures were destroyed, fifty women had died, and fifty more were imprisoned. In an attempt to appease the Igbo people, the colonial government outlawed the office of warrant chief. See H. A. Gailey, *The Road to Aba* (London: London University Press, 1970), 97–155; Margery Perham, *Native Administration in Nigeria* (London: Oxford University Press, 1937), 206–220; Elizabeth Isichei, *A History of the Igbo People* (London: Macmillan Press, 1976), 151–155; Mba, *Nigerian Women Mobilized*, 79–97; Sylvia Leith-Ross, *African Women: A Study of the Ibo of Nigeria* (London: Faber & Faber, 1938), 23–39; Audrey Wipper, "Riot and Rebellion among African Women: Three Examples of Women's Political Clout," in *Perspectives on Power: Women in Africa, Asia, and Latin America*, ed. Jean F. O'Barr (Durham, N.C.: Duke University Center for International Studies, 1982), 62–65; S. N. Nwabara, *Iboland: A Century of Contact with Britain, 1860–1960* (London: Hodder and Stoughton, 1977), 181–201; and Caroline Ifeka-Moller, "Female Militancy and Colonial Revolt: The Women's War of 1929, Eastern

Nigeria," in *Perceiving Women,* ed. Shirley Ardener (New York: John Wiley, 1975), 127–157.

77. Criminal Judgment Book, 1922, 118–119, NSUDIV 14/1/39, NAE.

78. Case 59, "Loose Papers: Sheet from Native Court Records Books 1926–30," two unnumbered pages, NSUDIV 13/1/3, NAE.

79. See the appendix, for the categories of civil and criminal cases that Ahebi presided over.

80. Meek, *Law and Authority,* 213; Afigbo, *The Warrant Chiefs,* 269.

81. Meek, *Law and Authority,* 207.

82. For an important collection of colonial court cases on law, property, and power in Africa, see Kristin Mann and Richard Roberts, eds., *Law in Colonial Africa* (Portsmouth, N.H.: Heinemann, 1991).

83. Afigbo, *The Warrant Chiefs,* 96.

84. The Ahebi Ugbabe Road took approximately two years to complete.

85. Even though Fabian Azegba says "all the men," the 1931 census was a count of all people.

86. Interview with Fabian Azegba (1998). Other support for Ahebi's taking charge of the 1931 census came from interviews with Boniface Abugu (1998), Michael Idoko (1996), Samuel Ezeja (1996), and Wilfred Ogara (1996).

87. Johnson, "Intelligence Report on People of Enugu-Ezike," paragraph 58.

88. J. S. Boston, *The Igala Kingdom* (Ibadan, Nigeria: Oxford University Press, 1968), 13. See also Austin J. Shelton, *The Ibo-Igala Borderland: Religion and Social Control in Indigenous African Colonialism* (Albany: State University of New York Press, 1971), 17; and Philip Adigwe Oguagha and Alex Ikechukwu Okpoko, *History and Ethnoarchaeology in Eastern Nigeria: A Study of Igbo-Igala Relations with Special Reference to the Anambra Valley,* Cambridge Monographs in African Archaeology 7 (Cambridge: Cambridge University Press, 1984), 12.

89. S. C. Ukpabi, "Nsukka Before the Establishment of British Administration," *Odu* 6 (October 1971): 105; Meek, *Law and Authority,* 166; P. A. Oguagha, "The Igbo and Their Neighbors: Some Patterns of Relationships in Pre-Colonial Southern Nigeria," in *Perspective[s] in History: Essays in Honor of Professor Obaro Ikime,* ed. A. E. Ekoko and S. O. Agbi (Ibadan, Nigeria: Heinemann Educational Books, 1992), 48; A. E. Afigbo, "The Nsukka Communities from Earliest Times to 1951: An Introductory Survey," in *The Nsukka Environment,* ed. G. E. K. Ofomata (Enugu: Fourth Dimension Publishers, 1978), 31; Lawrence Offie Ocho, "Nsukka: The Meeting Point of Four Civilizations," *Okikpe* 3, no. 1 (1997): 58.

90. Meek, *Law and Authority,* 153.

91. "Genealogy of Attah Kingship," in *Programme of Events for the 50th Anniversary of the Enthronement of His Royal Majesty Alh. (Dr.) Aliyu O. Obaje, Attah Igala and Chancellor, University of Lagos,* 19. Brochure in author's possession.

92. HRH Adebo Peter Obalua, interview with author, digital voice recording, Palace of HRH Ajeufo, Kogi State, Nigeria, July 8, 2007.

93. Oshageri Azegbo, interview with author, tape and video recording, Umuogbo Agu, Enugu-Ezike, Enugu State, Nigeria, December 6, 1998.

94. Ibid.; Abodo Nwa Idoko interview (1998); Selina Ugwuoke Adibuah, interview with author, tape recording, Trans-Ekulu, Enugu, Enugu State, Nigeria, October 23, 1996; Boniface Abugu interview (1998); Barnabas Obeta interview with author, video and tape recording, Umuida, Enugu-Ezike, Enugu State, Nigeria, November 25, 1996;

Barnabas Obeta interview (1998); Barnabas Obeta, interview with author, digital voice recording, Umuida, Enugu-Ezike, Enugu State, Nigeria, July 13, 2007; Fabian Azegba interview (1998); Ayogu Onu Odum, interview with author, tape recording, Umuida, Enugu-Ezike, Enugu State, Nigeria, September 29, 1998; Enwo Odo Nweze Nwaba, interview with author, tape recording, Umuida, Enugu-Ezike, Enugu State, Nigeria, September 29, 1998; Bernard Ameh, interview with author, tape recording, Unadu, Enugu-Ezike, Enugu State, September 29, 1998; Michael Idoko interview (1996); Wilfred Ogara interview (1996); Samuel Ezeja interview (1996); Uroke Nwa Iyida Oku (Raymond Iyida), interview with author, tape recording, Onitsha, Enugu-Ezike, Enugu State, Nigeria, September 28, 1998; Simeon Nweke interview (1996); Abugwu Eze Nwa Asanya, interview with author, tape recording, Umuida, Enugu-Ezike, Enugu State, Nigeria, September 29, 1998; Asanya Onu, interview with author, tape recording, Umuida, Enugu-Ezike, Enugu State, Nigeria, September 29, 1998; Chikere Abugwu, interview with author, tape recording, Umuida, Enugu-Ezike, Enugu State, Nigeria, September 29, 1998; Ogbu Nwa Abugwu Asenya Onu, interview with author, tape recording, Umuida, Enugu-Ezike, Enugu State, Nigeria, September 29, 1998; David Ugwuaku, interview with author, tape recording, Umuida, Enugu-Ezike, Enugu State, Nigeria, September 29, 1998; Jonathan Abugwu Asanya, interview with author, tape recording, Umuida, Enugu-Ezike, Enugu State, Nigeria, September 29, 1998; Enwo Nwa Odo Nweze Nwaba Osogwu, interview with author, tape recording, Umuida, Enugu-Ezike, Enugu State, Nigeria, September 29, 1998; Fabian Omeke, interview with author, tape recording, Umuida, Enugu-Ezike, Enugu State, Nigeria, September 29, 1998; Michael Omeke Onasanya, interview with author, tape recording, Umuida, Enugu-Ezike, Enugu State, Nigeria, September 29, 1998; Fidelis Eze Nwonu Asanya, interview with author, tape recording, Umuida, Enugu-Ezike, Enugu State, Nigeria, September 29, 1998; Oyima Obeta Nwa Ugbabe, interview with author, tape recording, Umuida, Enugu-Ezike, Nigeria, October 2, 1998; Ignatius Abugu, interview with author, tape recording, Imufu, Enugu-Ezike, Enugu State, Nigeria, September 28, 1998; Alice Akogu (formerly Ahebi) interview with author, tape recording, Ofante, Kogi State, Nigeria, October 5, 1998; Alice Akogu, interview with author, digital voice recording, Ofante, Kogi State, Nigeria, July 11, 2007; HRH Adebo Peter Obalua interview (2007); Onyima Obeta, interview with author, video and tape recording, Umuida, Enugu-Ezike, Enugu State, Nigeria, November 25, 1996; Onyima Obeta, interview with author, digital voice recording, Umuida, Enugu-Ezike, Enugu State, Nigeria, October 2, 1998; Elija Damasule, interview with author, digital voice recording, Attah's Palace, Idah, Kogi State, Nigeria, July 6, 2007; Agu Obaje, interview with author, digital voice recording, Attah's Palace, Idah, Kogi State, Nigeria, July 6, 2007; Friday O. Ocheni, handwritten communication to author, Attah's Palace, Idah, Kogi State, Nigeria, July 6, 2007.

95. *Agwogwu* is an expensive cloth with holes in it.

96. Oshageri Azegbo interview (1998). Azegbo's use of the term "gone astray" would refer to her stint as a prostitute in Igalaland.

97. "Isi na Ahebi abugu eze, gaje mijamaru Idah" was performed twice by Oshageri Azegbo: tape and video recording, Umuogbo Agu, Enugu-Ezike, Enugu State, Nigeria, November 19, 1998; and tape and video recording, Umuogbo Agu, Enugu-Ezike, Enugu State, Nigeria, December 6, 1998.

98. Abodo Nwa Idoko interview (1998); Alice Akogu interview (1998); Oshageri Azegbo interview (1998); Selina Ugwuoke Adibuah interview (1996); Boniface Abugu interview (1998); Ayogu Onu Odum interview (1998); Barnabas Obeta interviews

(1996 and 1998); Fabian Azegba interview (1998); Michael Idoko interview (1996); Samuel Ezeja interview (1996); Wilfred Ogara interview (1996); Enwo Odo Nweze Nwaba interview (1998); Bernard Ameh interview (1998); Uroke Nwa Iyida Oku (Raymond Iyida) interview (1998); Simeon Nweke interview (1996); Abugwu Eze Nwa Asanya interview (1998); Asanya Onu interview (1998); Chikere Abugwu interview (1998); Ogbu Nwa Abugwu Asenya Onu interview (1998); David Ugwuaku interview (1998); Jonathan Abugwu Asanya interview (1998); Enwo Nwa Odo Nweze Nwaba Osogwu interview (1998); Nwoyeja Obeta (Felicia Ugwu Agbedo), interview with author, tape recording, Umuida, Enugu-Ezike, Nigeria, October 4, 1998; Fabian Omeke interview (1998); Michael Omeke Onasanya interview (1998); Fidelis Eze Nwonu Asanya interview (1998); Oyima Obeta Nwa Ugbabe interview (1998); Ignatius Abugu interview (1998).

99. Song twice performed by Oshageri Azegbo: tape recording, Umuogbo Agu, Enugu-Ezike, Enugu State, Nigeria, November 19, 1998; and tape recording, Umuogbo Agu, Enugu-Ezike, Enugu State, Nigeria, December 6, 1998. Translation by Dr. Chris U. Agbedo, Department of Linguistics University of Nigeria, Nsukka.

100. The following collaborators provided supporting information on Ahebi's quelling of the resistance to her kingship and the fact that she was able to do so with the support of the British colonialists and Attah-Obaje: Ogbu Agashi interview (1996); Abodo Nwa Idoko interview (1998); Boniface Abugu interview (1998); Alice Akogu interview (1998); Nwoyeja Obeta (Felicia Ugwu Agbedo) interview (1998); Oshageri Azegbo tape and video interview (1998); Ayogu Onu Odum interview (1998); Barnabas Obeta interviews (1996, 1998, and 2007); Oyima Obeta Nwa Ugbabe interview (1998); Oyima Obeta Nwa Ugbabe, interview with author, digital voice recording, Umuida, Enugu-Ezike, Nigeria, July 13, 2007; Enwo Odo Nweze Nwaba interview (1998); Bernard Ameh interview (1998); Michael Idoko interview (1996); Wilfred Ogara interview (1996); Samuel Ezeja interview (1996); Fabian Azegba interview (1998); Uroke Nwa Iyida Oku (Raymond Iyida) interview (1998); Simeon Nweke interview (1996); Abugwu Eze Nwa Asanya interview (1998); Asanya Onu interview (1998); Chikere Abugwu interview (1998); Ogbu Nwa Abugwu Asenya Onu interview (1998); David Ugwuaku interview (1998); Jonathan Abugwu Asanya interview (1998); Enwo Nwa Odo Nweze Nwaba Osogwu interview (1998); Fabian Omeke interview (1998); Michael Omeke Onasanya interview (1998); Fidelis Eze Nwonu Asanya interview (1998); Ignatius Abugu interview (1998); Amos Abugu, interview with author, tape recording, Umuida, Enugu-Ezike, Enugu State, Nigeria, October 4, 1998.

101. HRH Adebo Peter Obalua interview (2007).

102. Oliefi Ugwu-Ogili, interview with author, digital voice recording, Umuida, Enugu-Ezike, Enugu State, Nigeria, July 13, 2007.

103. Case No. 134, Criminal Judgment Book, 1922, three illegibly numbered pages, NSUDIV 14/1/39, NAE. The preceding section on Ahebi's encounter with the occult was informed by interviews with the following collaborators: HRH Adebo Peter Obalua (2007); Abodo Nwa Idoko (1998); Boniface Abugu (1998); Barnabas Obeta (1996 and 1998); Bernard Ameh (1998); Fabian Azegba (1998); Samuel Ezeja (1996); Michael Idoko (1996); Oliefi Ugwu-Ogil, interview (2007); Oshageri Azegbo (1998); Alice Akogu (1998 and 2007); Boniface Abugu (1998); Ogbu Agashi (1996); Nwoyeja Obeta (Felicia Ugwu Agbedo; 1998); Ayogu Onu Odum (1998); Enwo Odo Nweze Nwaba (1998); Wilfred Ogara (1996); Uroke Nwa Iyida Oku (Raymond Iyida; 1998); Simeon Nweke (1996); Abugwu Eze Nwa Asanya (1998); Asanya Onu (1998); Chikere

Abugwu (1998); Ogbu Nwa Abugwu Asenya Onu (1998); David Ugwuaku (1998); Jonathan Abugwu Asanya (1998); Enwo Nwa Odo Nweze Nwaba Osogwu (1998); Fabian Omeke (1998); Michael Omeke Onasanya (1998); Fidelis Eze Nwonu Asanya (1998); Oyima Obeta Nwa Ugbabe (1998); Ignatius Abugu (1998).

104. Boston, *The Igala Kingdom*, 190; C. K. Meck, *An Ethnographical Report on the Peoples of Nsukka Division—Onitsha Province* (Enugu: Government Printer, 1930), page 34, paragraph 109.

105. See Obiukwu Nze (former warrant chief), transcribed interview with A. E. Afigbo, Umulolo, Awka Division, date unknown, in Afigbo, *The Warrant Chiefs*, 309.

106. The following collaborators spoke to me about the performance of King Ahebi's status by her flute blower and drum beater as well as the fact that she did not walk anywhere: Alice Akogu (1998 and 2007); Selina Ugwuoke Adibuah (1996); Oshageri Azegbo (1998); Abodo Nwa Idoko (1998); Boniface Abugu (1998); Ogbu Agashi (1996); Nwoyeja Obeta (Felicia Ugwu Agbedo, 1998); Ayogu Onu Odum (1998); Barnabas Obeta (1996 and 1998); Enwo Odo Nweze Nwaba (1998); Bernard Ameh (1998); Michael Idoko (1996); Wilfred Ogara (1996); Samuel Ezeja (1996); Fabian Azegba (1998); Uroke Nwa Iyida Oku (1998); Simeon Nweke (1996); Abugwu Eze Nwa Asanya (1998); Asanya Onu (1998); Chikere Abugwu (1998); Ogbu Nwa Abugwu Asenya Onu (1998); David Ugwuaku (1998); Jonathan Abugwu Asanya (1998); Enwo Nwa Odo Nweze Nwaba Osogwu (1998); Fabian Omeke (1998); Michael Omeke Onasanya (1998); Fidelis Eze Nwonu Asanya (1998); Oyima Obeta Nwa Ugbabe (1998); Ignatius Abugu (1998).

FOUR Inside King Ahebi's Palace

1. Samuel Apeh, interview with author, digital voice recording, Umuida, Enugu-Ezike, Enugu State, Nigeria, July 13, 2007. Corroborated also in Oliefi Ugwu-Ogili, interview with author, digital voice recording, Umuida, Enugu-Ezike, Enugu State, Nigeria, July 13, 2007; Alice Akogu (formerly Ahebi), interview with author, digital voice recording, Ofante, Kogi State, Nigeria, July 11, 2007; Fabian Azegba, handwritten conversation with author, Umuida, Enugu-Ezike, Enugu State, Nigeria, July 11, 2007; and Barnabas Akogu (formerly Ahebi), interview with author, digital voice recording, Ofante, Kogi State, Nigeria, July 11, 2007. A plot of land is about 150 x 60 feet. It is hard to say whether King Ahebi's palace grounds were as big as Apeh indicates. However, based on the information I gathered on the size of the land, Apeh is probably not too far off.

2. After King Ahebi died, many of the rightful owners of land Ahebi had acquired took it back.

3. Oliefi Ugwu-Ogili interview (2007).

4. King Ahebi had so many cows, according to Alice Akogu, that "if seven died a day, she would not have been able to tell." She also claimed that King Ahebi's cows tended to give birth almost daily. Alice Akogu interview (2007).

5. Samuel Apeh interview (2007).

6. Oliefi Ugwu-Ogili interview (2007).

7. Omabe was the fiercest masked spirit in Nsukka Division. Because it was owned by the community, the masked spirit would probably not have been housed in any individual man's house, let alone a woman's. I will discuss this in greater detail in chapter 6.

8. Alice Akogu interview (2007).

9.Ibid.

10. Samuel Apeh interview (2007).

11. *Oba ji iri na ahua* means twelve yam barns. *Ofu oba ji* is one yam barn, which typically contains enough yams to feed an entire polygamous family for a year. This barn would also contain the seed yams the farmer would plant the following year. Therefore, for King Ahebi to have over twelve barns of yam (*oba ji iri na abua*) was extraordinary. Many thanks to Chinua Achebe for providing me with this information; telephone conversation with author, October 20, 2008.

12. Alice Akogu, interview with author, tape recording, Ofante, Kogi State, Nigeria, October 5, 1998. Information was gathered from the following collaborators for the paragraphs on King Ahebi's farm workers: Oliefi Ugwu-Ogili interview (2007); Alice Akogu interview (2007); Barnabas Obeta, interview with author, tape and video recording, Umuida, Enugu-Ezike, Anambra (now Enugu) State, Nigeria, November 25, 1996; Barnabas Obeta, interview with author, tape recording, Umuida, Enugu-Ezike, Enugu State, Nigeria, October 2, 1998; Nwoyeja Obeta (Felicia Ugwu Agbedo), interview with author, tape recording, Umuida, Enugu-Ezike, Nigeria, October 4, 1998; Samuel Apeh interview (2007); Fabian Azegba, interview with author, Umuida, Enugu Ezike, Enugu State, Nigeria, October, 2, 1998; Bedford Okpe, interview with author, digital voice recording, Lagos, Lagos State, Nigeria, July 23, 2007; Bernard Ameh, interview with author, tape recording, Unadu, Enugu-Ezike, Enugu State, Nigeria, September 29, 1998; Michael Idoko, interview with author, tape recording, Umuida, Enugu-Ezike, Anambra (now Enugu) State, Nigeria, November 26, 1996; Oyima Obeta Nwa Ugbabe, interview with author, digital voice recording, Umuida, Enugu-Ezike, Enugu State, Nigeria, July 13, 2007. I also gathered information from Case No. 134, Criminal Judgment Book, 1922, three illegibly numbered pages, NSUDIV 14/1/39, NAE.

13. Which might be the reason that none of these homes, except the stone house for visitors, survived the Nigerian/Biafran Civil War.

14. Oliefi Ugwu-Ogili interview (2007).

15. For more on kingly taboos and the contaminating nature of menstrual blood, see the section on Ahebi's cooks later in this chapter.

16. Nwoyeja Obeta (Felicia Ugwu Agbedo) interview (1998).

17. Ibid.

18. Ibid.

19. Ibid.; Fabian Azegba interview (1998); Alice Akogu interviews (1998 and 2007); Bernard Ameh interview (1998).

20. Nwoyeja Obeta (Felicia Ugwu Agbedo) interview (1998). Additional collaborators provided information in interviews about the people who lived in Ahebi's palace. They are Fabian Azegba (1998); Barnabas Akogu (2007); Alice Akogu (2007); Samuel Apeh (2007); Oliefi Ugwu-Ogili (2007); Bernard Ameh (1998); and Christopher Akogu (formerly Ahebi), interview with author, digital voice recording, Ofante, Kogi State, Nigeria, July 11, 2007. I also relied on Moses Ogbu Apeh, handwritten piece on Ahebi, presented to author in Umuida, Enugu-Ezike, Enugu State, Nigeria, July 13, 2007.

21. On July 11, 2007, and July 13, 2007, Chinedu Chukwurah, a student at the University of Nigeria, Nsukka, worked with two groups of oral history collaborators

who had either lived in or close to King Ahebi's palace. They are Ahebi's adopted son, Stephen Akogu; his wife, Alice Akogu; and his eldest son, Barnabas Akogu; as well as Oliefi Ugwu-Ogili, the Honorable Fabian Azegba, retired army sergeant Samuel Apeh, and retired police constable Moses Ogbu Apeh, all of Umuida, Enugu-Ezike, Nigeria. Chukwurah accompanied me on a third trip to Umuida to sit with King Ahebi's nephew and nieces, Barnabas and Oyima Obeta, to capture their perspective on her palace, but they canceled the visit. Had Nwoyeja Obeta been alive, I am certain that she would have provided us with information.

22. Samuel Apeh interview (2007).

23. Oliefi Ugwu-Ogili interview (2007).

24. Alice Akogu interview (1998). Obaje Ocheji and Attah-Obaje were the same person. Attah-Obaje reigned from 1926 to 1945; Attah-Ameh reigned from 1946 to 1956.

25. Oliefi Ugwu-Ogili interview (2007).

26. Ibid.

27. Nwoyeja Obeta (Felicia Ugwu Agbedo) interview (1998).

28. Alice Akogu interview (1998).

29. Nwoyeja Obeta (Felicia Ugwu Agbedo) interview (1998).

30. Ibid.

31. Alice Akogu interview (1998).

32. Abodo Nwa Idoko, interview with author, tape recording, Ikpamodo, Enugu-Ezike, Anambra (now Enugu) State, Nigeria, September 26, 1998; Boniface Abugu, interview with author, tape recording, Umuida, Enugu-Ezike, Enugu State, Nigeria, October 4, 1998; Ogbu Agashi, interview with author, tape recording, Umuida, Enugu-Ezike, Anambra (now Enugu) State, Nigeria, September 26, 1996; Alice Akogu interview (1998); Nwoyeja Obeta (Felicia Ugwu Agbedo) interview (1998); Ayogu Onu Odum, interview with author, tape recording, Umuida, Enugu-Ezike, Enugu State, Nigeria, September 29, 1998; Barnabas Obeta interviews (1996 and 1998); Enwo Odo Nweze Nwaba, interview with author, tape recording, Umuida, Enugu-Ezike, Enugu State, Nigeria, September 29, 1998; Bernard Ameh interview (1998); Michael Idoko interview (1996); Wilfred Ogara, interview with author, tape recording, Umuida, Enugu-Ezike, Anambra (now Enugu) State, Nigeria, November 25, 1996; Samuel Ezeja, interview with author, tape recording, Umuida, Enugu-Ezike, Enugu State, Nigeria, November 25, 1996; Fabian Azegba interview (1998); Uroke Nwa Iyida Oku (Raymond Iyida), interview with author, tape recording, Onitsha, Enugu-Ezike, Enugu State, Nigeria, September 28, 1998; Simeon Nweke, interview with author, tape recording, Umuida, Enugu-Ezike, Anambra (now Enugu) State, Nigeria, November 25, 1996; Abugwu Eze Nwa Asanya, interview with author, tape recording, Umuida, Enugu-Ezike, Enugu State, Nigeria, September 29, 1998; Asanya Onu, interview with author, tape recording, Umuida, Enugu-Ezike, Enugu State, Nigeria, September 29, 1998; Chikere Abugwu, interview with author, tape recording, Umuida, Enugu-Ezike, Enugu State, Nigeria, September 29, 1998; Ogbu Nwa Abugwu Asenya Onu, interview with author, tape recording, Umuida, Enugu-Ezike, Enugu State, Nigeria, September 29, 1998; David Ugwuaku, interview with author, tape recording, Umuida, Enugu-Ezike, Enugu State, Nigeria, September 29, 1998; Jonathan Abugwu Asanya, interview with author, tape recording, Umuida, Enugu-Ezike, Enugu State, Nigeria, September 29, 1998; Enwo Nwa Odo Nweze Nwaba Osogwu, interview with author, tape recording,

Umuida, Enugu-Ezike, Enugu State, Nigeria, September 29, 1998; Fabian Omeke, interview with author, tape recording, Umuida, Enugu-Ezike, Enugu State, Nigeria, September 29, 1998; Michael Omeke Onasanya, interview with author, tape recording, Umuida, Enugu-Ezike, Enugu State, Nigeria, September 29, 1998; Fidelis Eze Nwonu Asanya, interview with author, tape recording, Umuida, Enugu-Ezike, Enugu State, Nigeria, September 29, 1998; Oyima Obeta Nwa Ugbabe, interview with author, tape recording, Umuida, Enugu-Ezike, Nigeria, October 2, 1998; Ignatius Abugu, interview with author, tape recording, Imufu, Enugu-Ezike, Enugu State, Nigeria, September 28, 1998; Ogbu Nwa Agashi interview, July 22, 1978, in Cyprian U. Agbedo, "Slavery and Slave Trade in Enugu-Ezike in the Pre-Colonial Period" (B.A. thesis, Department of History, University of Nigeria, Nsukka, June, 1979), 65.

33. Fabian Azegba interview (1998).

34. I differentiate human from spiritual "slaves" in my writing. Human "slaves" are bought or sold to individuals, whereas spiritual "slaves" are attached to deities, either as spouses or servants. See Nwando Achebe, *Farmers, Traders, Warriors, and Kings: Female Power and Authority in Northern Igboland, 1900–1960* (Portsmouth, N.H.: Heinemann, 2005), 72–73.

35. Alice Akogu interview (1998).

36. Ibid.

37. Ibid.; and Alice Akogu interview (2007).

38. Alice Akogu interview (1998).

39. Umuida is the natal village of Alice Akogu (née Abugu).

40. Alice Akogu interview (1998). Not having sons was deemed a problem in Igboland because without sons, one's name was not remembered. Sons also traditionally inherited land and other important possessions.

41. Ibid. "They were grabbing things at Umuida" is a reference to Ahebi's descendants dividing her possessions among themselves after her death. Even though Alice Akogu indicates that Stephen "was not worse off for returning," in fact Stephen did lose his status and access to Ahebi's wealth after her death.

42. Alice Akogu interview (1998).

43. Fabian Azegba interview (1998).

44. Samuel Apeh interview. "Settle them here" means "bribe them." Evidence for King Ahebi's *gago* force was gathered in interviews with the following oral history collaborators: Alice Akogu (1998 and 2007); Fabian Azegba (1998); Bedford Okpe (2007); Bernard Ameh (1998); Michael Idoko (1996); Uroke Nwa Iyida Oku (Raymond Iyida, 1998); Nwoyeja Obeta (Felicia Ugwu Agbedo, 1998); Simeon Nweke (1996); Boniface Abugu (1998); Abodo Nwa Idoko (1998); Barnabas Obeta (1996 and 1998); Ayogu Onu Odum (1998); Wilfred Ogara (1996); Samuel Ezeja (1996); Abugwu Eze Nwa Asanya (1998); Asanya Onu (1998); Chikere Abugwu (1998); Ogbu Nwa Abugwu Asenya Onu (1998); David Ugwuaku (1998); Jonathan Abugwu Asanya (1998); Enwo Nwa Odo Nweze Nwaba Osogwu (1998); Fabian Omeke (1998); Michael Omeke Onasanya (1998); Fidelis Eze Nwonu Asanya (1998); Oliefi Ugwu-Ogili (2007).

45. Native Court General Note Book, 1923–27, 47, NSUDIV 25/1/5, NAE.

46. Michael Idoko interview (1996).

47. For more on woman-to-woman marriages in Africa, see Beth Greene, "The Institution of Woman-Marriage in Africa: A Cross-Cultural Analysis," *Ethnology* 37, no. 4 (Fall 1998): 395–412; and Jean R. Cadigan, "Woman-to-Woman Marriage:

Practices and Benefits in Sub-Saharan Africa," *Journal of Comparative Family Studies* 29, no. 1 (Spring 1998): 89–99.

48. Nwoyeja Obeta (Felicia Ugwu Agbedo) interview (1998).

49. Fabian Azegba interview (1998).

50. Oliefi Ugwu-Ogili interview (2007).

51. Alice Akogu interview (1998).

52. Nwoyeja Obeta (Felicia Ugwu Agbedo) interview (1998).

53. Ibid.

54. *Obi fa sili ike* literally means "their hearts were strong."

55. Nwoyeja Obeta (Felicia Ugwu Agbedo) interview (1998). I gathered information on Ahebi's retraining house in interviews with the following other oral history collaborators: Bernard Ameh (1998); Oyima Obeta Nwa Ugbabe (2007); Boniface Abugu (1998); Oliefi Ugwu-Ogili (2007); Alice Akogu (1998 and 2007); Fabian Azegba (1998); and Uroke Nwa Iyida Oku (Raymond Iyida, 1998). I also drew on Moses Ogbu Apeh, handwritten piece on Ahebi, 2007.

56. Nwoyeja Obeta (Felicia Ugwu Agbedo) interview (1998).

57. Alice Akogu cooked for King Ahebi before she married Stephen Ahebi. At that time she was known as Alice Abugu. Alice Akogu interview (2007).

58. Nwoyeja Obeta (Felicia Ugwu Agbedo) interview (1998). By "brought," Nwoyeja meant paid as a cook. Her use of the words "move with the Attah" and "go with the Attah" are suggestive of a sexual relationship between Ahebi and Attah-Obaje.

59. Oyima Obeta Nwa Ugbabe interview (2007).

60. Ibid. *Okpa* is an Igbo delicacy prepared by steaming mashed *bambara* groundnut. The Igbo word for "smell" is *isi,* and "smelled" is *inu isi,* which means to "hear a smell."

61. Alice Akogu interview (2007).

62. Ibid. *Jiapa* and *alibo* are cassava flour.

63. Ibid.

64. Alice Akogu interview (1998).

65. Ibid. The Igbo language is tonal. A word spelled the same way could have as many as five different meanings. The word *eze* in this context refers to "teeth" rather than to "king." The tonal inflection in *eze* (teeth) is different from that in *eze* (king).

66. Onitsha Market was (and still is) the largest open-air market in West Africa and perhaps on the continent.

67. Alice Akogu interview (1998).

68. Alice Akogu could not remember Anekwe's last name but remembered that she was beautiful: "That Anekwe was exceedingly beautiful. Even when she was offered a husband, Ahebi's son who lived at Unadu refused to marry her for fear that she would intimidate him because she was too beautiful. Anekwe was too, too, beautiful, ah!" Alice Akogu interview (2007).

69. Alice Akogu interviews (1998 and 2007).

70. Oyima Obeta Nwa Ugbabe interview (2007). *Isi aka* literally means "hair made with the hands" and is used to denote braided as opposed to threaded hair.

71. Nwoyeja Obeta (Felicia Ugwu Agbedo) interview (1998).

72. Oliefi Ugwu-Ogili interview (2007). After Ahebi became king, she served her community as both warrant chief and king.

73. Ibid.

74. Alice Akogu interview (2007).

75. Oliefi Ugwu-Ogili interview (2007). Information for section on King Ahebi's palace court was gathered in interviews with the following oral history collaborators: Alice Akogu (1998 and 2007); Oyima Obeta Nwa Ugbabe (2007); Nwoyeja Obeta (Felicia Ugwu Agbedo, 1998); Bernard Ameh (1998); Boniface Abugu (1998); Fabian Azegba (1998); Ogbu Agashi interview (1996); Abodo Nwa Idoko (1998); Amos Abugu, interview with author, tape recording, Umuida, Enugu-Ezike, Enugu State, Nigeria, October 4, 1998; Oshageri Azegbo, interview with author, tape recording, Umuogbo Agu, Enugu-Ezike, Enugu State, Nigeria, November 19, 1998; Ayogu Onu Odum (1998); Barnabas Obeta (1996 and 1998); Enwo Odo Nweze Nwaba (1998); Michael Idoko (1996); Wilfred Ogara (1996); Samuel Ezeja (1996); Uroke Nwa Iyida Oku (Raymond Iyida, 1998); Selina Ugwuoke Adibuah, interview with author, tape recording, Trans Ekulu, Enugu, Anambra (now Enugu) State, Nigeria, October 23, 1996; Simeon Nweke (1996); Abugwu Eze Nwa Asanya (1998); Asanya Onu (1998); Chikere Abugwu (1998); Ogbu Nwa Abugwu Asenya Onu (1998); David Ugwuaku (1998); Jonathan Abugwu Asanya (1998); Enwo Nwa Odo Nweze Nwaba Osogwu (1998); Fabian Omeke (1998); Michael Omeke Onasanya (1998); Fidelis Eze Nwonu Asanya (1998); Oyima Obeta Nwa Ugbabe (1998); Ignatius Abugu (1998). I also drew on transcriptions of two interviews in Agbedo, "Slavery and Slave Trade in Enugu-Ezike in the Pre-Colonial Period": Ogbu Nwa Agashi, Ogrute, Enugu-Ezike, Anambra State, Nigeria, July 22, 1978 (page 64) and Onyeke Nwede, Ogurte, Enugu-Ezike, Anambra State, Nigeria, August 5, 1978 (page 73); and on Emmanuel Onoja Ugwu, interview with Remigius O. Agbedo, Amachalla, Enugu-Ezike, Anambra State, Nigeria, December 29, 1989, in Remigius O. Agbedo, "The Socio-Political and Economic Developments in Enugu-Ezike During the Colonial Period" (B.A. thesis, University of Nigeria, Nsukka, September 1990), 61. I also relied on page 12 of Agbedo's thesis.

76. Stephen and Onoja were Ahebi's "slave" children.

77. Infant school had three levels—levels 1, 2 and 3. Wilfred Ogara had attended infants 1, 2, and 3 at Ahebi's palace school.

78. There are differing dates for the end of World War II. Some sources date its ending on Victory in Europe Day, May 5, 1945, whereas others date it at the armistice of November 11, 1945, rather than the formal surrender of Japan, which took place on August 14, 1945. Wilfred Ogara's date falls within the accepted range of the period from May to November of 1945.

79. Wilfred Ogara interview (1996).

80. The British actually patrolled the area during the period 1909 to 1920; Nweke is off by one or two years. V. K. Johnson, "Intelligence Report on the People of Enugu-Ezike, Nsukka Division, Onitsha Province," paragraph 21, OP 1071 ONDIST 12/1/709, NAE.

81. Simeon Nweke interview (1996).

82. At the end of each interview, I typically give my oral history collaborators some money as a small token of my appreciation for their time; some collaborators spent several hours sharing their recollections with me. I do this not in an attempt to "buy" information from them (one cannot put a monetary amount on history) but to thank them for taking time out of their day for my study.

83. Barnabas Obeta interview (1996).

84. Barnabas Obeta interview (1998).

85. In the Igbo language one can refer to an older sister as a parent (especially if that sibling assumes the responsibility of parent), which is what Oyima does here.

86. Oyima's use of the term mother here is another acceptable Igbo reference to a close aunt.

87. These goods are called *ife eji edu uno* (literally, the things that a bride is ushered home with).

88. Part of the reason for this could have been a fear of being poisoned. Recall the case presented in chapter 3 about an alleged poisoning of her water pot.

89. Oyima is referring to what she considers their poverty.

90. Oyima Obeta Nwa Ugbabe interview (2007).

91. Nwoyeja Obeta (Felicia Ugwu Agbedo) interview (1998).

92. Ibid.

93. Barnabas Akogu interview (2007). *Obu* means "man's house"; that is how King Ahebi's house was referred to.

94. Agbedo, "The Socio-Political and Economic Developments in Enugu-Ezike," 22.

95. The Ahebi Palace School was a precursor to the Ahebi Primary School, which still exists in Umuida, Enugu-Ezike.

96. Nwoyeja Obeta (Felicia Ugwu Agbedo) interview (1998). Ahebi's palace school became a CMS school after a disagreement with the village elders (see below). Thus, the school that had started out as a Catholic school became a Protestant school.

97. For a good study of early mission education in colonial Nigeria, see La Ray Denzer, "Domestic Science Training in Colonial Yorubaland, Nigeria," in *African Encounters with Domesticity,* ed. Karen Tranberg Hansen (New Brunswick, N.J.: Rutgers University Press, 1992), 116–139.

98. Vincent and Godwin Aji Okegwu were sons of Headman Ugwu Okegwu.

99. Samuel Apeh interview (2007). "I used to follow Omabe" means that Samuel was one of the young children who followed the Omabe masquerade from place to place, enjoying its performance. He would not have been initiated into the masquerade cult because he was too young at the time.

100. Nwoyeja Obeta (Felicia Ugwu Agbedo) interview (1998).

101. Samuel Apeh interview (2007).

102. The first Igbo primer was published in 1857 by Samuel Crowther. His Isoama-Igbo primer was seventeen pages long and contained the Igbo alphabet and words, phrases, sentence patterns, the Lord's Prayer, the Ten Commandments, and translations of the first chapters of Matthew's gospel. See Frances W. Pritchett, comp., "A History of the Igbo Language," available at http://www.columbia.edu/itc/mealac/pritchett/00fwp/igbo/igbohistory.html.

103. F. Ugochukwu, "Dictionaries and Language Education—The Igbo Case," unpublished essay, available at www.pfi.uio.no/konferanse/LEA2006/assets/docs/Ugochukwu_paper.pdf.

104. Samuel Apeh interview (2007).

105. Ibid.

106. Ibid.

107. Ibid.

108. Mark 5:35–43.

109. Samuel Apeh interview (2007). My translation of "Talitha Koum!"

110. Samuel Apeh interview (2007).

111. My translation of "Oge Ezuwo, Anyi ga Ana." During our 2007 interview, Samuel Apeh sang both "Talitha Koum!" and "Oge Ezuwo, Anyi ga Ana" for me.

112. Samuel Apeh interview (2007).

113. This seems to be an adaptation of a practice of Igbo children *oge gbo* in which they visited the homes of prominent members of the community and danced for money during important festivals.

114. Samuel Apeh interview (2007).

115. Mrs. Rose Elam, interview with author, digital voice recording, Aku, Enugu State, Nigeria, July 20, 2007. Eleven years earlier, I interviewed Jacob and Rose Elam's adult daughter, Mrs. Christie Didiugwu, who also provided some information on her father's service as King Ahebi's teacher. Christie Didiugwu, interview with author, tape recording, Trans-Ekulu, Enugu, Anambra (now Enugu) State, Nigeria, November 1, 1996.

116. Wilfred Ogara interview (1996).

117. Information on missionary involvement in the setting up of schools in Enugu-Ezike was gathered from Ogbu U. Kalu, *The Embattled Gods: Christianization of Igboland, 1841–1991* (Lagos, Nigeria: Minaj Publishers, 1996), 118; and Remigius O. Agbedo, "The Socio-Political and Economic Developments in Enugu-Ezike," 22, 51. Information on the conflict between Jacob Elam and Ahebi was gathered from the following oral history collaborators: Nwoyeja Obeta (Felicia Ugwu Agbedo, 1998); Oliefi Ugwu-Ogili (2007); Samuel Apeh (2007); Fabian Azegba (1998); Boniface Abugu (1998); Wilfred Ogara (1996); Michael Idoko (1996); Ogbu Agashi (1996); Abodo Nwa Idoko (1998); Alice Akogu (1998 and 2007); Uroke Nwa Iyida Oku (Raymond Iyida, 1998); Oyima Obeta Nwa Ugbabe (1998 and 2007); Samuel Ezeja (1996); Simeon Nweke (1996); Samuel Ezeja (1996); Barnabas Obeta (1996, 1998, and 2007); Amos Abugu (1998); Enwo Nwa Odo Nweze Nwaba Osogwu (1998); and Bernard Ameh (1998). In addition, Vincent Aji Okegwu of Umuida, Enugu-Ezike, Enugu State, communicated with me in writing on July 11, 2007, as did Fabian Azegba on the same day.

FIVE Mastering Masculinities

1. Masquerades are the dead that have come back to life. Therefore, creating a masked spirit means that the person (through a ritual process that only full men can perform) fashions a physical representation of a community ancestor. Bringing the masquerade out is the introduction and performance of that masked spirit to members of the community.

2. Oshageri Azegbo, interview with author, tape recording, Umuida, Enugu-Ezike, Anambra (now Enugu) State, Nigeria, December 6, 1998.

3. Wilfred Ogara, interview with author, tape recording, Umuida, Enugu-Ezike, Anambra (now Enugu) State, Nigeria, November 25, 1996.

4. In this society, the more titles an individual takes (a feat that should, under normal circumstances, grant an individual increased power), the more restrictions the community applies to that person. For instance, certain titled men and women are not allowed to eat or sleep outside their homes; others are not even allowed to leave their

compounds. The *eze nri* (sacred "king"), for instance, was forced to plant his own yams! Leaders in this society were merely symbols of communal power and authority. Moreover, they were bound by an unwritten constitutional framework called *omenani* (taboos and observances) that imposed checks on a leader's power. In this system, therefore, a "king" could always be challenged by the community and was never above the law of the land. For more on this, see, T. Uzodinma Nwala, *Igbo Philosophy* (Lagos, Nigeria: Literamed, 1985), 172; and Ikenna Nzimiro, *Chieftaincy and Politics in Four Niger States* (London: Frank Lass, 1970), xvi and 253. Evidence was also gathered from Chinua Achebe, telephone conversation with author, October 13, 1999.

5. Chinua Achebe, "The Writer and His Community," in Achebe, *Hopes and Impediments* (New York: Anchor Books, 1989), 58.

6. Pius Charles Momoh, "The Social Functions of Masquerade in Enugu-Ezike: A Case Study of My Town Ogurute Enugu-Ezike in Igbo-Eze North L. G. A. of Enugu State" (B.A. thesis, University of Nigeria, Nsukka, February, 1994), 13–14.

7. Ibid., 22.

8. A. Talbot, *The Peoples of Southern Nigeria: A Sketch of Their History, Ethnology and Languages, with an Account of the 1921 Census*, vol. 3 (London: Oxford University Press, 1926), 767.

9. A. O. Onyeneke, *The Dead among the Living: Masquerades in Igbo Society* (Nimo, Nigeria: Holy Ghost Congregation, Province of Nigeria, and Asele Institute, 1987), 78.

10. Postmenopausal women in Igboland are considered gendered men. This is because they no longer menstruate—the crucial sign of womanhood.

11. Nwando Achebe, *Farmers, Traders, Warriors, and Kings: Female Power and Authority in Northern Igboland, 1900–1960* (Portsmouth, N.H.: Heinemann, 2005), 172.

12. See discussion of the society's use of masked spirits as instruments for admonishing offenders in chapter 3.

13. Momoh, "The Social Functions of Masquerade in Enugu-Ezike," 19–22.

14. Ibid., 15–16.

15. "A Owo Lee Leele" performed twice by Oshageri Azegbo: tape and video recording, Umuogbo Agu, Enugu-Ezike, Enugu State, Nigeria, November 19, 1998; and tape and video recording, Umuogbo Agu, Enugu-Ezike, Enugu State, Nigeria, December 6, 1998. Translated by Dr. Chris U. Agbedo of the Department of Linguistics, University of Nigeria, Nsukka.

16. I was able to determine that this event must have occurred sometime in 1939 because one of my collaborators, Boniface Abugu, remembered that this event happened in the same year that he started elementary school. Boniface Abugu, interview with author, tape recording, Umuida, Enugu-Ezike, Anambra (now Enugu) State, Nigeria, October 4, 1998.

17. Oshageri Azegbo interview (1998).

18. Amos Abugu, interview with author, tape recording, Umuida, Enugu-Ezike, Anambra (now Enugu) State, Nigeria, October 4, 1998. One other account claimed that Apeh Azegba spoke the following words directly to Ahebi's Ekpe: "Yes masquerade, you will go to the back," at which time it was escorted away. Boniface Abugu interview (1998). The events leading up to the seizure of Ekpe Ahebi were corroborated by Abodo Nwa Idoko, interview with author, tape recording, Umuida, Enugu-Ezike, Anambra (now Enugu) State, Nigeria, September 26, 1998; Wilfred Ogara

interview (1996); Samuel Ezeja, interview with author, tape recording, Umuida, Enugu-Ezike, Anambra (now Enugu) State, Nigeria, November 25, 1996; Fabian Azegba, interview with author, tape recording, Umuida, Enugu-Ezike, Anambra (now Enugu) State, Nigeria, October 2, 1998; and Uroke Nwa Iyida Oku (Raymond Iyida), interview with author, tape recording, Umuida, Enugu-Ezike, Anambra (now Enugu) State, Nigeria, September 28, 1998.

19. Elizabeth Isichei, *The Ibo People and the Europeans: The Genesis of a Relationship—to 1906* (New York: St. Martin's Press, 1973), 183.

20. Ibid., 158.

21. I began searching for this court case in 1996 at both the National Archives of Nigeria in Enugu and the Public Record Office now The National Archives in Kew, but unfortunately, despite numerous trips to both archives, I could not find it. In the approximately fifteen years since I started researching King Ahebi, I have combed through thousands of court cases. I am convinced that the case did go to the resident, as the people of Enugu-Ezike remembered, but I suspect it is now lost to history, perhaps due to the civil war or the deplorable condition in which documents are housed at the National Archives of Nigeria in Enugu, where this case most likely would have been deposited.

22. Fabian Azegba interview (1998); Bernard Ameh, interview with author, tape recording, Unadu, Enugu-Ezike, Enugu State, September 29, 1998.

23. "Ahebi akporo ifu ma woo ogbodu" performed twice by Oshageri Azegbo: tape and video recording, Umuogbo Agu, Enugu-Ezike, Enugu State, Nigeria, November 19, 1998; and tape and video recording, December 6, 1998. Translated by Dr. Chris U. Agbedo of the Department of Linguistics, University of Nigeria, Nsukka.

24. See narrative and tables of cases and dates that Chief Ahebi participated as member of the native courts of Nsukka Division in the appendix.

25. The following oral history collaborators spoke to me about the fact that Ahebi had to perform her burial rights while she was still living: Abodo Nwa Idoko interview (1998); Boniface Abugu interview (1998); Alice Akogu (formerly Ahebi), interview with author, tape recording, Ofante, Kogi State, Nigeria, October 5, 1998; Nwoyeja Obeta (Felicia Ugwu Agbedo), interview with author, tape recording, Umuida, Enugu-Ezike, Nigeria, October 4, 1998; Wilfred Ogara interview (1996); Fabian Azegba interview (1998); Simeon Nweke, interview with author, tape recording, Umuida, Enugu-Ezike, Enugu State, Nigeria, November 26, 1996; Abugwu Eze Nwa Asanya, interview with author, tape recording, Umuida, Enugu-Ezike, Anambra (now Enugu) State, Nigeria, September 29, 1998; Asanya Onu, interview with author, tape recording, Umuida, Enugu-Ezike, Anambra (now Enugu) State, Nigeria, September 29, 1998; David Ugwuaku, interview with author, tape recording, Umuida, Enugu-Ezike, Anambra (now Enugu) State, Nigeria, September 29, 1998; Jonathan Abugwu Asanya, interview with author, tape recording, Umuida, Enugu-Ezike, Anambra (now Enugu) State, Nigeria, September 29, 1998; Enwo Nwa Odo Nweze Nwaba Osogwu, interview with author, tape recording, Umuida, Enugu-Ezike, Anambra (now Enugu) State, Nigeria, September 29, 1998; Fabian Omeke interview with author, tape recording, Umuida, Enugu-Ezike, Anambra (now Enugu) State, Nigeria, September 29, 1998; Michael Omeke Onasanya, interview with author, tape recording, Umuida, Enugu-Ezike, Anambra (now Enugu) State, Nigeria, September 29, 1998.

26. Alice Akogu interview (1998). The details that Alice Akogu provided in this quote tell us that Ahebi's funeral lasted from morning until nighttime.

27. Ibid.

28. Nwoyeja Obeta interview (1998). As articulated in chapter 1, *igba* in Igbo means "the performance," "the procedure," "the investigation." It could also mean "to wear something." *Echi* is Igbo money. Therefore, *igba echi* in the context that Nwoyeja Obeta used it could mean either the "performance of money" or "the wearing of money" (in essence, the wearing of a ceremonial anklet). Southern Igbo people also evoke this distinction in the terms *igba nja* and *igba odu* (the wearing of a ceremonial anklet). Many thanks to Christie Chinwe Achebe for providing background information about this term. Christie Chinwe Achebe, telephone conversation with author, March 7, 2009.

29. Alice Akogu interview (1998).

30. Ibid.

31. Ibid.

32. Ibid. The sacrificing of human beings during the funeral services of royalty supposedly occurred in some of the centralized kingdoms in Nigeria *oge gbo gbo*, including the kingdoms of Benin and Oyo. The belief was that kings had a right to be accompanied into the world of the ancestors by their servants. See Alfred Burdon Ellis, *The Yoruba-Speaking Peoples of the Slave Coast of West Africa: Their Religion, Manners, Customs, Laws, Language, Etc.* (1894; repr., Chestnut Hill, Mass.: Adamant Media, 2003), 104; Bruce G. Trigger, *Understanding Early Civilizations: A Comparative Study* (London: Cambridge University Press, 2003), 89; and James D. Graham, "The Slave Trade, Depopulation and Human Sacrifice in Benin History," *Cahiers d'Études Africaines* 5 (1965): 317–334.

33. Alice Akogu interview (1998).

34. Oshageri Azegbo interview (1998).

35. "Igba naana eee" performed twice by Oshageri Azegbo: tape recording, Umuogbo Agu, Enugu-Ezike, Enugu State, Nigeria, November 19, 1998; and tape and video recording, December 6, 1998. Translated by Dr. Chris U. Agbedo of the Department of Linguistics, University of Nigeria, Nsukka.

36. "Onye Agbala Niya Uta" performed twice by Oshageri Azegbo: tape recording, Umuogbo Agu, Enugu-Ezike, Enugu State, Nigeria, November 19, 1998; and tape and video recording, Umuogbo Agu, Enugu-Ezike, Enugu State, Nigeria, December 6, 1998. Translated by Dr. Chris U. Agbedo of the Department of Linguistics, University of Nigeria, Nsukka.

37. Oliefi Ugwu-Ogili, interview with author, digital voice recording, Umuida, Enugu-Ezike, Enugu State, Nigeria, July 13, 2007.

Mmechi / The Conclusion

1. The buildings had doorways but no doors; I was able to walk right in.

2. During my fieldwork sponsored by the Ford Foundation in the fall of 1996, I journeyed into Enugu-Ezike with my driver Sir Christopher, stopping at the first elementary school that we saw. It was at this school that I first met Mr. Samuel Ezeja, who took a keen interest in my research and promised to accompany me into Umuida to meet with some of his contacts. Our first trip into Umuida was on Saturday, November 23, 1996.

3. Michael Idoko, interview with author, videotape recording, Umuida, Enugu-Ezike, Anambra (now Enugu) State, Nigeria, November 25, 1996.

4. Ibid.

5. In the Nigerian primary and secondary school system, each classroom has an elected class prefect, whose job it is to help the teacher keep order in the classroom. He or she typically does this by writing down the names of pupils who make noise when the teacher is away, or by copying lecture notes onto the chalkboard for his or her fellow classmates. It is the class prefect who rallies his or her classmates in greeting when a visitor enters their classroom.

6. My description of the class and its teachers is drawn from a videotape I recorded at the Ahebi School in Umuida on November 25, 1996.

7. "King" is a direct translation of the Igbo word *eze*. Most of the respondents used the term *eze* (king) as opposed to *eze nwanyi* (queen) when describing Ahebi Ugbabe.

8. It is most unlikely that Mr. Ene would have learned anything about King Ahebi in any of his social studies books, for very little had been written about her anywhere in 1996.

9. Barnabas Obeta, interview with author, tape and video recording, Umuida, Enugu-Ezike, Enugu State, Nigeria, November 25, 1996. Over the years, Nigerian currency has suffered a great devaluation. In the 1970s, the naira was much stronger than the dollar, with a 1976 exchange rate of 65 cents to ₦1. By 1996, when Barnabas said he loaned out King Ahebi's crown to people for ₦200.00, the naira had lost value and the dollar-to-naira exchange rate was only US$1 to ₦21.86. The naira has continued to plummet, and the 2010 exchange rate is now US$1 to ₦150.00. Information on the devaluation of the Nigerian naira was retrieved on January 10, 2009, from http://www.lonympics.co.uk/new/Naira.htm.

10. Barnabas Obeta interview (1996).

11. Two of Nigeria's most respected historians, A. E. Afigbo and Bolanle Awe, have bemoaned the propensity of some foreign "researchers" to "make away with" historical relics from Nigeria. Afigbo described this penchant as "grave robbery," whereas Awe called those responsible "smugglers and thieves." Speaking at a press briefing preceding the third anniversary celebrations of the Esie Soapstone Museum, Awe had this to say: "There is no doubt that they [foreigners] smuggled out our artifacts. Those who stole them in collaboration with our people did so for monetary gains. I came from African Studies of the University of Ibadan, so I know what I am talking about." Abiodun Fagbemi, "Bolanle Awe Alleges Stealing of Artefacts at Museum," *The Guardian*, January 28, 2009, available at http://odili.net/news/source/2009/jan/28/29.html (retrieved February 3, 2009).

12. For more on this see, Nwando Achebe, "'[T]he Real Rulers of [Nsukka] Town[s] are the Ancestors or Spirits . . . ': Understanding the Female Principle in Igbo Religion," in *Igbos in the Atlantic World*, ed. Toyin Falola and Matt Childs (Indiana University Press, forthcoming).

13. Francis Idoko, interview (2007). Francis Idoko is the other name of Priest Utubi.

14. Oshageri Azegbo, interview with author, tape and video recording. Umuogbo Agu, Enugu-Ezike, Enugu State, Nigeria, November 19, 1998.

15. *Onwuruchi* is a beautiful and expensive Igala robe that is patterned after the Igala Ekwe masquerade and is worn exclusively by affluent men and men of distinction.

Appendix

1. There were five civil and criminal judgment books in total: judgment books NSUDIV 15/1/1, NSUDIV 15/1/2, NSUDIV 15/1/3, NSUDIV 15/1/4, and NSUDIV 15/1/5. These judgment books were documentations of the earliest cases to go before the Nsukka Division native courts. Only case book, 15/1/5, covered cases in 1922 when Chief Ahebi was active.

2. There were a total of eighty-eight criminal judgment books housed at the archives (from NSUDIV 14/1/1 to NSUDIV 14/1/88). Of that total number, eighty judgment books fit in my time period (NSUDIV 14/1/8 to NSUDIV 14/1/88). Of these eighty, eight judgment books were missing: NSUDIV 14/1/67, NSUDIV 14/1/68, NSUDIV 14/1/77, NSUDIV 14/1/79, NSUDIV 14/1/80, NSUDIV 14/1/81, NSUDIV 14/1/87, and NSUDIV 14/1/88.

3. There were a total of thirty-one civil judgment books housed at the archives (from NSUDIV 16/1/1 to NSUDIV 16/1/31). Of that total number, twenty-seven judgment books fit in my time period (NSUDIV 16/1/5 to NSUDIV 16/1/31). Of these twenty-seven, two judgment books were missing: NSUDIV 16/1/24 and NSUDIV 16/1/28.

4. There were a total of six criminal cause books housed at the archives (NSUDIV 17/1/1, NSUDIV 17/1/2, NSUDIV 17/1/3, NSUDIV 17/1/4, NSUDIV 17/1/5, and NSUDIV 17/1/6). Of these six, two were missing: NSUDIV 17/1/1 and NSUDIV 17/1/2.

5. There were a total of seven civil cause books at the archives (NSUDIV 18/1/1, NSUDIV 18/1/2, NSUDIV 18/1/3, NSUDIV 18/1/4, NSUDIV 18/1/5, NSUDIV 18/1/6, and NSUDIV 18/1/7). Of these, two were missing: NSUDIV 18/1/5 and NSUDIV 18/1/7.

6. There were two Native Court general note books (NSUDIV 25/1/5 and NSUDIV 25/1/6). NSUDIV 25/1/6 was missing.

BIBLIOGRAPHY

Primary Sources

UNITED KINGDOM
The National Archives (TNA), Kew

Lloyd, W. H. "Annual Report on the Onitsha Province for the Year 1934," CO 583/204/BOX.

NIGERIA
National Archives of Nigeria (NAE), Enugu

"Annual Report N[sukka]D[ivision], 1937," NS 795 NSUDIV 8/1/190.

Barmby, J. "Intelligence Report on the Villages of Ede, Opi, Akwebe, Ohodo, Ozala and Lejja, Nsukka Division, Onitsha Province, 1934," EP 10862A CSE 1/85/5352.

———. "Intelligence Report on the Villages of Ukehe, Onyoho, Ochima, Ikolo, Aku, Ohebe, Umuna, Ngalakpu, Umunku and Idoha, Nsukka Division, 1934," OP 1029 ONPROF 8/1/4724.

Civil Judgment Book, 1922–1924, NSUDIV 16/1/23

Civil Judgment Book, 1923–1929, NSUDIV 16/1/24.

Civil Judgment Book, 1926–1927, NSUDIV 16/1/28.

Criminal Judgment Book, 1922, NSUDIV 14/1/39.

Criminal Judgment Book, 1925–1926, NSUDIV 14/1/67.

Criminal Judgment Book, 1925–1930, NSUDIV 14/1/68.

Criminal Judgment Book, 1928, NSUDIV 14/1/76 and NSUDIV 14/1/77.

Criminal Judgment Book 1929, NSUDIV 14/1/79.

Criminal Judgment Book, 1929–1930, NSUDIV 14/1/80 and NSUDIV 14/1/81.

Criminal Judgment Book, 1937–1943, NSUDIV 14/1/87.

Criminal Judgment Book, 1943–1954, NSUDIV 14/1/88.

Johnson, V. K. "Intelligence Report on the People of Enugu-Ezike, Nsukka Division, Onitsha Province, 1934," OP 1071 ONDIST 12/1/709.

"Loose Papers: Sheet from Native Court Records Books 1926–30," NSUDIV 13/1/3.

Native Court General Note Book, 1923–1927, NSUDIV 25/1/5.

OFFICIAL REPORTS

Federal Office of Statistics. "Census District NO: 305302, Census District Name: Nsukka North." In *Population Census of Nigeria, 1963,* vol. 1, part 4, *Census of Population, Eastern Nigeria, 1963.* Lagos, Nigeria: Federal Census Office, [1964–1965?].

Meek, C. K. *An Ethnographical Report on the Peoples of Nsukka Division—Onitsha Province.* Enugu: Government Printer, 1930.

ORAL INTERVIEWS
Interviews with Author

Abugu, Amos. Farmer. Tape recording. Umuida, Enugu-Ezike, Enugu State, Nigeria, October 4, 1998.

Abugu, Boniface. Ex-councilor and retired headmaster, now farmer. Tape recording. Umuida, Enugu-Ezike, Enugu State, Nigeria, October 4, 1998.

Abugu, Ignatius. Olu Oha and Onyishi Imufu. Tape recording. Imufu, Enugu-Ezike, Enugu State, Nigeria, September 28, 1998.

Abugwu, Chikere. Descendant of Ahebi Ugbabe. Tape recording. Umuida, Enugu-Ezike, Enugu State, Nigeria, September 29, 1998.

Abutu, Augustine. Onyishi Unadu. Digital voice recording. Unadu, Enugu State. Nigeria, July 15, 2007.

Adibuah, Selina Ugwuoke. Parasitologist and medical scientist. Tape recording. Trans-Ekulu, Enugu, Enugu State, Nigeria, October 23, 1996.

Afigbo, A. E. Professor Emeritus of History, University of Nigeria, Nsukka. Tape recording. Owerri, Imo State, Nigeria, October 3, 1996.

Agashi, Ogbu. Olu Oha. Tape recording. Enugu-Ezike, Enugu State, Nigeria, September 26, 1996.

Akogu (formerly Ahebi), Alice. Stephen Ahebi's wife. Ofante, Kogi State, Nigeria, October 5, 1998 (tape recording), and July 11, 2007 (digital voice recording).

Akogu (formerly Ahebi), Barnabas. Stephen Ahebi's first son. Digital voice recording. Ofante, Kogi State, Nigeria, July 11, 2007.

Akogu (formerly Ahebi), Christopher. Stephen Ahebi's second son. Digital voice recording. Ofante, Kogi State, Nigeria, July 11, 2007.

Akpanya, Alhaji Sarikin. Truck driver. Digital voice recording, Unadu, Enugu State, Nigeria, July 14, 2007.

Alaji, Idris. Brother of high priest of Oma Idoko Goddess. Digital voice recording. Bebejika, Kogi State, Nigeria, July 7, 2007.

Ameh, Bernard. Ahebi Ugbabe's great-great-grandson. Tape recording. Unadu, Enugu-Ezike, Enugu State, September 29, 1998.

Apeh, Moses Ogbu. Retired police constable. Digital voice recording. Umuida, Enugu-Ezike, Enugu State, Nigeria, July 13, 2007.

Apeh, Samuel. Retired army sergeant. Digital voice recording. Umuida, Enugu-Ezike, Enugu State, Nigeria, July 13, 2007.

Asanya, Abugwu Eze Nwa. Descendant of Ahebi Ugbabe. Tape recording. Umuida, Enugu-Ezike, Enugu State, Nigeria, September 29, 1998.

Asanya, Fidelis Eze Nwonu. Descendant of Ahebi Ugbabe. Tape recording. Umuida, Enugu-Ezike, Enugu State, Nigeria, September 29, 1998.

Asanya, Jonathan Abugwu. Descendant of Ahebi Ugbabe. Tape recording. Umuida, Enugu-Ezike, Enugu State, Nigeria, September 29, 1998.

Ayogu, Marford. Education secretary, Udeze Development Council, Enugu State, Nigeria. Digital voice recording. Unadu, Enugu State, Nigeria, July 15, 2007.

Azcgba, Fabian. Former councilor and headmaster. Umuida, Enugu-Ezike, Enugu State, Nigeria, October 2, 1998 (tape recording), and July 13, 2007 (digital voice recording).

Azegbo, Oshageri. Musician. Tape and video recording. Umuogbo Agu, Enugu-Ezike, Enugu State, Nigeria, November 19, 1998, and December 6, 1998.

Didiugwu, Christie. Businesswoman. Tape recording. Trans-Ekulu, Enugu, Enugu State, Nigeria. November 1, 1996.

Elam, Madam Rose. Jacob Elamu's wife. Interview with author. Digital voice recording, Aku, Enugu State, Nigeria, July 20, 2007.

Ezeja, Samuel. Schoolteacher. Interview with author. Tape recording. Umuida, Enugu-Ezike, Enugu State, November 25, 1996.

Idoko, Abodo Nwa. Herbalist and *dibia*. Interview with author. Tape recording. Ikpamodo, Enugu-Ezike, Anambra (now Enugu) State, Nigeria, September 26, 1998.

Idoko, Michael. Headmaster Ahebi Primary School. Interview with author. Tape and video recording. Umuida, Enugu-Ezike, Enugu State, November 25, 1996.

Idoko, Pius. Attama Ohe. Interviews with author. Tape recording. Imufu, Enugu-Ezike, Enugu State, Nigeria, November 23, 1996, and September 27, 1998.

Nwaba, Enwo Odo Nweze. Descendant of Ahebi Ugbabe. Tape recording. Umuida, Enugu-Ezike, Enugu State, Nigeria, September 29, 1998.

Nweke, Simeon. Former councilor. Tape recording. Umuida, Enugu-Ezike, Enugu State, Nigeria, November 26, 1996.

Obaje, Agu. Attah Obaje's aunt. Digital voice recording. Attah's Palace, Idah, Kogi State, Nigeria, July 6, 2007.

Obalua, HRH Adebo Peter. King of the Aju Amacho ruling house. Digital voice recording. Ajeufo, Kogi State, Nigeria, July 7, 2007.

Obeta, Barnabas. Biological nephew of Ahebi Ugbabe. Umuida, Enugu-Ezike, Enugu State, Nigeria, November 25, 1996 (tape and video recording), October 2, 1998 (digital voice recording), and July 13, 2007 (digital voice recording).

Obeta, Nwoyeja (Felicia Ugwu Agbedo). Biological niece of Ahebi Ugbabe. Tape recording. Umuida, Enugu-Ezike, Nigeria, October 4, 1998.

Odum, Ayogu Onu. Descendant of Ahebi Ugbabe. Tape recording. Umuida, Enugu-Ezike, Enugu State, Nigeria, September 29, 1998.

Ogara, Wilfred. Nonbiological son of Ahebi Ugbabe. Tape recording. Umuida, Enugu-Ezike, Enugu State, November 25, 1996.

Ogbonna, Josiah. Olu Oha of Nkofi Edem. Tape recording. Nkofi Edem, Enugu State, Nigeria, September 14, 1998.

Okpe, Bedford. Biological great-grandson of Ahebi Ugbabe. Interview with author. Digital voice recording. Lagos, Lagos Sate, Nigeria, July 23, 2007.

Oku, Uroke Nwa Iyida (Raymond Iyida). Former Igwe of Onitsha, Enugu-Ezike. Tape recording. Onitsha, Enugu-Ezike, Enugu State, Nigeria, September 28, 1998.

Okwoli, P. E. Igala Historian. Interview with author. Digital voice recording. Idah, Kogi State, Nigeria, July 7, 2007.

Omeke, Fabian. Descendant of Ahebi Ugbabe. Tape recording. Umuida, Enugu-Ezike, Enugu State, Nigeria, September 29, 1998.

Onasanya, Michael Omeke. Descendant of Ahebi Ugbabe. Tape recording. Umuida, Enugu-Ezike, Enugu State, Nigeria, September 29, 1998.

Onu, Asanya. Descendant of Ahebi Ugbabe. Tape recording. Umuida, Enugu-Ezike, Enugu State, Nigeria, September 29, 1998.

Onu, Ogbu Nwa Abugwu Asenya. Descendant of Ahebi Ugbabe. Tape recording. Umuida, Enugu-Ezike, Enugu State, Nigeria, September 29, 1998.

Oshidadama. Attama Oma Idoko. Digital voice recording. Agwa, Kogi State, Nigeria, July 7, 2007.

Osogwu, Enwo Nwa Odo Nweze Nwaba. Descendant of Ahebi Ugbabe. Tape recording. Umuida, Enugu-Ezike, Enugu State, Nigeria, September 29, 1998.

Sule, Alhaji Adama. Secretary, Attah-Igala Palace, Idah. Digital voice recording. Attah-Igala's Palace, Idah, Kogi State, Nigeria, July 6, 2007.

Ugbabe, Oyima Obeta Nwa. Biological niece of Ahebi Ugbabe. Tape recording. Umuida, Enugu-Ezike, Nigeria, October 2, 1998, and July 13, 2007.

Ugwoke, Victoria. Hairdresser and seamstress. Handwritten interview with author. Ikenga, Ogidi, Anambra State, Nigeria, September 24, 1999.

Ugwuaku, David. Descendant of Ahebi Ugbabe. Tape recording. Umuida, Enugu-Ezike, Enugu State, Nigeria, September 29, 1998.

Ugwu-Ogili, Oliefi. Elder, Umuida. Digital voice recording. Umuida, Enugu-Ezike, Enugu State, Nigeria, July 13, 2007.

Ugwuoke, Igwebueze. Retired headmaster and former councilor and chairman of Obukpa Development Committee. Tape recording. Ihe Obukpa, Enugu State, Nigeria, November 6, 1996.

Unsworth, Mike. History Librarian, Michigan State University. E-mail correspondence. October 2, 2008.

Utubi, a.k.a. Francis Idoko. Attama Ahebi Ugbabe Deity. Digital voice recording. Unadu, Enugu State, Nigeria, July 14, 2007.

Other Interviews

Abakwa, Hajia Salime. Iye-Ata Odo, the Attah-Igala's sister. Interview with Leonard Mbah and Winifred Nwaefido. Tape recording. Idah, Kogi State, Nigeria, January 31, 2008.

Achimugu, Lawrence. Principal, St. Peter's College, Idah. Interview with Leonard Mbah and Winifred Nwaefido. Tape recording. Idah, Kogi State, Nigeria, January 28, 2008.

Akpan (Bassey), Victor. Manager of Cliff Guest House and pimp. Interview with Leonard Mbah and Winifred Nwaefido. Handwritten interview. Idah, Kogi State, Nigeria, February 3, 2008.

Aliyu, Mohammed Balah. Retired police officer, Sokoto State. Interview with Leonard Mbah and Winifred Nwaefido. Tape recording. Idah, Kogi State, Nigeria, February 1, 2008.

Amanabu, HRH Chief S. U. The O-Dekina Ata-Igala. Interview with Leonard Mbah and Winifred Nwaefido. Tape recording. Attah-Igala's Palace, Idah, Kogi State, Nigeria, January 30, 2008.

Amodu, HRH Alahji Hayatu. The Nalogu Ata. Interview with Leonard Mbah and Winifred Nwaefido. Tape recording. Attah-Igala's Palace, Idah, Kogi State, Nigeria, January 30, 2008.

Ata, HRH Chief Omolobu. The Wada Omeje Igala. Interview with Leonard Mbah and Winifred Nwaefido. Tape recording. Attah-Igala's Palace, Idah, Kogi State, Nigeria, January 30, 2008.

Blessing (pseudonym). Igala hairdresser and prostitute. Interview with Leonard Mbah. Tape recording. Idah, Kogi State, Nigeria, January 29, 2008.

Charity (pseudonym). Igala saleswoman and prostitute. Interview with Leonard Mbah. Tape recording. Idah, Kogi State, Nigeria, February 1, 2008.

Edein, HRH Chief Ada. The Ekpa Ata. Interview with Leonard Mbah and Winifred Nwaefido. Tape recording. Attah-Igala's Palace, Idah, Kogi State, Nigeria, January 30, 2008.

Eje, Pius. Civil servant at Finance Department, Idah Local Government Area, Kogi State. Interview with Leonard Mbah and Winifred Nwaefido. Tape recording. Sabongeri area of Idah, Kogi State, Nigeria, February 1, 2008.

Etubi, Theresa. Principal, Holy Rosary College, Idah. Interview with Leonard Mbah and Winifred Nwaefido. Tape recording. Idah, Kogi State, Nigeria, February 3, 2008.

Haruna, HRH Amodo D. The Onuega/Egen-Ata-Igala. Interview by Leonard Mbah and Winifred Nwaefido. Tape recording. Attah-Igala's Palace, Idah, Kogi State, Nigeria, January 30, 2008.

Musa, HRH Chief E. O. The Ohe-Omogboro Ata. Interview with Leonard Mbah and Winifred Nwaefido. Tape recording. Attah-Igala's Palace, Idah, Kogi State, Nigeria, January 30, 2008.

Obaje, Grace Ajanigo (Akpata). Nurse. Interview with Leonard Mbah and Winifred Nwaefido. Tape recording. Idah, Kogi State, Nigeria, February 7, 2008.

Obaka, Atukolo. The Gago Ede-Alaba. Interview with Leonard Mbah and Winifred Nwaefido. Tape recording. Idah, Kogi State, Nigeria, February 7, 2008.

Ocheje, HRH Chief Abdullahi O. The Ochi Ata. Interview with Leonard Mbah and Winifred Nwaefido. Tape recording. Attah-Igala's Palace, Idah, Kogi State, Nigeria, January 30, 2008.

Odiba, HRH Jacob Osheni. The Odom Ata-Igala. Interview with Leonard Mbah and Winifred Nwaefido. Tape recording. Attah-Igala's Palace, Idah, Kogi State, Nigeria, January 30, 2008.

Ogah, (Mrs.). S. A. Teacher, Holy Rosary College, Idah. Interview with Leonard Mbah and Winifred Nwaefido. Tape recording. Idah, Kogi State, Nigeria, February 3, 2008.

Ogaji, HRH Chief Nuru I. The Amana Ata Okwuaja Idah. Interview with Leonard Mbah and Winifred Nwaefido. Tape recording. Attah-Igala's Palace, Idah, Kogi State, Nigeria, January 30, 2008.

Okwoli, P. E. Igala historian. Interview with Leonard Mbah and Winifred Nwaefido. Tape recording. Idah, Kogi State, Nigeria, January 30, 2008.

Omale, Ibrahim. Lecturer in public administration, Kogi State University, Anyingba. Interview with Leonard Mbah and Winifred Nwaefido. Tape recording. Anyingba, Kogi State, Nigeria, February 1 and February 2, 2008.

Sabime, HRH Odo. C. Hajia. The Abalaka Iye Ata. Interview with Leonard Mbah and Winifred Nwaefido. Tape recording. Attah-Igala's Palace, Idah, Kogi State, Nigeria, January 30, 2008.

Umonu, Mallam. Vice-principal of administration, Idah Commercial Secondary School. Interview with Leonard Mbah and Winifred Nwaefido. Tape recording. Idah, Kogi State, Nigeria, February 1, 2008.

PERSONAL COMMUNICATION

Achebe, Chinua. David and Marianna Fisher University Professor and Professor of Africana Studies, Brown University.

———. Telephone conversation with author. March 28, 1999.

———. Telephone conversation with author. October 13, 1999.

———. Telephone conversation with author. April 2, 2008.

———. Telephone conversation with author. April 4, 2008.

———. Written communication with author. April 10, 2008.

———. Telephone conversations with author. September 4, 2008

———. Telephone conversations with author. September 5, 2008.

———. Telephone conversation with author. September 24, 2008.

Achebe, Chinwe Christie. Professor of Education, Bard College, Annandale-on-Hudson, New York. Telephone conversation with author. April 4, 2008.

———. Handwritten communication with author. December 22, 2008.

———. Telephone conversation with author. March 7, 2009.

Afigbo, A. E. Professor Emeritus of History, University of Nigeria, Nsukka. E-mail correspondence with author. January 2, 2006.

Apeh, Apex. Lecturer, Department of History, University of Nigeria, Nsukka. Handwritten communication with Leonard Mbah. Nsukka, Enugu State, Nigeria, February 13, 2008.

Apeh, Moses Ogbu. Retired police constable. Handwritten piece on Ahebi. Presented to author in Umuida, Enugu-Ezike, Enugu State, Nigeria, July 13, 2007.

Chekaraou, Ibro. Visiting Assistant Professor of Linguistics and German, Slavic, Asian and African Languages, Michigan State University. E-mail correspondence with author. May 8, 2008.

Eze, Erobike. Retired civil servant and farmer. Handwritten communication with author. Trans Ekulu, Enugu, Enugu State, Nigeria, July 20, 2008.

———. Personal communication with author. Nsukka, Enugu State, Nigeria, September 26, 1998.

Ezema, Christopher. Retired timber dealer, now a farmer. Conversation with author. Ikenga, Ogidi, Anambra State, Nigeria, September 24, 1999.

Harrington, Peter. Curator of the Anne S. K. Brown Military Collection in the John Hay Library, Brown University, Providence, Rhode Island. E-mail correspondence with author. October 2, 2008.

Nnaemeka, Obioma. Chancellor Professor of French and Women's Studies, Indiana University. E-mail correspondence with author. April 3, 1999.

Nnaji, Amadi. Lecturer, Department of Linguistics, University of Nigeria, Nsukka. Handwritten communication with Leonard Mbah. Nsukka, Enugu State, Nigeria, February 3, 2008.

Ochenu, Friday O. Attah-Igala Palace receptionist/secretary. Handwritten communication with author. Attah-Igala's Palace, Idah, Kogi State, Nigeria, July 5, 2007.

Odamtten, Harry. Ph.D. candidate, Department of History, Michigan State University. Written communication with author. April 24, 2008.

Ogundimu, Folu. Professor of Journalism and Communications, Michigan State University. Conversation with author. Lansing, Michigan, May 8, 2008.

Okwoli, P. E. Igala historian. Telephone conversation with Leonard Mbah. February 5–6, 2008.

Onekutu, P. M. Lecturer, Department of Igala, College of Education, Ankpa. Handwritten communication with Leonard Mbah. Ankpa, Kogi State, Nigeria, February 3, 2008.

Umhey, Alfred. Uniformologist. E-mail correspondence with author. October 2, 2008.

Interviews in Published Sources

Nze, Obiukwu. Former warrant chief. Transcribed interview with A. E. Afigbo. Umulolo, Awka Division, date unknown. In A. E. Afigbo,. *The Warrant Chiefs: Indirect Rule in Southeastern Nigeria, 1891–1921.* Ibadan, Nigeria: Humanities Press, 1972, 309.

Oral Interviews Transcribed in Student Papers and Theses, Department of History, University of Nigeria, Nsukka

Agashi, Ogbu Nwa. Farmer. Ogrute, Enugu-Ezike, 22 July 1978. In Cyprian U. Agbedo, "Slavery and Slave Trade in Enugu-Ezike in the Pre-colonial Period." B.A. thesis, Department of History, University of Nigeria, Nsukka, June, 1979.

Eya, Abraham. Church and community leader. Amufie, Enugu-Ezike, Anambra [Enugu] State, Nigeria, August 15, 1978. In Patrick Odo Agashi, "Pre-Colonial Warfare in Enugu-Ezike. B.A. thesis, University of Nigeria, Nsukka, June 1979.

————. Amufie, Enugu-Ezike, August 17, 1978. In Cyprian U. Agbedo, "Slavery and Slave Trade in Enugu-Ezike in the Pre-Colonial Period." B.A. thesis, Department of History, University of Nigeria, Nsukka, June, 1979.

————. Amufie, Enugu-Ezike, October 29, 1977. In Christopher Uchechukwu Omeje, "The Establishment of British Rule in the Old Nsukka Division." B.A. History and Archaeology Special Project, University of Nigeria, Nsukka, June 1978.

Nwede, Onyeke. Wine-tapper. Ogrute, Enugu-Ezike, August 5, 1978. In Patrick Odo Agashi, "Pre-Colonial Warfare in Enugu-Ezike. B.A. thesis, University of Nigeria, Nsukka, June 1979.

Ozioko, Ugwokeja. Uzo Anyinya, Obukpa, Enugu State, Nigeria. October 10, 1983. In Aniemeka Michael Ugwu, "Some Aspects of Obukpa History before 1960." B.A. thesis, Department of History, University of Nigeria, Nsukka, June 1984.

Secondary Sources

BOOKS AND ARTICLES

Abangwu, C. A. *Nsukka Handbook.* Enugu, Nigeria: Federated Nsukka District Union, 1960.

Abu-Lughod, Lila. *Writing Women's Worlds: Bedouin Stories.* Berkeley: University of California Press, 1993.

Achebe, Chinua. "'Chi' in Igbo Cosmology." In *African Philosophy: An Anthology,* ed. Emmanuel Chukwudi Eze, 67–72. Malden, Mass.: Blackwell, 1998.

————. *Things Fall Apart.* New York: Doubleday, 1959.

————."The Writer and His Community." In Achebe, *Hopes and Impediments.* New York: Anchor Books, 1989.

Achebe, Nwando. "'And She Became a Man': King Ahebi Ugbabe in the History of Enugu-Ezike, Northern Igboland, 1880–1948." In *Men and Masculinities in Modern Africa,* ed. Stephan F. Miescher and Lisa A. Lindsay, 52–68. Portsmouth, N.H.: Heinemann, 2003.

————. "The Day I 'Met' Ahebi Ugbabe, *Female* King of Enugu-Ezike, Nigeria." *Journal of Women's History* 21, no. 4 (Winter 2009): 134–137.

————. *Farmers, Traders, Warriors, and Kings: Female Power and Authority in Northern Igboland, 1900–1960.* Portsmouth, N.H.: Heinemann, 2005.

————. "*Igo Mma Ogo:* The Adoro Goddess, Her Wives and Challengers—Influences on the Reconstruction of Alor-Uno, Northern Igboland, 1890–1994." *Journal of Women's History* 14, no. 4 (Winter 2003): 83–104.

————. "Murder in Ochima: Priestess Mgbafor-Ezira, Nwachukwu and the Circumstances Leading Up to the Death of Major G. L. D. Rewcastle." In *Emergent Themes and Methods in African Studies: Essays in Honor of Adiele*

Eberechukwu Afigbo, ed. Toyin Falola and Adam Paddock, 249–279. Trenton, N.J.: African World Press, 2008.

———. "Nwando Achebe—Daughter, Wife, and Guest—A Researcher at the Crossroads." *Journal of Women's History* 14, no. 3 (Autumn 2002): 9–31.

———. "'Ogidi Palaver': The 1914 Women's Market Protest." In *Nigerian Women in History, Culture and Development,* ed. Obioma Nnaemeka and Chima Korieh, 49–76. Trenton, N.J.: Africa World Press, 2009.

———. "'[T]he Real Rulers of [Nsukka] Town[s] are the Ancestors or Spirits . . .': Understanding the Female Principle in Igbo Religion." In *Igbos in the Atlantic World,* ed. Toyin Falola and Matt Childs. Bloomington: Indiana University Press, forthcoming.

———. "The Road to Italy: Nigerian Sex Workers at Home and Abroad." *Journal of Women's History* 15, no. 4 (Winter 2004): 177–184.

———. "West Africa." In *The Encyclopedia of Prostitution and Sex Work,* vol. 2, ed. Melissa Hope Ditmore, 532–536. Westport, Conn.: Greenwood, 2006.

———. "When Deities Marry: Indigenous 'Slave' Systems Expanding and Metamorphosing in the Igbo Hinterland." In *African Systems of Slavery,* ed. Stephanie Beswick and Jay Spaulding, 105–133. Trenton, N.J.: Africa World Press, 2010.

Achebe, Nwando, and Bridget Teboh. "Dialoguing Women." In *Africa After Gender?* ed. Catherine M. Cole, Stephan F. Miescher, and Takyiwaa Manuh, 91–113. Bloomington: Indiana University Press, 2007.

Ademola-Adeoye, F. F. "Language, Gender and Identity: A Social, Cultural and Psychological Study." Available at http://www.staff.hum.ku.dk/smo/smo2/RC-News-vi-ni/Art-Lg-Gender.htm (retrieved May 16, 2008).

Aderinto, Saheed. "Demobilization and Repatriation of "Undesirables: Prostitutes, Crime, Law and Reformers in Colonial Nigeria." In *Nigeria's Urban History: Past and Present,* ed. Hakeem Ibikunle Tijani, 99–118. Lanham, Md.: University of America Press, 2006.

———. "Prostitution: A Social Legacy of Colonialism in Nigeria." In *Nigeria's Urban History: Past and Present,* ed. Hakeem Ibikunle Tijani, 75–98. Lanham, Md.: University of America Press, 2006.

Afigbo, A. E. *The Igbo and Their Neighbors: Inter-Group Relations in Southeastern Nigeria to 1953.* Ibadan, Nigeria: Ibadan University Press, 1987.

———. "Nsukka from Earliest Times to 1951." In *The Nsukka Environment,* ed. G. E. K. Ofomata, 24–46. Enugu, Nigeria: Fourth Dimension Publishers, 1978.

———. "Oral Tradition and the History of Segmentary Societies." *History in Africa* 12 (1985): 1–10.

———. *An Outline of Igbo History.* Owerri, Nigeria: RADA Pub. Co., 1986.

———. "Precolonial Trade Links between Southeastern Nigeria and the Benue Valley." *Journal of African Studies* 4, no. 2 (1977): 119–139.

———. *Ropes of Sand: Studies in Igbo History and Culture.* Oxford: Oxford University Press, 1981.

————. "Southern Nigeria, the Niger-Benue Confluence, and the Benue in the Pre-colonial Period: Some Issues of Historiography." *History in Africa* 24 (1997): 1–8.

————. "Trade and Trade Routes in Nineteenth Century Nsukka." *Okikpe* 3, no. 1 (1997): 27–47.

————. "Traditions of Igbo Origins: A Comment." *History in Africa* 10 (1983): 1–11.

————. *The Warrant Chiefs: Indirect Rule in Southeastern Nigeria, 1891–1921.* Ibadan, Nigeria: Humanities Press, 1972.

————. "Women in Nigerian History." In *Women in Nigerian Economy,* ed. Martin O. Ijere, 22–40. Enugu, Nigeria: Acena Publishers, 1991.

Agbasiere, Joseph Therese. *Women in Igbo Life and Thought.* New York: Routledge, 2000.

Aguwa, Jude C. U. "Patterns of Religious Influence in Igbo Traditional Politics." In *The Igbo and the Tradition of Politics,* ed. U. D. Anyanwu and J. C. U. Aguwa, 89–99. Enugu, Nigeria: Fourth Dimension Publishing, 1993.

Akyeampong, Emmanuel. "Sexuality and Prostitution among the Akan of the Gold Coast, c. 1650–1950." *Past and Present* 156 (1997): 144–173.

Alagoa, E. J. "The Dialogue between Academic and Community History in Nigeria." In *African Words, African Voices: Critical Practices in Oral History,* ed. Luise White, Stephan F. Miescher, and David William Cohen, 91–102. Bloomington: Indiana University Press, 2001.

Allman, Jean, Susan Geiger, and Nakanyike Musisi. *Women in African Colonial Histories.* Bloomington: Indiana University Press, 2002.

Allen, Judith Van. "'Sitting on a Man': Colonialism and the Lost Political Institutions of Igbo Women." *Canadian Journal of African Studies* 6 (1972): 165–181.

Amadiume, Ifi. *Daughters of the Goddess, Daughters of Imperialism: African Women Struggle for Culture, Power and Democracy.* New York: Zed Books, 2000.

————. *Male Daughters, Female Husbands: Gender and Sex in an African Society.* London: Zed Books, 1987.

————. *Re-Inventing Africa: Matriarchy, Religion, and Culture.* New York: Zed Books, 1997.

Anarfi, John K. *Female Migration and Prostitution in West Africa: The Case of Ghanaian Women in Côte d'Ivoire.* Studies in Sexual Health no. 1. Accra: GTZ Regional AIDS Programme for West and Central Africa, 1995.

Arinze, Francis. *Sacrifice in Igbo Religion.* Ibadan, Nigeria: Ibadan University Press, 1970.

Asiegbu, Johnson U. J. *Nigeria and Its British Invaders, 1851–1920: A Thematic Documentary History.* Lagos: Nok Publishers International, 1984.

Awe, Bolanle, ed. *Nigerian Women in Historical Perspective.* Lagos, Nigeria: Sankore Publishers, 1992.

Awolalu, J., and P. Dopamu. *West African Traditional Religion.* Ibadan, Nigeria: Onibonoje Press, 1979.

Baral, M., I. Farley, M. Kiremire, and U. Sezgin. "Prostitution in Five Countries: Violence and Post-Traumatic Stress Disorder (South Africa, Thailand, Turkey, USA, Zambia)." *Feminism & Psychology* 8, no. 4 (1998): 405–426.

Basden, G. T. *Among the Ibos of Nigeria: An Account of the Curious and Interesting Habits, Customs and Beliefs of a Little Known African People by One Who Has for Many Years Lived amongst Them on Close and Intimate Terms.* London: Seely, Service & Co. Ltd, 1921.

———. *Niger Ibos: A Description of the Primitive Life, Customs and Animistic Beliefs, &c., of the Ibo Peoples of Nigeria by One Who, for Thirty-five Years, Enjoyed the Privilege of their Intimate Confidence and Friendship.* London: Frank Cass, 1966.

Belcher, Stephen. *African Myths of Origin.* London: Penguin Books, 2005.

———. *Epic Traditions of Africa.* Bloomington: Indiana University Press, 1999.

Bell, Diane Pat Caplan, and Wazir Jahan Karim, eds. *Gendered Fields: Women, Men and Ethnography.* London: Routledge, 1993.

Bloom, Leslie Rebecca. *Under the Sign of Hope: Feminist Methodology and Narrative Interpretation.* Albany: State University of New York Press, 1998.

Borgatti, Jean M. "Okpella Masking Traditions." *African Arts* 9, no. 4 (July 1976): 24–33, 90–91

Boston, J. S. "The Hunter in Igala Legends of Origin." *Africa: Journal of the International African Institute* 14, no. 2 (April 1964): 116–126.

———. *The Igala Kingdom.* Ibadan, Nigeria: Nigerian Institute of Social and Economic Research and Oxford University Press, 1968.

———. "Some Northern Ibo Masquerades." *Journal of the Royal Anthropology Institute* 90 (1960): 54–65.

Bozzoli, Belinda. *Women of Phokeng: Consciousness, Life Strategy, and Migrancy in South Africa, 1900–1983.* Portsmouth, N.H.: Heinemann, 1991.

Brodzki, Bella, and Celeste Schenck, eds. *Life Lines: Theorizing Women's Autobiography.* Ithaca, N.Y.: Cornell University Press, 1988.

Butler, Judith. *Gender Trouble: Feminism and the Subversion of Identity.* New York: Routledge, 1990.

———. "Performative Acts and Gender Constitution: An Essay in Phenomenology and Feminist Theory." In *Performing Feminisms: Feminist Critical Theory and Theatre,* ed. Sue-Ellen Case, 270–282. Baltimore, Md.: Johns Hopkins University Press, 1990.

Brownley, Martine Watson, and Allison B. Kimmich, eds. *Women and Autobiography.* Wilmington, Del.: SR Books, 1999.

Cadigan, R. Jean. "Woman-to-Woman Marriage: Practices and Benefits in Sub-Saharan Africa." In *Journal of Comparative Family Studies* 29, no. 1 (Spring 1998): 89–99.

Cameron, Elizabeth L. "Men Portraying Women: Representations in African Masks." *African Arts* 31, no. 2 (Spring 1998): 72–79.

Clark, Gracia. *Onions Are My Husband: Survival and Accumulation by West African Market Women*. Chicago: University of Chicago Press, 1994.

Cole, Catherine M., Stephan F. Miescher, and Takyiwaa Manuh, eds. *Africa after Gender?* Bloomington: Indiana University Press, 2006.

Cornwell, Andrea, ed. *Readings in Gender in Africa*. Bloomington: Indiana University Press, 2005.

Crais, Clifton, and Pamela Schully. *Sara Baartman and the Hottentot Venus: A Ghost Story and a Biography*. Princeton, N.J.: Princeton University Press, 2008.

Cromwell, Adelaide M. *An African Victorian Feminist: The Life and Times of Adelaide Smith Casely Hayford, 1868–1960*. Washington, D.C.: Howard University Press, 1992.

Davison, Jean. *Voices of Mutira: Lives of Rural Gikuyu Women*. Boulder, Colo.: Lynne Rienner Publishers, 1989.

Denzer, LaRay. "Domestic Science Training in Colonial Yorubaland, Nigeria." In *African Encounters with Domesticity*, ed. Karen Tranberg Hansen, 116–139. Piscataway, N.J.: Rutgers University Press, 1992.

Diouf, Sylviane A. "Introduction." In *Fighting the Slave Trade: West African Strategies*, ix–xxvii. Athens: Ohio University Press, 2003.

Ebron, Paulla A. "Constituting Subjects through Performative Arts." In *Africa after Gender?* ed. Catherine M. Cole, Takyiwaa Manuh, and Stephan F. Miescher, 171–190. Bloomington: Indiana University Press, 2007.

———. *Performing Africa*. Princeton, N.J.: Princeton University Press, 2002.

Edime, A. "The Rise and Fall of Igala State." *Nigerian Magazine* 80 (1974): 17–29.

Ejizu, C. "Continuity and Discontinuity in Igbo Traditional Religion." In *The Gods in Retreat: Continuity and Change in African Religions*, ed. Emefie Ikenga Metuh, 133–156. Enugu, Nigeria: Fourth Dimension Publishers, 1986.

Ekechi, F. K. "Gender and Economic Power: The Case of Igbo Market Women in Eastern Nigeria." In *African Market Women and Economic Power: The Role of Women in African Economic Development*, ed. Bessie House-Midamba and Felix. K. Ekechi, 41–57. Westport, Conn.: Greenwood Press, 1995.

———. "The Holy Ghost Fathers in Eastern Nigeria, 1885–1920: Observations on Missionary Strategy." *African Studies Review* 15, no. 2 (September 1972): 217–239.

———. *Missionary Enterprise and Rivalry in Igboland, 1857–1914*. London: Routledge, 1971.

Ekejiuba, F. Ifeoma."Omu Okwei, the Merchant Queen of Ossomari: A Biographical Sketch." *Journal of the Historical Society of Nigeria* 3, no. 4 (1967): 633–646.

Ellis, Alfred Burdon. *The Yoruba-Speaking Peoples of the Slave Coast of West Africa: Their Religion, Manners, Customs, Laws, Language, Etc.* 1894; repr., Chestnut Hill, Mass.: Adamant Media, 2003.

Epprecht, Marc. *Heterosexual Africa? The History of an Idea from the Age of Exploration to the Age of AIDS*. Athens: Ohio University Press, 2008.

———. *Unspoken Fact: A History of Homosexualities in Africa.* Zimbabwe: GALZ, 2008.

Etu, Yusufu. *Igala History in Questions and Answers.* Jos, Nigeria: New Concepts Incorporated Book House, 2001.

Fagbemi, Abiodun. "Bolanle Awe Alleges Stealing of Artefacts at Museum." *The Guardian,* January 28, 2009. Available at http://odili.net/news/source/2009/jan/28/29.html (retrieved February 3, 2009).

Falola, Toyin, and G. O. Ogunremi. "Traditional, Nonmechanical Transport Systems." In *Transport Systems in Nigeria,* ed. Toyin Falola and S. A. Olanrewaju, 17–30. Syracuse, N.Y.: Maxwell School of Citizenship and Public Affairs, Syracuse University, 1986.

Falola, Toyin, and S. A. Olanrewaju, eds. *Transport Systems in Nigeria.* Syracuse, N.Y.: Maxwell School of Citizenship and Public Affairs, Syracuse University, 1986.

FaSanto, Maria Eugenia G. Do Espirito, and Gina D. Etheredge. "And Then I Became a Prostitute . . . Some Aspects of Prostitution and Brothel Prostitutes in Dakar, Senegal." *Social Science Journal* 41 (2004): 137–146.

Forde, Daryll, and G. I. Jones. *The Ibo and Ibibio-Speaking Peoples of Southwestern Nigeria.* London: International African Institute by the Oxford University Press, 1950.

Gailey, H. A. *The Road to Aba.* London: London University Press, 1970.

Geiger, Susan. *TANU Women: Gender and Culture in the Making of Tanganyikan Nationalism, 1955–1965.* Portsmouth, N.H.: Heinemann, 1997.

Gevisser, Mark, and Edwin Cameron, eds. *Defiant Desire: Gay and Lesbian Lives in South Africa.* New York: Routledge, 1995.

Giles-Vernick, Tamara. "Lives, Histories, and Sites of Recollection." In *African Words, African Voices: Critical Practices in Oral History,* ed. Luise White, Stephan F. Miescher, and David William Cohen, 194–213. Bloomington: Indiana University Press, 2001.

Gluck, Sherna Berger, and Daphne Patai, eds. *Women's Words: The Feminist Practice of Oral History.* New York: Routledge, 1991.

Golden Jubilee Celebration of the Enthronement of His Royal Majesty Alhaji Aliyu O. Obaje. Lagos: Attah Igala and Chancellor, University of Lagos, n.d. In author's possession.

Graham, James D. "The Slave Trade, Depopulation and Human Sacrifice in Benin History." *Cahiers d'Études Africaines* 5 (1965): 317–334.

Green, M. M. *Igbo Village Affairs.* New York: Frederick A. Praeger, 1947.

Greene, Beth. "The Institution of Woman-Marriage in Africa: A Cross-Cultural Analysis." *Ethnology* 37, no. 4 (Fall 1998): 395–412.

Guyer, Jane I. "Women's Work in the Food Economy of the Cocoa Belt: A Comparison." *International Journal of African Historical Studies* 14, no. 2 (1981): 371–378.

Halberstam, Judith. *Female Masculinity.* Durham, N.C.: Duke University Press, 1998.

Harding, Frances. "To Present the Self in a Special Way: Disguise and Display in Tiv Kwagh-hir Performance." *African Arts* 31 (Winter 1998): 56–67.

Hawkins, E. K. *Road Transport in Nigeria: A Study of African Enterprise.* London: Oxford University Press, 1958.

Hill, Polly. "Markets in Africa." *The Journal of Modern African Studies* 1, no. 4 (December 1963): 441–453.

Hoad, Neville. *African Intimacies: Race, Homosexuality, and Globalization.* Minneapolis: University of Minnesota Press, 2007.

Hodder, B. W., and U. I. Ukwu. *Markets in West Africa: Studies of Markets and Trade among the Yoruba and Ibo.* Ibadan: Ibadan University Press, 1969.

Hodgson, Dorothy, and Sheryl McCurdy, eds. *"Wicked" Women and the Reconfiguration of Gender in Africa.* Portsmouth, N.H.: Heinemann, 2001.

Holmes, Rachel. *African Queen: The Real Life of the Hottentot Venus.* New York: Random House, 2007.

Hoppe, Kirk. "Whose Life Is It Anyway? Issues of Representation in Life Narrative Texts of African Women." *International Journal of African Historical Studies* 26, no. 3 (1993): 623–636.

Hunt, Nancy Rose, Tessie P. Liu, and Jean Quataert, eds. *Gendered Colonialisms in African History.* Malden, Mass.: Blackwell Publishers, 1997.

Ifeka-Moller, Caroline. "Female Militancy and Colonial Revolt: The Women's War of 1929, Eastern Nigeria." In *Perceiving Women,* ed. Shirley Ardener. New York: John Wiley, 1975.

Ilogu, Edmund. *Christianity and Ibo Culture.* Leiden: E. J. Brill, 1974.

———. *Igbo Life and Thought.* Onitsha, Nigeria: University Publishing, 1985.

———. "Ofo: A Religious and Political Symbol." *Nigerian Magazine* 82 (September 1964): 234–235.

Isichei, Elizabeth. *A History of the Igbo People.* London: Macmillan, 1976.

———. *The Ibo People and the Europeans.* New York: St. Martin's Press, 1973.

———. *Igbo Worlds: An Anthology of Oral Histories and Historical Descriptions.* London: MacMillan, 1977.

———. "Seven Varieties of Ambiguity: Some Patterns of Igbo Response to Christian Missions." *Journal of Religion in Africa* 3, no. 3 (1970): 209–227.

Johnson-Odim, Cheryl, and Nina Mba. *For Women and the Nation: Funmilayo Ransome-Kuti of Nigeria.* Chicago: University of Illinois Press, 1997.

Kalu, Ogbu U. *The Embattled Gods: The Christianization of Igboland, 1841–1991.* Lagos: Minaj Publishers, 1996.

Kaplan, Flora Edouwaye S., ed. *Queens, Queen Mothers, Priestesses, and Power: Case Studies in African Gender.* New York: New York Academy of Sciences, 1997.

Kellogg, N. D., T. J. Hoffman, and E. R. Taylor. "Early Sexual Experience among Pregnant and Parenting Adolescents." *Adolescence* 43 (1999): 293–303.

Leith-Ross, Sylvia. *African Women: A Study of the Ibo of Nigeria.* London: Faber & Faber, 1938.

Lindsey, Lisa A. *Working with Gender: Wage Labor and Social Change in Southwestern Nigeria.* Portsmouth, N.H.: Heinemann, 2003.

Lovejoy, Paul E. "Concubinage and the Status of Women Slaves in Early Colonial Northern Nigeria." *Journal of African History* 29 (1988): 245–266.

Lukman, Z. M. "Childhood Abuse among Children Involved in Prostitution in Malaysia." *The Social Sciences* 4, no. 6 (2009): 567–572.

Maathi, Wangari. *Unbowed: A Memoir.* New York: Vintage, 2007.

Mandela, Winnie. *Winnie Mandela: Part of My Soul Went with Him.* New York: W. W. Norton & Co., 1985.

Mann, Kristin, and Richard Roberts, eds. *Law in Colonial Africa.* Portsmouth, N.H.: Heinemann, 1991.

Mba, Nina. *Nigerian Women Mobilized: Women's Political Activity in Southern Nigeria, 1900–1965.* Berkeley: University of California Press, 1982.

Meek, C. K. *Law and Authority in a Nigeria Tribe: A Study of Indirect Rule.* London: Oxford University Press, 1937.

Metuh, Emefie Ikenga. *African Religions in Western Conceptual Scheme: The Problem of Interpretation.* Ibadan, Nigeria: Pastoral Institute, 1985.

———. *God and Man in African Religion.* London: Geoffrey Chapman, 1981.

Miachi, Tom A. "Introducing the Igala People." In *The Golden Jubilee Celebration of the Enthronement of His Royal Majesty Alhaji Aliyu O. Obaje.* Lagos, Nigeria: Attah Igala and Chancellor, University of Lagos. N.p.: n.d.

Miescher, Stephan F. *Making Men in Ghana.* Bloomington: Indiana University Press, 2005.

Miescher, Stephan F., and Lisa A. Lindsay, eds. *Men and Masculinities in Modern Africa,* Portsmouth, N.H.: Heinemann, 2003.

Mimiko, Femi. "Census in Nigeria: The Politics and the Imperative of Depoliticization." *African and Asian Studies* 5, no. 1 (2006): 1–21.

Mungia, Evelyn K., and Joy Awori, eds. *Kenya Women Reflections.* Nairobi: Lear Publishing Company, 1984.

Murray, Stephen O., and Will Roscoe, ed. *Boy-Wives and Female Husbands: Studies of African Homosexualities.* New York: St. Martin's, 1998.

Naanen, Benedict B. B. "'Itinerant Gold Mines': Prostitution in the Cross River Basin of Nigeria, 1930–1950." *African Studies Review* 34, no. 2 (September 1991): 57–79.

Nast, Heidi J. *Concubines and Power: Five Hundred Years in a Northern Nigerian Palace.* Minneapolis: University of Minnesota Press, 2005.

Ndambuki, Berida, and Claire Robertson. *We Only Come Here to Struggle: Stories from Berida's Life.* Bloomington: Indiana University Press, 2000.

Newell, Stephanie. *The Forger's Tale: The Search for Odeziaku.* Athens: Ohio University Press, 2006.

Njaka, Elechukwu Nnadibuagha. *Igbo Political Culture.* Evanston, Ill.: Northwestern University Press, 1974.

Noll, J. G., P. K. Trickett, and F. W. Putnam. "A Prospective Investigation of the Impact of Childhood Sexual Abuse on the Development of Sexuality." *Journal of Consulting and Clinical Psychology* 71 (2003): 575–586.

Northrup, D. *Trade without Rulers: Pre-Colonial Economic Development in Southeastern Nigeria.* Oxford: Clarendon Press, 1978.

Nwabara, S. N. *Iboland: A Century of Contact with Britain, 1860–1960.* London: Hodder and Stoughton, 1977.

Nwala, T. Uzodinma. *Igbo Philosophy.* Lagos, Nigeria: Literamed, 1985.

Nzimiro, Ikenna. *Chieftaincy and Politics in Four Niger States.* London: Frank Cass, 1970.

Oboni, Prince Idakwo Ameh. *Ameh the Great.* Ibadan, Nigeria: Intec Printers, 1989.

Ocho, Lawrence Offie. "Nsukka: The Meeting Point of Four Civilizations." *Okikpe* 3, no. 1 (1997): 48–78.

Ofomata, G. E. K., ed. *The Nsukka Environment.* Enugu, Nigeria: Fourth Dimension Publishers, 1978.

Ogbomo, Onaiwu W. *When Men and Women Mattered: A History of Gender Relations among the Owan of Nigeria.* Rochester, N.Y.: University of Rochester Press, 1997.

Ogbukagu, Ik. *Traditional Igbo Beliefs and Practices: A Study on the Culture and People of Adazi-Nnukwu.* Owerri, Nigeria: Novelty Industrial Enterprises, 1997.

Oguagha, Philip Adigwe. "The Igbo and Their Neighbors: Some Patterns of Relationships in Pre-Colonial Southern Nigeria." In *Perspectives in History: Essays in Honor of Professor Obaro Ikime,* ed. A. E. Ekoko and S. O. Agbi. Ibadan, Nigeria: Heinemann Educational Books, 1992.

Oguagha, Philip Adigwe, and Alex Ikechukwu Okpoko. *History and Ethnoarchaeology in Eastern Nigeria: A Study of Igbo-Igala Relations with Special Reference to the Anambra Valley.* Cambridge: Cambridge University Press, 1984.

Ogunyemi, Biodun. "Knowledge and Perception of Child Sexual Abuse in Urban Nigeria: Some Evidence from a Community-Based Project." *African Journal of Reproductive Health* 4, no. 2 (October 2000): 44–52.

Ohadike, Don. "The Decline of Slavery among the Igbo People." In *The End of Slavery in Africa,* ed. Suzanne Miers and Richard Roberts. Madison: University of Wisconsin Press, 1988.

Okeke, Uche. "The Art Culture of the Nsukka Igbo." In *The Nsukka Environment,* ed. G. E. K. Ofomata, 271–285. Enugu, Nigeria: Fourth Dimension Publishers, 1978.

Okonjo, Kamene. "The Dual-Sex Political System in Operation: Igbo Women and Community Politics in Midwestern Nigeria." In *Women in Africa: Studies in Social and Economic Change,* ed. N. J. Hafkin, and Edna G. Bay, 45–56. Stanford, Calif.: Stanford University Press, 1976.

Okorafor, A. E. "The Population of the Nsukka Area." In *The Nsukka Environment,* ed. G. E. K. Ofomata. Enugu, Nigeria: Fourth Dimension Publishers, 1978.

Okwoli, P. E. *The History of the Fifty Years Reign of the Attah Igala, Alhaji Aliyu Ocheja Obaje, 1956–2006.* Enugu, Nigeria: Snaap Press, 2006.

Olanrewaju, S. A. "The Nigerian Road Transport System." In *Transport Systems in Nigeria,* ed. Toyin Falola and S. A. Olanrewaju, 51–70. Syracuse, N.Y.: Maxwell School of Citizenship and Public Affairs, Syracuse University, 1986.

Omale, Ibrahim. *Igala, Yesterday, Today and Tomorrow: A Developmental Perspective.* Lagos, Nigeria: Summit Press, 2001.

Onyeneke, A. O. *The Dead among the Living: Masquerades in Igbo Society.* Nimo, Nigeria: Holy Ghost Congregation, Province of Nigeria, and Asele Institute, 1987.

Opata, Damian U. *Essays on Igbo World View.* Enugu, Nigeria: AP Express, 1998.

Oranekwu, George Nnaemeka. *The Significant Role of Initiation in the Traditional Igbo Culture and Religion: An Inculturation Basis for Pastoral Catechesis of Christian Initiation.* Frankfurt, Germany: IKO-Verlag, 2004.

Oriji, John Nwachimereze. *Traditions of Igbo Origin: A Study of Pre-Colonial Population Movements in Africa.* New York: Peter Lang, 1994.

Otieno, Wambui. *Mau Mau's Daughter: A Life History.* Boulder, Colo.: Lynne Rienner Publishers, 1998.

Oyewùmí, Oyèrónké. *African Gender Studies: A Reader.* New York: Palgrave Macmillan, 2005.

———. *The Invention of Women: Making an African Sense of Western Gender Discourses.* Minneapolis: University of Minnesota Press, 1997.

Paolucci, E. O., M. L. Genuis, and C. Violato. "A Meta-Analysis of the Published Research on the Effects of Child Sexual Abuse." *Journal of Psychology* 135 (2001): 17–36.

Parrinder, G. E. *West African Religion.* London: Epworth Press, 1969.

Perham, Margery. *Native Administration in Nigeria.* London: Oxford University Press, 1937.

Perschler-Desai, Viktoria. "Childhood on the Market: Teenage Prostitution in Southern Africa." *African Security Review* 10, no. 4 (2001). Available at http://www.iss.co.za/pubs/ASR/10No4/Perschler.html (retrieved October 9, 2009).

Personal Narratives Group. *Interpreting Women's Lives: Feminist Theory and Personal Narratives.* Bloomington: Indiana University Press, 1989.

Ramphele, Mamphela. *Across Boundaries: The Journey of a South African Woman Leader.* New York: The Feminist Press of CUNY, 1999.

Ray, Carina. "The Sex Trade in Colonial West Africa." *New African* 466 (October 2007): 80.

Richards, Polly. "Masques Dogons in a Changing World." *African Arts* 38, no. 4 (Winter 2005): 46–93.

Robertson, Claire. *Sharing the Same Bowl: A Socioeconomic History of Women and Class in Accra, Ghana.* Ann Arbor: University of Michigan Press, 1990.

Romero, Patricia C. *Profiles in Diversity: Women in the New South Africa.* East Lansing: Michigan State University Press, 1998.

Roscoe, Will, and Stephen O. Murray. *Boy-Wives and Female Husbands: Studies of African Homosexualities.* New York: Palgrave Macmillan, 2001.

Saewyc, E. M., L. L. Magee, and S. E. Pettingall. "Teenage Pregnancy and Associated Risk Behavior among Sexually Abused Adolescents." *Perspectives on Sexual and Reproductive Health* 36, no. 3 (2004): 98–105.

Shelton, Austin J. "Behavior and Cultural Value in West African Stories: Literary Sources for the Study of Culture Contact." *Africa* 34, no. 4 (October 1964): 353–359.

———. "Causality in African Thought: Igbo and Other." *Practical Anthropology* 15, no. 4 (Summer 1968): 157–169.

———. "The Departure of the Nshie: A North Nsukka Igbo Origin Legend." *Journal of American Folklore* 78, no. 308 (Spring 1965): 115–129.

———. *The Ibo-Igala Borderland: Religion and Social Control in Indigenous African Colonialism.* Albany: State University of New York Press, 1971.

———. "Igbo Child-Raising, Eldership, and Dependence: Further Notes for Gerontologists and Others." *The Gerontologist* 8, no. 4 (Winter 1969): 236–241.

———. "The 'Miss Ophelia Syndrome' in African Field Research." *Practical Anthropology* 2, no. 6 (November–December 1964): 259–265.

———. "The Meaning and Method of Afa Divination among the Northern Nsukka Igbo." *American Anthropologist* 67, no. 6 (December 1965): 1441–1455.

———. "On the Recent Interpretation of Deus Otiosus, the Withdrawal of High God in West African Religion." *Man* 64 (1964): 53–54.

———. "Onojo Ogboni: Problems of Identification and Historicity in the Oral Tradition of the Igala and Northern Nsukka Igbo of Nigeria." *Journal of American Folklore* 81, no. 321 (Summer 1968): 243–257.

———. "The Presence of the Withdrawn High God in North Ibo Religious Belief and Worship." *Man* 65, no. 4 (1965): 15–18.

Shostak, Marjorie. *Nisa: The Life and Words of a !Kung Woman.* New York: Vintage, 1981.

Siegel, Kristi. *Women's Autobiographies, Culture, Feminism.* New York: Peter Lang, 1999.

Smith, M. F. *Baba of Karo: A Woman of the Muslim Hausa.* London: Faber and Faber, Ltd., 1954.

Spurlin, William J. *Imperialism within the Margins: Queer Representation and the Politics of Culture in Southern Africa.* New York: Palgrave Macmillan, 2006.

Steady, Filomina Chioma. "An Investigative Framework for Gender Research in Africa in the New Millennium." In *African Gender Scholarship: Concepts, Methodologies and Paradigms,* ed. Signe Arnfred, Bibi Bakare-Yusuf, and Edward Waswa Kisiang'ani. Dakar, Senegal: CODESIRA Gender Series 1, 2004.

Strobel, Margaret. *Muslim Women of Mombasa, 1890–1975.* New Haven, Conn.: Yale University Press, 1979.

Strobel, Margaret, and Sarah Mirza. *Three Swahili Women: Life Histories of Mombasa.* Bloomington: Indiana University Press, 1989.

Talbot, Amaury P. *The Peoples of Southern Nigeria: A Sketch of Their History, Ethnology and Languages, with an Account of the 1921 Census.* 4 vols. London: Oxford University Press, 1926.

Trigger, Bruce G. *Understanding Early Civilizations: A Comparative Study.* London: Cambridge University Press, 2003.

Turrittin, Jane. "Men, Women, and Market Trade in Rural Mali, West Africa." *Canadian Journal of African Studies* 22, no. 3 (Summer 1988): 583–604.

Uchendu, V. C. "Concubinage among Ngwa Igbo of Southern Nigeria." *Africa* 35, no. 2 (April 1965): 187–197.

———. *The Igbo of Southeast Nigeria.* London: Holt, Rinehart and Winston, 1965.

Ugwu, D. C. *This Is Nsukka.* Apapa, Nigeria: Nigerian National Press, 1958.

———. *This Is Obukpa: A History of Typical Ancient Igbo State.* Enugu, Nigeria: Fourth Foundation Publishers, 1987.

Ukpabi, S. C. "Nsukka before the Establishment of British Administration." In *Nsukka Division: A Geographical Appraisal,* ed. P. K. Sircar, 26–36. Nsukka: University of Nigeria, Annual Conference of the Nigerian Geographical Association, 1965.

Undie, Chi-Chi. "My Father's Daughter: Becoming a 'Real' Anthropologist among the Ubang of Southeast Nigeria." *Anthropology Matters* 9, no. 1 (2007): 1–9.

VerEecke, Catherine. "Muslim Women Traders of Northern Nigeria: Perspectives from the City of Yola." *Ethnology* 32, no. 3 (Summer 1993): 217–236.

Walker, Gilbert James. *Traffic and Transport in Nigeria: The Example of an Under-developed Tropical Territory.* Research Studies No. 27. London: Colonial Office, 1959.

White, E. Frances. "Creole Women Traders in the Nineteenth Century." *The International Journal of African Historical Studies* 14, no. 4 (1981): 626–642.

White, Luise. *The Comforts of Home: Prostitution in Colonial Nairobi.* Chicago: University of Chicago Press, 1990.

White, Luise, Stephan F. Miescher, and David William Cohen, eds. *African Words, African Voices: Critical Practices in Oral History.* Bloomington: Indiana University Press, 2001.

Willis, B. M., and B. S. Levy. "Child Prostitution: Global Health Burden, Research Needs, and Interventions." *Lancet* 359, no. 9315 (April 2002): 1417–1422.

Wilson-Haffenden, J. R. "Ethnological Notes on the Kwottos of Toto (Panda) District, Keffi Division, Benue Province, Northern Nigeria: Part I." *Journal of the Royal African Society* 26, no. 104 (July 1927): 368–379.

Wipper, Audrey. "Riot and Rebellion among African Women: Three Examples of Women's Political Clout." In *Perspectives on Power: Women in Africa, Asia, and Latin America,* ed. Jean F. O'Barr. Durham, N.C.: Duke University Center for International Studies, 1982.

Wright, Marcia. *Strategies of Slaves and Women: Life-Stories from East/Central Africa.* London: James Currey, 1993.

THESES, DISSERTATIONS, AND OTHER UNPUBLISHED WORKS

Abugu, Jecinta Nneka. "The Worship of [a] Deity: A Case Study of Enwe Deity in Ogrute, Enugu-Ezike." Diploma Project in Religion, University of Nigeria, Nsukka, November 1998.

Afigbo, A. E. "Igbo Women, Colonialism and Socio-Economic Change." Paper presented at the Seminar on Igbo Women in Socio-Economic Change, Better Life Program for Rural Women, Imo State Wing, Owerri, and Institute of African Studies, University of Nigeria, Nsukka, April 3–5, 1990.

Agashi, Patrick Odo. "Pre-Colonial Warfare in Enugu-Ezike." B.A. thesis, Department of History, University of Nigeria, Nsukka, June 1979.

Agashi, P. O. "Government at Nsukka 1929–1979." M.A. history project, Department of History, University of Nigeria, Nsukka, 1986.

Agbedo, Cyprian U. "Slavery and Slave Trade in Enugu-Ezike in the Pre-colonial Period." B.A. thesis, University of Nigeria, Nsukka, June 1979.

Apeh, Gloria Nkeiru. "The Traditional Oracle and Culture in Enugu-Ezike." Diploma Programme/Certificate, Department of Religion, University of Nigeria, Nsukka, November 1997.

Dike, Paul Chike. "Symbolism and Political Authority in the Igala Kingdom." Ph.D. diss., University of Nigeria, Nsukka, 1977.

Makinwa-Adebusoye, P. K. "History and Growth of the Nigerian Census." President's address, delivered at the Seventh Annual Conference of the Population Association of Nigeria (PAN), University of Lagos, Lagos, Nigeria, December 6–10, 1988.

Momoh, Pius Charles. "The Social Functions of Masquerade in Enugu-Ezike: A Case Study of My Town Ogurute Enugu-Ezike in Igbo-Eze North L. G. A. of Enugu State." B.A. thesis, University of Nigeria, Nsukka, February 1994.

Nwodo, Stephen S. "African Traditional Religion in Enugu-Ezike." B.A. thesis, Department of Religion, University of Nigeria, Nsukka, February 2001.

Okwoli, P. E. "Igala Names: A Survey of Some Igala Names, Their Meanings, Relevance and Source." Unpublished manuscript.

Omale, Ibrahim. "The Igala Woman." Unpublished manuscript, Department of Public Administration, Kogi State University, Anyigba, Kogi State, Nigeria.

Onogu, Gertrude Ojochide. "The Place of Princess Inikpi in the Igala Traditional Belief System of Kogi State." Diploma Project, Department of Religion, University of Nigeria, Nsukka, September 1996.

INDEX

Page references in *italics* indicate information contained in figures.

NWANDO ACHEBE, Professor of History,
Michigan State University, received her Ph.D. from
the University of California, Los Angeles, in 2000.
She served as a Ford Foundation and Fulbright-Hays
Scholar-in-Residence at the Institute of African
Studies and History Department of the University
of Nigeria, Nsukka, in 1996 and 1998. Her research
interests involve the use of oral history in the study
of women, gender, and power in Eastern Nigeria. She
is the author of *Farmers, Traders, Warriors, and Kings:
Female Power and Authority in Northern Igboland,
1900–1960* (2005).

Printed and bound by CPI Group (UK) Ltd, Croydon, CR0 4YY

13/04/2025

14656552-0001